THE TEACHINGS OF THE REBBE

A Translation and adaptation
into English of

Sefer HaMa'amarim 5711

By

Our Master and Teacher
The Holy and Godly Tzaddik

Rabbi Menachem Mendel Schneerson
The Lubavitcher Rebbe

Adapted into English by:
Rabbi Amiram Markel
Rabbi Yehudah S. Markel

3

ISBN: 978-1-716-57458-0

Other books by the authors:

HaShem Is One – גנת אגוז

The Way of the Baal Shem Tov – צוואת הריב״ש

Gate of Unity-English translation – ספר שער היחוד

Gate of Unity with full commentary – שער היחוד המבואר

The Gateway to Understanding – פתח השער לאמרי בינה

The Principles of Religion – קונטרס עקרי הדת

On Divine Inspiration – קונטרס ההתפעלות

Going Kosher – ספר כשרון המעשה

Essential Faith – הקדמה לשער האמונה

Revealing the Infinite – המשך תרס״ו

The Path of Life – דרך חיים

The Knowledge of HaShem – ספר דעה את ה'

The Beginning of Wisdom – ספר התחלת החכמה

Praying with Passion-קונטרס ענין תפילה

Opening the Eyes-פוקח עיורים

The Book of Allegorics ספר המשלים

Available at
www.Neirot.com
&
www.Truekabbalah.com

Warning

The Holy Torah, the living words of the Living God, commands us,[1] "You shall not desecrate My Holy Name." In explaining the true unity and service of *HaShem*, blessed is He, this book necessarily and unavoidably makes use of His Holy Name. It therefore is holy and sacred and great care should be taken not to desecrate it in any way, shape or form.[2]

Now that we have entered the era of the true and complete redemption, it is our mitzvah and obligation to disseminate these teachings,[3] "So that all the peoples of the earth may know that *HaShem*, He is God, there is none else." Nevertheless, it behooves us to do so with the utmost reverence and care to sanctify His Great and Awesome Name. Therefore, wherever His Divine names are found in this book we have placed quotation marks between the letters, thus assuring that they are not the actual Divine names themselves.

In addition, it should be noted that the ineffable name of *HaShem* is not to be pronounced whatsoever. This is as stated by the Prophet Amos,[4] "Then he shall say: 'Silence, for we must not make mention of the name of *Hashem*!'" Rather, one must toil only to **know** *HaShem* and thereby know His name, as stated,[5] "For he has loved Me, therefore I shall deliver him; I

---

[1] Leviticus 22:32
[2] Talmud Bavli, Shabbat 115a
[3] Kings I 8:60
[4] Amos 6:10
[5] Psalms 91:14

5

will set him on high, because he knows My Name." The verse specifies, "because he **knows** My Name," and not because, "he says My Name," or because, "he uses My Name." As known, the Ten Commandments warns us that the only sin *HaShem* does not forgive, is the sin of bearing His Holy Name in vain.[6] It is thus of critical importance that we alert you to this.

Therefore, because the focus of this book is solely on the unity and service of *HaShem*, blessed is He, great care must be taken to treat it with the utmost respect. Be aware that it should not be defaced, destroyed or taken into any impure place, such as the toilet or bathroom. If, for whatever reason, you need to dispose of this book, do not discard it in the trash. Instead, drop it off at your local Orthodox Jewish Synagogue, where it can either be enjoyed by someone who will appreciate its value, or be respectfully disposed of, according to the manner prescribed by Torah law.

On the other hand, whosoever studies this work and contemplates its great depth, is assured abundant blessings from *HaShem.* This is as stated,[7] "Whosoever lengthens their contemplation of His Oneness shall be rewarded with length of days and years."

It is our sincere hope and prayer that our humble offering will find favor before *HaShem*, blessed is He, and that the dissemination of these teachings will be the final act that ushers in the true and complete redemption. May we fully

---

[6] Exodus 20:6
[7] Talmud Bavli, Brachot 13b

realize the time,[8] "When there will be neither famine nor war, envy nor competition, for goodness will flow in abundance and all delights will be as freely available as dust. The occupation of the **entire** world will be solely to know *HaShem*. Therefore, the Jews will be great sages[9] and know the hidden matters, grasping the knowledge of their Creator according to the full extent of human potential, as Isaiah (11:9) states, 'The world will be filled with the knowledge of *HaShem* as the waters cover the ocean floor.'"

The Translators

---

[8] Mishneh Torah, Melachim u'Milchamot 12:5

[9] Who will teach the entire world about *HaShem*, for all the nations will be thirsty for this knowledge and will greatly desire it.

Translators Forward

It is with tremendous joy and gratitude to *HaShem*, blessed is He, and blessed is His Name, and with awesome trembling and humility, that we have been graced with undertaking the translation of the Rebbe's Chassidic discourses (*Maamarim*) into English.

As known to all who have entered the gates of light of the Torah of Truth and the teachings of Chassidus, which are commonly known as "the words of the Living God," and as iterated by our holy Rebbes,[10] **all of it** is with one intention only. Namely, to embed the simple Oneness of *HaShem*, meaning, the matter of the Essential Light of the Unlimited One, blessed is He, into the minds and hearts of every single Jew, each according to his capacity and measure.

Like all his predecessors before him, this singular intention was conveyed to us by our holy master and teacher, the Rebbe, through his many teachings and explanations that illuminate the soul of whoever listens and receives them. It is with the same intention that we must endeavor to make these teachings directly available to the English-speaking public, to all who are unable to study them in the original language that they were said or written.

As well known, the true and complete redemption hinges upon the dissemination, study, and acquisition of the

---

[10] See the "Opening Words" of the Mittler Rebbe to Imrei Binah, in the name of his saintly father, the Alter Rebbe, Rabbi Schneur Zalman of Liadi, the author of Tanya and Shulchan Aruch and founder of the Chabad Chassidic movement, translated into English under the title, "The Gateway to Understanding."

knowledge of *HaShem*, blessed is He. In describing the times of Moshiach, Rambam[11] writes at the conclusion of his magnum opus, Mishneh Torah,[12] "The occupation of the entire world will be solely to know *HaShem*. Therefore, the Jews will be great sages[13] and know the hidden matters, grasping the knowledge of their Creator according to the full extent of human potential, as it states,[14] 'The world will be filled with the knowledge of *HaShem* as the waters cover the ocean floor.'" Moreover, Rambam clearly indicates that the acquisition of knowledge of *HaShem* is the most essential and primary aspect of the Messianic era, while all other aspects are entirely secondary to it.

Indeed, from its very inception, this has always been the essence and objective of the teachings of Chassidus, as illuminated by our holy Rebbes, beginning with the Baal Shem Tov himself, the first Baal Shem (Master of The Name *HaShem*) to come out and begin openly revealing the teachings of Chassidus.[15]

The Baal Shem Tov's ascent to the Garden of Eden on Rosh HaShanah of the year 5507, is documented in the only

---

[11] Maimonides

[12] Mishneh Torah, Melachim u'Milchamot 12:5

[13] Who will teach the entire world about *HaShem*, for all the nations will be thirsty for this knowledge and will greatly desire it.

[14] Isaiah 11:9

[15] As known, there was a chain of Baalei Shem (Masters of the Name *HaShem*) who preceded Rabbi Yisroel Baal Shem Tov. These were the leaders of the hidden *Tzaddikim* who paved the way for the knowledge of *HaShem* to be openly revealed in the world, through the teachings of Chassidus. To learn more about the historical account of these mystics, and the predecessors of the Baal Shem Tov, see *Sefer HaZichronot* translated under the title, The Lubavitcher Rabbi's Memoirs, by Rabbi Yosef Yitzchak Schneerson, the sixth Rebbe of Chabad.

manuscript that is confirmed to have been written by his holy hand. In it,[16] he describes his ascent through the various levels of the Garden of Eden, until he arrived at the palace of Moshiach himself. He asked Moshiach, "Master, when will you come?" To which Moshiach responded, "By this shall you know; It shall be at a time when your teachings will become famous and revealed in the world and your wellsprings will spread out; that is, what I have taught you and you grasped, so that they too will be able to effect unifications and ascents like you. In that time all the husks of evil (*klipot*) will cease to be, and it will be a time of grace and salvation."

The Baal Shem Tov continues and writes, "I was bewildered and greatly distressed about the length of time involved, and asked myself, "When could this possibly be?" However, while I was there, I learned three beneficial methods (*segulot*) and three Holy Names that are easy to learn and explain. My mind was then set at ease, and I thought that with these teachings, the people of my own generation might ascend and learn and attain the same level as myself, to be able to ascend and to learn and perceive as I do. However, I was not granted permission to reveal this during my lifetime."

However, now that we have entered the Messianic era, the time has come for all these holy teachings to be openly revealed in the world. As Moshiach told the Baal Shem Tov, every single Jew is capable of attaining the loftiest levels of

---

[16] Keter Shem Tov 1; For a translation of the complete letter of the Baal Shem Tov, see The Way of The Baal Shem Tov, a translation of a compilation of teachings from the Baal Shem Tov – Tzava'at HaRivash.

knowledge of *HaShem*, blessed is He, in ascending and unifying themselves to *HaShem*, just like the Baal Shem Tov.

It is to this end, that is, to spread the knowledge of *HaShem*, which is **the** essential component of the true and complete redemption, to which we all must endeavor. We have therefore been graced by *HaShem* to have translated a number of foundational works, critical to the acquisition of the knowledge of *HaShem* and how to put this knowledge into practice, in ascending and unifying ourselves to *HaShem*, blessed is He.

For, in order to derive the greatest possible benefit from the holy teachings of the Rebbe, it is important and quite helpful to, at least, possess a level of familiarity with the foundations of Torah and to have a basic understanding of the terms and order of the matters referred to in these teachings. That is, the Rebbe assumes that the student possesses some basic foundational knowledge and familiarity with the concepts and terms being discussed.[17] We have thus made the following works available to the English-reading public, so that everyone can derive the greatest possible benefit from them.

First and foremost, *HaShem* has graced us with the translation of *Ginat Egoz*, under the title "HaShem is One," by the great Rishon, Rabbi Yosef Gikatilla, of righteous memory. Born in Medinaceli, in Old Castille, Spain, in the year 1248, not long after the passing of the Rambam, Rabbi Yosef was the ultimate master of the knowledge of *HaShem*. The most famous

---

[17] See Igrot Kodesh of the Rebbe, Vol. 27, p. 133.

of all Kabbalists, Rabbi Yitzchak Luria, the Holy Ari, dubbed his work, *Shaarei Orah*-The Gates of Light, "The foundational key to all the teachings of Kabbalah."[18] If the Holy Ari regarded his *Shaarei Orah* as the foundational key to the received knowledge of Kabbalah, Rabbi Yosef himself writes that his Ginat Egoz (which he wrote first, at age twenty-six) is the foundation of all foundations.

Although this work was mostly hidden for almost 800 years, in it, he reveals the three methods and the three holy names hinted at by the Baal Shem Tov, which are the foundations of the teachings of Chassidus. It is no wonder then, that Rabbi Yitzchak of Acco, the successor of the Ramban,[19] wrote that, "if not for the work of Rabbi Yosef Gikatilla, Torah would have been forgotten from the Jewish people."[20] As the Rebbe points out in a discourse from the year 5720,[21] in this work, Ginat Egoz, Rabbi Yosef Gikatilla explains the ultimate and most essential knowledge of *HaShem*, and the Rebbe instructs us to draw these teachings forth into revelation.

No less critical to the serious student, is a study of the well-known work, *Shaar HaYichud* of the Mittler Rebbe, Rabbi DovBer of Lubavitch, the second Chabad Rebbe, which we

---

[18] See introductions to Shaarei Orah and Sefer HaMashalim of Rabbi Yosef Gikatilla, and elsewhere.

[19] Nachmanides

[20] See manuscript citation in the transcribers introduction to Sefer HaMashalim of Rabbi Yosef Gikatilla. Sefer HaMashalim is itself translated and available in English under the title The Book of Allegories.

[21] Discourse entitled "*Shiviti*" of Shabbat Parshat Naso 9 Sivan, 5720; Also see Shnei Luchot HaBrit 5a; Ohr HaTorah Yitro p. 836-839; Sefer HaMaamarim 5656 p. 381 and on; *Hemshech* 5666 p. 431; Sefer HaMaamarim 5677 p. 72 and on; Sefer HaMaamarim 5696 p. 73 and on, and elsewhere.

have translated and endeavored to elucidate under the title, "The Gate of Unity." As the sixth Lubavitcher Rebbe, Rabbi Yosef Yitzchak Schneerson, of blessed memory, said,[22] "In former generations, young men were not admitted to hear the Chassidic discourses being delivered by the Rebbe of their generation. They first had to be familiar with the order of the chaining down of the worlds (*Seder Hishtalshelut*), at least to know all its stations. This is what the Mittler Rebbe's book *Shaar HaYichud* is entirely about – it explains the nature of Chassidic contemplation (*Hitbonenut*), and the matters upon which one should contemplate."

This likewise was stated by the Rebbe himself, most notably in his first written work, *HaYom Yom*.[23] That is, that the Mittler Rebbe, Rabbi DovBer of Lubavitch, wrote specific works for each kind of student of Chassidic teachings, but his books, *Shaar HaYichud* and *Shaarei Orah*, are general works written for all students. As stated there, "*Shaar HaYichud* is the key to the teachings of Chassidus and *Shaarei Orah* is the *Aleph-Beit* of the teachings of Chassidus."

In another entry,[24] the Rebbe refers to the following teaching, relayed by Rabbi Shmuel of Lubavitch, the fourth Chabad Rebbe, to his son and successor, Rabbi Shalom DovBer of Lubavitch,[25] "The teachings of Chassidus must be studied in

---

[22] Sefer HaSichot 5691, p. 162-163
[23] HaYom Yom, 15 Adar II, Shushan Purim; Also see Sefer HaToldot Rebbe Maharash, Hosafa 2, p. 65; Igrot Kodesh of the Rebbe, Vol. 27, p. 133.
[24] HaYom Yom, 7 Tammuz
[25] Igrot Kodesh of the Rebbe Rayatz, Vol. 3, p. 404; Also see Sefer HaToldot Admor Maharash, p. 81;

an orderly fashion. This means that the first thing to know is the order of the chaining down of the worlds (*Seder HaHishtalshelut*) as our grandfather (referring to the Mittler Rebbe, Rabbi DovBer of Lubavitch) wrote in *Shaar HaYichud*."

However, it should be pointed out that, as the sixth Lubavitcher Rebbe continued to state, now that we are in the Messianic era, this is no longer a prerequisite. Rather, it now is our obligation and duty to fulfill the pledge to spread the wellsprings of these teachings outward and to open the doors to all who desire closeness to *HaShem*, blessed is He.[26] Nevertheless, it is clear from his words that the importance of these foundations is in no way diminished today, only that they no longer are prerequisites that might inhibit a person from beginning to study the words of the Living God, as conveyed in these teachings.

Of similar importance is the Mittler Rebbe's work *Kuntres HaHitpaalut*, translated into English under the title "Divine Inspiration." This book is well known[27] amongst Chassidim as the "Opening Gateway to the Service of *HaShem*." In it, the Mittler Rebbe sets forth all possible levels of attainment of Divine Inspiration, the manner of their attainment and the pitfalls that one may encounter along the way and how to avoid them. Thus, this work is invaluable to all who seek putting the teachings of Chassidus into practice.

---

[26] Sefer HaSichot 5691 ibid. p. 163
[27] Sefer HaToldot Rebbe Maharash Hosafa 2, p. 65.

Another important work, the Mittler Rebbe's Tract on Prayer (*Kuntres Inyan Tefillah*), has been translated under the title, "Praying with Passion," along with the Opening Gateway – *Petach HaShaar* to his famous work *Imrei Binah*, translated as "The Gateway to Understanding." Similarly, since the Rebbe often reiterated the Talmudic dictum that if the Jewish people do *Teshuvah*-repentance, they will immediately be redeemed,[28] we have made several foundational works available on the proper approach to *Teshuvah*-repentance, such as *Poke'ach Ivrim* of the Mittler Rebbe, translated as "Opening the Eyes of the Blind," as well as the first eleven chapters of his *Derech Chayim – Shaar HaTeshuvah*, under the title "The Path of Life," which the Rebbe encouraged the study of on a yearly basis.

Thus, having made these foundational works readily available, our approach in adapting the teachings of the Rebbe into English, is to convey these teachings as precisely as possible and in line with the above foundations that we have been given and upon which we must rely. In his discourses, translated here as, "The Teachings of the Rebbe," the Rebbe sheds light on the task and duty of **our** generation, the final generation of exile and the first generation of redemption, and the approach that we must adopt to attain and draw forth the revelation of *HaShem*, the Singular Intrinsic Unlimited Being Himself, blessed is He, in the here and now, culminating with the true and complete redemption for all mankind, literally.

---

[28] Talmud Bavli, Sanhedrin 97b; Rambam Hilchot Teshuvah 7:5

This having been said, we must state that although we have done our utmost to clarify the text itself and to incorporate elucidating notes wherever necessary, our explanations will be brief, as these matters have already been explained, at great length, in our other translations and commentaries.[29] We thus urge you, dear reader, to avail yourself of these foundational texts, which will surely open the gateways of knowledge and understanding to you and will greatly assist you in your path to attaining true closeness to *HaShem*, blessed is He.

In similar vein, it should be pointed out that the Chassidic discourses of the Rebbe are being presented here in the order that they were taught. Although it is not uncommon for Chassidim to study various Chassidic discourses at different times, not necessarily in the order that they were said, there nonetheless is added benefit in studying them in order. This is because it is often the case that a subsequent discourse further expounds on matters that were mentioned or touched upon in previous discourses. Thus, these teachings build upon each other, and questions that may arise in the mind of the reader in one discourse, will be explained by the Rebbe with greater clarity, in a subsequent discourse. Since we can be quite certain that the order in which they were said is not arbitrary, but that they are ordered according to the Supernal Intent, it is recommended that the approach to the study of these teachings also be orderly.

---

[29] See the copyright page above, for a list of available books.

It is our fervent hope and prayer that our efforts in making these teachings freely available, will illuminate the whole world with the knowledge of *HaShem*, blessed is He. May our humble offering find favor before *HaShem*, blessed is He and blessed is His name, and may the dissemination of these teachings be the final act that ushers in the true and complete redemption when,[30] "The earth will be filled with the knowledge of *HaShem* as the waters cover the ocean floor."

18th of Iyar, Lag B'Omer, 5781

ח"י אייר, ל"ג בעומר- הוד שבהוד, תשפ"א, שנת **פלאות אראנו**

The Translators

---

[30] Isaiah 11:9

Discourse 1

"*Bati LeGani* -
I have come to My garden"

Delivered on 10th of Shvat, 5711
By the grace of *HaShem,* blessed is He,

His honorable holiness, my father-in-law, our master, teacher and rabbi,[31] wrote as follows in his discourse,[32] dated for the day of his passing, the 10th day of *Shvat,* 5710:

"The verse states,[33] 'I have come to My garden My sister, My bride.' Midrash Rabbah comments,[34] 'The verse does not say, 'to a garden-*Gan*-גן,' but specifies, 'to My garden-*Gani*-גני,' meaning 'to My wedding canopy-*Genuni*-גנוני,' in that, at first, the essential root of the Indwelling Presence of *HaShem*-יהו"ה, the *Shechinah,* was in the lowest of worlds."

Now, we must understand why the term, "The **essential root** of the Indwelling Presence of *HaShem*-יהו"ה-*Shechinah,*" was used. In clarifying the term, "The Indwelling Presence-

---

[31] Rabbi Yosef Yitzchak Schneerson, the sixth Lubavitcher Rebbe.
[32] Discourse entitled "*Bati LeGani*" 5710 (*Sefer HaMaamarim* 5710. P. 111)
[33] Song of Songs 5:1
[34] Midrash Rabba, Shir HaShirim 5:1

19

Shechinah," our master, teacher and rabbi, the Alter[35] Rebbe,[36] explained that it is called the Indwelling Presence-*Shechinah*-שכינה because it dwells-*Shochenet*-שוכנת and is invested within, as in the verse,[37] "And I will dwell-*V'Shachanti*-ושכנתי **within** them**,**" this being the inception of the revelation of the Unlimited Light of *HaShem*-יהו"ה, (*Ohr Ein Sof*), blessed is He.

Now, from what he writes,[38] that the beginning of the revelation of the Unlimited Light of *HaShem*-יהו"ה (*Ohr Ein Sof*), is called, the Indwelling Presence-*Shechinah*-שכינה, it is understood that the matter of the Indwelling Presence-*Shechinah*-שכינה is much higher and loftier even than the world of Emanation-*Atzilut*,[39] and is an aspect of the light that even precedes the restraint-*Tzimtzum* of the light. For, the beginning of the revelation, is in the Unlimited Light of *HaShem*-יהו"ה (*Ohr Ein Sof*), that precedes the restraint-*Tzimtzum*.[40]

Now, his honorable holiness, our master, teacher, and rabbi, the Mittler[41] Rebbe, wrote[42] that relative to the essential

---

[35] The Elder Rebbe of the Chabad Chassidic Dynasty, the author of the Tanya and the Shulchan Aruch, Rabbi Schneur Zalman of Liadi.

[36] Tanya, Ch. 41

[37] Exodus 25:8

[38] Tanua, Ch. 52

[39] It is called Emanation, because it is the world of Godly revelation and light, and just like light, which when emanated from the luminary, reveals the luminary and has no existence without the luminary, so too with the world of Emanation-*Atzilut*.

[40] The Unlimited light and revelation of *HaShem* was restrained in order to make room, so to speak, for limited worlds. That is, by restraining the unlimited revelation of Godliness, the existence of limited worlds and beings becomes possible. (For a more extensive explanation of the first *Tzimtzum*-restraint, see Shaar HaYichud of the Mittler Rebbe, translated as The Gate of Unity, Ch. 12-13.)

[41] The *Mittler*-Middle Rebbe, Rabbi DovBer of Lubavitch.

[42] See the explanation of the verse (Psalms 118:7), "*HaShem*-יהו"ה is with me, to my aide" (cited in the long *Hemshech* discourse entitled "*Vakachah*" Ch. 27 –

Light of the Unlimited One, blessed is He, the radiance of the line and thread (*Kav V'Chut*)[43] is called by the term, "Indwelling Presence-*Shechinah*." It thus is a relative term that is applied according to the matter under discussion.

For example, relative to the world of Emanation-*Atzilut*, the attribute of Kingship-*Malchut* is called by the term Indwelling Presence-*Shechinah*. However, even in regard to this, his honorable holiness, our master, teacher and rabbi, the Tzemach Tzedek explained,[44] that the fact that the attribute of Kingship-*Malchut* of the world of Emanation-*Atzilut* is called by the term, Indwelling Presence-*Shechinah*, specifically refers to how the attribute of Kingship-*Malchut* of the world of Emanation-*Atzilut* descends to become the aspect of the crown of *Atik*[45] of the world of Creation-*Briyah*. However, as it is in Emanation-*Atzilut* it is unified with the *Sefirot* of Emanation-*Atzilut* and the term Indwelling Presence does not apply. However, this does not at all contradict what was said above,

---

Sefer HaMaamarim 5637 Vol. 2, p. 445 and on), also printed in Ohr HaTorah, Haazinu, p. 1,825; Maamarei Admor HaZaken, 5564, p. 235. Also see Biurei HaZohar of the Tzemach Tzeddek Vol. 2, p. 819 and on; Sefer HaMaamarim 5657 p. 199 and on; 5679 p. 100 and on.

[43] The limited revelation of Godliness that follows the restraint-*Tzimtzum* is called by the term "the line and thread" (*Kav V'Chut*) in that it is a thin band of revelation, as opposed to the unlimited revelation that preceded the restraint-*Tzimtzum*. (See Shaar HaYichud of the Mittler Rebbe, translated as The Gate of Unity, Ch. 14-17.)

[44] See Likkutei Torah, Shir HaShirim, the explanation of the verse, (Song of Songs 1:5) "I am blackened, but attractive," beginning of Ch. 2 (p. 8b).

[45] *Atik* of the world of Creation-*Briyah*, is the inner aspect of the crown-*Keter* of the world of Creation-*Briyah*. In general, *Atik* of Emanation-*Atzilut* refers to the pleasure to bring about the world of Creation (whereas, *Arich Anpin* refers to the desire). (See Shaar HaYichud of the Mittler Rebbe, translated as The Gate of Unity, Ch. 23-24.)

that the line and thread (*Kav V'Chut*) is called by the term, Indwelling Presence-*Shechinah*.

Nonetheless, when the sages, of blessed memory, made mention of the Indwelling Presence-*Shechinah*, they were referring to the aspect of Kingship-*Malchut* of the world of Emanation-*Atzilut*, and even then, only as it descends to become the aspect of *Atik* of the world of Creation-*Briyah*. But in its root, that is, relative to the Unlimited Light of *HaShem*-יהו״ה, even the line and thread (*Kav V'Chut*) is called, the Indwelling Presence-*Shechinah*.

His honorable holiness, our master, teacher and rabbi, the Rebbe Maharash, wrote[46] that the reason the line-*Kav* is called the Indwelling Presence-*Shechinah* is because it was drawn down in order to become invested within the worlds and within the souls of the Jewish people. Therefore, even at its inception, it is called by the term, Indwelling Presence-*Shechinah*.

Now, his honorable holiness, our master, teacher and rabbi, the Rebbe Rashab, whose soul is in Eden, explained[47] that the revelation of light, as it is even before the restraint-*Tzimtzum,* is called by the term, Indwelling Presence-*Shechinah*. That is, in the general light that precedes the restraint-*Tzimtzum,* there are three levels.[48] There is the essence

---

[46] In the *Hemshech* discourse entitled "*Vakachah*" ibid.

[47] In the discourse entitled "*Kodesh Yisroel*" in *Hemshech* 5666, p. 516 and on. Also see the discourse entitled *VaYedaber Elokim* of the year 5699, (Sefer HaMaamarim 5699 p. 175).

[48] See Shaar HaYichud of the Mittler Rebbe, translated as The Gate of Unity, Ch. 10-11 and the explanation of the three levels *Yachid*-Singular, *Echad*-One, and *Kadmon*-Preexistent. Also see Ginat Egoz of Rabbi Yosef Gikatilla, translated as

22

of the light (*Etzem Ha'Ohr*) and the light that spreads forth (*Hitpashtut Ha'Ohr*), and in the light that spreads forth itself, there also are two levels. That is, there is the revelation of the light as it is, in and of itself, which is the source of the light of how *HaShem*-יהו"ה transcends all worlds – *Sovev Kol Almin* – and there is the revelation of light that relates to worlds, which is the source of how *HaShem*-יהו"ה fills all worlds – *Memaleh Kol Almin*, and is the revelation of light that is called, the Indwelling Presence-*Shechinah*. In other words, even though it precedes the restraint-*Tzimtzum* and cannot be the direct source of the worlds, for which reason there needed to be a restraint-*Tzimtzum*, and moreover, the first restraint-*Tzimtzum* is specifically an aspect of withdrawal, nevertheless, this light is called, the Indwelling Presence-*Shechinah*.

Thus, through the above, we may understand why the terminology is specifically that, "The **essential root** of the Indwelling Presence – *Ikkar Shechinah* – was originally in the lower worlds." In other words, the revelation of the Indwelling Presence of *HaShem*-יהו"ה, as it originally was in the lower worlds, was not the Indwelling Presence as it relates to the world of Emanation-*Atzilut*, which is the aspect of Kingship-*Malchut*. It likewise was not the Indwelling Presence-*Shechinah* of the line-*Kav*, as it relates to the Unlimited light of *HaShem*-יהו"ה (*Ohr Ein Sof*). Rather, this refers to the essential

---

HaShem is One, The Gate of Intrinsic Being, and the explanation of the three names of Being-*Havayah* that are drawn forth from the Singular Preexistent Intrinsic Name of *HaShem*-יהו"ה, blessed is He.

23

and innermost aspect of *HaShem's*-יהו"ה Indwelling Presence-*Shechinah*, that was originally in this lowest world, specifically.

For, the light[49] that manifests within the worlds comes forth in a manner of order and gradation. In other words, there is great revelation above, and as it is drawn forth and chains down, the light becomes diminished. This principle applies to all the light generally throughout the entire chaining down of the worlds (*Hishtalshelut*). Thus, although before the sin of the tree of the knowledge of good and evil, there also was openly revealed light below, nevertheless, at the very same time, there was also a much greater revelation of light above. This is as our sages, of blessed memory, stated,[50] "He stretched forth His right hand and created the heavens, and He stretched forth His left hand and created the earth."[51]

Rather, the words, "The **essential root** of the Indwelling Presence – *Ikkar Shechinah* – was originally in the lowest world," are referring to the light that entirely transcends all worlds.

---

[49] See a lengthier discussion of this in the discourse entitled "*Eichah*," in the section on the Torah portion of *Devarim* from the year 5670 (Sefer HaMaamarim 5670, p. 215).

[50] Pirke D'Rabbi Eliezer Ch. 18; Zohar I 30a; Zohar II 20a, 37a, 85b

[51] The heavens were created with His right hand, referring to His attribute of *Chessed*-Kindness, which is an expansive revelation of Godly light, whereas, the left hand, by which the earth was created, refers to *Gevurah*-Might, which, in comparison, is a more restrained revelation of Godly light. We thus see that there was a greater degree of revelation in the heavens than in the earth.

2

Now, regarding this fact that the root of the Indwelling Presence-*Shechinah* of *HaShem*-יהו"ה, was in the lowest world, the Midrash explains that, "the lowest world," refers to this physical world. This is explained in the continuation of the Midrash there, that through the sin of the tree of the knowledge of good and evil, the Indwelling Presence of *HaShem*-יהו"ה withdrew from the earth to the firmament, and that at the giving of the Torah at Mount Sinai, "I came to My garden – to My wedding canopy."

Now, the primary withdrawal caused by sin, specifically resulted from the sin of the tree of the knowledge of good and evil. This is true of the matter of sin in general, in that the primary aspect of **all** sins was the sin of the tree of the knowledge of good and evil. This is because it was specifically this sin that gave "room" for all other sins. That is, the repercussions of this sin brought about the subsequent sins of Cain, the generation of Enosh, and so on.

The same is true of the **effect** of sin, which is the withdrawal of the Indwelling Presence of *HaShem*-יהו"ה, caused by sin. However, the primary withdrawal is what was withdrawn because of the sin of the tree of the knowledge of good and evil. For in that case, the withdrawal was specifically from this lowly world. In other words, just as the primary aspect of the Indwelling Presence of *HaShem*-יהו"ה was in the lowest world, specifically meaning this world, so likewise, this was so of the primary withdrawal.

That is, the primary withdrawal was specifically a withdrawal from the earth. This withdrawal was caused through the sin of the tree of the knowledge of good and evil, which caused the Indwelling Presence of *HaShem*-יהו"ה to be withdrawn from the earth to the firmament. This is also why the aforementioned discourse specifies this sin, in and of itself, thus separating between this sin and all other sins, such as those of Cain and the generation of Enosh etc.

This is because the sins of Cain and the generation of Enosh, caused the Indwelling Presence of *HaShem*-יהו"ה to be withdrawn from one firmament to a higher firmament. However, the sin of the tree of the knowledge of good and evil, caused His Indwelling Presence to be withdrawn from the earth to the firmament. In other words, besides the fact that the withdrawal from the earth directly affects us, in addition, it is **the** primary matter of withdrawal (*Siluk*).

The discourse[52] then continues and explains that subsequent to the withdrawal, there were seven righteous-*Tzaddikim* who drew the Indwelling Presence of *HaShem*-יהו"ה back down below. Avraham was meritorious and brought the Indwelling Presence down from the seventh firmament to the sixth firmament etc., until finally, Moshe, who was the seventh generation from Avraham (and "all sevens are beloved"[53]), brought the Indwelling Presence of *HaShem*-יהו"ה down below, to earth.

---

[52] The aforementioned discourse of Rabbi Yosef Yitzchak Schneerson, the sixth Lubavitcher Rebbe.

[53] Midrash Vayikra Rabba 29:11

That is, the primary matter of drawing down the Indwelling Presence was accomplished by Moshe, since it was specifically Moshe who brought it back down to earth. In other words, just as the primary aspect of withdrawal, from below to above, was through the sin of the tree of the knowledge of good and evil, wherein the withdrawal was from the earth, as said above, so likewise, the primary aspect of drawing down the Indwelling Presence, is specifically **to the earth**.

That is, besides the fact that this drawing down most directly affects and relates to us, in addition, it is **the** primary matter of drawing down His Indwelling Presence. This was accomplished specifically by Moshe. The reason for this was explained parenthetically in the (Previous Rebbe's) discourse, namely, that, "all sevens are beloved."

3.

Now, from the language of our sages, of blessed memory, that, "all sevens are beloved," and not, "all beloved are sevens," we must say that Moshe's primary advantage over and above the righteous-*Tzaddikim* who preceded him, was that he was the seventh. In other words, it is specifically because he was the seventh that he is beloved. That is, the reason he was beloved is not dependent on his choice, or his will, or his service of *HaShem*-יהו"ה, but rather, because he was the seventh generation. In other words, this is something that is dependent upon birth, and even so, "all sevens are beloved." This then, is why Moshe merited that the Torah was given by his hand.

His honorable holiness, my father-in-law, the Rebbe, explained (in a discourse said soon after his arrival to America)[54] that even in this matter of the seventh being beloved, we can recognize the greatness of the first. In other words, the entire matter of the seventh, is that he is seventh from the first. He thus explained the greatness of the first generation, that is, our forefather Avraham, and the greatness of his service of *HaShem-*יהו"ה, which was in a way of complete self-sacrifice.

However, he did not stop there, but continued to explain (even though it does not seem relevant to the subject) that the manner of Avraham's self-sacrifice was not that he sought out self-sacrifice. This is the difference between the self-sacrifice of our forefather Avraham and the self-sacrifice of Rabbi Akiva. That is, the self-sacrifice of Rabbi Akiva, was such, that he sought out self-sacrifice, and stated, "When will I be given the opportunity to fulfill the verse in *Shema,*[55] 'with all your soul'?"[56]

In contrast, the self-sacrifice of our forefather Avraham was a byproduct of his service of *HaShem-*יהו"ה. In other words, for Avraham, his primary service of *HaShem-*יהו"ה, was as stated,[57] "And he called-*Vayikra-*ויקרא there in the name of *HaShem-*יהו"ה, the God of the world," about which we are taught,[58] "Do not read, 'And he called-*Vayikra-*ויקרא' but read,

---

[54] At the end of the discourse entitled "*HaChodesh HaZeh Lachem*" 5700 (Sefer HaMaamarim 5700 p. 29 and on).
[55] Deuteronomy 6:5
[56] Talmud Bavli, Brachot 61b – "Even if He takes your soul."
[57] Genesis 21:33
[58] Talmud Bavli, Sota 10a

'and he caused others to call-*Vayakri*-ויקריא." That is, he realized that his primary service was to cause others to call out to *HaShem*-יהו"ה, and his service was such, that if this would entail self-sacrifice, he would be ready to serve *HaShem*-יהו"ה in this way too.

Now, Avraham's service and self-sacrifice for *HaShem*-יהו"ה was so great, that Moshe merited that the Torah be given by his hand only because he was the seventh generation from Avraham, who was the first. Thus, we find that even the Holy One, blessed is He, told Moshe,[59] "Do not stand in the place of great men," (referring to Avraham).

Now, although the seventh is more beloved, not by choice or through his own toil, but simply as a result of his birth, nonetheless, this is in an unrestricted manner. In other words, a person should not say to himself, "this is beyond me,"[60] or that, "this only applies to unique individuals."

Rather, as explained in Tanna D'Vei Eliyahu (Chapters 9 & 25) and cited throughout the words of the Living God,[61] **every single Jew**, even a servant or a maid,[62] is able to attain a manifestation of Divine inspiration through the Holy Spirit-*Ru'ach HaKodesh*. Additionally, every Jew is obligated to ask

---

[59] Midrash Dvarim Rabba 2:7; Proverbs 25:6

[60] Deuteronomy 30:11

[61] Chassidut

[62] The Rebbe adds: In Tanna D'Vei Eliyahu Ch. 9 it states that this applies even to an idolater. At first glance, this presents a difficulty when compared to what it states in Talmud Bavli, Bava Batra 15b, wherein it is evident that all opinions agree that the Divine Presence (*Shechinah*) does not dwell upon idolaters. See the Chiddushei Agadot and his citations there. Also see Iggeret Teiman of the Rambam, wherein it indicates that it is possible for there to be a prophet from amongst the idolaters. Thus, this requires further analysis.

29

himself, "When will my deeds reach the deeds of my forefathers, Avraham, Yitzchak and Yaakov?"[63]

Nevertheless, one must not delude himself in this, but must know that he, "should not stand in the place of great men." In other words, one must realize that the entire advantage of the seventh, is only in that he is seventh from the first, and that he thus has the ability to fulfill the service and mission of the first, which is, as stated above, "Do not read, 'and he called-*Vayikra*-ויקרא' but rather, 'and he caused others to call-*Vayakri*-ויקריא."

It is in this, specifically, that the seventh is the most beloved, since it is he who draws down the Indwelling Presence of *HaShem*-יהו"ה. More so, he draws down the, **"essential root** of the Indwelling Presence – *Ikkar Shechinah*," and moreover, he draws it **all the way down** into this lowest world!

This then, is demanded of each and every one of us who belong to this seventh generation. For, all sevens are beloved. In other words, even though we find ourselves in the seventh generation, not as a matter of choice and not because of our service of *HaShem*-יהו"ה, and there may be a number of things that are not according to our will, nevertheless, all sevens are beloved. That is, we find ourselves in the times of the, "heels of Moshiach."[64] Not only that, but at the end of the "heels." Thus, our service is specifically to **complete** the drawing down of Indwelling Presence of *HaShem*-יהו"ה-*Shechinah*, not merely the Indwelling Presence-*Shechinah*, but the **essential root** of

---

[63] Tanna D'Vei Eliyahu 25:1
[64] Talmud Bavli, Sotah 49b

His Indwelling Presence-*Ikkar Shechinah*, and to draw it down specifically into this lowest world.

4.

Now, after he explained in the aforementioned discourse that, at first, the essential root of the Indwelling Presence of *HaShem*-יהו"ה was in the lowest world, and that it was subsequently drawn down by Moshe (who was the seventh), specifically to the earth, he then states that the primary revelation of Godliness was in the Holy Temple, by citing the verse,[65] "They shall build a sanctuary for Me and I will dwell within them-*BeTocham*-בתוכם." The verse specifies, "within them-*BeTocham*-בתוכם," and not "within it-*BeTocho*-בתוכו," indicating that, "I will dwell within **each and every Jew**."[66] This is also the meaning of the verse,[67] "The righteous shall inherit the land, and dwell-*V'Yishkenu*-וישכנו upon it forever." That is, "the righteous shall inherit the land," refers to the Garden of Eden, which they inherit because they cause to dwell, (that is, they draw forth)[68] "He who dwells forever and Whose Name is exalted and holy,"[69] to be revealed below. (This matter

---

[65] Exodus 25:8

[66] Cited in the name of our sages, of blessed memory, in Likkutei Torah, Naso 20b; Reishit Chochmah, Shaar HaAhavah Ch. 6; Alshich to Exodus 25:8; Shnei Luchot HaBrit 69a; 201a; 325b; 326b; Likkutei Sichot, Volume 26, p. 173, note 45.

[67] Psalms 37:29; Midrash Rabba, Shir HaShirim 5:1; Bereishit Rabba 19:7; Bamidbar Rabba 13:2

[68] Also seee the commentary of the Maharzu to Bereishit Rabba ibid; and the Matnot Kehunah and Maharzu to Bamidbar Rabba ibid.

[69] See Shabbat prayer liturgy – "*Shochein Ad*-עד שוכן"; Isaiah 57:15

31

of, "He who dwells forever," was not explained in the aforementioned discourse, but was explained in Likkutei Torah,[70] according to the teaching of the Zohar.[71])

This then, is the meaning of,[72] "I have come to My garden,' meaning 'to My wedding canopy-*Genuni*-גנוני,' in other words, to the place where He originally dwelt." For, the essential root of the Indwelling Presence of *HaShem*-יהו"ה – the *Shechinah* – was originally in the lowest world, as explained above. The explanation (of why the essential root of His Indwelling Presence was specifically in the lowest world) is because *HaShem's*-יהו"ה ultimate intention in the creation and chaining down of the worlds, was that,[73] "The Holy One, blessed is He, desired to have a dwelling place in the lowest world."

The Alter Rebbe explains further,[74] that the ultimate purpose in the descent and chaining down of the worlds is actually not for the upper worlds, since for them, it is a great descent from the light of the Countenance of *HaShem*-יהו"ה, blessed is He, and it cannot be said that the purpose is for descent.[75] Moreover, as known, the creation of something out of nothing is only within the power of the Essential Self of *HaShem*-יהו"ה, blessed is He. This is as stated in Iggeret

---

[70] Likkutei Torah Pekudai 4d and on; 7b and on.
[71] Zohar II, beginning of Parshat Va'era; Also see Biurei HaZohar there.
[72] Song of Songs 5:1
[73] Midrash Tanchumah Naso 16; Bechukotai 3; Bereishit Rabba Ch. 3; Bamidbar Rabba Ch. 13; Tanya, Ch. 36
[74] Tanya Ch. 36
[75] Also see Ginat Egoz of Rabbi Yosef Gikatilla, translated as HaShem is One, Vol. 2, section entitled "The twelve letters ה"ו ז"ח ט"י ל"נ ס"ע צ"ק correspond to the twelve tribes of Israel"

HaKodesh,[76] in the section entitled, "He and His vitality are one." That is, it is only in the power of *HaShem*-יהו"ה, blessed is He, whose Essential Being is intrinsic to Him and who has no cause that precedes Him, to create something from absolute nothingness.[77]

In other words, the coming into being of novel existence is not from the revelations of His Godliness, but is from His Essential Self, blessed is He. Thus, it cannot be said that the ultimate purpose of novel existence is for the upper worlds, because even the world of Emanation-*Atzilut* is a revelation of that which is concealed (*Giluy HaHe'elem*).[78] This being so, it is a descent from the light of the Countenance of *HaShem*-יהו"ה, blessed is He. For, as the lights of the world of Emanation-*Atzilut* were still concealed in their source, they were on a significantly higher level and state. Moreover, since the world of Emanation-*Atzilut* is solely an aspect of revelation, it is not possible to say that the essence of creation is for revelations. Rather, the ultimate purpose is for this lowest world.

This is as stated by the Mittler Rebbe on the Torah portion of this week (the Torah portion of *Beshalach*),[79] regarding the difference between the upper worlds and this world. He explains that in this world, we feel ourselves to exist

---

[76] Tanya, Pg. 130b

[77] See Ginat Egoz ibid. translated as HaShem is One, Volume 1.

[78] For example, speech is a revelation and indication of the concealed intellect, but itself is not essential or necessary to the intellect at all, and is a complete diminishment relative to the intellect. For a lengthier explanation of the subject of "a revelation of that which is concealed" (*Giluy HaHe'elem*) see Shaar HaYichud of the Mittler Rebbe, translated as The Gate of Unity, Ch. 19.

[79] See Biurei HaZohar, Beshalach, at the end of the discourse entitled "*Kegavna d'L'Eyla*" (p. 43c).

independently. (This is similar to the explanations of the continuing discourses on Rosh HaShanah, printed this year,[80] regarding the difference between a creation-*Nivra* and a light-*Ohr*. That is, the existence of light is itself the proof that there is a luminary. Thus, when we see light, the light itself demonstrates and reveals that there is a luminary. However, such is not the case with tangible creations. Not only do they not reveal the Creator, but on the contrary, they actually conceal Him. This is because they actually experience themselves as existing independently (and it is only through intellect that it becomes obvious that this is not truly so).)[81] Although this sense of independent existence is solely within a person's sensory experience, nonetheless, the very fact that it seems to him that he exists intrinsically and independently, is specifically because he is rooted in the Essential Being of *HaShem*-יהו"ה, whose existence **is** intrinsic to Him.

It thus is understood that the intention in creation and in the chaining down of the worlds, is not for the upper worlds, which are the matter of revelations (*Giluyim*). Rather, the intention is specifically for this lowest world, which appears to be essential and intrinsic, rather than an aspect of revelations. That is, a person's experience of himself is that his existence is intrinsic and independent. Thus, it is through the service of *HaShem*-יהו"ה, blessed is He, in this world, through self-

---

[80] *Hemshech* Rosh HaShanah 5794, which was printed in 5711. Subsequently printed in Sefer HaMaamarim 5711 p. 4 and on (and see p. 37 and on).
[81] Also see Sefer HaMaamarim 5677 p. 150.

restraint (*Itkafia*) and self-transformation (*It'hapcha*), that the Essence, for which the chaining down of the worlds were created, is revealed.

5.

Now, it goes without saying, that according to the view cited by the Tzemach Tzedek,[82] even the vessels of the world of Emanation-*Atzilut* are in the category of a revelation of the concealed (*Giluy HaHe'elem*). Therefore, according to this view, the intention is certainly not for the world of Emanation-*Atzilut*, since it constitutes a descent, and is merely a matter of revelations (*Giluyim*).[83]

Rather, even according to the second opinion that he cites, that the vessels are in fact creations of something from nothing, it is explained in various places[84] that when we state that the vessels are creations of something from nothing, what is meant is not that they actually are created something from nothing, but that they only are called thus, relative to the light.

This is because the root of the vessels is in the impression-*Reshimu*,[85] which is the aspect of concealment, and

---

[82] Sefer HaMaamarim 5661 p. 178 and on.

[83] See Shaar HaYichud translated as The Gate of Unity, Ch. 19 ibid.

[84] See the discourse on "the three views" printed at the back of Sefer HaMitzvot of the Tzemach Tedek, Volume 2; Ohr HaTorah Inyanim p. 259 and on; The discourse entitled "*VaYedaber Elokim*" 5664, Sefer HaMaamarim 5664 p. 230 and on; Notes on the discourse entitled "*Patach Eliyahu*" in Torah Ohr, 56658 p. 9 and on; Discourse entitled "*Adam Ki Yakriv*" 5666, *Hemshech* 5666, p. 191 and on.

[85] The *Reshimu* is the impression of the, "empty space-*Makom Panuy*," that remained after the restraint-*Tzimtzum* of the Unlimited light and revelation, before the introduction of the line and thread-*Kav V'Chut*, which is the limited ray of light

therefore, their coming into existence is in such a way that their source is concealed. Thus, relative to the light, they are compared to the creation of something from nothing, but relative to the impression-*Reshimu*, they are the aspect of the revelation of the concealed (*Giluy HaHe'elem*).

With the above in mind, it is understood that the intention was not for the upper worlds, but rather, for our service of self-restraint (*Itkafia*) and self-transformation (*It'hapcha*) in this world. Now, it is indeed true that when we currently perform the commandments, we add additional light to the world of Emanation-*Atzilut*. This being so, how can we say that the primary intention is specifically for this world?

In response to this question, the Rebbe Maharash[86] explains that these lights that are added to the world of Emanation-*Atzilut* are like something that is placed in storage. That is, they in fact, are not for the world of Emanation-*Atzilut*, but are for this lowly world, and are not revealed in the world of Emanation-*Atzilut*.

This then, is what is explained by the Rebbe Rashab, whose soul is in Eden,[87] regarding this matter, that it is

---

and revelation that powers all the world. For a lengthier explanation of this subject, see *Shaar HaYichud* of the Mittler Rebbe, translated as The Gate of Unity, Ch. 12-13.

[86] In the discourse entitled "*Pizar Natan*" 5642; Also see the second note in Tanya Ch. 40; discourse entitled "*Erda Na*" 5648 (Sefer HaMaamarim 5648, p. 33); See Hemshech *Mi Yitenchah* 5642, Ch. 14 (Sefer HaMaamarim 5642 p. 313), founded on the discourse entitled "*Pizar Natan*" of the Alter Rebbe printed in Hanachot of R' Pinchas Reices of blessed memory, p. 57-58. Also see it with the glosses in Ohr HaTorah Bamidbar, Vol. 4, p. 1,487 and on.

[87] In the discourse entitled "*Mitzvatah MiShetishka*" 5678, Sefer HaMaamarim 5678 p. 112 and on; Also see the discourse entitled "*Erda Na*" 5658, p. 38.

impossible to say that the intention was for the upper worlds, since their existence constitutes a descent from the Countenance of *HaShem*-יהו"ה, blessed is He. The explanation is that the matter of the upper worlds is the matter of revelations (*Giluyim*), which is a descent from the Essential Being of *HaShem*-יהו"ה, since His Essential Being transcends and is removed from the matter of revelations (*Giluyim*).

Rather, the ultimate intention is for this lowly world, for thus it arose in His will, blessed is He, that He finds delight when we restrain the side of evil and transform darkness into light.[88] For, as explained in the discourse,[89] the whole of man's service of *HaShem*-יהו"ה, is to transform the foolishness (*Shtut*) of the side of evil into foolishness (*Shtut*) of holiness, and through this, "It causes satisfaction of spirit before Me, that I spoke and my will was actualized."[90]

Thus, it is through this that we draw forth that this world becomes a dwelling place for *HaShem*-יהו"ה, blessed is He. Just as a person's entire essence and being inhabits his dwelling place, it is the same way with this lowly world, which is the dwelling place of *HaShem*-יהו"ה, blessed is He.[91] In other words, His Divine intention is that we not only draw forth revelations, but beyond that, that the very Essential Self of *HaShem*-יהו"ה, the Unlimited One, blessed is He, will be within

---

[88] Zohar I 4a

[89] Chapter 3 and on; Sefer HaMaamarim 5710, p. 114 and on.

[90] Torat Kohanim and Rashi commentary to Leviticus 1:9

[91] See Maamarei Admor HaZaken 5565 Vol. 1, p. 489 (and with glosses printed in Ohr HaTorah, Shir HaShirim Vol. 2, p. 679 and on); Ohr HaTorah Balak p. 997 and on; Sefer HaMaamarim 5635 Vol. 2, p. 353; 5662 p. 335; *Hemshech* 5666 p. 3 & p. 445.

us. This then, is the ultimate purpose of the creation of the entire chaining down of the worlds.

6.

Now, at the conclusion of the discourse,[92] it is explained that the essential root of *HaShem's*-יהו"ה Indwelling Presence in this lowest world, was primarily revealed in the Holy Temple, and that because of this, the Tabernacle-*Mishkan* was built specifically of acacia wood (*Atzei Shittim*-עצי שטים). For, the intended purpose is to transform the foolish impulse (*Shtut*-שטות) for the opposite of holiness, such as the desires and passions of the animalistic soul, into foolish impulse for holiness.[93] This is like what our sages, of blessed memory, said about such conduct,[94] "The elder sage was well served by his foolishness (*Shtut*-שטות)." That is, he served *HaShem*-יהו"ה and was given over to Him, in a manner that transcended reasoning and knowledge.

Now, all matters that were demanded of us by his honorable holiness, my father-in-law, the Rebbe, and likewise, by all of the Rebbes that preceded him, were what they themselves fulfilled. This is similar to what our sages, of blessed memory, commented on the verse,[95] "He tells **His** word

---

[92] The aforementioned discourse of Rabbi Yosef Yitzchak Schneerson, the sixth Lubavitcher Rebbe, Chapter 5, Sefer HaMaamarim 5710, p. 117-118

[93] What is meant here by foolish impulse is that it is not subject to the calculations of rational measure, but is rather unrestrained and uncalculated.

[94] Talmud Bavli, Ketuvot 17a

[95] Psalms 147:19

to Yaakov, **His** statutes and ordinances to Israel." That is,[96] "that which He does, He tells the Jewish people to do and to keep." That is, that which He commands Israel to do, He does Himself. The same can be said about the instructions of our Rebbes; that which they demanded of those who were connected to them, they themselves fulfilled and did as well. Moreover, they revealed that they fulfilled these things, to make it easier for us to fulfill them too.

An example is the *mitzvah*-commandment to love of one's fellow Jew (*Ahavat Yisroel*). There are many anecdotes relating to the conduct of each Rebbe regarding this. For example, the Alter Rebbe once interrupted his prayers[97] and went to chop wood and cook soup for a woman who had just given birth, because there was no one at home to help her.

Similarly, during a private audience with the Mittler Rebbe, a young man bemoaned about what young men bemoan about, and the Rebbe uncovered his arm and said to him, "Do you see how my skin is shriveled upon my bones?[98] This is

---

[96] The Rebbe adds: Midrash Shmot Rabba 30:9; Talmud Yerushalmi Rosh HaShanah 1:3 – This refers to the awakening from Above (*It'aruta d'L'Eyla*) that precedes the awakening from below (*It'aruta D'L'Tata*). That is, first "He sanctified us with **His** commandments," and then afterwards, "whoever sits and studies Torah, the Holy One, blessed is He, sits and studies opposite him." That is, it is only afterwards that the donning of *Tzitzit*-fringes from below (for example) awakens the Supernal *Tzitzit*-fringes Above, to draw forth additional illuminations of light etc., through an awakening from below (*It'aruta D'L'Tata*) that subsequently affects an awakening from Above (*It'aruta d'L'Eyla*). This is the meaning of the words of the discourse that, "that which He commands Israel to do, He does Himself." See the explanation in Torah Ohr, in the discourse entitled "*Ki Imcha M'kor Chayim*" (p. 35c) and various other places. (Also see Sefer HaMaamarim 5636 Vol. 2, p. 327.)

[97] Torat Menachem Reshimat HaYoman p. 361

[98] Lamentations 4:8

because of the, 'sins of your youth!'"[99] Now, the Mittler Rebbe's exalted spiritual stature was so wondrously exalted beyond people who are drawn to such matters, in every way, both generally and particularly. Nevertheless, his bond with them was so great that their unsatisfactory behaviors even affected his health, to the point that his skin shriveled upon his bones.

It is related[100] that before his prayers, the Tzemach Tzedek, would go out of his way to make a charitable loan to a simple person in financial need.

It is related that the Rebbe Maharash once traveled[101] from a health spa to Paris, for the sole purpose of meeting with a certain young man. He told him, "Young man, forbidden wine spiritually dulls the mind and heart! Be a Jew!" The young man returned home and could not quiet his heart until he came to the Rebbe Maharash and fully repented. He subsequently became the head of a God fearing and observant family.

Moreover, it is known that time was extremely precious to the Rebbe Maharash, to such an extent that even when he would say a Chassidic discourse, he would do so briefly, and on certain known occasions, he had already concluded his morning prayers by eight in the morning. Nevertheless, as precious as time was for him, he traveled a great distance and stayed there

---

[99] Beit Rebbi Vol. 2, see note on p. 283
[100] Sefer HaSichot, Kayitz 5700, p. 98; Sefer HaMaamarim 5711 p. 153; Igrot Kodesh of the Previous Rebbe, Vol. 4, p. 522.
[101] See Sefer HaToldot Rebbe Maharash p. 77 at length. (Also printed in Sefer HaSichot 5705, p. 30 and on; Igrot Kodesh Vol. 15, p. 199.)

for an extended period of time, for the benefit of this young man.

Likewise, it is known that early in the reign of the Rebbe Rashab, whose soul is in Eden, an anti-Semitic decree was newly issued, and he wanted to travel to Moscow to work on nullifying it. His older brother, Rabbi Zalman Aharon, whose soul is in Eden, said to him, "Your time is very precious and you are not fluent in Russian, but you will need to make certain acquaintances there." (Rabbi Zalman Aharon was a linguist and spoke Russian fluently) "Let me go instead and deal with it according to your instructions."[102] The Rebbe Rashab, did not agree, traveled to Moscow himself and was successful.

There are many similar stories about how his honorable holiness, my father-in-law, the Rebbe, went out of his way and toiled to do a favor for another, even for single individuals, regardless of whether it involved a spiritual matter or a physical one. He set himself aside selflessly, both physically and spiritually, even when the recipient of his benevolence not only was not in the category of,[103] "your peer in Torah and *mitzvot*," but could not compare to him in any way.

---

[102] See Igrot Kodesh of the Rebbe Rashab Vol. 4, p. 245 where he indicates a deficiency in the language of the land. Also see the notes of the Rebbe Rayatz there, that the Rebbe Rashab was indeed fluent in the language, and was able to understand even deep matters that were read to him in that language, but that he did not wish to speak it. When the Rebbe Rayatz asked his father why he does not speak Russian, he gave three answers.

[103] See Tanya Ch. 32

7

Now, it is through self-restraint (*Itkafia*) and self-transformation (*It'hapcha*) from unholy foolishness to holy foolishness (*Shtut D'Kedusha*), that we fulfill the intention in creation, which is for *HaShem*-יהו"ה, blessed is He, to have a dwelling place in this lowest world. Moreover, when we say that it is through our self-restraint (*Itkafia*) and self-transformation (*It'hapcha*) that a dwelling place is made for Him below, that is, "I have come to My garden," this actually is in a way that is loftier than how the world was before the sin of the Tree of the knowledge of good and evil.

This is like demolishing a house in order to build a new one. Obviously, the new house must be an improvement over the old house. In the same way, we must say that the dwelling place for *HaShem*-יהו"ה that is made through our self-restraint (*Itkafia*) and self-transformation (*It'hapcha*) will be on a much higher level than it originally was before the sin.

This was explained in the aforementioned discourse,[104] that through the restraint (*Itkafia*) and transformation (*It'hapcha*) of the "other side-*Sitra Achara*,"[105] "the glory of the Holy One, blessed is He, is elevated-*Istalek* in all worlds."[106] This refers to the light that is in all worlds equally. In other words, although the language of the discourse seems to be

---

[104] The aforementioned discourse of Rabbi Yosef Yitzchak Schneerson, the sixth Lubavitcher Rebbe, Chapter 1, Sefer Hama'amarim 5710, p. 111-112.

[105] The "Other Side-*Sitra Achera*," means whatever is the opposite of holiness.

[106] Tanya Ch. 27 & Likkutei Torah, Parshat Pekudei cite Zohar II 128b, Zohar II 67b, Zohar II 184a; Torah Ohr Vayakhel 89d; Likkutei Torah Chukat 65c

referring to the light of how *HaShem*-יהו"ה, blessed is He, transcends all worlds-*Sovev Kol Almin*, nevertheless, we cannot say that the intention in creation is that there should be a drawing forth of light that is still in the category of worlds-*Almin*, only that it transcends and encompasses them. Rather, the intention is that there should be a drawing forth of the light of *HaShem*-יהו"ה, blessed is He, that is completely beyond the category of worlds, altogether.

It is for this reason that the revelation of this light is called elevation-*Istalek*-אסתלק, and this is likewise why the passing of the righteous-*Tzaddikim* is called, *Histalkut*-הסתלקות.[107] This is because the word *Histalkut*-הסתלקות refers to the revelation of a higher and more elevated light. There are two letters in Iggeret HaKodesh[108] that explain the matter of *Histalkut*-הסתלקות. In the second letter, the matter of *Histalkut*-הסתלקות is explained as it relates to the sin offering of the Red Heifer (*Parah Adumah*). It explains there that matters that are performed in an inner way cannot purify the three impure husks that are entirely evil (*Shalosh Kelipot HaTmei'ot*). To do so, requires matters that are performed specifically from the outside, just like the Red Heifer was offered outside the camps.

It is in this regard that a comparison is made to the passing of the righteous-*Tzaddikim*.[109] That is, nowadays we do not have the Red Heifer to purify us, since, "because of our sins," it became necessary that, "we were exiled from our

---

[107] See Torah Ohr, Vayakhel 89d
[108] Iggeret HaKodesh, Epistle 27 and 28.
[109] Talmud Bavli, Mo'ed Katan 28a; Talmud Yerushalmi Yoma 1:5

land."[110] However, we still have the passing of the righteous-*Tzaddikim*. Regarding the passing of the righteous-*Tzaddikim*, our sages, of blessed memory, taught us two things.[111] The first states, "The passing of the righteous-*Tzaddikim* is equal to the Temple of our God being burned down." The second states, "The passing of the righteous-*Tzaddikim* is worse than the destruction of the Holy Temple." Nevertheless, it is through this that the glory of the Holy One, blessed is He, is elevated-*Istalek*.

Now, the term *Histalkut*-הסתלקות, was explained by all the Rebbes. That is, this was explained by the Alter Rebbe, the Mittler Rebbe, the Tzemach Tzeddek, the Rebbe Maharash, the Rebbe Rashab, and my father-in-law, the Rebbe.[112] They all explained that the intention and meaning of the word *Histalkut*-הסתלקות is not that he withdraws and ascends above, God forbid. Rather, the intention is that he indeed is found below, but in an aspect of exaltedness.

This then, is what is demanded of each and every one of us who finds himself in the seventh generation from the Alter Rebbe. For, "all sevens are beloved," and therefore, although we have neither earned it, nor labored for it, nonetheless, "all sevens are beloved," and it thus is the mission and responsibility of this seventh generation to drawn down the Indwelling Presence of *HaShem*-יהו"ה into this lowly world, **literally**! That is, we must transform the foolishness and passions of our

---

110 Yom Tov Mussaf liturgy
111 Talmud Bavli Rosh HaShanah 18b; Midrash Eicha Rabba 1:37
112 Torah Ohr, Vayakhel; Ohr HaTorah, Shlach Vol. 6 p. 1,781; Sefer HaMaamarim 5671 p. 157 and on; and elsewhere.

44

animalistic soul, which each person knows he has, and transform it to foolishness for the holy (*Shtut D'Kedusha*).

8.

This then, is the matter of the passing of the righteous.[113] Although there were already numerous concealments, as well as many questions and matters that are not understood, all this was inadequate. That is, in order that the glory of the Holy One, blessed is He, be elevated in all the worlds, there was also the matter of the passing of the righteous-*Tzaddik*, which not only equals the destruction of the Temple, but is actually worse than it. However, the ultimate intention is that, through this, there is an elevation of the glory of the Holy One, blessed is He.

It is thus demanded of each and every one of us, to recognize that we find ourselves in the seventh generation, and that the elevated level of the seventh is that he is seventh from the first. The conduct of the first was that he did not seek anything for himself, not even self-sacrifice. For, he knew that the entire purpose of his being was as stated, "And he called there in the name of *HaShem*-יהו״ה, God of the world." An example of a person who conducts himself like our forefather Avraham, is that, if he arrives in a place where no one knows of Godliness and Judaism, or even knows the *Aleph-Beit*,[114] as long as he is there, he sets himself completely aside and fulfills

---

[113] Zohar III 71b; Iggeret HaKodesh, Ibid. (Epistle 27).
[114] The Hebrew alphabet.

the dictum,[115] "Do not read, 'and he called-*Vayikra*-ויקרא,' but rather read, 'and he caused others to call-*Vayakri*-ויקריא.'"

Now, as known,[116] whenever the sages expounded on biblical terms and used the principle of, "Do not read...but rather read..." both interpretations of the word are sustained intact. Here too, the written Torah explicitly states, "and he called-*Vayikra*-ויקרא in the name of *HaShem*-יהו״ה." Nevertheless, one must know that if he wants to succeed in the aspect of, "and he called-*Vayikra*-ויקרא in the name of *HaShem*-יהו״ה," he must necessarily have the aspect of, "and he caused others to call-*Vayakri*-ויקריא in the name of *HaShem*-יהו״ה," and he must therefore see to it that others not only know, but themselves, "call out in the name of *HaShem*-יהו״ה." In other words, even if until now, his fellow was entirely ignorant of *HaShem*-יהו״ה, one must now see to it that he now calls out to "*HaShem*-יהו״ה, God of the world-*E"l Olam*-א״ל עולם."

Moreover, the verse actually reads, "God world-*E"l Olam*-א״ל עולם" and not "God **of the** world-*E"l HaOlam*- א״ל העולם."[117] In other words, one must realize that Godliness is not one independent thing unto itself and the world is another independent thing unto itself, only that the Godliness has dominion and rule over the world. Rather, the world and Godliness are entirely one.

[115] Talmud Bavli, Sota 10a
[116] Halichot Elai Section 3
[117] Likkutei Torah Tavo 42d, 43a; Discourse entitled "*Anochi HaShem Elokecha*" 5673, *Hemshech* 567 Vol. 1, p. 257

9.

Now, although on the one hand,[118] "Who is he and where is he who dares to presume in his heart" to say "I will serve *HaShem*-יהו״ה like the service of our forefather Avraham," nevertheless, to a small extent this type of service is applicable to each and every one of us, and is obligatory.[119] Moreover, we are granted the power to do this through the conduct that was demonstrated by the first, and those who followed after him, up until and including the conduct demonstrated by his honorable holiness, my father-in-law, the Rebbe. They paved the way and granted us the necessary powers for this. This itself is what makes the seventh generation so beloved, in that so many powers were given and revealed for our sakes.

Thus, it is through service of *HaShem*-יהו״ה, in this manner, that we draw forth the primary aspect of the Indwelling Presence of *HaShem*-יהו״ה below, in this physical and material world. Moreover, this will be on an even higher level than before the sin, as stated about Moshiach,[120] "He will be exalted and high and exceedingly lofty," more than Adam, the first man, and even higher than he was before the sin.[121]

---

[118] Esther 7:5

[119] See Torah Ohr, Va'era (p. 55a), and Vayeitze (p. 23c and on).

[120] Isaiah 52:13

[121] Likkutei Torah of the Arizal, Tisa; Sefer HaLikkutim Shemot; This requires further analysis based on Sefer HaGilgulim Ch. 19 cited in Likkutei Torah Tzav 17a, but perhaps may be resolved by what it states in Sefer HaGilgulim, Ch. 7 cited in Likkutei Torah Shir HaShirim 51c.

His honorable holiness, my father-in-law, the Rebbe, who, "bore our ills and carried our suffering,"[122] and who "was anguished by our sins and crushed because of our iniquities," – just as he saw us in our afflictions, so will he redeem his flock from both spiritual and physical exile simultaneously, and uplift us to the rays of light, speedily in our days and rapidly in our times. However, all this is only the aspect of revelations (*Giluyim*) of Godliness. Beyond this, however, he will bond and unify us to the very Essential Self of *HaShem*-יהו"ה, the Unlimited One, blessed is He. For, this is the inner intent in the descent and chaining down of the worlds, as well as the matter of sin and its rectification, as well as the passing of the righteous, through which there will be an elevation of the Glory of the Holy One, blessed is He. When He redeems us from the exile "with an outstretched arm"[123] and "all the dwelling places of the children of Israel will be filled with light,"[124] "Then Moshe and the children of Israel shall sing... *HaShem*-יהו"ה will reign over the whole world forever,"[125] (as we recite in the prayer liturgy), and even in the language of translation,[126] "The Kingship of *HaShem*-יהו"ה is established forever, for all eternity." We conclude the prayer with the words,[127] "*HaShem*-יהו"ה will be King over all the earth, on that day *HaShem*-יהו"ה will be One and His Name One." That is, there will be no

---

[122] Isaiah 53:4-5
[123] Exodus 14:8
[124] Exodus 10:23
[125] Exodus 15:1, 15:18
[126] Targum Onkelos Ibid.; Also see Likkutei Torah, Shir HaShirim, discourse entitled "*Hinach Yafah*" Ch. 2 (p. 13d).
[127] Zacharia 14:9

difference between *HaShem*-יהו"ה and His Name.[128] All this is accomplished through the passing of the righteous, which is even harsher than the destruction of the Holy Temple. Since we have already experienced all these things, this matter is now entirely dependent on us, the seventh generation. May we merit to see[129] and meet with the Rebbe, here below in a physical body, below ten handbreadths (*Tfachim*),[130] and he will redeem us.

---

[128] Talmud Bavli Pesachim 50a; Also see Ginat Egoz of Rabbi Yosef Gikatilla, translated as HaShem is One, Volume 1.

[129] See the end of Sefer Chassidim (and Gilyon HaShas to Ketuvot 103a); Bamidbar Rabba 19:13.

[130] In regard to the laws of carrying on Shabbat, there are two primary domains, the private domain-*Reshut HaYachid*, and the public domain-*Reshut HaRabim*. It is explained that the space above ten handbreadths is not considered the public domain-*Reshut HaRabim* (See Shulchan Aruch of the Alter Rebbe, Orach Chaim 345:17). That is, the matter of the public domain-*Reshut HaRabim* is applicable only below ten handbreadths. The Arizal explains (and as cited in Tanya Ch. 33) that the public domain-*Reshut HaRabim* indicates the multiplicity of the separate worlds of Creation-*Briyah*, Formation-*Yetzirah*, and Action-*Asiyah* and the multiplicity indicated by the shared term God-*Elohi"m*-אלהי"ם, which is in the plural form and conceals the Singular Intrinsic and Essential Name of *HaShem*-יהו"ה Himself, blessed is He. In contrast, the world of Emanation-*Atzilut* is the world of the Oneness of the Singular Intrinsic Being, the private domain-*Reshut HaYachid*. This is further indicated by the fact that the minimum requirements of a private domain-*Reshut HaYachid* , is that has a minimum area of four handbreadths, and is surrounded by walls with a minimum height of ten handbreadths. These correspond to the four letters of the Singular Name *HaShem*-יהו"ה, blessed is He, which when spelled out as the Name of *Ma"H*-מ"ה-45, (יו"ד ה"א וא"ו ה"א) consists of ten letters that enliven the ten *Sefirot* of the world of Emanation-*Atzilut*. The ultimate intent, however, is that the Singularity of the Preexistent Intrinsic and Essential Being of *HaShem*-יהו"ה Himself, should be revealed in the lower world, specifically below ten handbreadths. (See the Sicha of Motzei Shabbat Parshat Bo, 10 Shvat 5737 toward the end. Also see Ginat Egoz of Rabbi Yosef Gikatilla, translated into English as HaShem is One, Volume 1.)

Discourse 2

"*HaYoshevet BaGanim* -
You who dwells in the gardens"

Delivered on the 13th of Shvat, 5711
By the grace of *HaShem*, blessed is He,

1.

The verse states,[131] "You who dwells in the gardens, the companions listen to your voice." His honorable holiness, my father-in-law, our master, teacher and rabbi, brings two seemingly contradictory explanations of this verse (in the discourse that continues from the discourse of the day of his passing.[132])

The first explanation of the term, "gardens-*Ganim*" is that it refers to this physical world,[133] and, "You who dwell in the gardens," refers to the Congregation of Israel who are scattered in exile, pasturing in the gardens of the other nations. Nevertheless, when they sit in the houses of worship and the houses of Torah study, the "companions," which refers to the ministering angels, who have neither jealousy, hatred or competition between them, "listen to your voice."

---

[131] Song of Songs 8:13
[132] See discourse entitled *HaYoshevet BaGanim* 5710, Sefer HaMaamarim 5710 p. 119.
[133] Rashi to Song of Songs 8:13; See also Midrash Shir HaShirim Rabba.

51

The second explanation is that the term "gardens-*Ganim*" refers to the Garden of Eden.[134] Now, although there are myriads of different levels of the Garden of Eden, to no end, they generally are divided into two levels that are called the lower Garden of Eden and the upper Garden of Eden.[135] According to this explanation, when the verse states, "the companions listen to your voice," it is referring to the souls in the Garden of Eden who are called by the term, "companions." This was explained in a parenthetical note in the aforementioned discourse, that at times, one soul is emanated of another soul.[136] It could be said that this parenthetical note

---

[134] Zohar I 77b; 92a; Zohar II 46a, and Mikdash Melech commentary there; Zohar III 13a; 213a; Also see the discourse entitled *HaYoshevet BaGanim* in Ohr HaTorah, Shir HaShirim, Vol. 2, p. 765-766 & p. 779, and elsewhere.

[135] See Torah Ohr, Tetzaveh 81c and elsewhere.

[136] Note of the Rebbe: In the prayer "*Ana Adon HaOlamim*" (*Ma'aneh Lashon* p. 10 [p.13]) it states: "For there are many times that a soul is emanated (*Ne'etzelet-*נאצלת) from a soul, like a branch that adheres (*Dvukah-*דבוקה) to a tree, clinging (*Chavukah-*חבוקה) like a link in a chain." It can be said that the reason for the use of these three terms is because the unity of souls that occurs when one prostrates at the gravesite of a *Tzaddik* (*Hishtatchut*) must be with the aspects of his *Nefesh, Ru'ach* and *Neshamah* bonding with the *Nefesh, Ru'ach* and *Neshamah* of the *Tzaddik*. (See Mishnat Chassidim, Mesechet Yichudim; Also see the discourse on prostrating at the gravesites of the righteous by Rabbi Hillel of Paritch.) Thus, the term emanated-*Ne'etzelet-*נאצלת corresponds to the *Neshamah*, the adhesion-*Dvukah-*דבוקה of the branch to the tree corresponds to the *Ru'ach* (since the emotive attributes correspond to the category of the vegetative-*Tzome'ach*) and the clinging-*Chuvukah-*חבוקה like a link in a chain, corresponds to the inanimate, which is the aspect of kingship-*Malchut*, and is the *Nefesh* level of the soul.

We possibly can also explain these three terms, emanated-*Ne'etzelet-*נאצלת, adhering-*Dvukah-*דבוקה and clinging-*Chuvukah-*חבוקה, and their relationship to the levels of *Nefesh, Ru'ach* and *Neshamah*, from Above to below, as follows: The matter of emanation-*Atzilut* is only the aspect of the revelation of the concealed (*Giluy HaHe'elem*). The matter of adhesion-*Dveikut* indicates that they are one essential and inner being, like the branch and the tree. The matter of clinging-*Chibuk* indicates a bond in a way of transcendence (*Makif*). (See the distinction between the term adhesion-*Dveikut-*דביקות and bonding-*Hitkashrut-*התקשרות elucidated in the discourse entitled "*VeHayah Eikev*" 5673 (*Hemshech* 5672 Vol. 1, p. 356 and on)).

comes to inform us that the relationship between souls is not arbitrary, but rather, that one soul is emanated from another soul.

We explained (in the previous discourse,[137] entitled "I have come to My garden,") that the matter of Emanation-*Atzilut* refers to the revelation of that which is concealed (*Giluy HaHe'elem*). In other words, it is one thing, except that it descends to be revealed from its state of concealment. This is comparable to the hidden powers of the soul that subsequently descend and become revealed from their concealment. Because of this, we cannot say that the intention of creation was for the world of Emanation-*Atzilut*, because, since the world of Emanation-*Atzilut* is the revelation of the concealed (*Giluy HaHe'elem*), it is only a matter of descent.[138]

Rather, the intention of creation is for this lowly world. We can likewise apply this to the aforementioned relationship between souls, since that too is a matter of emanation-*Atzilut* and the revelation of that which is concealed (*Giluy HaHe'elem*).

We can also connect this to the three categories of prayer, Torah which is the bond of spirit to spirit (*Rucha b'Rucha*), and the commandments, which are indicated by the verse (Song of Songs 2:6) "His right hand shall hug me-*Techabkeini*-תחבקני. (Also see the discourse later this year entitled "*VeHayah Eikev*" 5711 where this distinction of terms will be further elucidated.)

[137] See the previous discourse, Chapter 4.

[138] For example, speech is a revelation and indication of the concealed intellect, but it itself is not essential or necessary to the intellect at all, and is a complete diminishment in relation to the intellect. For a lengthier explanation of the subject of "a revelation of that which is concealed" (*Giluy HaHe'elem*) see Shaar HaYichud of the Mittler Rebbe, translated as The Gate of Unity, Ch. 19.

2.

Now, to understand the relationship between these two explanations, we should preface with what he explains earlier in his discourse.[139] Namely, that when the soul descends to manifest within the body, although the body indeed conceals and hides, nevertheless, through toil in the service of *HaShem-*יהו"ה, blessed is He, one eliminates the concealment and hiddenness. On the contrary, it is specifically through its descent and manifestation that the soul is actually strengthened with even greater strength.

Now, we can examine his use of the term, "On the contrary," specifically, and understand it in line with what the Alter Rebbe explains (in *Iggeret HaKodesh*, Epistle 25[140]) regarding the teaching of his honorable holiness, the Baal Shem Tov, about the matter of anger.[141] That is, if during prayer, a gentile[142] stands opposite a person and talks to him to confuse him, not only should he not be affected by him and continue to pray, as if the gentile was not disturbing him at all, but more so, it should affect him to have even greater strength and power in his prayers, when he contemplates and considers that the exile

---

[139] That is, in the discourse of Rabbi Yosef Yitzchak Schneerson, Ch. 9 (Sefer HaMaamarim 5710 ibid. p. 124).

[140] Pg. 141a

[141] See Tzava'at HaRivash, translated into English under the title, The Way of The Baal Shem Tov, Teaching 120.

[142] Note from the Rebbe: It should be pointed out that in the correct version of Tanya, towards the end of Chapter Twenty-Eight, the word used here is an "uncircumcised one," (meaning any gentile), but that due to censorship it was replaced with the term "idolater." This being the case, we can be certain that this is in fact also the correct word in the aforementioned epistle in Iggeret HaKodesh.

of the Indwelling Presence of *HaShem*-יהו"ה, is to such an extent, that it is exiled into this disturbing speech. We thus find that it is specifically through the opposition of the disturbance, that he is awakened to an even greater extent, specifically because of the disturbance.

His honorable holiness, the Mittler Rebbe, explains this the same way. (In Torah Ohr[143] this matter is only touched upon in short, but in Torat Chaim of the same Torah portion,[144] it is explained at great length.) There it is explained in regard to the verse,[145] "And it came to pass, when Pharaoh sent the people," that this means that not only did the external husk of evil, known as Pharaoh, not conceal and hide, but on the contrary, it actually assisted. This is as stated,[146] "And when Pharaoh came near-*Hikriv*-הקריב," about which the Midrash states,[147] "The word '*Hikriv*-הקריב means, 'brought close,' that is, he brought the hearts of Israel close to their Father in heaven." Moreover, the continuing words of the verse are understood to mean that Pharaoh himself went with the nation, meaning that the sparks that had fallen into this husk, ascended with them.

This then, also explains why the term, "On the contrary," was specifically used. In other words, not only does the body not conceal and hide over the soul, which remains in its original condition, as if there is no concealment or

---

[143] Torah Ohr, Beshalach 61a-61c

[144] Torat Chaim, Beshalach 169b and on; 174a; Also see Ohr HaTorah Beshalach p. 363 and on.

[145] Exodus 13:17

[146] Exodus 14:10

[147] Shmot Rabba 21:5; Tanchuma Beshalach 8; Pirke D'Rabbi Eliezer Ch. 42; Zohar II 47b

hiddenness, but on the contrary, it is specifically because there is concealment at first, that a person fortifies himself with even greater strength to overcome it. Moreover, this is the primary intention in the creation of the worlds, to restrain (*Itkafiah*) and transform (*Ithafcha*) the foolishness of the opposing side and the drive of the animalistic soul for worldly matters – into holiness.

Although it indeed is explained in various places that the performance of the *mitzvot*-commandments is in order to add additional illumination in the world of Emanation-*Atzilut*, it was already explained before[148] that the essential purpose in this, is for this world. This is as stated by his honorable holiness, the Tzemach Tzeddek and his honorable holiness, the Rebbe Maharash,[149] that as the lights are in the world of Emanation-*Atzilut*, they are comparable to something that is placed in storage. More so, the essential revelation and root of the Indwelling Presence of *HaShem*-הו"ה, is specifically in this world. This accords with what we previously explained at length in the name of his honorable holiness, the Rebbe Rashab,[150] whose soul is in Eden, regarding the term, "the **essential root** of the Indwelling Presence – *Ikkar Shechinah*." This was expressed to an even greater degree by his honorable

---

[148] In the previous discourse entitled "*Bati LeGani*," Ch. 5

[149] See Hemshech *Mi Yitenchah* 5642, Ch. 14 (Sefer HaMaamarim 5642 p. 313), founded on the discourse entitled *Pizar Natan* of the Alter Rebbe printed in Hanachot of R' Pinchas Reices of blessed memory, p. 57-58. Also see it with the glosses in Ohr HaTorah Bamidbar, Vol. 4, p. 1,487 and on.

[150] In the previous discourse, "*Bati LeGani*," Ch. 1

holiness, the Alter Rebbe,[151] and his honorable holiness the Maggid of Mezhritch,[152] where they explained the teaching of our sages, of blessed memory,[153] "Know what is above you." They explained that, "You should know that, that which is above, is from you," meaning that all matters that are above, are from and of your doing, and are entirely dependent upon you.

3.

This then, explains of the matter of, "You who dwell in the gardens." Namely, that the souls who dwell in the lower Garden of Eden and the upper Garden of Eden, come to hear the voices of the Jewish people below. This includes both the souls as they are above,[154] before descending into bodies, as well as souls that have been in bodies and already have attained the advantage brought about through the service of *HaShem*-יהו"ה within a body. For, about the time that they were in the body, the verse states,[155] "though they are fashioned in many days, to Him they are one."[156] That is, these souls drew forth the Oneness of, "*HaShem* is One-*HaShem Echad*-יהו"ה אחד" into themselves and completed all their service, for which

---

[151] See Igrot Kodesh of the Rebbe Rayatz, Vol. 3, p. 303; HaYom Yom 13 Iyyar.

[152] Likkutei Amarim of the Maggid of Mezhritch p. 198; Also see Tzava'at HaRivash translated into English as The Way of The Baal Shem Tov, Num. 142.

[153] Mishnah Avot 2:1

[154] See Likkutei Torah, Shir HaShirim, "*Tzena U're'ena*" (p. 22b).

[155] Psalms 139:16

[156] See Likkutei Torah ibid. as well as the end of Shlach; Also see the discourse entitled "*Tov Li*" and "*Beyadcha Afkeed*" (Sefer HaMaamarim Yiddish, p. 82, p. 102).

reason the Jewish people are called,[157] "The legions of HaShem-*Tziv'ot HaShem*-יהו״ה צבאות." (as explained by my father-in-law, the Rebbe, in the aforementioned discourse.[158])

That is, the term "*Tzva*-צבא" has three meanings. The first meaning is, "army," and refers to accepting the yoke of Heaven. The second meaning is, "an appointed time," which means that in the fixed time that was apportioned to them, they completed all their service of HaShem-יהו״ה. The third is that it is a term for, "colors-*Tzivyon*-צביון," meaning beauty. In other words, it does not just mean, "desirable," but "beautiful," indicating that it comes from the innermost aspect of the crown-*Keter* and causes pleasure. It is for these reasons that the Jewish people are called by the title "*Tziv'ot HaShem*-יהו״ה צבאות."

Nevertheless, even these souls come to hear the voices of souls that are manifest within bodies, even if their service is not yet completed to perfection. That is, they have not perfected their service according to the first explanation of the word, "army-*Tzva*-צבא," referring to accepting the yoke of Heaven. Nor have they attained the second meaning of the term, "time-*Tzva*-צבא," meaning the attainment of complete and perfect days, that are not wasteful and lacking.[159] They also have not attained the third meaning of "*Tzva*-צבא," which is "beauty."

This is as mentioned in his aforementioned discourse, that when we learn Torah unconditionally and when we fulfill the commandments-*mitzvot* unconditionally, we then transform

---

[157] Exodus 12:41

[158] Discourse entitled *HaYoshevet BaGanim* 5710, Sefer HaMaamarim 5710.

[159] Zohar I 224a; Torah Ohr Chayeh Sarah, *Yafe Sha'a Achat*, p. 16a.

the "treason-*Kesher*-קשר" and "lies-*Sheker*-שקר," referring to the falseness of the world, into the "boards-*Keresh*-קרש" of the Tabernacle, about which the verse states[160] "And you shall make the boards for the Tabernacle of acacia-wood-*Shitim*-שטים, standing up."

That is, the standing boards of acacia-wood-*Shitim* bond the light of the Unlimited One, *HaShem*-יהו״ה, blessed is He, with the world, and transform it from one extreme to the other extreme. For, one of the letter permutations of the word, "board-*Keresh*-קרש," is "bond-*Kesher*-קשר," which in holiness, refers to the matter of bonding-*Hitkashrut*-התקשרות to *HaShem*-יהו״ה. In contrast, regarding the opposing side, the word means, "a treasonous conspiracy-*Kesher*-קשר," as in the verse,[161] "Do not speak treasonous conspiracy-*Kesher*-קשר, for everything this people speaks of is treasonous conspiracy-*Kesher*-קשר." In other words, the opposing side is the matter of separation and division.[162]

However, in the "bonding-*Hitkashtrut*-התקשרות" of the side of holiness, all are called "companions," and thus, "the companions listen to your voice." That is, the souls that are yet above, as well as the souls that have already been in a body and already have the advantage of the service of *HaShem*-יהו״ה that is attained through the body, having already completed all their work in this world, according to all three aforementioned

---

160 Exodus 26:15
161 Isaiah 8:12; Talmud Bavli, Sanhedrin 26a
162 Also see Ginat Egoz of Rabbi Yosef Gikatilla, translated as HaShem is One, Volume 4, The Gate of the Vowels, section on the *Shoorook*-שרק vowel.

meanings of the term *"Tzva-צבא,"* all come to listen and receive the voice of the souls that are manifest within bodies.

This is so, even if they have not yet completed their work. For, although they are scattered in exile and are, "pasturing in the gardens of others," even so, they raise themselves above the world and take their bodies and their animalistic souls to the houses of worship and houses of Torah study, and recite *Shema* and are involved in the study of Torah. This literally is the matter of self-sacrifice (*Mesirat Nefesh*),[163] which is only possible to attain in this world. Thus, even the "companions," which refers to the souls in the Garden of Eden,[164] listen to their voice. Moreover, even the Holy One, blessed is He, states, "I and My entourage come to listen to your voice."

This itself is the meaning of the verse, "though they are fashioned in many days, to Him-*Lo*-לו they are one." That is, the verse is written as "naught-*Lo*-לא," but is read, "to Him-*Lo*-לו."[165] In other words, it is specifically through the service of *HaShem*-יהו״ה with the soul as it is invested within the body, both in the body and with the body, that they draw forth He who is higher than the whole chaining down of the worlds to below the chaining down of the worlds. That is, they draw the "One-

---

[163] See Tanya, end of Ch. 41

[164] Note: The relationship between the two explanations of the term "companions" - the angels, and the souls in the Garden of Eden – is understood according to that which is well known. Namely, that in order for there to be an ascension of the letters of the words of Torah study and prayer, it is necessary for the words to be refined by the angelic beings "who hug and kiss them" (See Zohar I 23b; Zohar II 201b; Torah Ohr 42b; Sefer HaMaamarim 5708 p. 202.) It is in this merit that the angels likewise listen (as explained in Torat Shalom end of p. 85 and on.)

[165] See Torah Ohr, beginning of Parshat Lech Lecha.

Echad-אחד within them,"[166] in order to fulfill,[167] "*HaShem* is One-*HaShem Echad*-יהו"ה אחד and His Name is One-*Echad*-אחד."

---

[166] See the introduction and Petach HaShaar to Imrei Binah of the Mittler Rebbe, translated into English as The Gateway to Understanding. Also see Ginat Egoz of Rabbi Yosef Gikatilla, translated as HaShem is One, Volume 1.

[167] Zachariah 14:9; Talmud Bavli, Pesachim 50a

Discourse 3

"V'Eleh HaMishpatim -
These are the ordinances"

Delivered on Shabbat Mevarchim Adar I, 5711
By the grace of *HaShem*, blessed is He

1.

It states,[168] "And these are the ordinances that you shall place before them: If you acquire a Hebrew servant etc." Now, the discernment of the terms in this verse is well known.[169] Namely, the term "before them-*Lifneihem*-לפניהם" is in the plural form, whereas it then states, "If you acquire-*Ki Tikneh-* כי תקנה" in the singular form. It is explained that the singular "If you acquire-*Ki Tikneh*-כי תקנה" (is not associated with those referred to by the word, "before them-*Lifneihem*-לפניהם," but rather) refers to the words, "that you shall place-*Asher Tasim-* אשר תשים," meaning that it refers specifically to our teacher Moshe. That is, the words, "If you acquire a Hebrew servant," were said in relation to our teacher Moshe, and the reason given for this is because it is he who draws down knowledge-*Da'at* of *HaShem*-יהו"ה within the souls of the Jewish people.

---

[168] Exodus 21:1-2
[169] See Torah Ohr, Mishpatim 74c; Torat Chaim Mishpatim 409a; Maamarei Admor HaZaken 5565 Vol. 1 p. 247 and on; Derech Mitzvotecha 80a and elsewhere.

Now, to summarize the explanation of this matter, it is written,[170] "'Behold, days are coming' – the word of *HaShem*-יהו"ה – 'when I shall sow the House of Israel and the House of Judah – the seed of man and the seed of animal.'" In general, the souls of the Jewish people are divided into two categories that are called, "the seed of man," and, "the seed of animal." "The seed of man" refers to souls of the world of Emanation-*Atzilut*, of which there are very few, even in previous generations. "The seed of animal" refers to souls of the worlds of Creation-*Briyah*, Formation-*Yetzirah*, and Action-*Asiyah*, and thus, virtually all the souls of our generation are in the category of, "the seed of animal."[171] They are thus called because they do not possess knowledge-*Da'at* of *HaShem*-יהו"ה.

Now, the primary matter of our teacher Moshe is to draw knowledge of *HaShem*-דעת יהו"ה into the souls that are in the aspect of, "the seed of animal." This is because Moshe is one of the seven shepherds[172] who draw vitality and Godliness to all the souls of the Jewish people, which is why they are called, "shepherds." Moshe includes them all and is thus called, "The Shepherd of Faith," for he draws forth the aspect of

---

[170] Jeremiah 31:26

[171] See Torah Ohr Ibid. which cites Zohar II 94b and the Ramaz commentary there. Sefer HaMaamarim 5713 p. 89.

[172] Talmud Bavli, Sukkah 52b

knowledge of *HaShem*-יהו"ה דעת, since he corresponds to the level of the upper knowledge-*Da'at*.[173]

3.

We must understand this in greater detail and understand why the matter of knowledge of *HaShem*-יהו"ה דעת is so necessary. After all, the faculty of knowledge-*Da'at* is only one of the three intellectual faculties of the mind, and is the final one.

Now, the advantage of the faculty of knowledge-*Da'at* is that it is specifically through it that the emotions are born and aroused. This accords with the explanation in Tanya[174] that if a person does not bind and attach the faculty of the knowledge-*Da'at* of his mind and thoughts to the greatness of the Unlimited One, *HaShem*-יהו"ה, blessed is He, with a firm and strong bond, then although he may indeed possess the aspects of wisdom-*Chochmah* and understanding-*Binah* of the greatness of *HaShem*-יהו"ה, blessed is He, he will nonetheless not give rise to true love and fear of *HaShem*-יהו"ה in his soul, but only false delusions. Thus, it is the faculty of knowledge-*Da'at* that gives existence to the emotions and vitalizes them, and it is comprised of both kindness-*Chessed* and judgment-*Gevurah*, meaning, love of *HaShem*-יהו"ה and its offshoots, and fear of *HaShem*-יהו"ה and its offshoots.

---

[173] Tanya, Ch. 42
[174] Tanya, Ch. 3 and Ch. 42

This is why[175] a child is not obligated in the responsibilities of Torah and *mitzvot*-commandments. In other words, though he may be intelligent, even having a sharp mind, nevertheless, he is neither obligated to do the positive commandments nor to desist from the prohibitive ones, because he is not considered to have knowledge-*Da'at*. In other words, though he may indeed know and understand the ideas, nevertheless, he is lacking in this matter of knowledge-*Da'at*, in that it does not touch or move him to conduct himself according to this understanding (that is, it does not affect him emotionally, that he should act accordingly).

This matter may be further explained as follows: The mind of wisdom-*Chochmah*, is the beginning of the intellect. (There is another, higher aspect of wisdom-*Chochmah*, which is the source of the intellect, but what is relevant to the actual service of *HaShem*-יהו"ה is the beginning of actual intellect, which is called the **point** of the wisdom-*Chochmah* and is its fundamental axiom or premise-*Hanachah*.) Now, although this intellectual point includes many details in it, they all are included within the single point of the intellect. There likewise are intellectual leanings in this point, towards either kindness-*Chessed* or judgment-*Gevurah*, but they are hidden within it.

The mind of understanding-*Binah*, is the discernment and specification of all the particular matters included in the point of wisdom-*Chochmah*, as well as the revelation of its various leanings, either towards kindness-*Chessed* or

---

[175] See Sefer HaMaamarim 5670, p. 115; Kuntres HaTefilah Ch. 5; Discourse entitled Bati Legani 5713, Ch. 7 and elsewhere.

judgment-*Gevurah*. However, in this stage, these matters can easily be reversed from one leaning to its opposite.

In contrast, the term knowledge-*Da'at* is actually a term of bonding, recognition, and feeling,[176] which are the three levels of *Da'at*, one above the other. That is, at first, he binds his mind to the subject matter, through which he comes to have a recognition of the truth of it, until he comes to have feelings about it. That is, his recognition of the truth of it becomes so strong, that it no longer is just intellectual recognition, but that even in his heart he feels that this is how it is. Once a person arrives at this state of recognition, we already know his position and standing etc. (In other words, we then know what his position is and where his mind is holding.)

Through the above we may understand the difference between the souls of the world of Emanation-*Atzilut*, who are called, "the seed of man," and souls of the worlds of Creation-*Briyah*, Formation-*Yetzirah*, and Action-*Asiyah*, who are called, "the seed of animal." That is, in the worlds of Creation-*Briyah*, Formation-*Yetzirah*, and Action-*Asiyah*, the sublimation to *HaShem*-יהו"ה is only in a way of the sublimation of tangible beings to the intangible Godliness (*Bitul HaYesh*). In other words, although there is an aspect of grasping the reality of Godliness with the intellect and they know that this is how it must be etc., nonetheless, in relation to action, their sublimation is only the sublimation of the tangible to the intangible Godliness (*Bitul HaYesh*). In other words, their

---

[176] Bonding-*Hitkashrut*-התקשרות, recognition-*Hakarah*-הכרה, and feeling-*Hargashah*-הרגשה.

knowledge of reality does not affect that they experience that reality themselves. This is because they are lacking in the matter of knowledge of *HaShem*-יהו״ה דעת. This is why the angelic beings are called, "animals-*Chayot*" and "beasts-*Behemot*,"[177] because they too lack this matter of knowledge-*Da'at*. As a result, their sublimation too is only the sublimation of the tangible to the intangible Godliness (*Bitul HaYesh*).

In contrast, the sublimation of the world of Emanation-*Atzilut* is the nullification of any sense of separate existence (*Bitul B'Metziut*) at all. For, the matter of the world of Emanation-*Atzilut* is that, not only is there an understanding and grasp that, "this is how it must be," but rather that, "this is how it actually is," (that is, this indeed **is** the true reality). This is brought about through the matter of knowledge-*Da'at*, and because of this, the souls of the world of Emanation-*Atzilut* are called, "the seed of man." For, the numerical value of, "man-*Adam*-אדם-45" is the same numerical value of "*Ma"h*-מ״ה-45,"[178] which refers to the fact that they are truly sublimated to *HaShem*-יהו״ה, blessed is He, as a consequence of knowledge-*Da'at* of Him. This then, is the matter of Moshe, about whom it states, "If you acquire a Hebrew servant," because it is he who

---

[177] Torah Ohr Ibid. 75b; Torat Chaim Ibid. p. 410a.

[178] Pardes Rimonim, Shaar Erchei HaKinuyim, Adam-אדם and elsewhere; That is, the aspect of *Ma"h*-מ״ה-45 which refers to the Power of What-*Koach Ma"h*- כח מ״ה of the perception of wisdom-*Chochmah*-חכמה, is the recognition of the true reality of the inner name of *Ma"h*-מ״ה-45 which is the inner Name of *HaShem*-יהו״ה as expanded with the letters *Aleph*-א as follows יו״ד ה״א וא״ו ה״א-45, the ten letters of which enliven the ten *Sefirot* of the world of Emanation-*Atzilut*. (Zohar introduction to Tikkunim 17a; Also see Ginat Egoz of Rabbi Yosef Gikatilla, translated as HaShem is One.)

draws the aspect of knowledge of *HaShem*-יהו"ה to the souls that are in the category of, "the seed of animal."

4.

Now, this must be further understood. For, how is it possible to draw forth this aspect of knowledge-*Da'at* to souls that are in the category of "the seed of animal," when it is something that is specifically applicable only to souls in the category of "the seed of man"? However, it is in regard to this that the verse specifies, "If you acquire a Hebrew-*Ivri*-עברי servant." The Jewish people are called by the title, "Hebrews-*Ivri*-עברי," which stems from the verse,[179] "Your forefathers dwelt over-*Ever*-עבר the river," meaning that they are from above the aspect called, "the river-*Nahar*-נהר."

Regarding the aspect of, "the river-*Nahar*-נהר," the verse states,[180] "A river-*Nahar*-נהר issues forth from Eden to water the Garden and from there it divides to becomes four headwaters." From this verse it is understood that the aspect referred to as, "a river-*Nahar*-נהר," is higher than the aspect of the division indicated by the words, "from there it divides." It likewise is understood that the aspect of, "over the river-*Ever HaNahar*-עבר הנהר" is even higher than the aspect known as, "the river-*Nahar*-נהר."

---

[179] Joshua 24:2
[180] Genesis 2:10

This then, is the meaning of the verse,[181] "Your forefathers dwelt over-*Ever*-עבר the river." In other words, the souls of all the Jewish people, including the souls that are in the aspect of, "the seed of animal," are rooted in the aspect of, "over the river-*Ever HaNahar*-עבר הנהר," which is even higher than the aspect known as, "the river-*Nahar*-נהר." Thus, when they were in that state originally, they certainly possessed very great knowledge of *HaShem* יהו"ה and therefore, the aspect of this knowledge-*Da'at* can be drawn forth even to them.

This then, is the meaning of the words "If you acquire a Hebrew-*Ivri*-עברי servant etc." Moreover, the verse specifies, "If you acquire," since the acquisition of something does not indicate the introduction of any novelty in the existence of the thing, nor does any change take place in the thing itself. Rather, it is just a transference from the possession of the seller to the possession of the buyer. The same matter apples to the drawing forth of knowledge of *HaShem*-יהו"ה to souls who are in the category of, "the seed of animal." In other words, there is no change to their essential being, but rather, there is only a revelation of that which is concealed and of what they already possessed because they are rooted in the aspect of, "over the river-*Ever HaNahar*-עבר הנהר."

Now, this is accomplished specifically by Moshe, since Moshe is likewise of that level ("over the river-*Ever HaNahar*-עבר הנהר"). In fact, the reason he is named Moshe is as the verse specifies,[182] "And she called his name Moshe-משה, and said:

---

181 Joshua 24:2
182 Exodus 2:10

70

'Because I drew him-*Mesheeteehu*-משיתיהו from the water,'"
about which it is explained that he is rooted in the waters of the
first Sabbatical (*Shmitah*) of creation.[183]

Additionally, it is noteworthy that the matter of "waters"
is not alluded to in his name, but rather, the "drawing forth-
Mesheeteehu-משיתיהו," which indicates his drawing forth from
the waters. The reason for this is because the aspect of "waters"
refers to the aspect of wisdom-*Chochmah*, whereas Moshe is
rooted higher than the aspect of wisdom-*Chochmah*. (From this
it is understood that, actually, Moshe is even higher than the
souls in the category of, "the seed of man." Thus, since Moshe
transcends the limitations of both, "the seed of man," and, "the
seed of animal," it is also within his ability to draw forth
knowledge of *HaShem*-יהו"ה to the souls in the category of "the
seed of animal.")[184]

However, we must understand this further. For, all the
above is regarding the soul, in that since it is rooted in the aspect
of, "the other side of the river-*Ever HaNahar*-עבר הנהר," it thus
is possible for the knowledge of *HaShem*-יהו"ה to be drawn
forth to them. However, we know that the giving of the Torah
was specifically to souls in bodies, and that the primary
intention in drawing forth the knowledge of *HaShem*-יהו"ה to
the Jewish people, is to draw forth the knowledge of Him
specifically to souls as they are manifest within bodies. We
must therefore understand how it is possible that this knowledge

[183] See Torah Ohr Ibid. 76b and on; Torat Chaim Ibid. 412a; Maamarei Admor
HaZaken Ibid. p. 262 and on; Torah Ohr Shemot 51d; Torat Chaim Shemot 59a and
on.
[184] See Derech Mitzvotecha Ibid.

of *HaShem*-יהו"ה can possibly be drawn forth even to the body of man.

The explanation is that even the body of man is from this level. That is, the body of man is rooted in the two-hundred and eighty-eight (רפ״ח) sparks of the world of *Tohu*-chaos, which itself is the first Sabbatical (*Shmitah*) of creation that preceded this world, only that due to the shattering of the vessels (*Shevirat HaKeilim*), they fell and descended further down.[185] Nevertheless, because the body is also rooted in this first Sabbatical (*Shmitah*) of creation, "over the river-*Ever HaNahar*-עבר הנהר," it therefore is possible for the knowledge of *HaShem*- יהו"ה to be drawn to the body by Moshe, who is likewise of that level, as explained above.

5.

Now, from the language of the verse, "And these are the ordinances that you shall place before them," wherein it simply states, "before them," it seems to clearly indicate that this includes all the Jewish people. In other words, this includes not only the souls in the category of, "the seed of animal," but also the souls in the category of, "the seed of man." However, at first glance, this is not understood. For, it indeed makes sense that it should refer to and include the souls of the "seed of animal," who lack knowledge of *HaShem*-יהו"ה, to whom Moshe draws forth the aspect of knowledge of *HaShem*-יהו"ה,

---

[185] See Torah Ohr Ibid. 76c; Torat Chaim Ibid. 410b; Maamarei Admor HaZaken Ibid. p. 255.

blessed is He. However, the souls of the "seed of man" indeed possess knowledge of *HaShem*-יהו"ה. This being the case, to what end is this knowledge drawn to them by Moshe, that they need to be included in the words, "that you shall place before them"?

The explanation is as follows: In the matter of knowledge of *HaShem*-יהו"ה דעת itself, there are two aspects. There is the knowledge that one arrives at after thought and contemplation, through which one grasps the subject matter. In other words, after he thinks deeply and contemplates the matter to the point that he understands it well, he comes to the recognition of the reality of it and develops a sensitivity and feel for it. This level of recognition is specifically according to the degree of his grasp.[186]

However, there is a higher level of knowledge of *HaShem*-יהו"ה that transcends tangible grasp.[187] This is the recognition of the Essential Self of *HaShem*-יהו"ה Himself, who is not graspable through comprehension, neither in a way of positive grasp, nor in grasp through negation, nor through any form of intellectual endeavor. Rather, this level is only attained through the recognition of the reality of His Essential Being, blessed is He. It is about this that it states,[188] "The ultimate

---

[186] See the Mittler Rebbe's Kuntres HaHitpaalut, translated into English as Divine Inspiration for lengthier explanations of all levels of attainments of knowledge of *HaShem*-יהו"ה that result from study contemplative thought (*Hitbonenut*).

[187] See Sefer HaMaamarim 5670, p. 129 and on; 5677 p. 93 and on, and elsewhere.

[188] Bechinat Olam, Section 7, Ch. 2; Ikarim Discourse 2, Ch. 30; Shnei Luchot Habrit 191a

knowledge is that You are beyond our knowledge," which is the recognition of His Essential Being, blessed is He.

It is this aspect of knowledge of HaShem-יהו"ה דעת that must be drawn forth, even to the souls of, "the seed of man," who are souls of the world of Emanation-*Atzilut*. This is because the knowledge of HaShem-יהו"ה that the souls of the world of Emanation-*Atzilut* possess, is knowledge that is acquired through grasp and comprehension. For, the world of Emanation-*Atzilut* is the world of revelations, meaning that it is a world that already is in the category of revelation and concealment. It therefore is necessary to draw knowledge of HaShem-יהו"ה to them that, "The ultimate knowledge is that You are beyond our knowledge," which is the recognition of His Essential Being.

However, even this aspect is drawn forth through our teacher Moshe, since he is from the aspect of,[189] "I drew him-*Mesheeteehu*-משיתיהו from the water." That is, he is rooted higher than the aspects of revelation and concealment. Thus, Moshe has the ability to draw forth the recognition of the Essential Being of HaShem-יהו"ה, even to souls that are "the seed of man."

Now, we have already explained the matter of the drawing forth of knowledge-*Da'at* of HaShem-יהו"ה in the souls of "the seed of animal," which is possible due to the fact that they possess this matter due to their root. We explained this with respect to both the souls of "the seed of animal" about

---

[189] Exodus 2:10

74

which it states,[190] "Your forefathers dwelt over-*Ever*-עבר the river," as well as with respect to the body itself, which is rooted in the world of *Tohu*-chaos. It is in this same manner that we may understand the matter of the drawing forth of the ultimate knowledge, "that You are beyond our knowledge," to all the souls of the Jewish people, including the souls of, "the seed of man." For, this too is only possible because of their root.

This matter is understood by way of the known[191] explanation of the teaching,[192] "Israel arose in thought," that the root of the souls of the Jewish people (including the souls of the aspect of "the seed of animal") is from the most elevated level of thought. It therefore is possible to draw forth a recognition of the Essential Being of *HaShem*-יהו"ה, of "the ultimate knowledge is that You are beyond our knowledge," to them.

This matter is likewise drawn forth by Moshe, specifically, since in Moshe there was an illumination of the Supernal Essence. This is as stated,[193] "And Moshe said: 'Six-hundred-thousand foot-soldiers of the people in whose midst I am-*Anochi b'Keerbo*-אנכי בקרבו.'" That is, "in the midst" of Moshe there was an illumination of the aspect of, "I am who I am-*Anochi Mi SheAnoichi*-אנכי מי שאנכי," which refers to the Essential Self of *HaShem*-יהו"ה Himself, blessed is He.[194]

---

[190] Joshua 24:2

[191] Likkutei Torah, Shir HaShirim 17d and on; Sefer HaMaamarim 5700, p. 17 & p. 27, and elsewhere.

[192] Midrash Bereishit Rabba 1:4

[193] Numbers 11:21

[194] See Ginat Egoz of Rabbi Yosef Gikatilla, translated into English as HaShem is One, Volume 1, The Gate of The Name.

(Moreover, it should be pointed out that the revelation of this aspect within Moshe was specifically through the Jewish people. For, as explained elsewhere,[195] the revelation of, "I am-*Anochi*-אנכי" within Moshe is specifically through the "six-hundred-thousand foot-soldiers of the people.")

This, then, is the meaning of the verse,[196] "And these are the ordinances that you shall place before them-*Lifneihem*-לפניהם," meaning, "to their innerness-*LiPnimiyutam*-לפנימיותם." This is to say that it is Moshe who binds the inner essence of the souls of the Jewish people to the aspect of the Inner Essential Being of the Unlimited One, *HaShem*-יהו״ה Himself, blessed is He. It is for this reason that it is he who draws forth the aspect of knowledge of *HaShem*-יהו״ה to the Jewish people, to the point of even drawing forth the ultimate knowledge of *HaShem*-יהו״ה that, "You are beyond our knowledge."

We may say that it is for this reason that the verse specifies that it is, "ordinances-*Mishpatim*-משפטים that you shall place before them." As known, "ordinances-*Mishpatim*-משפטים" refer to the commandments-*Mitzvot* that are understood logically according to the intellect. It thus is understood that even in the commandments that are understood intellectually, Moshe drew forth the aspect of knowledge of *HaShem*-יהו״ה, including even the, "ultimate knowledge that You are beyond our knowledge."

---

[195] Sefer HaMaamarim 5687 p. 115; 5705 p. 134; Torah Ohr Bereishit 1b
[196] Exodus 21:1-2

6.

Now, the explanation of this matter in man's service of HaShem-יהו"ה, blessed is He, in actuality, even in our generation, is as follows: On a more detailed level, every single Jew possesses both the aspect of "the seed of man" and "the seed of animal." That is, when he is occupied with the study of Torah and prayer, then he is in a state of, "the seed of man," whereas when he is occupied throughout the day with mundane affairs, even though they are permissible, he is in a state of, "the seed of animal."

However, the substance of the objective of man's service of HaShem-יהו"ה, blessed is He, is to draw forth knowledge of HaShem-יהו"ה, even into the aspect of "the seed of animal." In other words, he is to draw forth awareness and knowledge of HaShem-יהו"ה, blessed is He, even while he is occupied with mundane affairs. Beyond that, even in his service of HaShem-יהו"ה in the aspect of "the seed of man," such as when he is occupied with Torah study and prayer, he is to draw forth the aspect of, "the ultimate knowledge is that You are beyond our knowledge."

In other words, he should not satisfy himself with Torah study and prayer that is solely in a way of comprehension and grasp. Rather, he should draw forth this knowledge of HaShem-יהו"ה, which is the aspect of the bond of faith-Emunah. For, when there is this bond of faith-Emunah, questions cannot cause any weakness, nor can seeing cause any strengthening.

It is this level that is drawn forth through our teacher Moshe. Now, it is true that the Jewish people stated,[197] "You speak with us, and we shall hear; Let God not speak to us lest we die," which seems to indicate that the speech of Moshe is a descent in relation to the words of HaShem-יהו"ה. Nevertheless, it is specifically Moshe who draws forth the aspect of knowledge of HaShem-יהו"ה that is beyond comprehension and grasp, even to the souls of "the seed of animal."

The same applies to the Moshe of our generation. For,[198] "there is an offshoot of Moshe in every generation." All those who were bonded to him are still bonded to him now, and the same applies to all those who will be bonded to him in the future. It is Moshe who is the one who bonds the essence of their souls, the aspect of their singular-*Yechidah* essence, with his own singular-*Yechidah* essence. Through this, "she is bonded and cleaves to You, a singular one to unify You,"[199] in a manner that is entirely beyond reason and knowledge.

7.

The verse then continues,[200] "he shall work for six years; and in the seventh he shall go free, for no charge." That is, through the completion of our service of HaShem-יהו"ה now, during the "six thousand years of the world,"[201] even though it

---

[197] Exodus 20:15
[198] Tikkunei Zohar, Tikkun 69, 112a
[199] Hosha'anot Liturgy for the third day.
[200] Exodus 21:2
[201] Talmud Bavli, Rosh HaShanah 31a; Also see Torah Ohr Mishpatim 76c

is only a limited span of time, nevertheless, we will complete all the work that is to be done. Through this we will arrive at the time in which,[202] "the earth will be filled with the knowledge of *HaShem*-יהו"ה," wherein the verse specifies "knowledge-*De'ah*-דעה," meaning the aspect of knowledge of *HaShem*-יהו"ה. Moreover, this will be in such a way that,[203] "They will all know Me, from their smallest to their greatest." For although he may be small, and even in the coming future he will continue to be small, nevertheless, he will possess this matter of knowledge of *HaShem*-יהו"ה. For, this will be in such a way that, "the waters will cover the ocean floor,"[204] in that the illumination and revelation will be in everyone equally.

Now, we may connect all this to what was explained in the discourse of the *Hilulah*,[205] regarding the fact that the Jewish people are called, "the legions of *HaShem*-*Tzivot HaShem*-יהו"ה צבאות." That is, the term "*Tzva*-צבא" has three interpretations. One is a terminology of a "limited appointed time," the second is a terminology of "beauty," and the third means "army," which refers to the acceptance of the yoke of Heaven.

We may apply these three explanations to our subject here as well. That is, our service of *HaShem*-יהו"ה is in the "six thousand years of the world,"[206] which is a limited set time, that relates to the term "*Tzva*-צבא" as a language of "an appointed

[202] Isaiah 11:9
[203] Jeremiah 31:33
[204] Isaiah 11:9
[205] Bati Legani 5710, Ch. 10, Sefer HaMaamarim 5710 p. 125.
[206] Talmud Bavli, Rosh HaShanah 31a; Also see Torah Ohr Mishpatim 76c

fixed time." Nevertheless, we shall come to the perfection and completion of our service of *HaShem*-יהו"ה in a way of "beauty." That is, all of one's service shall be in a way of completion and perfection, with all of the inner powers (*Kochot Pnimiyim*) of one's soul, as well as all the encompassing powers (*Kochot Makifim*) of the soul, and even those levels that are beyond the encompassing lights of the soul. Beyond that, the service of *HaShem*-יהו"ה, blessed is He, should be in a way of the acceptance of the yoke of His Kingship, as in the third explanation of the term "*Tzva*-צבא," which is the matter of the "Hebrew servant-*Eved Ivri*-עבד עברי," as explained above.

It is through this kind of service of *HaShem*-יהו"ה, that we affect a transformation of the "treason-*Kesher*-קשר" and "lies-*Sheker*-שקר" of the world, into the "boards-*Keresh*-קרש" of the Tabernacle.[207] Then, the Moshe of our generation, his honorable holiness, my father-in-law, the Rebbe, will "bind-*Yekasher*-יקשר" the singular-*Yechidah* essence of our souls to His singular-*Yechidah* essence. This demands that, "she bears Your yoke," through which, "She is singular in unifying You."[208] Thus, it is through this that the conclusion of the verse is realized, that, "in the seventh he shall go free, for no charge." This refers to the revelation of the coming future, which is brought about by Moshe who, "is the first redeemer and the last redeemer."[209] May this occur speedily in our times, and may

---

[207] See *"Bati Legani"* 5710, Ch. 6 and on.
[208] See Hayom Yom, 17 Tishrei
[209] Midrash Shmot Rabba 2:4; Zohar I 253a; Shaar HaPesukim of the Arizal, Parshat Vayechi, Torah Ohr Ibid. 75b.

he redeem us from this final bitter exile, wherein the darkness is doubled and quadrupled. May He redeem us!

Discourse 4

"Ki Tisa et Rosh B'nei Yisroel -
When you take a census of the Children of Israel"

Delivered on Shabbat Parashat Vayakhel, Parashat Shekalim, Shabbat
Mevarchim Adar II 5711
By the grace of *HaShem*, blessed is He,

1.

The verse states,[210] "When you uplift the head-*Ki Tisa
et Rosh*-כי תשא את ראש of the children of Israel." Now, we must
understand[211] why the verse specifically uses the term, "when
you uplift-*Ki Tisa*-כי תשא," rather than simply stating, "when
you count-*Ki Tifkod*-כי תפקוד." Additionally, why does it
specify, "When you uplift the head-*Tisa et Rosh*-תשא את ראש,"
specifically mentioning the "head-*Rosh*-ראש?"

Now, Rashi explained this as follows: "When you wish
to take a census of their numbers to know how many they are,
do not count them by the head (so that there should not be a
plague amongst them). Rather, each one should give a half-
shekel, and you shall count the shekels, and thereby you will
know their number." According to this explanation, it seems
apparent that the words "When you take a census-*Ki Tisa et*

---

[210] Exodus 30:12

[211] See discourse entitled *Ki Tisa* 5658, Sefer HaMaamarim 5658 p. 146; 5675
(*Hemshech* 5672 Vol. II) p. 893 and elsewhere.

Rosh" indicate that this is not something that we are commanded to do as a *Mitzvah*, but that it is optional. However, in the Midrash[212] it states, "The Holy One, blessed is He, said to Moshe, 'Go and count the Jewish people etc.,'" seeming to indicate that this was indeed a commandment-*Mitzvah*. (The method of the count should be through the half-shekel, in order that they should not be afflicted by plague.) Nevertheless, even according to the Midrash, it is clear that this was a commandment-*Mitzvah* specific to that time, and not something commanded for all generations. On the contrary, it is understood from the response of Yo'av to King David that one is to avoid such a count, when he responded,[213] "May *HaShem*-יהו"ה your God, increase the number of the people over and over a hundred times, while the eyes of my lord the king live to see it." That is, he tried to avoid counting the Jewish people.

Now, there are also a number of other matters that are learned from this Torah portion. It states,[214] "You shall take the silver of atonements from the Children of Israel and give it for the work of the Tent of Meeting etc." Rashi comments, "This silver was used for the production of the base sockets." In other words, although the giving of the half-shekel for the purpose of the base sockets (*Adanim*-אדנים) only occurred once, meaning that it was something temporary, nevertheless, something permanent was produced through it, since the Tabernacle (*Mishkan*) was preserved for eternity.[215]

---

[212] Yalkut Shimoni beginning of Parshat Ki Tisa
[213] Samuel II 24:3 and on; Also see Torah Sheleima Vol. 21, Miluim 61
[214] Exodus 30:16, and Rashi commentary there.
[215] Talmud Bavli, Sota 9a and elsewhere.

In this Torah portion, we also learn that the commandment of the half-shekel was indeed commanded for all generations (as also necessitated by Chronicles II 24:9).[216] That is, there is a constant and ongoing commandment for all generations,[217] to give the half-shekel each and every year for the coffers of the Holy Temple, which was used to pay for the communal offerings, as clearly elucidated in the Mishnah in Shekalim.[218] However, the distinction is that when it comes to the commandment of the half-shekel that applies to all generations, the obligation is solely in regard to giving the half-shekel, but is not accompanied by any command to count the Jewish people or to know their number. Furthermore, as indicated in several places, they specifically did not count them.

This being the case, our difficulty is as follows: From the superficial reading of the language of the Torah portion, it seems to indicate that all these matters discussed in the Torah portion require being prefaced by the verse,[219] "When you uplift the head-*Ki Tisa et Rosh*-כי תשא את ראש of the children of Israel." In other words, this matter seems to be a precondition and primary aspect to all the other matters discussed in the Torah portion, and must therefore be understood.

---

[216] Also see Talmud Yerushalmi, Shekalim 1:1 and Ramban commentary to Exodus 30:12.

[217] Rambam Hilchot Shekalim, Ch. 1

[218] Mishnah Shekalim 4:1

[219] Exodus 30:12

2.

Now, the explanation of the matter is that the general purpose of the half-shekel is to fund the communal offerings. The general explanation of this in man's service of *HaShem*-יהו"ה, blessed is He, is that through bringing the offerings on the altar to become included in the upper fire, which is the aspect of, "the lion that consumed the offerings,"[220] the animal souls of every Jew were also diminished and became included in holiness.[221] This affected that each and every Jew would be able to bind his faculties of knowledge-*Da'at* and understanding-*Binah* to the greatness of *HaShem*-יהו"ה, blessed is He, and become sublimated to Him.

Nowadays, this is accomplished through the prayers, which were established in place of the offerings.[222] However, it first is necessary for strength and assistance to be given for this from Above. This is accomplished through the matter of "uplifting the head of the Jewish people," which is accomplished through Moshe, as well as the offshoot of Moshe that exists in every generation. For, Moshe is called the, "shepherd of faith" (*Ra'aya Mehemna*),[223] in that he is the shepherd who grazes the flock, (meaning that he provides them

---

[220] Zohar I 6a; Zohar III 32b; 211a; Discourse entitled *Ki Tisa* in the addendums to Torah Ohr 111c; Likkutei Torah Bamidbar 11a; Sefer HaMaamarim 5698 p. 229; 5709 p. 30 and elsewhere.

[221] See Sefer HaMaamarim 5698 p. 232

[222] Talmud Bavli, Brachot 26a-b

[223] Throughout the Zohar; See Tanya Ch. 42 and citations there.

with their sustenance), of faith-*Emunah*. This is as stated,[224] "Nourish faith," through Torah study and acts of lovingkindness. By means of this, there is an elevation and uplifting of the head of the Jewish people, meaning that there is an ascent caused from below to Above by means of the offerings and through prayer.

3.

Now, we must further understand the relationship between this matter to Moshe, "the shepherd of faith," specifically, since it is regarding him that it states,[225] "When you uplift the head-*Ki Tisa et Rosh*-כי תשא את ראש of the children of Israel." The reason that Moshe is called, "the shepherd of faith" (*Ra'aya Mehemna*), is because it is he who nourishes the faith of the Jewish people, sustaining and enlivening it. This is because faith-*Emunah*, on its own, can remain transcendent and encompassing.[226]

This is like the teaching,[227] "A thief, when standing on the threshold, calls out to the Merciful One for assistance." In other words, we are discussing a thief-*Ganav* who is even worse

---

[224] Psalms 37:3 – The term for nourish-*Re'eh*-רעה shares the same root as shepherd-*Ro'eh*-רועה.

[225] Exodus 30:12

[226] See discourse entitled *Ki Tisa* Sefer HaMaamarim 5679, p. 267 and on; Additions to Torah Ohr, 111a and on; Maamarei Admor HaZaken 5563 Vol. 1, p. 176 and on; Maamarei Admor HaEmtza'ee Shmot Vol. 2, p. 619 and on; Ohr HaTorah Tisa p. 1,838 and on & p. 1,879 and on; Sefer HaMaamarim 5630 p. 108 and on; 5654 p. 181 and on; 5687 p. 113 and on; 5711 p. 183 and on; Likkutei Torah VeEtchanan, first discourse entitled *VeYada'ata* and its explanation there.

[227] Talmud Bavli, Brachot 20a

than a robber-*Gazlan*. This is as our sages, of blessed memory, taught,[228] "Why is the Torah stricter with a thief-*Ganav* than with a robber-*Gazlan*? Because this one (the robber-*Gazlan*) equates the honor of the servant to the honor of his Master, whereas that one (the thief-*Ganav*), does not equate the honor of the servant to the honor of his Master."[229] (That is, he gives greater honor to the servant than to his Master, in that he has fear of man, but is not concerned by the fact that he is being watched from Above.) In other words, the concealment and hiddenness of Godliness is so great in him, that although he does have sensitivity and is embarrassed of his deeds (in that he fears man), he nonetheless thinks that he can deceive *HaShem*-יהו"ה, blessed is He. Even so, while he is on the threshold, he calls out to the Merciful One, blessed is He, for assistance. In other words, even as he is perpetrating an act that is the diametric opposite of *HaShem's* Supernal will, he actually requests that *HaShem*-יהו"ה, blessed is He, give him success in this matter itself, a matter that is the diametric opposite of *HaShem's* will.

Now, in a refined manner, every single person can find this in himself. This applies whether he is a businessman or a Torah scholar, meaning those who are found within the four

---

228 Talmud Bavli, Bava Kamma 79b and Rashi there.

229 That is, the robber-*Gazlan* acts in a public manner, in that he has neither fear of the Holy One, blessed is He, nor fear of man, and thus, at the very least he equates them. In contrast, the thief-*Ganav* acts in a hidden manner, which indicates that he fears man to a greater extent than he fears the Holy One, blessed is He, and thus, he does not even equate the Holy One, blessed is He, to man, but considers *HaShem* inferior. In this respect the thief-*Ganav* is therefore actually considered worse than the robber-*Gazlan*.

cubits of Torah and within the four cubits of prayer. That is, they too possess this aspect of, "A thief, when standing on the threshold, calls out to the Merciful One for assistance."

For example, this matter can be found within businessmen, in that, although he believes that it is *HaShem*-יהו"ה, blessed is He, "who gives the strength to make wealth,"[230] nevertheless his mind will delve into all kinds of schemes that distract him from Torah study, the service of *HaShem*-יהו"ה, and from having fixed times for Torah study, as required even of businessmen. On an even more particular level, when he is indeed successful in business, but then encounters problems in his business that are not as they should be, his thoughts then become drawn into new schemes etc. In other words, the Holy One, blessed is He, has made him successful in his business, and he too has transformed the physical into spiritual through giving a tenth or a fifth (or something in between) of his profits to charity. Moreover, the commandment of charity is the single commandment about which *HaShem*-יהו"ה, blessed is He, states,[231] "'Test Me, if you will, in this,' says *HaShem Tzva'ot*-יהו"ה צבאות, 'see if I do not open up the windows of the heavens for you and pour blessings upon you without end.'" *HaShem*-יהו"ה, blessed is He, is certainly trustworthy to fulfill this, and yet, the businessman draws his thoughts into all kinds of schemes. We thus observe one thing and its diametric opposite,

---

[230] Deuteronomy 8:12
[231] Malachi 3:10; Talmud Bavli, 9a; Tur and Shulchan Aruch, Yoreh De'ah end of Siman 247.

just like the "thief, who when standing on the threshold, calls out to the Merciful One for assistance."

Similarly, this can even be found in those who are occupied with the study of Torah. That is, he fully believes that the Torah is the wisdom and will of the Holy One, blessed is He. Yet, if he is successful in his studies and shows off his prowess, he becomes boastful in this. It goes without saying that this is the diametric opposite of *HaShem's* Supernal intent, especially if he studies for this very purpose. The automatic result, is that, at times, he will bend the subject to his own will, just to have the upper hand in the debate. Thus, on numerous occasions, he may transgress the laws of the Shulchan Aruch (The Code of Torah Law) specifically **because** of his occupation in studying Torah.

There likewise are Torah scholars who do not occupy themselves with the service of *HaShem*-יהו"ה by praying at length, and certainly do not involve themselves with the contemplations (*Hitbonenut*) that should precede prayer. Or they may not occupy themselves with the three preparations for prayer, as explained in Likkutei Torah,[232] namely, the study of the inner aspects of Torah, purity and charity.

All this is because he thinks the Torah that he studies is his own, meaning, it is his Torah, in the sense that he thinks he must come up with novel insights in Torah from his own human intellect. He thus abstains from all the aforementioned matters, since they require a significant expenditure of his time. He,

---

[232] Likkutei Torah Tavo 43b and on.

however, feels that he needs this time to come up with novel insights in Torah.

If, on the other hand, he would study Torah because it is the wisdom and will of the Holy One, blessed is He, then he would surely understand that it is not applicable that matters that the Holy One, blessed is He, Himself commanded, would be an obstruction to his Torah study. For example, the study of the teachings of Chassidut, immersing in the Mikvah, and giving charity, cannot possibly obstruct the study of Torah, since that itself is the wisdom and will of the Holy One, blessed is He.

All these circumstances are brought about because his faith-*Emunah* is in an aspect of transcendence (*Makif*), just like the, "thief, who when standing on the threshold, calls out to the Merciful One for assistance." It is because of this that the influence of Moshe, the shepherd of faith, is necessary. For, it is he who nourishes and sustains the faith of the Jewish people. That is, he draws the faith-*Emunah* from its transcendence to become manifest in the inner powers of the soul, so that a person actually conducts himself in alignment with his faith. This is accomplished through true reflection and contemplation in one's soul, strongly affixing one's thoughts to *HaShem*-יהו״ה, blessed is He, with great strength, so that his contemplation will not result in false self-delusions.[233]

---

[233] See Tanya, Ch. 3

4.

Now, regarding what one should contemplate, there is a well-known difference between the faith that comes about through the wisdom of philosophical inquiry, which is the wisdom of the pious of the nations of the world,[234] and the faith of the Jewish people. The faith of the pious of the nations of the world is solely in the aspect of how *HaShem*-יהו"ה, blessed is He, fills the worlds (*Memale Kol Almin*). This refers to the vitality and life-force that manifests within all the details within creation. The resultant view of this perspective is that the world does indeed have an existence, although it is sublimated and dependent upon the vitality that is manifest within it. This perspective arises from the name, "God-*Elohi"m*-אלהי"ם."

In contrast, the faith of the Jewish people is in the aspect of how *HaShem*-יהו"ה, blessed is He, utterly transcends the worlds (*Sovev Kol Almin*), which is the general transcendence of *HaShem*-יהו"ה that encompasses all of existence, and is beyond reason, knowledge, and division.

In even greater detail, there actually are three levels of faith. There is the faith in the aspect of how *HaShem*-יהו"ה, blessed is He, fills all worlds (*Memale Kol Almin*). Then there is the faith in how *HaShem*-יהו"ה, blessed is He, utterly transcends all worlds (*Sovev Kol Almin*). Then there is the faith

---

[234] See Siddur Im Divrei Elokim Chaim, Shaar Chag HaMatzot p. 284c & 287b and on. Sefer HaMitzvot of the Tzemach Tzeddek, p. 23a; Sefer HaMaamarim 5626 p. 244; Likkutei Sichot, Vol. 3, p. 1,015.

in the aspect of the Singular Intrinsic Essential Being of
HaShem-יהו״ה Himself, which utterly transcends any relation to
worlds altogether, and is beyond both transcending all worlds
(*Sovev Kol Almin*), and filling all worlds (*Memale Kol Almin*).

In other words, there is the faith that comes through
philosophical inquiry, which even the pious of the nations of
the world possess. Then there is a higher level of faith, which
is specifically the faith of the Jewish people, because of which
they are called, "the faithful-*Ma'aminim.*" There is yet a higher
level, which is that the Jewish people are also called, "the
children of the faithful-*Bnei Ma'aminim.*"[235] This third level
refers to the faith that comes to us as an inheritance from our
forefather Avraham, peace be upon him.

The explanation is that the first level, is faith that is also
graspable with human intellect. This is the faith-*Emunah* in the
aspect of how *HaShem*-יהו״ה, blessed is He, fills all worlds
(*Memale Kol Almin*). This is like the teaching of our sages, of
blessed memory,[236] "Just as the soul fills the body, so too the
Holy One, blessed is He, fills the earth." For, man is called a
microcosm of the world.[237] This is likewise stated in Otiyot
D'Rabbi Nathan that,[238] "everything that was created in man
was likewise created in the world," and the world is likewise
called a "large body,"[239] or "macrocosm."

---

[235] Talmud Bavli, Shabbat 97a; Midrash Shmot Rabba 23:5

[236] Midrash Vayikra Rabba, end of Ch. 4; Midrash Tehillim 103:1; Talmud
Bavli, Brachot 10a

[237] Midrash Tanchumah, Pekudei 3; Tikkunei Zohar, Tikkun 69 100b & 101a

[238] Otiyot D'Rabbi Nathan, end of Ch. 31

[239] Moreh HaNevuchim Vol. 1, Ch. 72

Thus, "just as the soul fills the body," in that the body, in and of itself, is entirely inanimate and all its vitality is from the soul, so likewise, the vitality of the worlds is the Godly vitality that manifests within them. In other words, the very same proofs that demonstrate that the existence of the soul vitalizes the body, are used to demonstrate that Godly vitality vitalizes the world.

Now, although this is something that the intellect can comprehend, it nevertheless requires the matter of faith-*Emunah*. The reason is because the substance and physicality of the body covers over and conceals the intellect. For example, we clearly observe that when a person becomes heavily invested in the pursuit of his lusts, God forbid, he will act irrationally and not according to intellect at all. It goes without saying that he is not acting according to the Godly intellect of the Jewish people.

It is about this that our sages, of blessed memory, stated,[240] "A person commits a transgression only if a spirit of folly enters him." This applies even to the human intellect of the nations of the world. That is, when a person is ruled by his lusts, they have dominion over him and his intellect has no control at all. Therefore, this type of comprehension alone is inadequate in keeping a person from sin and must be conjoined to the matter of faith-*Emunah*. Nevertheless, this kind of faith is understandable, even by the intellect.

---

[240] Talmud Bavli, Sotah 3a

Above this is the level of faith-*Emunah* in the aspect of how *HaShem*-יהו״ה, blessed is He, transcends all worlds (*Sovev Kol Almin*), in that He encompasses and surrounds them all equally. (This is unlike the aspect of how He fills all the worlds, wherein there are divisions and differences between one world and another.) In the soul of man, an example of this would be the general life force that vitalizes the totality of his body equally, in which there is no distinction between the head and the foot. It is in regard to this aspect that the Jewish people are called, "the faithful-*Ma'aminim*," since they have faith in this aspect of how *HaShem*-יהו״ה, blessed is He, transcends and encompasses all worlds (*Sovev Kol Almin*).

Now, there is yet another aspect of faith-*Emunah* which is even loftier than this. This is the faith-*Emunah* in the aspect of the Godliness that is even beyond *HaShem*'s transcendence over all worlds (*Sovev Kol Almin*). For, in the aspect of how *HaShem*-יהו״ה, blessed is He, transcends all worlds, there still, at the very least, is some relation to worlds, even if only in a manner of negation. In other words, when we say that this aspect of *HaShem's* Godliness is not in the category of worlds, nevertheless, in the very statement itself, that "He is not related to worlds," there is some relation to worlds, at least in a way of negation.

In truth, however, the fact that He brings the worlds into existence, is not at all of His Essential Self.[241] Rather, what is understood from this, is that His Singular Intrinsic Essential

---

[241] See Torah Ohr, Megilat Esther 99b; Likkutei Torah Shir HaShirim 8a, See Ginat Egoz, translated as, HaShem is One, volume one.

Being, blessed is He, as He is, in and of Himself, is beyond even a negative relation to worlds. The Jewish people are thus called "sons of the faithful-*Bnei Ma'aminim,*" in relation to our faith in the Singular Essential Intrinsic Being of the Unlimited One, *HaShem*-יהו"ה, blessed is He, who even transcends the aspect of transcending all worlds (*Sovev Kol Almin*). This faith is our inheritance from our forefather Avraham, peace be upon him, who is called, "the first of the faithful."[242]

We should add that even in the aspect of the faith in how *HaShem*-יהו"ה, blessed is He, fills all worlds (*Memale Kol Almin*), there is a vast difference between the faith of Jewish people and the faith of other nations. This may be likened to the fact that there is no comparison between the world of Action-*Asiyah* of the three worlds of Creation-*Briyah*, Formation-*Yetzirah*, and Action-*Asiyah*, to the aspect of Action-*Asiyah* of the world of Emanation-*Atzilut*. For, as is simply understood, there is a screen (*Parsa*) between the world of Emanation-*Atzilut* and the worlds of Creation-*Briyah*, Formation-*Yetzirah*, and Action-*Asiyah*, and the light that comes through that screen is the aspect of a secondary, novel light.[243]

The same applies to the matter of faith-*Emunah*. Namely, since the Jewish people possess faith in the aspect of how *HaShem*-יהו"ה, blessed is He, transcends all worlds (*Sovev Kol Almin*) and even higher, it is self-understood that their faith

---

[242] Midrash Shir HaShirim Rabba 4:8

[243] Etz Chaim, Shaar 42, Ch. 13; Torah Ohr Vayera 14a and on. Also see Shaar HaYichud of the Mittler Rebbe, translated as The Gate of Unity, Ch. 51.

in the aspect of how *HaShem*-יהו"ה fills all worlds, (*Memale Kol Almin*) is of an altogether different level and category.

5.

The explanation is as follows: The aspect of how *HaShem*-יהו"ה, blessed is He, fills all worlds (*Memale Kol Almin*) is called, "the Supernal speech."[244] That is, it is similar to speech, which is to one's fellow, in that speech is the aspect of revelation to another person, and is in the category of relating to others. Additionally, speech can cease, as it states,[245] "There is a time to keep silent and a time to speak." The same applies to the aspect of how *HaShem*-יהו"ה, blessed is He, fills all worlds (*Memale Kol Almin*), which is revelation to another, in which there is division.

Now, the world of speech (*Olam HaDibur*) is called by the term,[246] "the city of our God-*Elohei"nu*-אלהינ"ו,"[247] in that it is related to the title God-*Elohi"m*-אלהי"ם. In other words, when the essential name *HaShem*-יהו"ה is concealed, and the title God-*Elohi"m*-אלהי"ם is revealed, then it is called, "the city of our God-*Eer Elohei"nu*-עיר אלהינ"ו," which is the aspect of the world of speech (*Olam HaDeebur*) wherein there is division etc.

---

[244] Sefer HaMitzvot of the Tzemach Tzeddek Ibid.

[245] Ecclesiastes 3:7

[246] Psalms 48:2

[247] See Torah Ohr Veyera 56b and on; Sefer HaMaamarim 5700 p. 139 and on;

It is with this in mind that we may understand the Halachic ruling[248] (cited in the teachings of Chassidut[249]), that the sons of Noah were not commanded against the conjoining or partnering of *HaShem* with matters in creation (*Shituf*). At first glance, however, if the Jewish people were indeed commanded against conjoining or partnering *HaShem* with matters in creation (*Shituf*) since the reality is that indeed *HaShem*-יהו"ה is utterly beyond creation and has no partner, since this is so, why is it that the sons of Noah were not commanded against such partnering (*Shituf*)?

The explanation is that the sons of Noah are rooted in the aspect of how *HaShem*-יהו"ה, blessed is He, fills all worlds (*Memale Kol Almin*), and in this aspect, which is the world of speech, there indeed is a matter of division-*Hitchalkut*-התחלקות. This is indicated by the verse,[250] "And lest you raise your eyes to the heavens and you see the sun and the moon and the stars – the entire legion of the heavens – and you be drawn astray to bow to them and worship them, which *HaShem*-יהו"ה, your God, has apportioned-*Chalak*-חלק to all the other nations under the entire heaven." Because of this view of the nations of the world, they have turned it into a matter of partnering (*Shituf*), in that they call Him the, "God of the gods."[251]

---

[248] Rama to Orach Chaim 156:1 and the Darkei Moshe there

[249] Sefer HaMitzvot of the Tzemach Tzeddek 59b; Ohr HaTorah Noach Vol. 3, p. 658a and on; Ohr HaTorah Bereishit Vol. 7 p. 1,164b; Sefer HaMaamarim 5626 p. 18 & 187; 5629 p. 155 and on; Bati Legani 5713 Ch. 3; Mayim Rabim 5717 Ch. 3; and elsewhere.

[250] Deuteronomy 4:19; Also see Ramaz commentary to Zohar III 286b cited in the Sefer HaMitzvot and Torah Ohr ibid.

[251] Talmud Bavli, Menachot 110a

Now, all the above is in regard to the matter of speech (*Dibur*), which is the aspect of how *HaShem*-יהו"ה, blessed is He, fills all worlds (*Memale Kol Almin*). However, the aspect of how *HaShem*-יהו"ה, blessed is He, transcends all worlds (*Sovev Kol Almin*) is the matter of thought (*Machshavah*). Unlike speech, thought never ceases, but rather, constantly flows. Additionally, the "garment" of thought is unified with the soul.

This then,[252] is why the faith of the nations is only in the aspect of how *HaShem*-יהו"ה, blessed is He, fills all worlds (*Memale Kol Almin*), whereas the faith-*Emunah* of the Jewish people is in the aspect of how *HaShem*-יהו"ה, blessed is He, transcends all worlds (*Sovev Kol Almin*). For, the nations of the world are rooted in the title God-*Elohi"m*-אלהי"ם, which is the aspect of how *HaShem*-יהו"ה, blessed is He, fills all worlds (*Memale Kol Almin*) and is the world of speech (*Olam HaDibur*). In contrast, the Jewish people are rooted in the aspect of how *HaShem*-יהו"ה, blessed is He, transcends all worlds (*Sovev Kol Almin*), and is the world of thought (*Olam HaMachshavah*), for, as we are taught,[253] "Israel arose in thought."

Now, in regard to the faith that the Jewish people have in the aspect of the Essential Self of *HaShem*-יהו"ה Himself, blessed is He, who transcends relation to worlds **altogether**, including the aspect that He transcends all worlds (*Sovev Kol*

---

[252] See Siddur Im Divrei Elokim Chaim, Shaar Lag Ba'Omer 305a and on; Ohr HaTorah Na"ch, Vol. 2, p. 956 and on.

[253] Midrash Bereishit Rabba 1:4

Almin), this is because "Israel arose-*Alu*-עלו" – that is, ascended – "in thought." This is according to the well-known explanation[254] of the teaching that, "Israel arose-*Alu*-עלו in thought," meaning that they ascended-*Alu*-עלו to the loftiest level of thought, which transcends all revelations (*Giluyim*) entirely. Moreover, in reality, they even are rooted higher than thought (*Machshavah*) altogether.

For, even this aspect of, "they ascended in thought," is already within the category of thought, albeit, the loftiest level of thought. This is like our sages, of blessed memory, stated,[255] "The thought for the Jewish people preceded everything." In other words, although it preceded everything, they nevertheless related this thought to everything, only that it was first and preceded everything. However, the true root of the souls of the Jewish people is entirely beyond thought, and even beyond the loftiest level of thought, to the point that it is not even applicable to say about it, that it "preceded everything," since really, there is no relativity between them and "everything," whatsoever.

It is about this that our sages, of blessed memory, stated,[256] "The Holy One, blessed is He, consulted the souls of the righteous to create the world." In other words, even the consideration and consultation to create the thought itself, arose with the council of the souls of the Jewish people. It thus is understood from this that the souls of the Jewish people entirely transcend even the matter of thought-*Machshavah*. In other

---

[254] Likkutei Torah Shir HaShirim 17d and on; Sefer HaMaamarim 5700 p. 17 & p. 27; 5703 p. 74 and elsewhere.

[255] Midrash Bereishit Rabba 1:4 Ibid.

[256] Midrash Ruth Rabba 2:3

words, the matter that,[257] "Israel arose in thought" is only how this comes forth into revelation, but their essential root is actually higher than this, about which it states, "The Holy One, blessed is He, consulted the souls of the righteous to create the world." Thus, because of their root in this higher aspect, their faith-*Emunah* is even in the Essential Intrinsic Preexistent Being of the Unlimited One, *HaShem*-יהו"ה Himself, blessed is He.

6.

Now, although the Jewish people have all aspects of faith-*Emunah*, not only faith in how *HaShem*-יהו"ה, blessed is He, fills all worlds (*Memale Kol Almin*), and not only faith in how *HaShem*-יהו"ה, blessed is He, transcends all worlds (*Sovev Kol Almin*), but even faith-*Emunah* in the aspect of the Essential Intrinsic Preexistent Being of the Unlimited One Himself, *HaShem*-יהו"ה, blessed is He, they nevertheless need Moshe, the "shepherd of faith," to sustain and nourish them with faith-*Emunah*. What this means is that even faith in the Essential Intrinsic Preexistent Being of the Unlimited One, *HaShem*-יהו"ה Himself, blessed is He, is insufficient. For, since it is only in a manner of inheritance, it is entirely possible for it to remain dormant. Thus, Moshe is needed to reveal it from concealment into revelation.

---

[257] Midrash Bereishit Rabba 1:4

Moreover, it even is possible for the faith-*Emunah* in how *HaShem*-יהו"ה, blessed is He, transcends all worlds (*Sovev Kol Almin*) to remain in an encompassing aspect of transcendence. It thus is necessary for Moshe to draw forth this faith for it to penetrate internally.

Beyond even this, it is quite possible that even in the aspect of the faith of how *HaShem*-יהו"ה, blessed is He, fills all worlds (*Memale Kol Almin*), which the intellect can grasp, there still must be an aspect of, "nourishing faith," so that these matters penetrate all of one's inner being, to the point that the true reality of *HaShem*-יהו"ה manifests in ones thought, speech, and action.

Without this, it is entirely possible for a person to find himself in the category of,[258] "A thief, when standing on the threshold, calls out to the Merciful One for assistance," as understood quite simply from what we explained before. In other words, because one is so invested into the lusts of this world, it is possible for him to do things that even the pious of the nations would not do.

This is why the actions of Moshe, the shepherd of faith, are so needed, for it is he who sustains and nourishes faith-*Emunah*. This is because it states about Moshe,[259] "Because I drew him-*Mesheeteehu*-משיתיהו from the water," which refers to the aspect of the Supernal waters that even transcend the aspect of,[260] "Even the heavens and the heavens of the heavens

---

[258] Talmud Bavli, Brachot 20a

[259] Exodus 2:10; Torah Ohr Mishpatim 76c; Also see chapter 4 of the prior discourse of this year.

[260] Kings I 8:27

cannot contain You," which is the aspect how *HaShem*-יהו"ה, blessed is He, transcends all worlds (*Sovev Kol Almin*).

It is for this reason that Moshe is able to even draw forth faith-*Emunah* in the aspect of the very Essential Intrinsic Preexistent Being of the Unlimited One, *HaShem*-יהו"ה Himself, blessed is He. Moshe specifically draws this faith-*Emunah* to the fore in the Jewish people, since because of their essential root, they already possess this aspect of faith-*Emunah*.

(This is as previously explained[261] regarding the matter of the verse,[262] "If you acquire a Hebrew servant etc.," which is like the acquisition of something, wherein there is no novelty or change to the existence of the thing itself, but only a transference from one domain to the other, from concealment into revelation.)

7.

Based upon all the above we may now also understand the matter of the half-shekel. For, about the half-shekel, our sages, of blessed memory, stated,[263] "The Holy One, blessed is He, showed Moshe a coin of fire, and told him, 'Like this one they shall give.'" In other words, by giving the half-shekel here below, which is the aspect of the awakening from below, we draw forth the aspect of the, "coin of fire," from Above, which

---

[261] See the prior discourse entitled "These are the ordinances-*V'Eleh HaMishpatim*" 5711, where this was explained.

[262] Exodus 21:2

[263] Talmud Yerushalmi Shekalim 1:4; Midrash Tanchumah Tisa 9; Rashi to Exodus 30:13, and elsewhere.

is the aspect of the awakening from Above. However, this is only the aspect of the awaking from Above that is affected and reached by the awakening from below. Nevertheless, it is through this that there subsequently is a drawing down of the aspect of an awaking from Above, that is entirely beyond the reach of the awakening from below.

This accords with what is explained regarding the matter of the desire of the heart (*Re'uta D'Leeba*), that there are two levels in it. The first is the aspect of the desire of the heart (*Re'uta D'Leeba*) that is roused through contemplation-*Hitbonenut*. In other words, although it itself is beyond comprehension, nevertheless, it is drawn forth by means of the contemplation-*Hitbonenut*. Then, there is the aspect of the desire of the heart (*Re'uta D'Leeba*) that is not drawn forth through any contemplation-*Hitbonenut*, but is of the essence of the soul itself.

It is this latter aspect that is the matter of the "half-shekel of the sacred-*Kodesh*-קדש shekel." That is, the verse specifies "sacred-*Kodesh*-קדש" without the letter *Vav*-ו, which is loftier than "holy-*Kadosh*-קדוש." As known, the difference between the term "sacred-*Kodesh*-קדש" and "holy-*Kadosh*-קדוש," is that the term "holy-*Kadosh*-קדוש" with the letter *Vav*-ו indicates the expressions and descent of drawing down. This is as explained regarding *HaShem*'s title, "The Holy One, blessed is He-*HaKadosh Baruch Hoo*-הקדוש ברוך הוא."

In other words, although holiness-*Kadosh*-קדוש is likewise a term of separation, in that He is holy and transcendent, nevertheless, He is also blessed-*Baruch*-ברוך,

which means that He is drawn down. This is further hinted at in the fact that the term "holy-*Kadosh*-קדוש," has the *Vav*-ו present, which indicates a drawing down from Above to below.[264]   In other words, the term "holy-*Kadosh*-קדוש," with the *Vav*-ו, at the very least denotes the aspect of how *HaShem*-יהו"ה, blessed is He, transcends the worlds (*Sovev Kol Almin*), in which there is already a relation to worlds, even if only in a way of negation.

In contrast, the term "sacred-*Kodesh*-קדש" is as stated,[265] "*Kodesh*-קדש is a matter entirely unto to itself," indicating the aspect that transcends even the aspect of how *HaShem*-יהו"ה, blessed is He, transcends all worlds (*Sovev Kol Almin*).

This, then, explains the continuation of the verse,[266] "every man shall give *HaShem*-יהו"ה an atonement for his soul." In other words, through giving this half-shekel, there is a drawing down of the aspect of the Intrinsic Preexistent Essential Being of the Unlimited One, *HaShem*-יהו"ה Himself, blessed is He, since this is from the aspect of the singular-*Yechidah* essence of the soul. As known,[267] the aspect of the Singular One-*Yachid*-יחיד,[268] blessed is He, manifests within the singular-*Yechidah* essence of the soul, since it is rooted in the

[264] Likkutei Torah Tazria 22c & 24b; Shir HaShirim 40c and on.
[265] Zohar III 94b
[266] Exodus 30:12
[267] Likkutei Torah, Re'eh 25a; Sefer HaMaamarim 5696 p. 57
[268] See Shaar HaYichud of the Mittler Rebbe, translated as The Gate of Unity, Chapters 10 & 11.

Essential Self of the Unlimited One, *HaShem*-יהו״ה Himself, blessed is He, as explained before.

It is about all this that the verse states, "When you uplift the head of the children of Israel," referring to Moshe, who uplifts and elevates the head of the Jewish people. It is through this, that the matter of the "atonement of his soul," is possible, which is the matter of drawing down the Singular Intrinsic Being of the Unlimited One, *HaShem*-יהו״ה Himself, blessed is He.

From all the above we can also understand what our sages, of blessed memory, stated in the Midrash. That is,[269] "Moshe asked the Holy One, blessed is He, about the commandment of the half-shekel, 'What will be with it in the coming generations?' The Holy One, blessed is He, responded, 'This is why it states, 'When you uplift,' in the future tense.'"

Now, at first glance, it is not understood why Moshe specifically asked about this commandment. However, the explanation is that within this commandment-*Mitzvah* the entirety of the matter of man's service of *HaShem*-יהו״ה, blessed is He, is included. This refers to the sacrificial offerings that were funded by the half-shekel, through which the animalistic souls of the Jewish people become diminished and included in holiness. That is, that which cannot be purified becomes diminished, and that which can be purified becomes included in holiness, to the point that the service of *HaShem*-יהו״ה is such,

---

[269] Midrash Tanchumah Tisa 3; Torah Sheleima Tisa 30:12, Ch. 38

that "every man shall give *HaShem*-יהו"ה an atonement for his soul."

It is through this that we then arrive at the aspect of the "sacred-*Kodesh*-קדש shekel," which is the aspect of, "*Kodesh*-קדש is a matter entirely unto itself." In other words, not only do we draw forth the aspect of how *HaShem*-יהו"ה, blessed is He, fills all worlds (*Memale Kol Almin*), and not only the aspect of how *HaShem*-יהו"ה, blessed is He, transcends all worlds (*Sovev Kol Almin*), but even the aspect of the Singular Essential Intrinsic Being of the Unlimited One Himself, *HaShem*-יהו"ה, blessed is He, "before Whom all is as nothing."[270] It is because of this that Moshe specifically asked about this particular commandment and what would be of it in future generations.

Thus, the Holy One, blessed is He, answered him that He wrote in the Torah the words, "When you uplift," in the future tense. In other words, it applies to all generations, since there is an offshoot of Moshe in each and every generation. That is, the Moshe of each generation must draw forth not only the aspect of how *HaShem*-יהו"ה, blessed is He, fills all worlds (*Memale Kol Almin*), and not only the aspect of how *HaShem*-יהו"ה, blessed is He, transcends all worlds (*Sovev Kol Almin*), but even the aspect of the Singular Intrinsic Essential Being of the Unlimited One, *HaShem*-יהו"ה Himself, blessed is He, "before Whom all is as nothing,"[271] and,[272] "There is nothing aside for Him."

---

[270] Zohar I 11b; Daniel 4:32
[271] Zohar I 11b; Daniel 4:32
[272] Deuteronomy 4:35

Discourse 5

"VeKeebel HaYehudim et Asher Hecheilu La'asot -
The Jews undertook that which they had begun to do"

Delivered on Purim, 5711

By the grace of *HaShem*, blessed is He,

1.

The verse states,[273] "The Jews undertook that which they had begun to do." His honorable holiness, my father-in-law, the Rebbe, explains this in his discourse[274] that begins with these words (recently printed and publicized).[275] That is, the Jews undertook that which they had begun at the time of the giving of the Torah. For, when the Jewish people said,[276] "All that *HaShem*-יהו״ה has spoken, we will do and we will hear," that was only the beginning ("they had begun to do"). It was specifically in the days of Achashverosh (during the period of the decree of Haman) that the "undertaking-*Kabbalah*-קבלה"[277]

---

[273] Esther 9:23

[274] Of Purim Katan 5687

[275] This discourse was printed in 5711, and is printed in Sefer HaMaamarim 5711 p. 180 and on; 5787 p. 110 and on

[276] Exodus 24:7

[277] Note: This is similarly stated in the discourse by the same title in Torah Ohr, Megillat Esther 96c; Shaarei Orah of the Mittler Rebbe, Shaar HaPurim 88b; Torah Ohr Ibid. 90a, 98a; Shaarei Orah 54a; Sefer HaMaamarim 5678 p. 196 discourse of this title, and various other places. To add further clarity, in the Torah Ohr ibid. (98a) and in the (beginning of the) discourse of 5678 (Ibid. p. 197), it is similar to what our sages, of blessed memory, stated (Shabbat 88a) regarding the verse (Esther 9:27) "The Jews undertook upon themselves – that which they had

took place, as it states, "The Jews undertook-*VeKeebel HaYehudim*-ויקבל היהודים."

Now, (in his discourse) he analyses this with precision, since at first glance this is an extremely wondrous thing.[278] For, during the time of the giving of the Torah, the Jewish people were in a state of the utmost elevation. This is true both physically, that they were in an extremely prosperous and excellent state, on account of their freedom,[279] and also spiritually, that they had a revelation of the loftiest level of Godliness.[280]

In contrast, in the days of Achashverosh, the Jewish people were in a state of ultimate descent. For, in addition to the concealment and hiddenness that takes place in all exiles, during which time, "darkness covers the whole earth,"[281] nevertheless, during that time (of the decree of Haman) there was an even greater concealment and hiddenness.[282] For, even

---

already undertaken." [Now, although at first glance it seems that they are two opposite matters, meaning, that the words "The Jews undertook that which they had begun to do" seems to indicate that they only undertook this at the time of Purim. In contrast, the words "They fulfilled that which they had previously undertaken" indicates that even at the giving of the Torah they did indeed receive and undertake this, only that it was not yet everlasting. For a more complete explanation see Ch. 12 of this discourse.] Likewise, see Shaarei Orah ibid. (both citations) as well as the discourse by this title in 5678, where this distinction and explanation is stated in the same manner, in the name of our sages, of blessed memory.

[278] For the explanation of this precise language, see the discourse with the same title, Purim Katan 5738, Ch. 1.

[279] Midrash Shmot Rabba 41:7; VaYikra Rabba 18:3; Zohar II 113b and on; Talmud Bavli, Eruvin 54h

[280] See Tanya Ch. 36 that the revelation at the time of the giving of the Torah was a foretaste of the revelation of the coming future.

[281] Isaiah 60:2

[282] Note: To further illuminate from the words of our sages, of blessed memory, who stated (Talmud Bavli, Chullin 139b), "From where do we know of Esther-אסתר in the Torah? From the verse that states (Deut. 31:18) 'I shall surely hide My face-

physically, they were in a state of utmost lowliness and there was a decree, "to destroy, to slay and to exterminate all the Jews, from young to old, children and women, in one day."[283]

Even so, during the time of the giving of the Torah, when the Jewish people were in a state of utmost elevation, that was only the beginning ("they had begun to do"), whereas in the time of the decree of Haman, when they were in a state of the utmost lowliness, it was specifically then that they, "undertook to do that which they had begun," at the giving of the Torah!

He continues and explains[284] that during the time of the decree, their fulfillment of Torah and *mitzvot* was in a way of self-sacrifice (*Mesirat Nefesh*). [To further clarify, it is explained in Torah Ohr[285] that the self-sacrifice (*Mesirat Nefesh*) they had was as follows: If they would have renounced their faith, nothing would have been done to them, since the decree was only against the Jews. Nevertheless, it never entered their minds to consider such a thing, God forbid. Moreover, it is further explained that their self-sacrifice was (not only to not renounce the true faith in *HaShem*-יהו"ה, God forbid, but also)

Aster Asteer-אסתיר אסתר'" In other words, even after the miracle of Purim (due to the fact that the miracle manifests within the natural order) the Jewish people were still called Esther-אסתר, as a terminology of, "I shall surely hide-אסתיר אסתר." (See Torah Ohr, Megillat Esther 90d and on). This being so, this was certainly the case during the time of the decree itself.

[283] Esther 3:13

[284] In the aforementioned discourse, chapter 3 and on.

[285] Torah Ohr ibid. 91b, 97a, 99b; Also see Shaarei Orah Ibid. Ch. 68, p. 90b; Sefer HaMaamarim 5678 p. 204, end of the discourse by this title; Discourse entitled "*Chayav Inish*" 5679, Ch. 4, p. 306; 5671, Ch. 5, p. 191; 5708 p. 118; Discourse entitled "*BaLaylah HaHoo*" 5700 Ch. 5, p. 9; Also see Megillat Setarim on the verse in Esther Ibid.

that they had literal self-sacrifice in the fulfillment of Torah and *mitzvot*,[286] to the extent that they **publicly** gathered by the multitudes to study Torah with self-sacrifice.]

The awakening of their self-sacrifice (*Mesirat Nefesh*) was through Mordechai the Jew-*HaYehudi*, who is called the Moshe of his generation,[287] who publicly gathered the multitudes to strengthen their faith-*Emunah*. However, Mordechai's principal work, is that he taught and studied Torah with the schoolchildren, who are the foundation of the whole Jewish people. [This is explained at length in the discourse about the great level of the breath of schoolchildren when they learn Torah].

This is as stated in Midrash,[288] "Mordechai gathered twenty-two thousand pupils and taught them Torah with self-sacrifice. When Haman arrived, Mordechai instructed them, 'Run away, so as not to be burned by my coals.' They responded, 'We stand together with you, whether for life or for death.'" In other words, they accepted upon themselves whatever punishments might come, so long as they would not be separated from the holy Torah.

---

[286] Note: This is an even more wondrous thing, because when it comes to the faith-*Emunah*, even the simplest of Jews will have self-sacrifice and give up his life for the sanctification of the Name of *HaShem* (see Tanya Ch. 18 and various other places).

[287] Note: In other words, in addition to the fact that there is an offshoot of Moshe in each generation (as stated in Tikkunei Zohar Tikkun 69 – 112a; 114a), and that Mordechai was the offshoot of Moshe in his generation (See the aforementioned discourse Ch. 15) – in addition, it states in the Midrash (Esther Rabba 6:2 cited in the discourse Ch. 3) that "Mordechai in his generation, was equal to Moshe in his generation."

[288] Midrash Esther Rabba 10:4; Yalkut Shimoni Esther Remez 1,058; Vayikra Rabba 28:6; Yalkut Shimoni Emor Remez 643 to Lev. 23:11; Psikta Rabbati Ch. 18.

This then, is what is meant by the fact that they[289] "undertook that which they had begun to do," and that the giving of the Torah was only the beginning, whereas the "undertaking" was at the time of the decree of Haman. For, through the **actual** self-sacrifice (*Mesirat Nefesh*) that they had for the fulfillment of Torah and *mitzvot*, they were elevated (in a certain respect) to an even higher level than at the time of the giving of the Torah. This is the reason why the "undertaking-*Kabbalah*-קבלה" was specifically then, such that it states, "The Jews undertook that which they had begun to do."

2.

Now, we must further understand this. For, the main point of the explanation in the discourse, is that the reason that this "undertaking" occurred at the time of the decree, was because of their self-sacrifice at that time. This being the case, of what relevance is it that their awakening to self-sacrifice was by the hand of Mordechai, or that his primary work was learning Torah with the schoolchildren?

We also must explain why it was specified (at the beginning of the discourse) that at the giving of the Torah, the Jewish people were in the most elevated state, whereas at the time of the decree they were in a state of utmost lowliness, both spiritually and physically. At first glance, when we examine the discourse, it explains how it was that when they were at the

---

[289] Esther 9:23

height of elevation, it was only "the beginning," whereas when they were in the utmost lowliness, that is specifically when they took on this "undertaking." The relevance of their elevation or lowliness thus makes sense, in that it relates to their spiritual standing. However, to what end does the discourse specify their physical elevation at the time of the giving of the Torah and their physical lowliness at the time of the decree?

3.

Now, in addition to the points mentioned above, we must also understand the general theme of the explanation (in the discourse), namely, that the reason the "undertaking" specifically took place at the time of the decree, is because of their self-sacrifice for Torah and *mitzvot* at that time. Now, this must be better understood. For, at first glance, regarding almost all the commandments, the verse states,[290] "You shall live by them."

Even the three cardinal commandments about which it states,[291] "one should rather be killed, than to transgress," are not actually one and the same as the matter of self-sacrifice (*Mesirat Nefesh*). Rather, it only is that the manner of fulfilling these commandments entails that one must never transgress

---

[290] Leviticus 18:5; See Rambam Hilchos Yesodei HaTorah 5:1; (Yoma 85b; Sanhedrin 74a; Tosefta Shabbat, end of Ch. 16) – "You shall live by them, and you should not die by them."

[291] Rambam Hilchos Yesodei HaTorah 5:2 (Cited from Yoma 82a, and Sanhedrin & Tosefta Ibid.)

them, even if it means that he will be killed as a result of it,[292] whereas the commandment of self-sacrifice (*Mesirat Nefesh*) for the sanctification of the Name *HaShem*-יהו"ה, blessed is He, is only a single commandment. Why then is this self-sacrifice (*Mesirat Nefesh*) a prerequisite to the "undertaking" ("The Jews undertook") of the Torah as a whole?

Now, it does state in Tanya,[293] that the reason that Moshe commanded the generation that was entering the land of Israel to recite the *Shema* twice daily and to accept the yoke of the Kingdom of Heaven upon themselves with self-sacrifice, is because the fulfillment of Torah and *mitzvot* is dependent upon the constant remembrance of the matter of self-sacrifice of one's soul to *HaShem*-יהו"ה, blessed is He. (This is so, even though he also promised them that,[294] "*HaShem*-יהו"ה your God, shall place the fear of you and the dread of you upon all the land that you shall tread upon etc.") However, what we see from this is that the self-sacrifice (*Mesirat Nefesh*), upon which the fulfillment of Torah and *mitzvot* are dependent, is self-sacrifice in potential (*BeKoach*), rather than self-sacrifice in actuality (*BePo'el*). (In other words, if he should ever need to have self-sacrifice in fulfilling Torah and *mitzvot*, he is prepared to do so.)

This being so, then even at the giving of the Torah, when the Jewish people said,[295] "All that *HaShem*-יהו"ה has spoken, we will do and we will hear," (and certainly after they were commanded the *mitzvah* of *Shema* recital twice daily) they

---

[292] See Sefer HaMaamarim 5709, p. 123 and in the note there, at greater length.
[293] Tanya, Ch. 25
[294] Deuteronomy 11:25
[295] Exodus 24:7

accepted upon themselves to fulfill all that they were commanded, even if it would require self-sacrifice (*Mesirat Nefesh*). However, even so, the "undertaking" (when "the Jews undertook") was not complete until the time of the decree of Haman, when they had self-sacrifice in actuality (*BePo'el*).[296]

Now, it is generally known that there were two times in history that (the Jewish people as a whole) had actual self-sacrifice for Torah and *mitzvot*. One was on Chanukah (at the time of the decrees of the Greeks), and the other was on Purim (at the time of the decrees of Haman). Since all matters in Torah are with ultimate precision, we must say that the fact that this matter of, "the Jews undertook," was specifically accomplished through the self-sacrifice of Purim, was (not only because the self-sacrifice of Purim preceded the self-sacrifice of Chanukah, but also) because the self-sacrifice of Purim was more closely related to the (completion) of receiving the Torah. We must therefore understand the difference between the self-sacrifice of Chanukah and the self-sacrifice of Purim.[297] For, it is due to

---

[296] Note: In Shaarei Orah ibid. (61a; 90b) it is explained that the fact that the "undertaking-*Kabbalah*" of the giving of the Torah was completed specifically through the actual self-sacrifice that they had in the days of Purim (even though when they said "we will do and we will hear" they certainly did so with their whole hearts and with a willingness to have complete self-sacrifice in actuality) is because of the advantage of self-sacrifice in actuality, which reaches and elicits an even higher aspect of Godliness than Torah and the commandments themselves. Nevertheless, this still requires explanation, for, why is it necessary to reach a higher level than the Torah and the commandments, in order to receive the Torah?

[297] Note: In the introduction to Shaarei Orah it is explained that the self-sacrifice of Purim was from the "strength of the influencer-*Mashpia*" whereas the self-sacrifice of Chanukah was "from the recipient-*Mekabel*." However, this distinction seemingly is not coming to explain the fact that the "reception" and "undertaking" was accomplished through the self-sacrifice of Purim specifically. Moreover, according to what is explain in Torah Ohr ibid. (92b and on) and in

this difference that the completion of the receiving of the Torah occurred specifically by means of the self-sacrifice of Purim.

4.

Now, this will be understood by prefacing[298] with the well-known explanation[299] regarding the novelty that occurred with the giving of the Torah, in comparison to the Torah and commandments, as they were, before the giving of the Torah. That is, the *mitzvot* that were fulfilled by our forefathers, peace be upon them (and in general – all those who preceded the giving of the Torah), were only performed and fulfilled spiritually (such as *Tefillin,* through which we recall the exodus from Egypt, whereas at that time, the exile in Egypt had not yet happened) and even in the commandments that they fulfilled physically, the drawing forth of holiness-*Kedushah* only occurred spiritually, and was not transferred to the physical object through which the mitzvah was done.[300] For, before the giving of the Torah, there was a Divine edict that, "the upper

---

Shaarei Orah ibid. (97a and on), the reason that at the giving of the Torah there was only the aspect of, "they had begun to do," is because the self-sacrifice at the giving of the Torah was due to the revelations from Above, which was not the case with the self-sacrifice of Purim. Nevertheless, it seems that if the self-sacrifice of Chanukah was from the angle of "the recipient-*Mekabel*" then it would have been more fitting that the "receiving" and "undertaking" of "*VeKeebel*-וקבל" should have occurred through the self-sacrifice of Chanukah.

[298] Note: See the discourse entitled "*VeKeebel*" in Torah Ohr (96c), and Shaarei Orah (88b), that this matter (that in the days of Achashverosh they undertook that which they began at the giving of the Torah) is understood through a preface of an explanation of the matter of the giving of the Torah itself.

[299] See at length in Likkutei Sichot Vol. 5, p. 88 and on, and pg. 79.

[300] See Sefer HaMaamarim 5710 p. 223 and the notes there.

ones shall not descend below and the lower ones shall not ascend above."[301] Therefore, there was no bond between the holiness of the *mitzvah* ("the upper ones") with the physical object through which the *mitzvah* was performed ("the lower ones").

This is not the case, with the *mitzvot*[302] that followed the giving of the Torah. For, at that time, the Divine edict that separated between, "the upper ones and the lower ones," was nullified, and a bond was made between the physical object (through which the *mitzvah* is performed) and the holiness-*Kedushah* of the *mitzvah*. This is to such a degree, that in some *mitzvot*, the physical object becomes a "Holy *Mitzvah* Object."[303] Now since, as known, a bond between two opposites only happens through something that is higher than both, it therefore is understood that the bond between, "the upper ones" and "the lower ones" that came about at the giving of the Torah, was because the giving of the Torah was a drawing forth of the Unlimited Light of *HaShem*-יהו"ה, who transcends the categories of up and down altogether.

What we understand from all this is that there are three aspects in the commandments-*mitzvot*, after the giving of the

---

[301] Midrash Shmot Rabba 12:3; Tanchuma Va'era 15

[302] Note: It is this same way with the Torah itself, that specifically through the giving of the Torah, power was given to the study of Torah to transform the man who studies it. See at length in Likkutei Sichot Vol. 16, p. 214. Nevertheless, the primary matter in this is in the commandments-*Mitzvot* – See Hadran al HaShas (in Torat Menachem – Hadranim on the Rambam and Shas, p. 418) note 31.

[303] See Likkutei Sichot Vol. 16, p. 213, note 16 (There are various different levels of holy objects. See Talmud Bavli, Megilla 26b; Rambam Hilchot Sefer Torah 10:3 and on; Tur and Shulchan Aruch Orach Chaim 154; Yoreh De'ah 282; Shulchan Aruch of the Alter Rebbe 42:6)

Torah. There is the aspect of "below," [for even after the giving of the Torah, the physical object with which the *mitzvah* is done, is not transformed into spirituality, but remains physical, even though it now has become a "Holy *Mitzvah* Object"]. The second is the aspect of "above," [for even after the giving of the Torah, when the holiness of the *mitzvah* is drawn forth and embedded in the physical object, nonetheless, the holiness itself remains spiritual]. The third and highest aspect is the nullification of "Above" and "Below," since the very fact that Above and Below bond to each other [though they are opposites] is through the nullification of their parameters and limitations, which is done through drawing forth the Unlimited Light of *HaShem*-יהו"ה, blessed is He, who transcends them both.

It can be said that these three matters may also be found in how a person fulfills the *mitzvot*. If he fulfills them, "as commands people do by rote,"[304] it is because he has become accustomed to it out of habit.[305] Since the habit has become naturally ingrained in him,[306] his fulfillment of the *mitzvot* also becomes due to the nature of his body and natural soul, which is the lower aspect in man.[307]

However, when he fulfills the commandments of *HaShem*-יהו"ה, blessed is He, because he loves Him and desires

---

[304] Isaiah 29:13

[305] Tanya Ch. 39 (p. 53b)

[306] Tanya Ch. 44 (p. 63b), end of Ch. 14, Ch. 15 (21a); Shvilei Emunah, Netiv 4, Shaar 2; Shu"t HaRama MiPano 36

[307] Midrash Bereishit Rabba 8:11; 12:8; Torah Ohr Bereishit 3d and on; Kuntres U'Maayon discourse 15; Hemshech 5666 p. 495 and elsewhere.

to cleave to Him, and since it is not possible to truly cleave to Him except through the fulfillment of the "two-hundred and forty-eight commands-*Pekudin,*" which are the "two-hundred and forty-eight organs of the King,"[308] then his fulfillment of the commandments is due to his (Godly) soul, the upper aspect of man.

However, if he fulfills the *mitzvot* for the Sake of the Name *HaShem-*יהו"ה alone, meaning that he does not do them because of any benefits that he may gain from them (not even spiritual benefits), but rather, only because they are the will of *HaShem-*יהו"ה, blessed is He, then his fulfillment of the commandments is not due to his own existence at all (not even the existence of his soul), but instead, he does them with complete sublimation to *HaShem-*יהו"ה. This is because his only interest (when doing the *mitzvah*) is entirely to fulfill *HaShem's-*יהו"ה Supernal will, blessed is He.

5.

We should add, that the root of these three ways of fulfilling the commandments is because the *mitzvot* themselves possess these three aspects (corresponding to the three ways of fulfilling the commandments). To further explain the giving of the commandments below, our sages, of blessed memory, stated,[309] "The Torah was only given in order to refine the

---

[308] Tanya Ch. 4

[309] Midrash Tanchumah 8 (and see 7); Bereishit Rabba beginning of Ch. 44; Moreh HaNevuchim Vol. 3, Ch. 26

creatures." In other words, the intention in the giving of the commandments-*mitzvot* is (not for the commandments themselves, but rather) for the purification and refinement of the faculties and organs of the person who fulfills them, as well as for the purification and refinement of the physical things of the world through which the commandments are performed.[310]

However, there is a loftier aspect to the *mitzvot*, which is that they are the commands of the Holy One, blessed is He. This is as our sages, of blessed memory, stated[311] about the verse,[312] "He relates **His** Words to Yaakov, **His** statutes and **His** judgments to Israel," that, "What He Himself does, He instructs Israel to do." In other words, the fact that the Holy One, blessed is He, fulfills the *mitzvot* (prior[313] to instructing the Jewish people to do them), means that He does them of His own accord (from "Above"). [As is also understood from this, that the "two-hundred and forty-eight commands-*Pekudin*" are the "two-hundred and forty-eight organs of the King." In other words, when we say that the *mitzvot* are His organs, so to speak, this is from the aspect of what He determined Above.]

Thus, when the Jewish people fulfill the commandments that "He does," they are walking on the ways of the Holy One,

---

[310] See at length in Tanya Ch. 37
[311] Midrash Shmot Rabba 30:9; Talmud Yerushalmi Rosh HaShanah 1:3
[312] Psalms 147:19
[313] Note: That is, since He is above time altogether, the explanation of "prior" here means that it precedes them in level.

blessed is He,[314] and cleave to Him.[315] Through this, vitality is drawn to the person who fulfills them, as it states,[316] "You shall do My ordinances and keep My statutes, to walk therein, which if a man shall do, he shall live by them." For, through the performance of the *mitzvot*, he cleaves to the Holy One, blessed is He, (as mentioned before), which is the fulfillment of the verse,[317] "But you who cleave to *HaShem*-יהו״ה your God – are all alive today."

Now, this aspect of the *mitzvot* (that they are the pathways of the Holy One, blessed is He, in that the Holy One, blessed is He, Himself performs the *mitzvot*) is higher than any relation to worlds. Therefore, the vitality that is drawn to the person who performs them, comes to him from the aspect of how *HaShem*-יהו״ה, blessed is He, transcends all worlds (*Sovev Kol Almin*). In other words, by itself, it is holy and transcends

---

[314] Note: As known, the commandments-*Mitzvot* are called "the paths of *HaShem*-יהו״ה, blessed is He (See the end of Hosea; Talmud Bavli Nazir 23a; Horayot 10b; Zohar I 175b "these are the pathways and passageways of the Torah" and various other places). It was already explained on a number of occasions (See Torat Menachem Sefer HaMaamarim Cheshvan p. 255; Likkutei Sichot Vol. 34 p. 153 and on) that the explanation of the words "to go in all of His ways" (Deut. 10:12) is that it refers to the actual performance of the commandments-*Mitzvot*. When our sages, of blessed memory, explained that the words "to go in all of His ways" refers to the attributes of the Holy One, blessed is He (in that "just as He is compassionate, so likewise you be compassionate"), they said so in regard to the verse at the end of Parshat Ekev (Deut. 11:22).

[315] Note: This can be further illuminated by the words of Rashi to the words (Deut. 13:5) "to Him you shall cleave," who states, "Cleave to His ways: bestow kindness, bury the dead, and visit the sick, just as the Holy One, blessed is He, did." (Sota 14a). It is through this that one "cleaves **to Him**."

[316] Leviticus 18:5; Likkutei Torah Shir HaShirim 2a [See also Derech Chaim Ch. 75, p. 82a and on where this is similarly stated.] – "You shall live by them – meaning that you shall derive vitality from them."

[317] Deuteronomy 4:4; See Avot D'Rabbi Nathan end of Ch. 34.

worlds, but nonetheless, through doing the *mitzvot*, "he lives by them," and draws forth inner vitality.[318]

Nonetheless, even this aspect of the *mitzvot* has form, and therefore the *mitzvot* of this level are in a manner of division. That is, they are called, "the **ways** of *HaShem-Darchei HaShem*-ה"דרכי יהו" (in the plural),[319] and thus correspond to the division of the two-hundred and forty-eight "organs of the King." In other words, the drawing forth of vitality affected by each particular *mitzvah* is unique to that *mitzvah*. (This is similar to the differences between the power of sight in the eye and the power of hearing in the ear.)

This is why it is possible for a person to perform *the mitzvot* that the Holy One, blessed is He, does Himself, because the two-hundred and forty-eight organs of man below, correspond to the, "two-hundred and forty-eight organs of the King," as stated,[320] "Let us make man in our form and in our likeness."

However, there is an even loftier aspect in the commandments-*mitzvot*, which is that they are *HaShem's*-ה"יהו Supernal will, blessed is He (a desire that transcends reason),

---

[318] Note: We may further illuminate this based on Tanya, Ch. 36 (p. 66a) from the explanation of the words of our blessings, "that He has sanctified (and betrothed) us with His commandments," as follows: "This is the holiness of the Holy One, blessed is He, Himself... the aspect of how *HaShem*-ה"יהו, blessed is He, transcends all worlds (*Sovev Kol Almin*)... (nevertheless,) she (referring to the soul of man who performs the commandments) attains the quality and level of holiness of the Singular Infinite One, Himself, blessed is He, literally, since she unifies herself to Him and becomes included in His unity, and they become literally one."

[319] Note: This is further illuminated by Likkutei Torah Re'eh 21d with respect to the matter of the 613 pathways.

[320] Genesis 1:26

123

in that *HaShem's*-ה"יהו desire is in all six-hundred and thirteen commandments equally (higher than the division into two-hundred and forty-eight organs). Now, since this desire for the commandments is entirely beyond any comparison to the human being who fulfills them (which is certainly the case, since it even is beyond the form of Supernal Man), therefore, relative to this level[321] (as it is, in and of itself) man takes up no space at all.

This sublimation, that before *HaShem*-ה"יהו, blessed is He, one literally takes up no space, is the nullification of one's very existence (*Bitul B'Metziut*).[322] Moreover, even after the matter of a command to man, through which he indeed is given existence, nonetheless, his entire existence is solely to fulfill the command. Thus, through fulfilling the *mitzvah* (in that the term "*mitzvah*-מצוה" means[323] "binding and bonding-*Tzavta v'Chibur*-צוותא וחיבור") he becomes bound to the Commander of the *mitzvah* (who is totally and completely beyond comparison to him altogether).

---

[321] With respect to this section (until the end of this chapter), see Igrot Kodesh of the Rebbe Rayatz, Vol. 10, p. 369 and on, as well as Sefer HaMaamarim 5698, 5700, and 5710 cited below in the coming note.

[322] See the discourse ibid. (entitled "*VeKeebel*" 5677) Ch. 12 and on.

[323] Note: Likkutei Torah, Bechukotai 45c; Derech Chaim Shaar HaTefilah (p. 52b); Sefer HaMaamarim 5698 p. 52; 5700 p. 73 and on; 5710 p. 71 and on; Likkutei Sichot Vol. 7, p. 30 and on; Likkutei Torah Chukat 57d on the words "*Asher Tzeevah*-אשר צוה-that He commanded." Also see the aforementioned discourse Ch. 4 on the explanation of "And you shall command-ואתה תצוה" that "command-*Tzivuy*-צווי is a term of "binding and bonding-*Tzavta v'Chibur*-צוותא וחיבור," and is a term of connection between two things, "*Hitkashrut*-התקשרות." Also see Pri Etz Chaim, Shaar 29 (Shaar HaLulav) Ch. 3: The term "He will command-*Yetzaveh*-יצוה" is as our sages, of blessed memory stated, (Brachot 6b) "The whole world was only created to command-*Letzavot*-לצוות to this one" which is a term of bonding-*Chibur*-חיבור.

6.

Now, the same principle also applies to the study of Torah, in that there likewise are three approaches to the study of Torah. This is to say that in addition to the three ways that exist in the commandment to study Torah (just like all other commandments), in Torah study itself there also are these three ways (in a similar manner).

If one learns Torah because of the wisdom and intellect that is in it, for the Torah is,[324] "Your wisdom and your understanding (even) in the eyes of the nations," then his Torah study is due to the nature of his body and natural soul, in that he is an intellectual by nature and loves ideas.

If one's Torah study is because the Torah is the intermediary that binds the Jewish people to the Holy One, blessed is He, as Zohar states,[325] "There are three bonds that are tied to one another, the Jewish people are bound to the Torah and the Torah is bound to the Holy One, blessed is He." Thus, through Torah study, we bind ourselves to the Torah and to the Holy One, blessed is He. In such a case, one's Torah study is due to the soul that resides within him. In other words, even this level of Torah study is due to his own existence (in that his motivation is that **he** should be bonded to the Holy One, blessed is He).

However, there is an even higher level of Torah study. This is when one studies Torah (not because of any elevation

---

[324] Deuteronomy 4:6
[325] Zohar III 73a; Sefer HaMaamarim 5657 end of p. 28.

that he will derive through it, but rather) because of the Torah itself. That is, he studies it because, "The Torah and the Holy One, blessed is He, are entirely one,"[326] so much so, that it actually is one with His Essential Self, blessed is He.

This is as our sages, of blessed memory, stated,[327] "The word, 'I am-*Anochi*-אנכי'[328] is an acronym for, "I have placed My soul in My writings-*Ana Nafshi Katavit Yahavit*- אנא נפשי כתבית יהבית." The words "I-*Ana*-אנא" (and "my soul-*Nafshi*-נפשי") refer to the Essential Self of *HaShem*-יהו"ה Himself, blessed is He. Thus, the meaning of, "I have placed My soul in My writings," is that He has written and given us His Singular Essential Self, blessed is He,[329] "My soul-*Ana Nafshi*-אנא נפשי," and therefore, through Torah study, "it is Me that you are taking."[330]

Therefore, just as the Holy One, blessed is He, is not an intermediary to anything, God forbid, but is the ultimate end, in and of Himself, in the same way,[331] this is how it is with this level of Torah study. That is, when a person learns in this manner, his perspective is that the ultimate purpose of his Torah study is Torah itself. In other words, because he realizes that,

---

[326] Tanya Ch. 4 and beginning of Ch. 23 in the name of the Zohar; See citations in Maamarei Admor HaEmtza'ee Vayikra Vol. 1 p. 285; Zohar I 24a; Zohar II 60a; Tikkunei Zohar Tikkun 6, 21b; Tikkun 22, 64a; Likkutei Torah Netzavim 46a, and elsewhere.

[327] Talmud Bavli Shabbat 105a (Ein Yaakov version of the text).

[328] The first word of the Ten Commandments that states, "I am *HaShem*, your God-*Anochi HaShem Elohe"cha*-אנכי יהו"ה אלהי"ך."

[329] Likkutei Torah Shlach 58d and on.

[330] See Midrash Shmot Rabba 33:1 & 6; Tanchuma Terumah 3; Tanya Ch. 47; Likkutei Torah ibid.

[331] See Likkutei Sichot Vol. 19, p. 182.

"The Torah and the Holy One, blessed is He, are entirely one," this realization compels him to fully invest himself into the study of Torah without any calculations (even the calculation that through this he will bond with the Holy One, blessed is He). Through this, he studies Torah in a state of utter nullification of self.

These three ways of Torah study are drawn from the three matters that exist in Torah itself. That is, the Torah is wisdom and intellect (meaning that it is the wisdom of the Holy One, blessed is He, that subsequently descends and becomes manifest within the intellect of man).[332] Additionally, it is an intermediary that binds the Jewish people to the Holy One, blessed is He. Beyond that, "the Torah and the Holy One, blessed is He, are entirely one."

7.

Now, the three above mentioned matters are also found in the laws and *halachot* of Torah study. That is, the obligation to study the laws that apply to the actual performance[333] of the commandments, in order to know how and what to do, is similar to studying Torah from the angle of the (nature of the) body and the natural soul. This is because the performance of the commandments (as well as commandments that apply to

---

[332] See Tanya Ch. 4

[333] Note: That is, they take a certain amount of precedence over and above the study of laws that do not relate to practical action to such a great extent. See Hilchot Talmud Torah of the Alter Rebbe 2:9.

speech)[334] is done with the physical body and the natural soul that vitalizes it.

On the other hand, the commandment to **know** the Torah, that is, to know all of Torah in its entirety (including matters that are not directly connected to the active performance of the *mitzvot*), is similar to the study of Torah for the benefit of the soul, since the substance of this commandment is specifically the **knowledge** of Torah.

It can therefore be said, that this is why there indeed is measure to the commandment to know Torah. [For the verse that states,[335] "It's measure is longer than the earth and wider than the sea," is referring to the **reasons** of the laws. However, the laws themselves, as well as the Midrashim etc., indeed have a fixed measure and number to them,[336] and there indeed have been a number of people who have learned and known the entire Torah.[337]] For, since this obligation to know the whole Torah is upon a person, that he must know the Torah, and since man is limited, therefore the Torah that he must know (as it relates to this commandment) has measure and limit.

Then there is the obligation of,[338] "You shall toil in it day and night." [This applies even after one has learned the

---

[334] Tanya Ch. 37 (p. 47a); However, in Tanya, Ch. 35 (p. 45a) it seems to state this differently. However, this is not the place for the extended explanation.

[335] Job 11:9

[336] See Hilchot Talmud Torah Ibid. 1:5

[337] Talmud Bavli, Menachot 99b; Kuntres Acharon Hilchot Talmud Torah Ibid. Ch. 3, 1:1 (p. 1686).

[338] Note: Joshua 1:8; Also see at length in the Kuntres Acharon Ibid. that the commandment of knowing the Torah and the commandment of "you shall toil in it, day and night," are two distinct matters. Although the Kuntres Acharon states that the knowledge of Torah is greater than the commandment of "you shall toil in it" this

entire Torah, and also to those who do not have the attention span to come to know the entire Torah.[339]] That is, this is the obligation to study Torah because of what Torah itself is. Now, since Torah (as it is, in and of itself) is beyond all measure and limitation ("It's measure is longer than the earth"), so likewise, the commandment to study Torah (because of what Torah itself is), is that he should be involved in its study constantly, day and night, and at every free moment, beyond measure and limitation.[340]

8.

Now, we can state with even greater depth, that even regarding the commandment of, "you shall toil in it, day and night," since it is a commandment that man is commanded to do [and is not like the Torah, as it is, in the wisdom of the Holy One, blessed is He (that transcends all relation to worlds), that subsequently descended below], therefore, Torah that is learned because of the *mitzvah* of, "you shall toil in it day and night," (is not the same as Torah is, in and of itself, but is rather) as it relates to man.

---

is not a contradiction to what we are stating here. For, the commandment of knowing the Torah is only greater in the sense that it is not pushed off by any other commandments.

[339] Hilchot Talmud Torah Ibid 3:3-4

[340] Note: Now, although it is explained in Hilchot Talmud Torah Ibid. (Ch. 3) that there are various ways to fulfill this commandment of "You shall toil in it" to the point that in extenuating circumstances it may be fulfilled through the recital of the *Shema* in the morning and in the night (Hilchot Talmud Torah Ibid. 3:4) – nevertheless, these differences only apply when he is extremely preoccupied with the pursuit of his livelihood. However, when it comes to a person's spare time, this commandment of "You shall toil in it" applies at every moment.

Therefore, the **true** matter of Torah study, as it is, (meaning, as it transcends all relation to man), is the study of the Torah of *HaShem*-יהו"ה for the sake of its Name, in that it is the Torah of *HaShem*-יהו"ה, blessed is He. This type of Torah study is not solely in order to fulfill the *mitzvah* of Torah study, but is because of what Torah itself is.

We should add that the advantage of Torah study for the sake of the Name *HaShem*-יהו"ה, over and above the study of Torah to fulfill the *mitzvah* of Torah study, is not only in one's intention during study, but also, in the actual study itself. For, when Torah study is only to fulfill the commandment of Torah study, the study is in a limited manner. Even in the commandment of, "you shall toil in it, day and night," there are various restrictions and limitations, as explained in the laws of Torah study.

This is not so with the study of Torah for the sake of the Name *HaShem*-יהו"ה, blessed is He, wherein there is no consideration of any measure or limitations whatsoever (including whether or not he is obligated to study in this way or not).[341] Thus, his Torah study will transcend the measures and limitations of time, and will likewise transcend the measures and limitations of space. This is as our sages, of blessed

---

[341] Note: See at length in Likkutei Sichot Vol. 2, p. 304 and on; Also see Kuntres Acharon Ibid. (p. 1688) in explanation of the teaching of our sages, of blessed memory, (Avot 6:4) "Such is the way of [a life of] Torah: You shall eat bread with salt, and rationed water shall you drink; you shall sleep on the ground, your life will be one of privation, and in Torah you shall labor etc." It is clarified there that this is not obligatory, but rather "such is the way of Torah." Even so, see the beginning of section 3:3 there, that states, "One whose heart is roused within him to fulfill this **commandment-*Mitzvah*** as is fitting... will live a life of privation."

memory, stated,[342] "One whose studies are beyond his control is different."

The (inner) reason for this is that, because the *mitzvah* of, "you shall toil in it" is a commandment that was given to man, it therefore has limitations (according to the limitations of man). This is not the case, however, with the study of Torah for the sake of the Name *HaShem-*יהו״ה, blessed is He. This is because the Torah (as it is, in and of itself) transcends all measure and limitations ("its measure is longer than the earth"), and therefore, when man studies Torah in this way, namely, that his study is for the sake of the Name *HaShem-*יהו״ה (meaning, because of what Torah itself **is**), then he too exits the limitations of time and space.

9.

Now, we may state that the novel bond between "the upper ones" and "the lower ones" that occurred at the giving of the Torah, is specifically revealed in **this** aspect of Torah study, that is, for the sake of the Name *HaShem-*יהו״ה, blessed is He, that is within it.

That is, there is an additional aspect to this, beyond the fact that in order for there to be a bond between, "the upper,

---

[342] Talmud Bavli, Kiddushin 33a; Hilchot Talmud Torah Ibid. end of Ch. 3 (This teaching was stated relative to one who inadvertently comes to contemplate matters of Torah even in places that it is not permissible to do so, because he is so absorbed in Torah, to the point that, "it is beyond his control." Thus, this demonstrates an aspect of Torah study that transcends the restrictions of time and space.)

ones," and, "the lower ones," there must be a nullification of the categories of upper and lower, by drawing forth the light of the Unlimited One, blessed is He, that transcends them both (as explained before in chapter four). The example for this, in man, is that when a person is involved in Torah study for the sake of the Name *HaShem*-יהו"ה, there is a nullification of his awareness of separate existence (*Bitul B'Metziut*), both with respect to his body ("the lower"), as well as with respect to his soul ("the upper"). Thus, this bond of, "the upper ones" and "the lower ones" is specifically revealed in this manner of Torah study. That is, the Unlimited aspect of Torah ("the upper ones") affects man ("the lower ones"), such that his study of Torah itself transcends all limitation.

We may further add to this, that through the limitlessness of Torah effecting man (and this also applies to the descent of Torah below to this world, in general), there is a revelation of the limitlessness of Torah to an even **greater** extent. For, the limitlessness of Torah is not only in regard to its place and position, in terms of its level, but rather, the very fact that it is drawn down below, is an indication of its limitlessness.[343] This is to say that even as it is drawn down

---

[343] Note: This is similar to the difference between the revelation of the Limitlessness of *HaShem*-יהו"ה, blessed is He, that is revealed in the world of Emanation-*Atzilut*, and between the Limitlessness of *HaShem*-יהו"ה Himself, as He transcends the world of Emanation-*Atzilut*. That is, although the light of the world of Emanation-*Atzilut* is described as, "There is no limit to its spreading forth," nevertheless, "This remains in the world of Emanation-*Atzilut* itself, and is not revealed outside of the world of Emanation-*Atzilut*." In contrast, the Light of the Singular Intrinsic Being of the Infinite One, *HaShem*-יהו"ה Himself, blessed is He, who transcends the world of Emanation-*Atzilut*, is "in an aspect of total limitlessness

below, there is a felt revelation of the Unlimited One, blessed is He, Who is in it, such that even man's study of Torah is in a way of limitlessness.[344]

10.

Based on all the above, we may now explain why the completion of receiving the Torah ("the Jews undertook") depends on self-sacrifice (*Mesirat Nefesh*). This is because the bond between "the upper ones" and "the lower ones" comes about through the nullification of the boundaries and existence of the upper and lower (as explained before). Therefore, in order for the receiving of the Torah to be completed to perfection, the nullification (*Bittul*) of self-sacrifice (*Mesirat Nefesh*) is necessary.

Although it is true that at the time of the giving of the Torah, when the Jewish people said,[345] "All that *HaShem*-יהו״ה has spoken, we will do and we will hear," they did indeed accept upon themselves to do all that they would be commanded, even should it require having total self-sacrifice in doing so, nevertheless, as long as self-sacrifice is only in potential

---

to His spreading forth, such that He is drawn forth in the totality of the chaining down of the worlds." (See *Hemshech* 5666 p. 500 and on.)

[344] Note: The fact that man retains his existence (limitation) and even so, his Torah study transcends all limitation, this itself further reveals the light of the Limitless One, *HaShem*-יהו״ה, that is within the Torah. This is as explained in *Hemshech* 5666 ibid. (p. 501), that "the true matter of 'there is no limit to His spreading forth' is that, on the one hand He, illuminates all space and place with literal open revelation, nevertheless, at the very same time the worlds remain at the level and state of existence, in which He brings them forth into being."

[345] Exodus 24:7

(*BeKo'ach*) it is only from the angle of the soul, and is not the body.

However, because the nullification (*Bittul*) (through which a bond is affected between "the upper ones" and "the lower ones"), needs to be both in the upper and the lower, therefore the completion of the receiving of the Torah depends upon self-sacrifice (*Mesirat Nefesh*) in actuality (*BePo'el*), because self-sacrifice is actualized[346] (*BePo'el*) with the body and the natural soul.

Based on this, we may also understand the advantage of the self-sacrifice of Purim, over and above, the self-sacrifice of Chanukah. This is because even self-sacrifice (*Mesirat Nefesh*) in actuality (*BePo'el*) is primarily due to the soul. In other words, it is the self-sacrifice of the soul that even affects the body and the natural soul. Nevertheless, because the body and the natural soul (in relation to themselves) remain in their state of existence, therefore it is the same with the revelation at the giving of the Torah, that (the bond between "the upper ones" and "the lower ones") that was drawn forth to them, through the nullification of the self-sacrifice of the soul, was something that is superimposed upon them.

This then, is the advantage of the self-sacrifice of Purim over and above the self-sacrifice of Chanukah. That is, on Purim they had the ultimate self-nullification (and lowliness)

---

[346] See Shaarei Orah, Shaar HaChanukah discourse entitled "On the twenty-fifth of Kislev" Ch. 19 (8a) and on; Also see at length in the discourse entitled "*VeHayah Ekev*" 5726 Ch. 5.

even from the angle of the body,[347] in that they were entirely abandoned to be killed by whoever desired to do so, and according to the natural order, there was no way for them to be saved from the decree. [Although the decree was only against the Jewish people, and had they renounced their faith, God forbid, nothing would have been done to them (as mentioned before in Chapter 1, from Torah Ohr), nevertheless, since the decree was not only against Torah and *mitzvot*, but also against the body, "to slay and cause all the Jews to perish,"[348] God forbid, it thus came about that their very bodies were in a state of ultimate lowliness at that time.

For, when the decree was only against Torah and *mitzvot* (as occurred during the time of Chanukah, when the decree was, "to cause them to forget Your Torah and to remove them from the laws that You desire[349]), this meant that they would only be killed if they fulfilled Torah and *mitzvot*. In that case, the body, in and of itself, is not abandoned to destruction.

This was not the case, however, when the decree was to "to slay and cause all the Jews to perish,"[350] God forbid, when the only possibility of being saved from the decree, was through renouncing the true faith in *HaShem*-יהו"ה, God forbid. In this case, because the decree to kill him is (not because he doesn't want to renounce his faith, but rather) upon his body, we find

---

[347] See at length Shaarei Orah, discourse entitled "*VeKeebel*", Ch. 11 (although the explanation there is in another manner).

[348] Esther 3:13

[349] See the liturgy of the *Al HaNissim* prayer of thanks recited on Chanukah.

[350] Esther 3:13

that the body (as it is, in and of itself) was abandoned to destruction.[351]]

Thus, it is for this reason that it was specifically the self-sacrifice of Purim that affected the perfect completion of receiving of the Torah. For, because at that time, their nullification of self was from the aspect of the body, they therefore were fitting receptacles for the revelation of the giving of the Torah, both from the angle of the soul, as well as the angle of the body. We may say that this is why the discourse specifies that at the time of Haman's decree, the Jewish people were in a state of utter lowliness, even physically. For it is through this that he hints at the reason that they then were receptacles for the giving of the Torah, even from the angle of the body.

11.

Now, according to what was explained before (in chapter four) that in the bond between the upper and the lower, there are three matters; the upper, the lower and their nullification, it is understood that to merit the completion and perfection of the receiving of the Torah, the nullification

---

[351] Note: To further illuminate the difference between these two ways from the angle of *Halachah*-Jewish law: Even those who are in a situation in which they are *Halachically*-legally required to be killed rather than to transgress, if they do indeed transgress under duress, they are not punished for it. (See Rambam Hilchot Yesodei HaTorah 5:4.) Nevertheless, in a case where one transgressed them as a method of healing (See ibid. Halachah 6) and was indeed healed, he is indeed punished. Amongst the various reasons for this, is that the sick person did so willingly. (See at length in "Teshuvot u'Biurim p. 14 and the notes there, as well as several other examples of this.)

(*Bittul*) of the soul and the body is insufficient. Rather, it is necessary that even their existence, as they are, should be in a state of ultimate perfection, in that their very existence is tied to and bonded with the Torah.

This is similar to what we explained before (in chapters six and eight) that the advantage of Torah study for the sake of the Name *HaShem*-יהו"ה, is not only in regard to his nullification of self (that is, that his pursuit of Torah is not for the attainment of his own perfection, nor even to attain the perfection of his soul), but also, that the very existence of the one who is learning Torah (both in soul and body) is completely bonded to Torah. Through this, he escapes his limitations and ascends to the limitlessness of the Torah.

We may therefore say that this is why he states in the discourse that it was specifically Mordechai, the Moshe of his generation, who awakened self-sacrifice in the Jewish people, because the Torah study of Mordechai was of the utmost elevation. Therefore, through awakening the Jewish people to study Torah with self-sacrifice (*Mesirat Nefesh*) [and this was especially true of Mordechai who was the head of the generation (like Moshe), thus it is through him that vitality was drawn to all the other limbs and organs], he therefore drew into them (not only the nullification of the sense of separateness (*Bittul*), but also) the elevated level of Torah study, as it is in the most perfected state of man, the perfection of both soul and body.

Based upon this we may also explain what he cites in the discourse, that Mordechai gathered twenty-two thousand schoolchildren and taught them Torah. For, this elevated level of Torah study (which is from the aspect of the perfection of the soul and of the body), is primarily found in schoolchildren.

This may be understood through what our sages, of blessed memory, taught,[352] "'The world only exists because of the breath of the schoolchildren.' Rav Pappa said to Abaye, 'If so, what is the status of my Torah study and yours?' He responded: 'Breath that is tainted by sin cannot be compared to breath that is not tainted by sin.'"

In other words, although the Torah study of Rav Pappa and Abaye was (most certainly) for the sake of the Name *HaShem*-יהו"ה at the highest of levels, whereas the Torah study of schoolchildren is out fear of punishment,[353] nevertheless, the "breath of the schoolchildren" has an advantage, in that the world is sustained in its existence specifically by this breath.

The explanation is well known,[354] that the advantage of the breath of schoolchildren is because of both their souls and their bodies. That is, they are closer to Godliness because they have only recently arrived here from the spiritual world. Additionally, their bodies which have not yet become coarse through indulging in food and drink and the various lusts of the world, as explained elsewhere at greater length.

Based in the above, we may therefore state, that the reason the discourse cites the fact that during the time of the decree, Mordechai gathered twenty-two thousand

---

[352] Talmud Bavli, Shabbat 119b

[353] See Tanya Kuntres Acharon, "To understand that which is written in *Shaar HaYichudim*" (p. 155a).

[354] Derech Chaim, Ch. 76 (84d)

schoolchildren and taught them Torah, is to explain and highlight that their study of Torah at that time was (not only the nullification of the sense of self of the soul and of the body, but) was also in the state of the utmost perfection of the soul and body.

[However, the advantage of the soul of the schoolchildren was not really related to their Torah study. This is because their Torah study was out of fear of punishment (which is the nature of the body), and is not related to the soul. Moreover, their Torah study had no nullification of sense of self, to the point of self-sacrifice (*Mesirat Nefesh*). This is the reason why he cites in the discourse that it was specifically Mordechai who taught the schoolchildren Torah. For, it is specifically through him that their Torah study too, rose to the level of self-sacrifice, as explained in the discourse.]

It should also be added that through Mordechai gathering the twenty-two thousand schoolchildren, he too gained the additional, elevated aspect of the breath of the schoolchildren,[355] and thus[356] was able to draw this forth in all of the Jews of his generation.

---

[355] Note: See the explanation in the discourse regarding the fact that it was specifically "through the six-hundred foot-soldiers of the nation... that additional light and illumination was added to Moshe."

[356] Note: To further clarify based upon what it states at the end of the discourse, that "Mordechai got up... and gathered the multitudes in public in order to strengthen their faith in *HaShem*-יהו״ה, blessed is He (that is, the faith of the Jewish people in general) *through the study of Torah of the school-children.*"

12.

Based upon all the above, we can also explain the reason that[357] "a person is obligated to become intoxicated on Purim until he does not know the difference between cursed is Haman and blessed is Mordechai." For, every year, on Purim there is a renewed awakening of this matter that the Jews "undertook," just as on the first occasion. On the contrary – it is in a way of "ascension in holiness."[358]

[We may thus add that the novelty of the days of Purim, over and above the giving of the Torah, is in two matters: In the days of Purim there was a completion and perfection of the receiving of the Torah ("the Jews received"), as explained before at length. Moreover, even in the fulfillment of Torah there was an advantage, as stated in Talmud[359] on the verse,[360] "The Jews fulfilled and undertook," that they, "Fulfilled that which they already undertook to do at Sinai."

In other words, that which they undertook to do at Sinai was not in a manner that was everlasting, because after they sinned with the golden calf[361] "the Jewish people stripped themselves of their ornaments, from Mt. Horeb onward." In contrast, it states about the days of Purim,[362] "And these days of Purim shall not cease from amongst the Jews, nor shall the

---

[357] Talmud Bavli, Megilla 7b; See Sefer HaMaamarim 5681 p. 179 note 1.
[358] Talmud Bavli, Brachot 28a
[359] Talmud Bavli, Shabbat 88a
[360] Esther 9:27
[361] Exodus 33:6; Shabbat ibid.
[362] Esther 9:28

memory of them perish from their offspring." In other words, that which they "received" and "undertaken" at the time of Purim, is established for eternity.[363]

Likewise, each and every year, the days of Purim possess these two matters. That is, every year there is additional perfection in the receiving of the Torah (as explained above), and secondly, this addition perfection is established forever.]

This is why our service of *HaShem*-יהו"ה on Purim, is in this way of, "not knowing the difference." That is, one must go entirely out of himself, since receiving the Torah only comes about through the total nullification of sense of self (*Bittul*). This is also why the manner through which one goes out of his sense of independent existence ("to the point that he does not know") must be through, "becoming intoxicated with (physical) wine."[364]

This is because the nullification of sense of self (*Bittul*) that is to be attain (on Purim) must also be from the angle of the body, as explained before at length. This draws out the ability and strength that, throughout the year, matters of the body will take up no space for him, and he will automatically have no obstructions to his Torah study on account of his body.

According to what we explained before regarding the elevated level of Torah study for the sake of the Name *HaShem*-יהו"ה, blessed is He, and that this is not only a matter of nullification of sense of self (*Bittul*), but beyond, that one's study of Torah also becomes in a way of limitlessness, we may

---

[363] See Shaarei Orah discourse entitled "*VeKeebel*" Ch. 20 (94a) at length.
[364] Rashi to Tractate Megillah Ibid. (7b)

say that it is the same way in the matter of "becoming intoxicated until one does not know the difference." This is to say that it (subsequently) affects an ascension even in one's knowledge [since Torah study must specifically be in a way of understanding and comprehension]. That is, he will understand matters in Torah that he would have been incapable of knowing and understanding previously.

This was explained by his honorable holiness, my father-in-law, the Rebbe, in one of his Purim talks.[365] That is, through attaining the state of, "not knowing," the "knowing" that subsequently follows, is of a different order and quality altogether. In general, this is because the limited intellect of man becomes one with the limitless Torah that he learns, through which he becomes one with the Holy One, blessed is He, Himself. For, "the Jewish people, the Torah, and the Holy One, blessed is He, are entirely one."[366]

---

[365] See the Sicha of Purim 5706 Ch. 2 (Sefer HaSichot 5706 p. 23 and on.)

[366] Tanya Ch. 4 and beginning of Ch. 23 in the name of the Zohar; See citations in Maamarei Admor HaEmtza'ee Vayikra Vol. 1 p. 285; Zohar I 24a; Zohar II 60a; Tikkunei Zohar Tikkun 6, 21b; Tikkun 22, 64a; Likkutei Torah Netzavim 46a, and elsewhere.

Discourse 6

"Zot Chukat HaTorah -
This is the decree of the Torah"

Delivered on Shabbat, Parshat Shemini, Parshat Parah,
Shabbat Mevarchim Nissan 5711
By the grace of *HaShem,* blessed is He,

1.

The verse states,[367] "And *HaShem*-יהו״ה spoke to Moshe and to Aharon, saying: This is the decree of the Torah, which *HaShem*-יהו״ה has commanded, saying: Speak to the Children of Israel, and they shall take to you a completely red heifer, which is without blemish, and upon which a yoke has not come etc." Now, we must understand[368] the reason for the repetitive language used in this verse. Namely, it states, "And *HaShem*-יהו״ה spoke," and then repeats, "which *HaShem*-יהו״ה commanded saying." At first glance, it looks like the verse could have simply stated, "And *HaShem*-יהו״ה spoke to Moshe and to Aharon saying: Speak to the Children of Israel etc." Additionally, we must understand why the Name *HaShem*-יהו״ה is repeated twice, as opposed to simply stating, "And *HaShem*-

---

[367] Numbers 19:1-2
[368] See Likkutei Torah Chukat 56a; Ohr HaTorah Chukat (Vol. 5) p. 1,617 and 1,621; Discourse entitled *"Zot Chukat"* 5629 (Sefer HaMaamarim 5629, p. 258); 5672 (*Hemshech* 5672 Vol. 1, p. 41); 5665 (Sefer HaMaamarim 5665, p. 224) and elsewhere.

יהו״ה spoke... This is the decree of the Torah that I have commanded," or something to that effect.

Now, about this commandment-*mitzvah* the Midrash relates,[369] "Solomon said, 'About all these things (that is, all the other commandments of the Torah) I have knowledge (that is, he grasped the reasoning) for all these. But in the case of the red heifer, I have investigated it, inquired into it, and examined it,[370] 'I thought I could fathom it, but it eludes me.'" This must be better understood, because of the various commandments of the Torah, a number of them are also in the category of "decrees-*Chukim*." In what way does the commandment of the red heifer differ from them? That is, when it came to grasping the reasons for the other *mitzvot*, including the decrees-*Chukim*, King Solomon was indeed able to grasp them. However, it is specifically about the *mitzvah* of the red heifer (*Parah Adumah*) that he stated, "It eludes me."

Additionally, it is stated in Midrash,[371] regarding the verse,[372] "Speak to the Children of Israel, and they shall take to you a completely red heifer," that, "The Holy One, blessed is He, said to Moshe, 'To you I will reveal the reason for the red heifer, but for others it will be a decree without reason." This too requires explanation,[373] for it seems to indicate that when it comes to all the other decrees-*Chukim* of Torah, there are others who knew their reasons, even if they were only special

---

[369] Midrash Bamidbar Rabba 19:3
[370] Ecclesiastes 7:23
[371] Midrash Bamidbar Rabba 19:6
[372] Numbers 19:2
[373] Also see Likkutei Sichot Vol. 18, p. 230

individuals. Therefore, it is not understood why it is specifically the commandment of the red heifer that they were incapable of knowing its reasons, and that the reason was revealed to Moshe only.

2.

Now, the explanation[374] of the matter may be understood through understanding the verse,[375] "And the *Chayot*-חיות were running and returning." The simple interpretation of this verse is that it refers to the holy living angels (*Chayot HaKodesh*-חיות הקודש) that are in a state of "running" (*Ratzo*) and "returning" (*Shov*). However, there is another explanation of this verse,[376] namely that it refers to the light and Godly vitality (*Chayut*-חיות) that likewise is in a state of "running" (*Ratzo*) and "returning" (*Shov*). Nevertheless, these two interpretations convey the same point, which is that the reason that the holy living angels-*Chayot*-חיות are in a state of "running" (*Ratzo*) and "returning" (*Shuv*) is because the Godly vitality-*Chayut*-חיות that brings the worlds into existence and enlivens them, is in a state of "running" (*Ratzo*) and "returning" (*Shuv*).

This vitality is in all worlds, from the beginning of all levels to the end of all levels, which therefore also includes the

---

[374] See discourse entitled *Zot Chukat HaTorah* 5665 (p. 225 and on; Discourse entitled "*Ohr L'Arba'ah Asar*" 5677 (Sefer HaMaamarim 5677 p. 143 and on).

[375] Ezekiel 1:14; Likkutei Torah Chukat 56b and on.

[376] See Ohr HaTorah Terumah p. 1,357 and on; Bamidbar (Drushim L'Shavuot) p. 139 and on; Sefer HaMaamarim 5629 p. 203, and elsewhere.

angelic beings known as the holy living angels-*Chayot HaKodesh*-חיות הקודש. Now, since every action brings about a reaction that is similar to the action, therefore the Godly vitality-*Chayut*-חיות that enlivens them, causes them to be in a state of "running" (*Ratzo*) and "returning" (*Shov*). This is likewise the case with the lower creatures who appear to exist as independent beings. They too, possess this aspect of "running" (*Ratzo*) and "returning" (*Shov*), which is the matter of "the beating of the heart."[377]

Nevertheless, there is a difference between the lower creatures and the holy living angels-*Chayot HaKodesh*. That is, the holy living angels-*Chayot HaKodesh* (and this applies to all supernal creations), sense the Godly vitality, and as a byproduct, they thus also sense the "running" (*Ratzo*) and "returning" (*Shov*) that is within it. Thus, for them, the experience of "running" (*Ratzo*) and "returning" (*Shov*) is openly revealed. This is not the case, however, with the lower creatures, who do not sense the Godly vitality-*Chayut*-חיות that brings them into existence and enlivens them. Thus, the experience of the "running" (*Ratzo*) and "returning" (*Shov*) is concealed from them. In other words, it is latently there in matters that are not tied to their choice, such as the involuntary beating of the heart, wherein we see that they do indeed possess this matter of "running" (*Ratzo*) and "returning" (*Shov*). However, when it comes to matters that are tied to their own

---

[377] Tikkunei Zohar, Tikkun 69 (105a); Likkutei Torah Pekudei 5d, 7d and on, and elsewhere; Also see Shaar HaYichud of the Mittler Rebbe, translated as The Gate of Unity, Chapter 37, and the notes there.

toil in the service of *HaShem*-יהו"ה, blessed is He, they do not possess this matter of "running" (*Ratzo*) and "returning" (*Shov*) – (at least not in a revealed way).

3.

The explanation of the matter is as follows: It is known that the light and vitality that enlivens the worlds and brings the creatures into being is only the aspect of a glimmer of the light of *HaShem*-יהו"ה, blessed is He. This is as stated,[378] "Your Kingship is the kingship of all worlds," and as known, the aspect of Kingship-*Malchut* is only a glimmer of the light of His Being, blessed is He. This is like what we recite,[379] "then His Name as King was coronated over them." Now, just as a name is but a mere glimmer, that does not reach the very Essence of His Being at all, so likewise, in regard to the Godly vitality that enlivens the worlds and brings them into existence, it is a mere glimmer of His vitality.

Now, with respect to this glimmer of illumination that is drawn forth to the worlds, since it is only a glimmer, we must say that it has a root and source from which it is drawn forth, and that, as it is included in its source, it is in a much loftier state. Thus, this glimmer that is drawn forth, is in a state of "running" (*Ratzo*), in that it desires to ascend and become included in its root and source. This aspect of "running" (*Ratzo*), however, is then followed by the matter of "returning"

---

[378] Psalms 145:13
[379] In the *Adon Olam* liturgy

(*Shov*). This is to say that since *HaShem's*-יהו"ה Supernal intention is that there should be an illumination of light below that illuminates within the worlds, it is thus drawn to "return" (*Shov*) to the worlds. We thus find that the very same cause that creates the motion of "running" (*Ratzo*), namely, the awareness of one's Source, is the very same cause for the "returning" (*Shov*), since the Source, *HaShem*-יהו"ה blessed is He, desires that there should be an illumination of light below.

Now, the fact that there are beings who are not in a state of "running" (*Ratzo*) and "returning" (*Shov*), is because they do not have awareness of their Source and are not in a state of adhesion (*Dveikut*) to their Source. The same applies to human souls. For, although it is known[380] that souls are Godliness that has been transformed into created beings, nevertheless, they are in the category of novel created beings, and as such, they are not in constant motion of "running" (*Ratzo*) and "returning" (*Shov*). That is, at times souls are at motion in their service of *HaShem*-יהו"ה, blessed is He, and at times they are not. As explained above, the reason is that this vitality-*Chayut*, which is in a state of "running" (*Ratzo*) and "returning" (*Shov*), is only the aspect of a glimmer. Thus, though this vitality is indeed a cause for them to be capable of entering into a state of, "running" (*Ratzo*) and "returning" (*Shov*), it also is necessary to have a sense and awareness of one's Source, that is, *HaShem*-יהו"ה, blessed is He, and to adhere (*Dveikut*) to Him. Thus, those creatures who do not possess an awareness and sense of

---

[380] See Biurei HaZohar of the Mittler Rebbe, p. 114d and on; Biurei HaZohar of the Tzemach Tzeddek Vol. 1, p. 546 and on.

their Source, are not in a state of "running" (*Ratzo*) and "returning" (*Shov*).

Now, all the above was stated in regard to the manifest soul, known as the *Neshamah*. As known, the soul is called by five names: *Nefesh, Ru'ach, Neshamah, Chayah* and *Yechidah*.[381] The transcendent aspects, which are the *Chayah* and the *Yechidah* of the soul, "are bonded and cleave to You,"[382] in a state of constant motion of "running" (*Ratzot*) and "returning" (*Shov*). However, this is not the case regarding the manifest aspects of the soul, which are the *Nefesh, Ru'ach* and the *Neshamah*. They are not in a constant state of "running" (*Ratzot*) and "returning" (*Shov*). It thus is necessary for them to serve *HaShem*-יהו״ה, blessed is He, specifically by way of toil.

The same is true of lights (*Orot*) and vessels (*Keilim*). That is, the lights (*Orot*) are in a state of recognizable adhesion to their Source, and are thus in a state of "running" (*Ratzot*) and "returning" (*Shov*). In contrast, the receptacles (*Keilim*) are not in a recognizable state of adhesion to their Source, and therefore, in and of themselves, are not in a state of "running" (*Ratzot*) and "returning" (*Shov*). It is only when the light becomes revealed and illuminates within the vessels that they too come to a state of "running" (*Ratzot*) and "returning" (*Shov*). Furthermore, this matter, that, in and of themselves, the receptacles are not in a state of "running" (*Ratzot*) and

---

[381] Midrash Bereishit Rabba 14:9; Dvarim Rabba 2:37; Also see Ginat Egoz of Rabbi Yosef Gikatilla, translated as HaShem is One, Volume 2.

[382] *Hosha'anot* liturgy (day 3).

"returning" (*Shov*), is an additional cause for the matter of "running" (*Ratzot*) and "returning" (*Shov*) of the light (*Ohr*). Namely, because the receptacles are not in a state of "running" (*Ratzot*) and "returning" (*Shov*), they clearly are something of an opposing force to the lights. Because of this, the light comes to be in a state of "running" (*Ratzo*), to return to its Source wherein the Godly vitality is felt. Moreover, even as the light is drawn forth to manifest within the receptacles (*Keilim*) in a way of "returning" (*Shov*), since it becomes manifest in something that is its opposite, it cannot become truly settled within the vessels. Thus, because of this, the manifestation is only temporary.

This is comparable to the relationship between the body and the soul. Since they are two opposites, their bond is only through the power of, "He who does wondrous things,"[383] blessed is He. Thus, the vitality of the soul within the body is likewise in a way of "running" (*Ratzot*) and "returning" (*Shov*). The same is true of the relationship between lights (*Orot*) and vessels (*Keilim*). Since the vessels are the opposite of the lights, therefore the drawing forth of light to manifest within them is in a manner of "running" (*Ratzot*) and "returning" (*Shov*). This "running" (*Ratzot*) and "returning" (*Shov*) of the lights causes a revelation of the aspects of "running" (*Ratzot*) and "returning" (*Shov*), even in the vessels themselves.

---

[383] See Rama to Shulchan Aruch, Orach Chaim 6

4.

Based on the above, we may understand the verse, "This is the decree-*Chukat*-חוקת of the Torah." The word "*Chukah*-חוקה" is a term that also means "conduct,"[384] as we see from the verse,[385] "Were it not for My covenant[386] day and night, I would not have established the laws by which I conduct-*Chukot*-חקות the heaven and the earth." In other words, the conduct of the Torah is likewise in a way of "running" (*Ratzot*) and "returning" (*Shov*).[387] This is as stated,[388] "From His right hand, a fiery law unto them," and as known, the "right" is the aspect of the drawing forth of influence,[389] which is the aspect of "returning" (*Shov*). In contrast, the "fiery law" is an aspect of ascension, like fire, the nature of which is to ascend.[390] It therefore indicates the aspect of, "running" (*Ratzo*).[391]

These aspects are likewise drawn forth in the performance of the *mitzvot* themselves. For, as known,[392] "Torah study is greater because it leads to the performance of the commandments in action." Thus, the *mitzvot* are likewise in a state of "running" (*Ratzot*) and "returning" (*Shov*), these

---

[384] Likkutei Torah, Chukat Ibid. 57b

[385] Jeremiah 33:25

[386] The Torah

[387] Likkutei Torah Ibid. 56b; Sefer HaMaamarim 5665 Ibid. p. 224 and on.

[388] Deuteronomy 33:2

[389] That is, the right corresponds to kindness-*Chessed*-חסד, which indicates the bestowal of influence to below.

[390] Rambam Hilchot Yesodei HaTorah 4:2

[391] That is, the "fiery law" corresponds to the attribute of might-*Gevurah*-גבורה and the withdrawal and ascension to one's source Above; the desire to ascend and cleave to the Singular Preexistent Intrinsic Being of *HaShem*-יהו״ה, blessed is He.

[392] Talmud Bavli, Bava Kamma 17a

being the two aspects of the positive commandments (*Mitzvot Aseh*) and the prohibitive commandments (*Mitzvot Lo Ta'aseh*). That is, the positive commandments (*Mitzvot Aseh*) which bear the responsibility to actively do them, are in a way of "returning" (*Shov*). In contrast, the prohibitive commandments (*Mitzvot Lo Ta'aseh*) are fulfilled by desisting from doing, and thus are an aspect of withdrawal and "running" (*Ratzo*).

This may likewise be applied to the matter of the red heifer, which also involves this matter of "running" (*Ratzot*) and "returning" (*Shov*). For, the purifying waters of the sin offering, contain the burnt ashes and the living spring waters.[393] The ashes were made by burning the red heifer, and is the matter of "running" (*Ratzo*), whereas the living spring waters, are the aspect of "returning" (*Shov*), since the nature of water is to descend from a high place to a low place.[394]

Now, the reason the commandment of the red heifer is specifically called, "The decree-*Chukat* of the Torah," is because the aspects of "running" (*Ratzot*) and "returning" (*Shov*) of the red heifer have an advantage over and above the "running" (*Ratzot*) and "returning" (*Shov*) of all the other commandments. For, in regard to all other commandments, each one is a particular, in that there are *mitzvot* that are in the aspect of "running" (*Ratzo*) and there are *mitzvot* that are in the aspect of "returning" (*Shov*). In contrast, the commandment of the red heifer is a single general commandment that includes

---

[393] Numbers 19:17
[394] Talmud Bavli, Taanit 7a

both aspects of "running" (*Ratzot*) and "returning" (*Shov*) as one.

Notwithstanding all the above, we still do not understand how this matter applies to Moshe and King Solomon. Namely, they grasped the reasons for all the other *mitzvot*, but about the commandment of the red heifer, the Holy One, blessed is He, said to Moshe, "To you I will reveal the reason for the red heifer, but to others, it will be a decree without reason," and King Solomon stated,[395] "I thought I could fathom it, but it eludes me." At first glance, if the advantage of the red heifer, over and above the other *mitzvot,* is like the advantage of a general principle (*Klal*) over and above a particular principle (*Prat*), then if King Solomon grasped all the other *mitzvot,* that is, the particulars, should he not have also automatically grasped the general principle (*Klal*)? For, as known,[396] "the general principle (*Klal*) is the sum total of its particulars (*Prat*)."

In addition, it is not understood why the Holy One, blessed is He, said to Moshe, "To you I will reveal the reason for the red heifer," but not to anyone else. For if it is indeed the case that there are others who comprehended all the particular details, then what exactly is the novelty in the fact that the general principle (*Klal*) was revealed to Moshe only? Therefore, we must say that the "running" (*Ratzo*) and "returning" (*Shov*) of the red heifer, is in a way that is entirely beyond all other *mitzvot*.

---

[395] Ecclesiastes 7:23
[396] Talmud Bavli, Bechorot 6a

5.

The explanation of the matter is as follows:[397]   We explained before that the cause of the "running" (*Ratzo*) and "returning" (*Shov*) is in having a sense of one's Source. However, there is a limitation to this, since it all depends on the manner that one senses his Source and according to the elevation of the Source.   In other words, all this is only applicable when the Source has some relation to an "other," which is the light of how *HaShem*-יהו״ה, blessed is He, fills all worlds (*Memale Kol Almin*). For, as known regarding the light of how *HaShem*-יהו״ה, blessed is He, fills all worlds, even the loftiest level in this, has some relation to an "other."   This is because the drawing forth of the light of *HaShem*-יהו״ה that fills all worlds, is by means of the restraint (*Tzimtzum*) of the light. For, even the first revelation of the line (*Kav*), is by means of and follows the first restraint (*Tzimtzum HaRishon*),[398] which is the matter of the withdrawal of light. Only afterwards was there a drawing forth of a line of revelation (*Kav*), in a way of leap (*Dilug*).[399]

Though it is true that the drawing forth of the line (*Kav*) is due to the fact that there was a return and illumination of the aspect of the light of the Unlimited One, blessed is He, that preceded the restraint (*Tzimtzum*), nevertheless, this itself is

---

[397] See Sefer HaMaamarim 5665 Ibid. p. 227 and on; 5677 p. 144 and on; Sefer HaSichot Torat Shalom p. 181 and on; 5689 p. 359 and on.

[398] Etz Chaim, Shaar 1 (Drush Igullim V'Yosher) Anaf 2.

[399] See Shaar HaYichud, translated as The Gate of Unity, Ch. 12-14.

specifically through the separation affected by the restraint (*Tzimtzum*).[400] Thus, in regard to the line (*Kav*), although it is drawn from the light of the Unlimited One, blessed is He, that precedes the restraint (*Tzimtzum*), which is the meaning of the subsequent return and illumination of light, nevertheless, it is in the aspect of a constricted line (*Kav*) of illumination that is tailored according to the capacity of the worlds, and thus comes forth in a manner of the divisions and gradations, of upper and lower.

Now, because even as it is in its root, the light of *HaShem*-יהו״ה, blessed is He, that fills all worlds (*Memale Kol Almin*) is the aspect that gives room and possibility for the existence of an "other," thus, the aspect of "running" (*Ratzo*) that is within it (whether it is the desire to become totally included in the Source, or whether it is the desire for the Source to become revealed in the place of the light), is not a complete and total nullification of the sense of separate existence (*Bitul B'Metziut*). For, even as it is in its Source, it has an aspect that gives room for the possibility of the existence of an "other." The same is true of the aspect of "returning" (*Shov*) that is in it, which is the manner in which lights become manifest and settled in the vessels, in that they are literally manifest and settled within them (*Hityashvut*).

In contrast, the "running" (*Ratzo*) and "returning" (*Shov*) that is from the aspect of how *HaShem*-יהו״ה, blessed is He, utterly transcends all worlds (*Sovev Kol Almin*), is entirely

---

[400] See Sefer HaMaamarim 5665 and 5677 ibid. Also see Sefer HaMaamarim 5661 p. 166 and on; 5698 p. 41 and on.

different. For, the light of *HaShem*-יהו״ה that transcends all worlds (*Sovev Kol Almin*), even though it too is drawn down by means of the line (*Kav*), since all of the circles of *Iggulim* are drawn forth by means of the line (*Kav*),[401] nonetheless, their root is in the light of the Unlimited One, blessed is He, that precedes the restraint and lessening (*Tzimtzum*). That is, they are from the general great circle (*Igul HaGadol*) that precedes the line (*Kav*). Thus, the restraint and lessening (*Tzimtzum*) does not affect them to such a great extent. Thus, the "running" (*Ratzo*) of this state, is such that he desires to become entirely nullified of his existence, since in his Source, there altogether is no room for the existence of an "other." Additionally, even in the aspect of the "returning" (*Shov*), it is not a matter of light manifesting and becoming settled within receptacles at all, but is rather, the nullification and sublimation of the receptacles to the lights.

These matters may be understood through how they are in man's service of *HaShem*-יהו״ה, blessed is He. That is, the experience of "running" (*Ratzo*), that is brought about from the aspect of how *HaShem*-יהו״ה, blessed is He, fills all worlds (*Memale Kol Almin*), is that he has a desire for Godliness and desires nothing apart from Godliness. However, it is in such a way that his sense of separate existence is not nullified (*Bitul B'Metziut*). Rather, it only is the experience of,[402] "Coming close to God is good for **me**," or it may be the realization that closeness to God is essentially good. However, this is

---

[401] See Shaar HaYichud – The Gate of Unity, Ch. 16-17.
[402] Psalms 73:28

experienced in such a way, that his sense of self and separate existence is not nullified. The same is true of his "returning" (*Shov*), in that the light illuminates within him in a settled manner (*Hityashvut*).

Such is not the case regarding the "running" (*Ratzo*) and "returning" (*Shov*) that is due to an illumination from the light of *HaShem*-יהו״ה, blessed is He, that transcends all worlds (*Sovev Kol Almin*). The "running" (*Ratzo*) of this aspect, is in a way that his sense of self and separate existence becomes entirely and completely nullified (*Bitul B'Metziut*). Likewise, the "returning" (*Shov*) is not in a way that the lights are settled within the receptacles, meaning that the receptacles do not impede or encumber the light, because they absorb and retain the light, but rather, it is the complete nullification of the receptacles to the light.

This then, is the "running" (*Ratzo*) and "returning" (*Shov*) of the red heifer, which is higher than the "running" (*Ratzo*) and "returning" (*Shov*) of all other *mitzvot*.[403] For, the "running" (*Ratzo*) and "returning" (*Shov*) of the red heifer is from the aspect of how *HaShem*-יהו״ה, blessed is He, transcends all worlds (*Sovev Kol Almin*). Because of this, we find both motions of "running" (*Ratzo*) and "returning" (*Shov*) in the singular matter of the red heifer, these being the two aspects of, "the ashes" and "the living spring waters," that are found together. That is, the ashes alone cannot render purity, nor can the living spring waters alone render purity. Rather, it is only

---

[403] Sefer HaMaamrim 5665 p. 209 and on.

when both are found together at once, indicating that this is specifically from the transcendent aspect of how *HaShem*-יהו״ה, blessed is He, utterly transcends all worlds (*Sovev Kol Almin*).

6.

This then, explains the aforementioned verses,[404] "And *HaShem*-יהו״ה spoke to Moshe and to Aharon, saying: This is the decree of the Torah, which *HaShem*-יהו״ה has commanded, saying: Speak to the Children of Israel, and they shall take to you a completely red heifer, which is without blemish, and upon which a yoke has not come etc." The first time it states, "And *HaShem*-יהו״ה spoke," refers to the aspect of the lower name *HaShem*-יהו״ה, which is the name *HaShem*-יהו״ה as it is expressed in the chaining down of the worlds (*Hishtalshelut*). This is the aspect of how *HaShem*-יהו״ה, blessed is He, fills all worlds (*Memale Kol Almin*). The verse thus informs us that it is from this aspect that the speech came forth to Moshe and Aharon.

The continuation of the verse, "which *HaShem*-יהו״ה has commanded," refers to the upper Name *HaShem*-יהו״ה, that is, the Essential Name *HaShem*-יהו״ה of the most Ancient One (*Atik*), who entirely transcends the chaining down of the worlds (*Hishtalshelut*). In this Essential Name *HaShem*-יהו״ה, there is

---

404 Numbers 19:1-2

no room for the existence of any "other" at all,[405] and thus, it is from there that the matter of the red heifer is drawn forth.

This is also why it is called, "the decree (*Chukat*-חוקת) of the Torah." That is, the term decree-*Chukah*-חוקה is of the same root as "engraving-*Chakikah*-חקיקה."[406]   Now, the difference between letters that are engraved (*Chakikah*) and letters that are written (*Ketivah*) is well known.   Namely, written letters are essentially extraneous to the parchment, even though they become bonded to it by being written upon it.   In contrast, letters that are engraved (*Chakikah*) are not extraneous to the thing upon which they are engraved.   This is the reason that the commandment of the red heifer is called, "the engraving-*Chukat*-חוקת of the Torah," in that it is from the aspect of the upper essential Name *HaShem*-יהו"ה, that is, the most Ancient One (*Atik*), in Whom there is no possibility of any "other" whatsoever.

This also explains what our sages, of blessed memory stated in Midrash:[407] "When Moshe arrived at the Torah portion that discusses impurity that is contracted from a corpse, Moshe inquired (of the Holy One, blessed is He), 'Master of the world, if [a Kohen-priest] becomes impure [through touching a human corpse], what means is there for his purification?'   When the Holy One, blessed is He, did not reply, the face of Moshe turned yellow at that time.   When they subsequently reached the Torah

---

[405] See Ginat Egoz of Rabbi Yosef Gikatilla, translated as HaShem is One, Volume 1, The Gate of Intrinsic Being; Also see the Rebbe's discourse entitled "*Shiviti*" of the year 5720.

[406] Likkutei Torah ibid. 56a

[407] Midrash Bamidbar Rabba 19:4; Likkutei Torah ibid. 59d and on.

portion of the red heifer, the Holy One, blessed is He, said to him, '…This is his purification: they shall take some ashes from the burning of the sin offering…'"

The reason Moshe's face turned yellow is as follows: When it comes to all other matters of impurity, there still remains some Godly vitality in them,[408] and therefore, they can be purified. However, such is not the case with the impurity contracted from a corpse, which is the father of all the fathers of impurity,[409] in which there is no vitality at all. Thus, Moshe questioned how this kind of impurity could possibly become purified. For, when it comes to the order of the gradation of the chaining down of the worlds, there indeed is no possible way to purify such an impurity. However, since the red heifer is rooted in the aspect of the Upper Name *HaShem*-יהו"ה, which is the aspect of engraved letters (*Chakikah*) that altogether do not exist separately from their source in a way of an "other," there are no such limitations, and they can therefore even purify the impurity contracted from a corpse.

This is also the meaning of what King Solomon said,[410] "I thought I could fathom it, but it eludes me." For, the commandment of the red heifer is rooted in the aspect of how *HaShem*-יהו"ה, blessed is He, utterly transcends all worlds (*Sovev Kol Almin*), which is the aspect of the engraved letters (*Chakikah*).

---

[408] See Likkutei Sichot Vol. 8, p. 326; Vol. 18, p. 223
[409] That is, the source of all the sources of impurity.
[410] Ecclesiastes 7:23

Now, in regard to how this relates to man's service of HaShem-יהו״ה, blessed is He, the verse states,[411] "You shall love HaShem-יהו״ה your God, with all your heart, with all your soul and with all your might." The beginning of a person's service of HaShem-יהו״ה is, "with all your heart." However, even though this "running" (Ratzo) is complete, in that it is with **all** his heart-לבבך (which is in the plural form and includes both inclinations),[412] nevertheless, it does not extend beyond the capacity of the heart to contain. That is, it only is with the vessel of the heart itself, and not beyond that.

However, there is a loftier level of service of HaShem-יהו״ה, which is, "with all your might." This kind of service is in such a way that one exits the restrictions and parameters of the vessel, and thus transcends all limitation.

This corresponds to the order of the verses mentioned above,[413] "And HaShem-יהו״ה spoke... which HaShem-יהו״ה has commanded..." In other words, the order of one's service of HaShem-יהו״ה begins from below to Above. That is, one must first serve HaShem-יהו״ה from the angle of the lower name HaShem-יהו״ה, which is service in a manner of limitation, within the order of the chaining down of the worlds (Hishtalshelut). This is the aspect of the "running" (Ratzo) and "returning" (Shov) of the aspect of how HaShem-יהו״ה, blessed is He, fills all worlds (Memale Kol Almin). It is about this that our sages, of blessed memory, stated,[414] "At the outset, when a

---

[411] Deuteronomy 6:5
[412] Brachot 54a; Sifri and Rashi to Deuteronomy 6:5
[413] Numbers 19:1-2
[414] Talmud Bavli, Pesachim 68b

161

person does the *mitzvah*, he does it for his own soul." In other words, he does it in order to rectify his own soul, so that he should come to be in a state "running" (*Ratzo*) and "returning" (*Shov*), through first accepting the yoke of the Kingship of Heaven upon himself.

Afterwards, he can come to the matter of, "This is the decree-*Chukat*-חוקת of the Torah that *HaShem*-יהו״ה has commanded," which is the upper, essential Name of *HaShem*-יהו״ה Himself, blessed is He. This is the aspect of the "running" (*Ratzo*) and "returning" (*Shov*) that arises from the grasp of how *HaShem*-יהו״ה, blessed is He, utterly transcends all worlds (*Sovev Kol Almin*). In this case, he completely exits the parameters of limitation entirely. This is like what the Alter Rebbe said about the verse,[415] "Who do I have in the heavens? And but for You, I do not desire anything on earth." He would say,[416] "I do not want anything – I desire neither Your Garden of Eden, nor Your World to Come. I want nothing more than You alone," and he had no interest in limited, expressive revelations (*Giluyim*). This is the "running" (*Ratzo*) and "returning" (*Shov*) that arises from the aspect of how *HaShem*-יהו״ה, blessed is He, utterly transcends all worlds, which is the matter of the red heifer.

Through all the above we can also understand why we read the portion of the red heifer (*Parshat Parah*) prior to the week when we read the portion of the *mitzvah* of the new moon

---

[415] Psalms 73:25

[416] Sefer HaMitzvot of the Tzemach Tzeddek, Shoresh Mitzvat HaTefilah Ch. 40 (Derech Mitzvotecha p. 138a); Also see HaYom Yom 18 Kislev.

(*Parshat HaChodesh*). For it is through our service of *HaShem*-יהו״ה in the manner conveyed by the mitzvah of the red heifer, which is the "running" (*Ratzo*) and "returning" (*Shov*) in a manner that transcends all limitation, that there is a subsequent revelation of the Singular Intrinsic Essential Being of *HaShem*-יהו״ה Himself, blessed is He, which is the matter of the redemption (conveyed in the portion of the commandment of the new moon (*Parshat HaChodesh*)) and the true and complete redemption, may it be speedily in our days.

Discourse 7

"VeHeineef Yado al HaNahar -
And He shall wave His hand over the river"

Delivered on the final day of Passover-
Acharon Shel Pesach, 5711
By the grace of *HaShem,* blessed is He,

1.

The verse states,[417] "*HaShem*-יהו"ה will dry up the gulf of the Sea of Egypt and He will wave His hand over the River with the power of His breath; He will break it into seven streams and lead [the people] across in [dry] shoes." This verse refers to the times of Moshiach, as indicated by the verse at the beginning of the chapter, that states,[418] "A staff will grow from the stump of Yeshai and a shoot will sprout from his roots. The spirit of *HaShem*-יהו"ה will rest upon him – a spirit of wisdom and understanding, a spirit of counsel and strength, a spirit of knowledge and the fear of *HaShem*-יהו"ה. He will be imbued with a spirit of fear of *HaShem*-יהו"ה; and will not need to judge by what his eyes see nor decide by what his ears hear. He will judge the destitute with righteousness, and with fairness rebuke the humble of the earth etc."

---

[417] Isaiah 11:15
[418] Isaiah 11:1-4

Now, we must understand this matter that, "He will be imbued with a spirit of fear of *HaShem-VeHaricho B'Yirat HaShem*-יהו״ה בריאת בריאת," which our sages, of blessed memory, explained to mean,[419] "He will smell and judge-*Morach VeDa'in*-ודאין."[420] At first glance, this is not understood, since the whole matter of judgment is the process of clarifying the matter. What then is the relevance of "scent-*Rei'ach*-ריח" in regard to judgment?

In addition, we must understand why, of all the things listed, this is the primary, elevated characteristic of Moshiach, to the extent that when it is necessary to test Moshiach, he is tested to see if he can, "smell and judge-*Morach VeDa'in*-מורח ודאין."[421] In other words, all the other characteristics that were listed, such as, "a spirit of wisdom and understanding, a spirit of counsel and strength, a spirit of knowledge and the fear of *HaShem*-יהו״ה" are insufficient on their own, and instead, the primary, elevated characteristic of Moshiach is that, "he will be imbued with a spirit-*VeHaricho*-והריחו of fear for *HaShem*-יהו״י," which means that, "he will smell and judge-*Morach VeDa'in*-מורח ודאין." Because of this, although the verse specifies his other characteristics in the affirmative; that he will possess a spirit of wisdom and understanding, a spirit of counsel and strength, a spirit of knowledge and the fear of *HaShem*-יהו״י," it is only in regard to this characteristic that, "he will be imbued with a spirit-*VeHaricho*-והריחו of the fear of *HaShem*-

---

[419] Talmud Bavli, Sanhedrin 93b

[420] That is, the word "*VeHaricho*-והריחו" shares the same root as "*Rei'ach*-ריח" which means "smell."

[421] See Talmud Bavli, Sanhedrin 93b ibid. with respect to Bar Kochba.

יהו״ה," that it also specifies it in the negative, "he will not need to judge by what his eyes see nor decide by what his ears hear." In other words, this further indicates that this quality, specifically, is the primary, elevated characteristic of Moshiach.

2.

The explanation[422] is as our sages, of blessed memory, stated,[423] "What is something that the soul derives benefit from, but the body does not derive benefit from? You must say: This is scent." Indeed, this is the primary difference between eating and drinking, and scent. That is, eating and drinking are activities that the body derives benefit from. Scent, on the other hand, is an activity that the soul derives benefit from.

Since they are different, their effects, that is, how they impact the bond between the soul and the body, are also different. This is because the essential self of the soul is very distant from the physicality of the body, and its bond with the body is only through the power of, "He who does wonders,"[424] and can bind two opposites, the spiritual with the physical. Thus, because of their essential difference and distance from each other, at times, there can be a concealment or weakening of that bond. Nonetheless, the consumption of food and drink strengthens the bond between the soul and body, as in the well-

---

[422] See *Hemshech* 5672 Vol. 1, Ch. 13, 18, 22 & 23. Also see *Sefer HaMaamarim* 5722 p. 228 and on - discourse entitled *"VeHayah BaYom Hahoo"* 5722.
[423] Talmud Bavli, Brachot 43b
[424] See Rama to Shulchan Aruch Orach Chaim 6:1

known[425] explanation of the verse,[426] "Not by bread alone does man live, but by everything that issues from the mouth of *HaShem*-יהו״ה does man live." In other words, what is meant by this verse, is that it is, "that which emanates from the mouth of *HaShem*-יהו״ה," which is in the bread, that enlivens and vitalizes man, meaning that there is a spark of Godliness in the bread, that enlivens and vitalizes man. In other words, because it is rooted in the aspect of the inner light (*Ohr Pnimi*), it thus has the power to strengthen the bond between the soul and the body in a way of inner vitality (*Chayut Pnimi*).

In contrast, when there is a withdrawal of the soul from the body, for example, when a person faints, God forbid, then eating and drinking are of no use to revive him. Rather, it is specifically the power of scent that has the capacity to draw out the essence of his soul. This is because the power of scent (*Rei'ach*-ריח) is rooted in the aspect of the transcendent, encompassing lights (*Ohr Makif*) of the soul. For the same reason, smelling something causes no diminishment in the thing being smelled, for which reason we are taught that,[427] "The sound [of the musical instruments] and the sight and smell [of the incense] are not subject to [the prohibition of] misuse of consecrated property." This is because they only are from the aspect of the transcendent, encompassing lights (*Ohr Makif*). Thus, because scent is from the aspect of the transcendent encompassing light (*Ohr Makif*), it therefore is capable of

---

[425] Likkutei Torah of the Arizal to Deut. (*Ekev*) 8:3; Keter Shem Tov No. 194; Likkutei Torah Tzav 13b, and elsewhere.

[426] Deuteronomy 8:3

[427] Talmud Bavli, Pesachim 26a; Keritot 6a

reaching and affecting a drawing forth from the essence of the soul.

For the same reason we are taught,[428] "If a person is buried under a collapsed building, one is required to check [if he is alive] until checking [the breath of] his nostrils." The Bachaya[429] states that the reason is because, just as the drawing down of the soul into the body is through the nostrils, as it states,[430] "and He blew into his nostrils the soul of life," so also, its withdrawal is likewise through the nostrils. Therefore, even if all of his other organs have been checked, including his heart, and no signs of life have been found, this is inadequate, and they must uncover and check him until the breath of his nostrils have been checked. This is because as long as there still is some vitality in the nostrils, which is the essential vitality, it still is possible to draw it out into revelation by various means.

This is also the reason that the nostrils are called, "The Gate of the Brain" (Shaar HaMochin).[431] What is meant is that it is the gateway to the inner aspect of the brain, as indicated by the fact that the nose and nostrils are designated as, "The Gate of the Brain." In contrast, the "Gate of the Heart" is the mouth, which is the matter of speech, since the emotions are revealed through speech. Additionally, the very existence of speech

---

[428] Talmud Bavli, Yoma 85a and Rashi there; Sota 45b; See Reshimot Vol. 15 p. 65 and on.

[429] Rabbeinu Bachaye to Genesis 2:7

[430] Genesis 2:7

[431] See Hemshech 5672 ibid. citing the Talmud in Yoma ibid. Also see the discourse of the Alter Rebbe by this same title, 5662 Vol. 1, p. 63 and on; Ohr HaTorah Bereishit Vol. 3, p. 520b; Bamidbar Vol. 4, p. 1,464.

itself is rooted in the breath of the heart.[432] However, at first glance, one might think that speech is also, "The Gate of the Brain," since intellect is also revealed through speech. However, the revelation that occurs through speech is only from the external aspect of the brain, which is the intellect. This is to say that the bestowal of intellectual influence to another is only an external bestowal. Therefore, intellectual influence can only be conveyed to a person who also is intellectual. However, the bestowal of intellect cannot help a person who is not intellectual. This is because the bestowal of intellect does not engender any novelty, but is merely an external transference and bestowal. Thus, when they stated that the nose and nostrils are, "The Gate of the Brain," they were referring to the inner aspect of the brain.

Now,[433] in the nose itself there are two levels. This is as stated in Idra Rabba,[434] that the nose has two nostrils, the right nostril and the left nostril, "from one nostril (the right nostril) comes life (Chayin-חיין), and from the other nostril (the left nostril) comes the life of all life (Chayin D'Chayin- חיין דחיין)." It is explained that in the right nostril there is a drawing forth of the aspect of the encompassing light (Ohr Makif) of direct illumination (Ohr Yashar), that reaches the aspect of "life," which is the externality of the Ancient One (Atik), blessed is He. In the left nostril, however, there is a drawing

---

432 See at greater length Shaar HaYichud – The Gate of Unity, Ch. 37.

433 See Siddur (Im Divrei Elokim Chaim) 9b and on; Imrei Binah Shaar HaTefillin (Vol. 3) p. 151-154.

434 Zohar III 130b – This section is further elucidated in the citations in the prior note.

170

forth of the aspect of the encompassing light (*Ohr Makif*) of the rebounding illumination (*Ohr Chozer*), that reaches all the way to, "the life of all life," which is the inner aspect of the Ancient One (*Atik*) blessed is He.

In man's service of *HaShem*-יהו״ה, blessed is He, the explanation is that the encompassing light (*Ohr Makif*) of the direct illumination (*Ohr Yashar*) refers to the drawing forth of a revelation of Godliness within the physical, and thus reaches to the aspect of "life." In contrast, the encompassing light (*Ohr Makif*) of the rebounding illumination (*Ohr Chozer*), refers to the matter of making the physical world itself a receptacle for Godliness, and thus reaches to the aspect of, "the life of all life."

On the physical level, this is analogous to the fact that for a regular faint or dizzy spell, even a scent that is not overly strong will be effective. However, if a person falls into a deep faint, a regular scent will not be effective. Specifically a strong and sharp scent, like vinegar or ammonia, must be used, which has the power to revive the soul even from a deep faint, because it reaches to an even deeper level of the soul.

It is the same way in man's service of *HaShem*-יהו״ה, blessed is He. That is, when a person's service is in a manner of direct illumination (*Ohr Yashar*), in which there are not so many concealments and Godliness is not as hidden, then it can reach the aspect of "life," which is the aspect of the encompassing light of the *Chayah* level of the soul. This is the aspect of the desires of the heart (*Re'uta D'Leeba*), which although, in and of itself, transcends intellect and reason, nevertheless, is tied to intellect and reason, in that the intellect

(*Sechel*) is the receptacle for the aspect of the desires of the heart (*Re'uta D'Leeba*). However, it is specifically when a person's service is in a manner of the rebounding light (*Ohr Chozer*), meaning that there are concealments and Godliness is hidden, that his service reaches the aspect of, "the life of all life," which is the inner aspect of the Ancient One (*Atik*), blessed is He.

Now, the drawing forth of the inner aspect of the Ancient One (*Atik*) also effects the intellect (*Sechel*), so that the intellect is caused to operate in an entirely different manner. This refers to the matter of, "The inner aspect of the father-*Abba* is the inner aspect of the Ancient One-*Atik*."[435] The explanation is as follows:[436] The drawing forth of intellect (*Sechel*) is from the power of intellect (*Ko'ach HaMaskeel*). However, this drawing forth is not imperative, and we thus see that, at times, the intellect is not drawn forth from the power of intellect (*Ko'ach HaMaskeel*). When this happens, the solution is the faculty of desire (*Ratzon*), as our sages, of blessed memory, stated,[437] "A person should always learn Torah from a place that his heart desires." In other words, it is the desire (*Ratzon*) that draws the power of the intellect (*Ko'ach HaMaskeel*) into revelation.

However, at times, it is quite possible for various reasons, whether circumstantial ones or internal ones (such as

---

[435] See Likkutei Torah Netzavim 49d; Sefer HaMaamarim 5700 p. 49 and on; Also see Shaar HaYichud – The Gate of Unity, Ch. 24 through 26.

[436] See *Hemshech* 5672 ibid. Ch. 23; Likkutei Torah Matot 87c; *Hemshech V'Kachah* 5637 Ch. 76; *Hemshech* 5666 p. 428.

[437] Talmud Bavli, Avoda Zarah 19a

the mind being muddled by impurity), that even desire (*Ratzon*) is ineffective in drawing out the intellect. The solution is to occupy oneself in Torah study, in a manner of accepting the yoke of Heaven upon himself. In other words, he must force himself and invest himself entirely, with the totality of his being, into his study of Torah, through which the intellect will be caused to be revealed.

However, the root of this revelation is a higher source than the power of intellect (*Ko'ach HaMaskeel*) itself. Rather, it is from the aspect of, "the air that is above the membrane that hovers over the brain,"[438] which is the aspect of the intellect of the Ancient One-*Atik*, blessed is He. This is because the knowledge-*Da'at* of the Ancient One-*Atik* takes hold and illuminates in this air,[439] and penetrates the membrane and draws forth from the aspect of the concealed wisdom (*Chochmah Stima'ah*). Through this, there is a revelation of intellect that is of an entirely loftier order. It is this aspect that is referred to in the matter of, "The inner aspect of the father-*Abba* is the inner aspect of the Ancient One-*Atik*." That is, when there is a revelation of the inner aspect of the Ancient One-*Atik*, this necessitates a drawing forth of the existence of the intellect, however, the intellect that is drawn forth due to the inner aspect of the Ancient One-*Atik*, transcends all limitations.

To further clarify, the intellect (*Sechel*) that is drawn forth from the power of intellect (*Ko'ach HaMaskeel*) by means

---

[438] Etz Chaim, Shaar 13 (Shaar Arich Anpin), Ch. 3; Also see Shaar HaYichud – The Gate of Unity, Ch. 21 and the notes there, as well as Ch. 25 & 26 ibid.

[439] See Etz Chaim Ibid. Ch. 4 & 6.

of the desire (*Ratzon*), is limited according to the limits of the desire. Even the intellect that is drawn forth from the externality of the faculty of pleasure (which is tied to the desire) is also limited according to the measure of the perfection of the intellect itself and its adhesion to the externality of the pleasure (*Ta'anug*). In contrast, when the study of Torah is in a way of accepting the yoke of the Kingdom of Heaven upon oneself, this affects a drawing forth from the inner aspect of the pleasure (*Pnimiyut HaTa'anug*), and the intellect (*Sechel*) that is drawn forth from this transcends all limitations. In other words, even though it is drawn into the existence of revealed intellect, nevertheless, it is unlimited.

3.

Based on the above, we may now understand why the primary characteristic by which Moshiach is elevated, is specifically in the matter of, "scent-*Rei'ach*-ריח," that he will "smell and judge-*Morach VeDa'in*-מורח ודאין."[440] This is because of the elevated level of scent-*Rei'ach*-ריח, in that it reaches to the very Essence, to the inner aspect of the Ancient One-*Atik*, blessed is He, and does so in such a way, that it also affects a drawing forth into wisdom-*Chochmah* and revealed intellect (*Sechel*). This itself is the meaning of the fact that he will, "smell and judge-*Morach VeDa'in*-מורח ודאין." In other words, although there is a matter of judgment, nevertheless, "he

---

[440] See Talmud Bavli, Sanhedrin 93b ibid. with respect to Bar Kochba.

will not need to judge by what his eyes see nor decide by what his ears hear." In other words, he will not render judgment based upon understanding (*Havanah*) and comprehension (*Hasagah*), nor even according to the powers of intellectual insight (*Haskalah*), and not even according to the sight of the power of wisdom (*Re'iyah D'Chochmah*). Rather, he will "smell and judge-*Morach VeDa'in*-ודאין מורח," meaning that the judgment will be according to scent that reaches all the way to the Essential Self, and from there affects a drawing forth of influence, even to the revealed intellect.

This is also the substance of the words of his honorable holiness, my father-in-law, the Rebbe, in his talk,[441] in which he explained this verse regarding Moshiach that, "He will be imbued with a spirit of the fear of *HaShem*-יהו"ה and will not need to judge by what his eyes see nor decide by what his ears hear." He explains that the judgments of Moshiach will be in such a way, that he will know the underlying causes that brought a person to the state that he finds himself in. This is like the teaching,[442] "Do not judge your fellow until you have reached his place," meaning that a person recognizes in himself and knows the causes that brought him to his present condition. The same principle applies to one's judgment of his fellow. He should know the underlying causes that brought his fellow to such a condition. In other words, he should recognize that his fellow is essentially good and the fact that he finds himself in

---

[441] Sichat Simchat Torah 5690 Ch. 39 and on, and Ch. 46 (Likkutei Dibburim Vol. 2, p. 317 and on; p. 322b, Sefer HaSichot 5690 p. 117 and on, & p. 123).
[442] Mishnah Avot 2:4

an undesirable state, is only due to secondary reasons and circumstances.

To preface, there are those who think that a Torah talk is nothing more than words of exposition. However, in reality, "Even the conversations of Torah scholars require study," as our sages, of blessed memory, explained[443] about the verse,[444] "and his leaf does not wither." How much more so is this certainly the case when a Rebbe, the prince and leader of the generation, speaks. (For this, one does not even have to rely on this teaching of our sages, of blessed memory.) Certainly, his words are founded on the depths of the received knowledge (*Kabbalah*). In other words, based on the above explanation about the advantage of scent-*Rei'ach*-ריח, in that it reaches the very essence, it is understood that the judgments of Moshiach will be rendered in such a way, namely, that he will see the very essence of the person and that he is essentially good.

This is further understood from what is explained elsewhere[445] about Rabbi Yochanan ben Zachai's statement,[446] "I do not know on which path they are leading me." He said this, even though[447] "he did not neglect either the smallest minutiae of Torah, nor the greatest matters in Torah etc." This is because the revealed powers of the soul are not indicative of

---

[443] Talmud Bavli, Sukkah 21b; Avoda Zarah 19b – further explained in Sefer HaMitzot of the Tzemach Tzeddek 105a and on, and elsewhere.

[444] Psalms 1:3

[445] Likkutei Torah Vayikrah, Hosafot 50d; Maamarei Admor HaZaken, HaKetzarim p. 309; Ohr HaTorah beginning of Parshat Pinchas (p. 1,059 and on). Discourse entitled "*Ach B'Goral*" 5626 (Sefer HaMaamarim 5626 p. 171); Sefer HaMaamarim 5696 p. 50 and note 1 there.

[446] Talmud Bavli, Brachot 28b

[447] Talmud Bavli, Sukkah 28a

the essence of the soul. In other words, it is entirely possible that a person's revealed powers are as they should be, whereas his essence can be entirely sunken in the depths of the external husks of evil (*Kelipot*). Proof of this, is the case of Yochanan the High Priest (*Kohen Gadol*), who served as the High Priest for eighty years, but ultimately became a heretical Sadducee. The fact that he served as High Priest for eighty years demonstrates that, during that time, he was a righteous *Tzaddik*, since, as known, if a High Priest who was not as he should be, entered the Holy of Holies on Yom Kippur, he would not live out the year.[448]

Nevertheless, because his essence was in the depths of the external husks of evil (*Kelipah*), over time, this was drawn out, even into the revealed powers of his soul, to the point that, ultimately, he became a heretical Sadducee. This demonstrates that the revealed powers of the soul are not indicative of the essence of the soul. Thus, due to the great his humility, Rabbi Yochanan ben Zachai, was fearful about the essence of his soul.

However, from the above, we also can understand the inverse in relation to Moshiach, that he will not judge based on the external condition of the person, but will judge according to the essence of the person. This then, is the meaning of, he will "smell and judge-*Morach VeDa'in*-מורח ודאין."[449]

---

[448] See Talmud Bavli, Yoma 8b and Rashi there.
[449] See Talmud Bavli, Sanhedrin 93b ibid. with respect to Bar Kochba.

4.

This also explains the verse,[450] "*HaShem*-יהו"ה will dry up the gulf of the Sea of Egypt and He will wave His hand over the River with the power of His breath; He will break it into seven streams and lead [the people] across in [dry] shoes." The explanation is as follows:

As known,[451] just as the splitting of the sea was in preparation for the giving of the Torah, so too, the splitting of the river that will happen in the coming future will be preparatory to the revelation of the inner teachings of Torah that will come about by the hand of Moshiach. This was explained by his honorable holiness, my father-in-law, the Rebbe, in the discourse that was printed for the holiday of Passover.[452] He explains that the splitting of the sea was not to facilitate their subsequent travels through the desert, because in fact, they came up from the sea on the same side that they descended into the sea.[453] Rather, the splitting of the sea was preparatory to the giving of the Torah.

Now, about the giving of the Torah, it states in Midrash,[454] "This is analogous to a king who decreed, 'The Romans shall not descend to Syria and the Syrians shall not ascend to Rome.' Likewise, when the Holy One, blessed is He,

---

[450] Isaiah 11:15

[451] Discourse entitled "*VeHeineef Yado*" in Likkutei Torah Tzav 17a and on, and is explained in various other places as well.

[452] Discourse entitled "*Vayolech HaShem*" 5704, subsequently printed in Sefer HaMaamarim 5711, p. 229 and 5704 p. 179.

[453] See Talmud Bavli, Arakhin 15a, Tosefot entitled "*K'Sheim.*"

[454] Midrash Tanchuma Va'era 15; Shmot Rabba 12:3

created the world, He decreed,[455] 'The heavens are the heavens of *HaShem*-יהו"ה, and the earth he gave to mankind.' However, when He gave us the Torah, He nullified the decree and said, 'The lower ones shall ascend above and the upper ones shall descend below.'" This is the novelty of the commandments-*mitzvot* once the Torah was given. That is, even though, before the giving of the Torah, there also was a matter of fulfilling *mitzvot*, and our forefathers, peace be upon them, fulfilled them physically, for example, Avraham performed the *mitzvah* of welcoming guests (*Hachnasat Orchim*), Yitzchak served *HaShem*-יהו"ה, blessed is He, with the digging of the wells, and Yaakov served *HaShem*-יהו"ה with the act of peeling the sticks etc. These all were physical acts with physical objects. Nevertheless, the act of the *mitzvah* did not remain manifest in the physical objects, and the *mitzvot* they did, only affected the upper, spiritual worlds.[456]

In contrast, the novelty of the giving of the Torah, is that the fulfillment of the *mitzvot* causes a change in the physical object itself. Moreover, the drawing down of holiness into the physical happens at the moment the object is prepared for the fulfillment of the commandment, even before it is actually done. (This is explained in Shaarei Orah of the Mittler Rebbe, in the discourse entitled, "*Yaviyu Levush Malchut*.")[457] The preparation for this was through the matter of the splitting of the sea. For, through the splitting of the sea there was a

---

[455] Psalms 115:16

[456] See Sefer HaMaamarim 5665 p. 220 and on; Likkutei Sichot Vol. 15, p. 57 and on, and elsewhere.

[457] Chapter 5 and on, and Ch. 87, and the summaries there.

penetration of the upper aspect of, "the sea-*HaYam*-הים," which refers to the aspect of kingship-*Malchut* of the world of Emanation-*Atzilut*, through which there subsequently was a bond between the world of Emanation-*Atzilut* and the worlds of Creation-*Briyah*, Formation-*Yetzirah*, and Action-*Asiyah*.[458]

Now, there are two opinions about this. [However, there is no actual dispute between them. They both are true, however they each indicate a different matter.][459] The view presented by the Arizal[460] is that the splitting of the sea is the matter of the drawing forth and descent of the world of Emanation-*Atzilut* to the worlds of Creation-*Briyah*, Formation-*Yetzirah* and Action-*Asiyah*. The view presented in Zohar,[461] is that the splitting of the sea is the matter of the ascension of the worlds of Creation-*Briyah*, Formation-*Yetzirah*, and Action-*Asiyah* to the world of Emanation-*Atzilut*.

We may say that these two views are similar to the distinction between the two forms of service of *HaShem*-יהו"ה. Namely, one view is that, "Godliness is everything." The alternative view is that, "Everything is Godliness."[462] This is known to be the general distinction between the perspective of the Maggid of Mezhritch and the perspective of the Alter

---

[458] See citations in the next note, and as is discussed elsewhere.

[459] See Siddur Im Divrei Elokim Chaim 290a; Shaar HaEmunah of the Mittler Rebbe, Ch. 54.

[460] Pri Etz Chaim, Shaar Chag HaMatzot, Ch. 8; Shaar HaKavanot, Inyan Sefirat HaOmer, Drush 12.

[461] Zohar II 48b

[462] See *Hemshech* 5666 p. 568; Sefer HaSichot Torat Shalom p. 63 and on; Sefer HaMaamarim 5700 p. 141; Igrot Kodesh of the Rebbe Rayatz, Vol. 3, p. 539; Sefer HaSichot 5680-5687 p. 229; 5690 p. 86; 5701 p. 47; 5703 p. 25.

Rebbe.[463] Beyond this, however, the matter of the splitting of the sea is not only the penetration of the aspect of Kingship-*Malchut* of the world of Emanation-*Atzilut*, which is the intermediary that affects the bond between the world of Emanation-*Atzilut* and the worlds of Creation-*Briyah*, Formation-*Yetzirah*, and Action-*Asiyah*. Rather, there also is an aspect of the penetration of the Crown-*Keter*,[464] which is the intermediary between the world of Emanation-*Atzilut* and the worlds that transcend the world of Emanation-*Atzilut*. (This is the matter of the two aspects of the *Sefirah* of Crown-*Keter*, which are called *Atik* and *Arich*. That is, on the one hand, it is the lowest aspect of the upper level, but on the other hand, it is the highest aspect of the lower level.)

However, even beyond all the above, the matter of the splitting of the sea is the aspect of the penetration of the aspect of Kingship-*Malchut* of the Unlimited One, blessed is He,[465] which is the intermediary between the light of the Unlimited One that precedes the restraint (*Tzimtzum*) and the order of the chaining down of the worlds (*Hishtalshelut*) that follows the restraint (*Tzimtzum*). The matter of this, "penetration" (*Bekiyah*), is to bring about a bond between He who precedes the restraint (*Tzimtzum*) and that which follows the restraint (*Tzimtzum*).

Now, just as at the time of the exodus from Egypt it was necessary for there to be this matter of the splitting of the sea,

---

[463] See *Hemshech* 5666 ibid.; Sefer HaSichot Torat Shalom ibid.

[464] See Ohr HaTorah Beshalach p. 572 and on; Sefer HaMaamarim 5677 p. 163 and on; 5680-5681 p. 16 and on, and elsewhere.

[465] See *Hemshech* 5672 Vol. 2, p. 942 and elsewhere.

as a preparation for the giving of the revealed Torah, so it is in regard to the coming redemption, about which it states,[466] "As in the days when you left the land of Egypt, I will show you wonders." That is, before the revelation of the inner aspects of Torah, which will occur by the hand of Moshiach, it first will be necessary for there to be this matter of the, "splitting of the river."

In this too, there also are two opinions.[467] The first is that the, "splitting of the river," will be in such a manner that the river itself will become dry land, which is the matter of drawing Godliness down. The second is that the river will remain a river, only that it will split, which is the matter of the ascension and elevation of the lower level to the higher level.

Now, one of the differences between the splitting of the sea at the time of the exodus, compared to the splitting of the river in the coming future, is that the splitting of the sea at the time of the exodus was done with the staff.[468] In contrast, in the coming future, the splitting of the river will be by hand,[469] as it states, "He will wave His hand."

The reason is because, initially, the work of preparing the physical and making it into a receptacle for Godliness requires that the penetration is specifically by means of the staff. This is understood from the teaching of our sages, of

---

[466] Micah 7:15

[467] See *Hemshech VeHechereem* 5631 p. 1

[468] Exodus 14:16

[469] See *Hemshech VeHechereem* 5631, p. 24 and on; *Hemshech V'Kachah* 5637 p. 16 and on.

blessed memory, about the verse,[470] "Take your staff," about which they said,[471] "The Holy One, blessed is He, does not discipline the wicked except with a staff. Why is this? Because the wicked are compared to dogs, as it states,[472] 'And they return each evening, crying like dogs.' Just as one normally strikes a unruly dog with lashes, so too, they are lashed."

However, this is not true of the coming redemption, for that will be the conclusion and completion of the work. Therefore, the splitting of the river will not require the use of a staff. Instead, "He will wave His hand over the river," through which there will be an ascension of the physical, so that it will become a receptacle for Godliness, to the point that it will be in such a way that there will be an actual perception of Godliness.

The Torah teachings of Moshiach will be in the same manner, for Moshiach will teach Torah to the entire Jewish people.[473] Now, at first glance, how is it possible for Moshiach to teach Torah to the entire Jewish people? However, the explanation is that Moshiach will teach them in a manner of "seeing" the actual **being** of Godliness. Right now, we cannot even imagine this, since our entire grasp is only of the **existence** of Godliness (*Hasagat HaMetziut*), but not a grasp of His Being itself (*Yediyat HaMahut*). However, with the coming of

---

[470] Exodus 7:9
[471] Midrash, Shmot Rabba 9:2
[472] Psalms 59:15
[473] Rambam, Hilchot Teshuvah 9:2

Moshiach, the novelty will be that we will have perception and sight into the actual Being of *HaShem*-יהו"ה, blessed is He.[474]

5.

Based on all the above,[475] we may also understand the statement of our sages, of blessed memory,[476] "Moshiach will cause the righteous *Tzaddikim* to repent." At first glance, this teaching is not understood. How does the matter of repentance relate to the righteous *Tzaddikim*? However, as known, the matter of repentance (*Teshuvah*) does not only apply to repentance from sins and transgressions. Rather, the matter of repentance is that one leaves his state and standing, because he is dissatisfied by his present state, in that it does not fulfill his ultimate desire. This matter is even applicable to righteous *Tzaddikim* who have no relation to matters of sin or transgression. They too can to leave their previous state and standing, as our sages, of blessed memory, taught,[477] "If he is accustomed to learning one chapter, he should learn two chapters etc."

We may apply this to our understanding of Moshiach as well. Since, by his hand, there will be the matter of the "sight"

---

[474] See the Introduction and Petach HaShaar to Imrei Binah translated into English as The Gateway to Understanding.

[475] See *Hemshech* 5672 Vol. 1, 222; This will also be discussed at greater length in the next discourse.

[476] Zohar III 153b; See Likkutei Torah Drushim L'Shmini Atzeret 92b; Shir HaShirim 50b

[477] Cited from Tana d'Vei Eliyahu in Tanya Iggeret HaTeshuva, Ch. 9; Also see Vayikra Rabba 25:1

of the Being of *HaShem*-יהו"ה, and he will, "smell and judge," which itself is a revelation of the Essential Being of the Unlimited One, blessed is He, then in relation to the Essential Being of *HaShem*-יהו"ה, blessed is He, "even in His angels He finds fault."[478] Thus, at that time, the righteous *Tzaddikim* will also repent, in that they will leave their previous state and standing, as a result of the revelation of the Essential Being of *HaShem*-יהו"ה Himself, in relation to which, "even in His angels He finds fault."

It is about this that it states,[479] "Now the man Moshe was exceedingly humble, more than any person on the face of the earth." It is explained[480] that Moshe saw the generation of the of the heels of Moshiach and that they would be incapable of even understanding and comprehending.[481] He saw that it would be a time of concealment and hiddenness and that darkness would be doubled and quadrupled. Albeit, he saw that the Jewish people would nevertheless fulfill the commandments with self-sacrifice. In other words, not only will the concealments not obstruct their service of *HaShem*-יהו"ה, blessed is He, but more so, specifically because of the hiddenness, they would strengthen themselves with even greater fortitude to fulfill them. This is what caused a state of nullification (*Bittul*) and humility in Moshe.

---

[478] Job 4:18

[479] Numbers 12:3

[480] See Sefer HaMaamarim 5679 p. 464; 5689 p. 299 and on.

[481] The generation of Moshe is called, דור דעה-The generation of knowledge of *HaShem*, and is like the brain relative to the generations immediate to the coming of Moshiach, who are called the heels and have very diminished awareness of Godliness in comparison.

Based on the above, we may present a possible explanation, that Moshe became aware of the tremendous elevation of Moshiach, which is the matter of the revelation of the Essential Being of the Unlimited One Himself, *HaShem-יהו"ה*, blessed is He, that even causes, "the righteous to repent." This even affected Moshe to be roused and moved to repent (*Teshuvah*).

6.

It is about this that the verse states,[482] "I thank You *HaShem-יהו"ה*, for You were angry with me, and now Your wrath has subsided and You have comforted me." What is meant by this is that the thankfulness should specifically be over the very fact that, "You were angry with me." This is as explained before about the advantage of serving *HaShem-יהו"ה* from the angle of the rebounding light (*Ohr Chozer*). That is, it is specifically through the concealment and hiddenness of Godliness that one reaches a much higher state. Thus, "I thank You *HaShem-יהו"ה*, for You were angry with me." For, ultimately, at the end of it all, through the service of *HaShem-יהו"ה* in the manner of the rebounding light (*Ohr Chozer*), there will be the revelation of Moshiach. Thus, (the one) who "was pained because of our rebellious sins and oppressed through our iniquities,"[483] and "who bore our ills and carried our pains,"[484]

---

[482] Isaiah 12:1
[483] Isaiah 53:5
[484] Isaiah 53:4

will lead us to welcome the true and complete redemption, at which time, there will be a revelation of the advantage of servicing *HaShem*-יהו"ה in the manner of the rebounding light (*Ohr Chozer*),[485] and we will then arrive at the time that,[486] "Your wrath has subsided and You have comforted me."

---

[485] Also see the end of the prior discourse *Bati LeGani* 5711, Ch. 9
[486] Isaiah 12:1

Discourse 8

"Machar Chodesh - Tomorrow is the New Moon"

Delivered on Shabbat Mevarchim, Parashat Acharei
Erev Rosh Chodesh Iyar, 5711
By the grace of *HaShem,* blessed is He,

1.

The verse states,[487] "Yehonatan said to him, 'Tomorrow is the New Moon, and you will be missed because your seat will be empty.'" We read this *Haftorah* on a Shabbat that falls on the day before the New Moon (*Rosh Chodesh*).[488] The reason is because Yehonatan said these words to David on the day before the New Moon (*Rosh Chodesh*). He therefore said, "Tomorrow is the New Moon." Now, this must be better understood. For, at first glance, the connection is quite weak, especially since the rest of the *Haftorah* itself has no bearing or connection to the day before the New Moon (*Rosh Chodesh*). In other words, on its surface, it appears that the entire connection is only the two words, "Tomorrow is the new moon-*Machar Chodesh*-מחר חודש."

Moreover, it is not understood for yet another reason. Namely, that the *Halachic* legal ruling, is that the *Haftorah*

---

[487] Samuel I 20:18
[488] Talmud Bavli, Megillah 31a; Tur & Shulchan Aruch Orach Chaim 425:2

must be related to the subject matter of the Torah portion (*Parshah*) read in the Torah scroll. In fact, the *Haftorah* should not only be related to the general subject of the Torah portion (*Parshah*), but it must be related to the subject matter at the **conclusion** of the Torah portion (*Parshah*).[489] This is why, if the Shabbat of Chanukah falls out on the New Moon (*Rosh Chodesh*), the *Haftorah* that takes precedence is,[490] "Sing and be glad-*Rani Ve'Simchi*-רני ושמחי,"[491] which relates both to the end of the Torah portion, as well as to Chanukah.[492]

This being the case, our question is compounded. Why is it that on every Shabbat that falls on the day before the New Moon (*Rosh Chodesh*), we read the *Haftorah* of, "Tomorrow is the New Moon," which does not seem to have any relation to the subject of the Torah portion? Nonetheless, we read it as the *Haftorah,* on every Shabbat that falls out the day before the New Moon (*Rosh Chodesh*) irrespective of what Torah portion is being read on that Shabbat.

This being so, we are forced to conclude that the relationship between this particular *Haftorah* and the Shabbat that precedes the New Moon (*Rosh Chodesh*) is so strong, that it actually pushes aside the obligation to read a *Haftorah* that relates to the subject matter of the Torah portion. We must therefore understand this.

---

[489] See Beit Yosef to Tur Orach Chaim 283; Shulchan Aruch of the Alter Rebbe Orach Chaim Ibid. citing Tosefot to Megillah 23a.

[490] Zachariah 2:14-4:7

[491] Shulchan Aruch Orach Chaim 684:3

[492] See Tosafot to Shabbat 23b; Ohr Zarua Vol. 2, No. 394

We also must understand the details of the *Haftorah*, namely, that Yehonatan told David,[493] "I will shoot three arrows in that direction... If I say to the lad, 'Look, the arrows are on this side of you!' then you yourself may take the arrows and return, for it is well with you and, as *HaShem*-יהו"ה lives, there is nothing to be concern about. But if I say this to the boy, 'Behold, the arrows are beyond you!' then go, for *HaShem*-יהו"ה has sent you away." Why did he specifically give him a sign that involved arrows and not a different sign, perhaps something that would be a bit clearer?

2.

Now, to understand all this, we must preface with what we explained before[494] about the elevated level of Moshiach. That is, it states about Moshiach that,[495] "he will be imbued with a spirit of the fear for *HaShem*-*VeHaricho B'Yirat HaShem*-והריחו ביראת יהו"ה," which our sages, of blessed memory, explained to mean,[496] "He will smell and judge-*Morach VeDa'in*-מורח ודאין."[497] Additionally, our sages, of blessed memory, stated that,[498] "Moshiach will cause the righteous *Tzaddikim* to repent." It was explained[499] that these two aspects

---

[493] Samuel I 20:21-22

[494] In the previous discourse entitled "*VeHeineef*."

[495] Isaiah 11:3

[496] Talmud Bavli, Sanhedrin 93b

[497] That is, the word "*VeHaricho*-והריחו" is of the same root as "*Rei'ach*-ריח" which means "smell."

[498] Zohar III 153b; See Likkutei Torah Drushim L'Shmini Atzeret 92b; Shir HaShirim 50b

[499] In the prior discourse. Also see *Hemshech* 5672 Vol. 1 Ch. 22.

of Moshiach that relate to his essential being, namely, that the primary aspect of his elevation is that, "He will be imbued with a spirit of fear for *HaShem-VeHaricho B'Yirat HaShem-* והריחו ביראת יהו״ה," and that "Moshiach will cause the righteous *Tzaddikim* to repent," are related to each other.

It was explained that the matter of, "He will smell and judge-*Morach VeDa'in-*ומורח ודאין," means that, "He will not need to judge by what his eyes see," but will judge, "not as man sees with his eyes,"[500] since the eyes only perceive matters that are revealed. Instead, the judgments of Moshiach will be in such a way that he will know the causes that brought a person to the undesirable state he finds himself in.

This is like the teaching,[501] "Do not judge your fellow until you have reached his place." In other words, we explained that the truth of this matter is that it reaches to the very essence. For, as explained before,[502] the state and standing of the revealed powers of the soul are not indicative of the essence of the soul. An example of this was given from Rabbi Yochanan ben Zachai,[503] "who did not neglect either the smallest minutiae of Torah, nor the greatest matters in Torah etc." Nevertheless, because of his great humility, he said,[504] "I do not know on which path they are leading me."

---

[500] Samuel I 16:7

[501] Mishnah Avot 2:4

[502] Likkutei Torah Vayikrah, Hosafot 50d; Maamarei Admor HaZaken, HaKetzarim p. 309; Ohr HaTorah beginning of Parshat Pinchas (p. 1,059 and on). Discourse entitled "*Ach B'Goral*" 5626 (Sefer HaMaamarim 5626 p. 171); Sefer HaMaamarim 5696 p. 50 and note 1 there.

[503] Talmud Bavli, Sukkah 28a

[504] Talmud Bavli, Brachot 28b

Thus, for Moshiach to render true judgment he must know all these matters, including the aspect of the essential self of the person, and it specifically is then that, "he will judge the destitute with righteousness." This then, is the matter of, "he will smell and judge-*Morach VeDa'in*-מורח ודאין," since the aspect of scent-*Rei'ach*-ריח reaches the very essence of the soul. This was previously explained about the nostrils being, "The Gate of the Brain," referring to the inner aspect of the brain. More specifically, as explained in Idra Rabba,[505] the left nostril reaches the aspect of, "the life of all life-*Chayin D'Chayin*- חיין דחיין," which is the inner aspect of the Ancient One (*Atik*), and is the Essence. Thus, because of this matter of scent-*Rei'ach*-ריח, he reaches knowledge of all matters relating to his fellow, including to his essential self.

The same matter explains why, "Moshiach will cause the righteous *Tzaddikim* to repent." For, since his judgment will be from the aspect of the essence, he thus will cause the matter of repentance (*Teshuvah*) even in the righteous *Tzaddikim*. This is because, as explained before, the revealed powers of the soul are not indicative the state of the essential self of the soul, to the degree that even if the revealed powers are entirely good, it is possible that the essence of the soul is sunken into the depths of the extraneous husks of evil (*Kelipah*) (as demonstrated by the aforementioned statement of Rabbi Yochanan ben Zachai.) Thus, even in the *righteous* Tzaddikim, the aspect of repentance (*Teshuvah*) is necessary.

---

[505] Zohar III 130b

Now, this must be further understood. That is, this teaching makes sense regarding regular *Tzaddikim*, meaning those who are righteous in the revealed powers of their souls. In other words, because their revealed powers do not indicate their essence, it is necessary for them to have this aspect of repentance (*Teshuvah*). However, the statement that, "Moshiach will cause the righteous *Tzaddikim* to repent," is a general statement about **all** *Tzaddikim*, including *Tzaddikim* who are righteous to the very essence of their souls. This is the very reason why the example brought, is specifically from our teacher Moshe, who attained the level of repentance (*Teshuvah*) before his passing,[506] since there was an illumination of the revelation of Moshiach in him. However, Moshe certainly was a *Tzaddik* of the highest order, even in the essence of his soul and it cannot be said that his essential self was sunken into the extraneous husks of evil (*Kelipot*), God forbid. On the contrary, his essence was most certainly of the loftiest levels of holiness! Therefore, this teaching is not understood, and we must understand what the matter of repentance (*Teshuvah*) is relative to such souls.

As we explained before, the matter of repentance (*Teshuvah*) is that one's desire is no longer satisfied with his previous state and standing. This is something that applies even to the most righteous *Tzaddikim*. For, since the essence of the soul is in a constant state of adhesion to the Essential Being of the Unlimited One, *HaShem*-יהו״ה, blessed is He, as it states,[507]

---

[506] Likkutei Torah, Shmini Atzeret 92b
[507] Deuteronomy 4:4; Avot D'Rabbi Nathan end of Ch. 34

"You who adhere to HaShem-יהו"ה your God, are all alive today," and since the Light of the Unlimited One, HaShem-יהו"ה, blessed is He, is, "to the highest heights to no end,"[508] therefore, the matter of repentance (*Teshuvah*) is a constant. That is, no matter the level and state one finds himself in, he should desire to ascend to an even higher level.

Nevertheless, this still is not understood, because generally, this matter exists even before the coming of Moshiach. This being the case, what exactly is the great novelty of it (that it is such a wondrous thing) that it will specifically be introduced by Moshiach?

3.

Now, the explanation[509] is that the general matter of the work of clarification (*Avodat HaBirurim*) is the matter of, "including the left within the right."[510] In general, this is one of the main functions of Torah, namely, to clarify and elevate all matters that are undesirable, due to the "left side," so that they become included in "the right side."

Now, there are two aspects in this; the first being the **restraint** of the opposing side of evil (*Itkafia*), and the second being the **transformation** of darkness to light (*It'hapcha*), each of these aspects having an advantage over the other.

---

[508] Tikkunei Zohar, end of Tikkun 57; Zohar Chadash Yitro 34c
[509] See *Hemshech* 5672 Vol. 3, p. 1,306 and on; p. 1,315 and on; p. 1,321 and on; Also see Maamarei Admor HaEmtza'ee Bamidbar Vol. 2, p. 486 and on.
[510] Zohar III 176a, 178a

Serving HaShem-יהו"ה in a manner of restraint (*Itkafia*) is through drawing out the good to manifest within the evil and battle with it. This, primarily, is the service of HaShem-יהו"ה performed by intermediates (*Beinonim*),[511] and is attainable by every person. It therefore is something that everyone should strive for.[512] This kind of service of HaShem-יהו"ה is in a manner of battle, as the verse states,[513] "and a man wrestled with him." However, through this battle, the evil in oneself is proportionally nullified, by being reduced in relation to the good, until there is sixty times more good in him than bad, or a thousand or ten thousand times more good than bad, and so on.[514]

The advantage of this kind of service of HaShem-יהו"ה is that through it, the evil inclination itself, comes to recognizes and acknowledge the advantage and benefit of the good, that one must be good, to the point that it too agrees to do good. Nevertheless, the deficiency of this service of HaShem-יהו"ה, blessed is He, is that the evil inclination itself is not transformed to good. In other words, it is nullified and sublimated, due to the overwhelming preponderance of good, but the evil inclination itself, remains in the same state of being as before.

There is yet another deficiency in this, which is that, in order for the good to clarify the evil, the good must manifest within the evil. That is, the one who does the clarification must don the "garments" of the one being clarified. Because of this,

---

[511] Tanya Ch. 27
[512] Tanya Ch. 14
[513] Genesis 32:25
[514] Tanya Ch. 10; *Hemshech* 5672 Ibid. p. 1,316.

the evil causes a diminishment and weakening of the good, in that the good must give consideration to the existence of evil.

An example of this may be understood by the sweetening of bitter waters by adding an abundance of sweet waters to them. It is easily understood that the bad waters are not actually transformed by sweet waters, but remain bitter, as before. In truth, they only have become proportionally nullified because of the overwhelming abundance of sweet waters. However, it is likewise understood that the bitter waters also cause a weakening of the sweet waters, in that their sweetness is diminished compared to their original sweetness, since they now are mingled with a diminished proportion of bitter waters. In contrast, the service of *HaShem*-יהו״ה, blessed is He, in a manner of transformation (*It'hapcha*), is that, as a result of the abundant revelation of light of an entirely loftier order and illumination, the evil inclination itself is transformed to good. This fact, that the evil inclination itself is transformed to good (not just neutralized and sublimated in proportion to the good) is the advantage of this mode of service. In addition, it does not cause any weakening of the good whatsoever, since in this case, the good does not need to manifest within the evil to transform it. Instead, it automatically is transformed, by virtue of the revelation of light of an entirely loftier order and illumination.

However, the deficiency of this, is that the evil inclination, in and of itself, has no awareness of the transformation, to even recognize it. For, since its transformation to good was through the illumination of a loftier order of light, it is not that the evil inclination agreed to be

197

nullified and sublimated to the good. Rather, it was automatically transformed by virtue of the higher revelation and illumination of light.

This may be understood by way of analogy[515] to a court case, in which there is a prosecuting council and a defending council. The nullification of the arguments of the prosecutor can occur in two possible ways. The first is through the arguments of the defending council, in that he presents so many reasons and proofs on the side of merit and innocence of the defendant, that not only does he affect the judges, but even affects the prosecuting council. That is, as a result of his arguments, the position of the prosecutor is nullified.

However, it is understood, that the prosecutor himself is not transformed to also argue the merits of the defendant. Rather, because of the strong arguments of the defending council, he is forced to concede and cease arguing guilt. Moreover, it is understood that this approach causes a weakening to the defending council as well, for he is, at the very least, required to hear out the arguments of the prosecution for a period of time, and thus, although he himself argues on the side of merit and innocence, he must, nevertheless, take into account that there is an opposing council, who presents arguments of guilt.

However, there is another loftier way in which the prosecutor is nullified. This is through a revelation of the fact that, "In the light of the King's countenance is life."[516] In other

---

[515] See *Hemshech* 5672 Ibid. p. 1315 and on (citing Zohar II 60b); p. 1,317.
[516] Proverbs 16:15

words, this is like when the king himself enters the court, in which case, both the prosecuting council and defending council are utterly nullified. (There no longer is a prosecutor or defender.) In this case, even the prosecutor takes the position of the defender. However, although in this manner the prosecutor himself is transformed into a defender, this matter is only because of the revelation of, "the light of the King's countenance." In other words, it is not because of himself at all, since he has no understanding or grasp of the, "light of the King's countenance." Rather, he is automatically nullified by the revelation of the light of the King's countenance, whereas, in and of himself, he would have remained a prosecutor.

However, there is yet another manner of transformation (*It'hapcha*) that has both advantages. That is, the evil inclination himself is transformed entirely to good, and this even is done of his own accord, not just because of a revelation that is beyond him. This happens when the evil inclination himself grasps, recognizes (and deeply understands) that he is evil, and this realization of his standing and position, pains him (and brings him anguish), until he leaves his state of evil and becomes transformed to good.

This is caused through a revelation of the Hidden Essential Self (*He'elem HaAtzmi*). In other words, it is not a matter of revelation of light and illumination, like the "light of the King's countenance," which the verse specifies as an aspect of "light," indicating that it only is a ray and illumination alone. Rather, this comes about from the aspect of the inherently concealed Essential Self of the King, blessed is He.

4.

This then, is the meaning of the verse,[517] "They came to Marah, but they could not drink the waters of Marah because they were bitter; therefore, they named it, 'Marah-מרה-bitter.' The people complained against Moshe, saying, 'What shall we drink?' He cried out to HaShem-יהו״ה and HaShem-יהו״ה showed him a tree; he threw it into the water and the water became sweet." Now, we find two views regarding the tree. The view of the Zohar,[518] is that the "tree" refers to Torah, as it states about Torah,[519] "It is a tree of life for those who hold on to it." The view of the Midrash,[520] is that this was an Oleander Tree (Hardufni), which is poisonous.[521]

Now, these two views reflect the two aforementioned approaches of transformative service of HaShem-יהו״ה, blessed is He (It'hapcha). For, all views agree that the bad waters were not nullified through an addition of an overabundance of good waters. (Since, in that case, no change would take place in their essential state of being at all, as explained above.) Rather, it was through throwing the tree into the waters that the bitter waters were actually transformed, as it states, "the water became sweet."

---

[517] Exodus 15:23-25
[518] Zohar II 60b
[519] Proverbs 3:18
[520] Midrash Shemot Rabba 23:3; 50:3
[521] See Matnat Kehunah commentary to Shemot Rabba 23:3 and 50:3 ibid. Also see Mishnah Chullin 3:5 and elsewhere.

However, in this itself there are two views. According to the view of the Zohar, that the tree refers to Torah (since Torah is the Tree of Life, that has no admixture of good and evil and no connection to the tree of death), we find that the sweetening of the waters was accomplished through the revelation of the light of Torah. That is, it was due to this revelation that the bitter waters were transformed to sweet waters.

In contrast, according to the view of the Midrash, that the tree itself was also a bitter poison, we find that the act of throwing the tree into the waters, was to reveal the bitterness in the waters themselves. That is, the sweetening of the waters was accomplished by the bitter waters themselves. Now, although this was specifically accomplished by Moshe, as it states, "and *HaShem*-יהו"ה showed him a tree," this is because it is not applicable for evil to come to a recognition or feeling that it is evil, in and of itself. It therefore is necessary for this to be revealed specifically from above.

Nevertheless, this is not a matter of a revelation of light and illumination, but rather, the action here is that he showed them their own bitterness, through which evil itself leaves its former state of being and becomes transformed to good. In other words, this is not a matter of revelations of light, but rather, a revelation of the inherently Concealed Essential Self of *HaShem*-יהו"ה (*He'elem HaAtztmi*), blessed is He, the

201

Concealment of all Concealments, about Whom it states,[522] "He made darkness His concealment."

5.

The explanation of this matter in man's service of HaShem-יהו"ה, blessed is He, is as follows: The verse states,[523] "As HaShem-יהו"ה, the God of Israel, lives – before Whom I stood etc." It is explained that this refers to the soul as it is above, before to its descent, that stands before HaShem-יהו"ה, blessed is He, with love and fear of Him, and knows of nothing except for Godliness.

However, when it descends to manifest within the body and animalistic soul, it then comes to have some relation to human intellect, the grasp of physical matters, and even lesser matters. For, two concealments occur with the descent of the soul into the body. The first, is that the body covers over and conceals the light of the soul, and the second, is the inherent concealment of the body itself.

These two aspects also exist within darkness (Choshech-חושך) itself. Namely, darkness is the absence of light, and beyond this, it is the novel creation of darkness, in and of itself. In other words, the concealment of the light of the soul is like the matter of the absence of light, whereas the concealment of the body itself, is like the existence of darkness as a created thing, in and of itself. For, the absence of light is

[522] Psalms 18:12
[523] Kings I 17:1 (Also see Likkutei Sichot Vol. 25, p. 147, note 53.)

only applicable when first there is an existence of light, after which, the darkness causes the absence of the light, or at the very least, a diminishment, dimming and concealment of the light.

It thus is understood that the concealment of the body itself is not just a matter of the absence of light, since the formation of the body preceded the formation of the soul.[524] It is for this reason that the root of the existence of the body is not from the aspect of the Light (*Ohr*), but rather, from the aspect of the Impression (*Reshimu*).[525] Rather, the concealment of the body itself, is similar to the matter of the existence of darkness as a novel creation, in and of itself.

Now, in both above-mentioned aspects of darkness, it is necessary for there to be the service of *HaShem*-יהו"ה, blessed is He, according to both modes of service, that is, the service of restraint (*Itkafia*), as well as the service of transformation (*It'hapcha*). The service of restraint (*Itkafia*) is a kind of service that goes according to reason and intellect. In other words, through the many manners of contemplation (*Hitbonenut*) explained in many written works of Torah, especially in books of Chassidic teachings, one affects that the evil is nullified to the good.

The mode of service of transformation (*It'hapcha*), on the other hand, is in such a manner that one does not even want to enter into argument or response to the side of evil altogether.

---

[524] See Torah Ohr Bereishit 3d and on.

[525] See Siddur Im Divrei Elokim Chaim 166a; Sefer HaMaamarim 5670 p. 27; 5710 p. 59; Also see Shaar HaYichud – The Gate of Unity, Ch. 12-13.

As his honorable holiness, my father-in-law,[526] the Rebbe, said in the name of his honorable holiness, the Alter Rebbe, "A Jew has neither the desire nor the ability to be separated from Godliness." In general, this is the result of strengths granted from Above, such as the powers that a Rebbe bestows on a person. In other words, this is not because of one's own strenuous toil in himself (with his own strengths), but rather, because of strengths that were given to him by the Rebbe. Nevertheless, as a result of these strengths he does not enter into matters of argument or conflict with evil whatsoever.

However, there is an even higher level of transformation (*It'hapcha*) that comes about as a result of the revelation of the inherently concealed Essential Self of *HaShem*-יהו"ה (*He'elem HaAtzmi*). This matter is entirely beyond the category of understanding and comprehension (*Havanah*), for we have no understanding or comprehension in it, nor any recognition or sense, not in an inner way (*Pnimi*), nor in an encompassing, transcendent way (*Makif*). Rather, because of the adhesion of his soul to the Singular Essential Preexistent Intrinsic Being of *HaShem*-יהו"ה Himself, blessed is He, nothing whatsoever is obstructed from him and he is even granted a revelation of the inherently Concealed Essential Self of *HaShem*-יהו"ה Himself, blessed is He; something that cannot be drawn forth to either the inner powers of the soul or to the transcendent powers of the soul!

---

[526] Sefer HaMaamarim 5684 p. 215 & p. 243; 5710 p. 115 & 117; Igrot Kodesh of the Rebbe Rayatz Vol. 4, p. 384; HaYom Yom 25 Tamuz

This matter is specifically brought to the fore through the realization that,[527] "your forsaking of HaShem-יהו״ה your God, is evil and bitter." In other words, although a person may possess no knowledge of "HaShem-יהו״ה your God," and may have no knowledge of matters of holiness altogether, nevertheless, he feels deeply that, "it is evil and bitter to have forsaken HaShem-יהו״ה your God." Beyond that, he may not even know the reason that he is in this state of bitterness and evil, but nonetheless, he feels that he is in a state of bitterness and evil, and feels it so deeply that it literally touches the very essence of his soul, so that he makes a determination that, come what may, he cannot continue in this way going forward. He thus necessarily, "turns aside,"[528] and although he does not even know what it means to come close to HaShem-יהו״ה, blessed is He, he nevertheless knows that it is impossible for him to continue to be the way he was.

It is specifically in this kind of service that there is a revelation of the inherently Concealed Essential Self of HaShem-יהו״ה Himself, blessed is He. For, in this kind of service of HaShem-יהו״ה, the body itself is transformed to good. In other words, the cause of his transformation to good is not because of any revelations or illuminations of light, but rather, because of the body itself. Thus, this matter results from the revelation of the Concealed Essential Self of HaShem-יהו״ה (He'elem HaAtzmi), since the revelation of the True Something

---

[527] Jeremiah 2:19
[528] Rashi to Exodus 3:3

(*Yesh HaAmeetee*) is specifically in the created something (*Yesh HaNivra*).[529]

6.

From all the above, we may now understand[530] the statement that,[531] "Moshiach will cause the righteous *Tzaddikim* to repent." For, the novelty that will be introduced in the days of Moshiach is that the tangible something (*Yesh*) will itself be transformed to good, in and of itself. This is the advantage of what will be revealed by Moshiach, over and above the revelation that took place at the splitting of the sea. For although, at the splitting of the sea, there also was a transformation of darkness to light, in that the darkness itself illuminated, as stated,[532] "And there were cloud and darkness, and it illuminated the night," nevertheless, this matter was because of the revelation of light.[533] As we recite,[534] "The King, King of kings, the Holy One, blessed is He, was revealed to them," and,[535] "I and not an angel... I and no other." In other words, this revelation illuminated the darkness.

---

[529] See Biurei Zohar of the Mittler Rebbe, Beshalach 43c; Sefer HaMaamarim 5661 p. 191 and on.

[530] See *Hemshech* 5672 ibid. p. 1,342 and on.

[531] Zohar III 153b; See Likkutei Torah Drushim L'Shmini Atzeret 92b; Shir HaShirim 50b

[532] Exodus 14:20

[533] *Hemshech* 5672 ibid. p. 1,323 & 1,328

[534] Haggadah for Pesach – "*Matza Zu*"

[535] Haggadah for Pesach – "*VaYotzi'einu*"

However, about the coming future it states,[536] "Night shines like the day; darkness and light are the same." In other words, although at night it is dark, nevertheless, in and of itself, "it will shine like the day." This matter is only possible specifically through a revelation of the True Something (*Yesh HaAmeetee*), which is the advantage of the revelation of the coming future. In contrast, at the time of the splitting of the sea the revelation was only from the aspect of the intangible nothingness (*Ein*) of the True Something (*Yesh HaAmeetee*).

Thus, this matter is also the novelty through which "Moshiach will cause the righteous *Tzaddikim* to repent." For, the *Tzaddik* serves HaShem-יהו"ה, blessed is He, with abundant love and delight (*Ahavah Rabba B'Ta'anugim*), and is thus in the category of a tangible something with a sense of self (*Yesh*),[537] in that there is the one who loves.[538] Even though his sense of self is that he loves HaShem-יהו"ה, blessed is He, nevertheless, he is within the category of a tangible something (*Yesh*) with a sense of self.

The novelty of Moshiach that will cause even the *Tzaddikim* to repent (*Teshuvah*) is that the *Tzaddik* will himself become aware of his sense of self, and will automatically desire to be rid of his sense of self. This is because, at that time, there will be a revelation of the True Something (*Yesh HaAmeetee*), blessed is He, within the created something (*Yesh HaNivra*), for Whom there is no "other."

---

[536] Psalms 139:12; *Hemshech* 5672 ibid. p. 1,345
[537] See Tanya Ch. 35 (44a); Ch. 37 (48a)
[538] See Torah Ohr 114d

7.

Based on all the above, we now may understand the verses of the *Haftorah*, that,[539] "Yehonatan said to him, 'Tomorrow is the New Moon' etc." For, "Tomorrow is the New Moon-*Machar Chodesh*," refers to the renewal of the moon, which is similar to the revelations of the coming future. This is as we recite in the blessing of the sanctification of the moon (*Kiddush Levanah*) that, "the light of the moon shall be as the light of the sun,[540] like the light of the seven days of creation, as it was before being diminished etc."

This is why the verse specifies,[541] "Tomorrow-*Machar*-מחר is the New Moon," similar to the statement of our sages, of blessed memory,[542] "Today to do them,[543] and tomorrow-*Machar*-מחר to receive their reward." In other words, right now, the general service of *HaShem*-יהו"ה, blessed is He, is like the service that precedes the New Moon (*Rosh Chodesh*), upon which all the revelations of the coming future are dependent.[544] Thus, this is what is meant by, "Tomorrow is the New Moon-*Machar Chodesh*-מחר חודש."

Now, this matter is also hinted at in the particulars that Yehonatan said to David,[545] "I will shoot three arrows in that direction... If I say to the lad, 'Behold, the arrows are on this

---

[539] Samuel I 20:18

[540] Isaiah 30:26

[541] See Sefer HaMaamarim 5631 p. 355

[542] Talmud Bavli, Eruvin 22a; Avodah Zarah 3a; Rashi to Deuteronomy 7:11

[543] Deuteronomy 7:11

[544] See Tanya Ch. 37

[545] Samuel I 20:21-22

side of you!' then you yourself may take the arrows and return, for it is well with you and as *HaShem*-יהו"ה lives, there is no concern. But if I say this to the boy, 'Behold, the arrows are beyond you!' then go, for *HaShem*-יהו"ה has sent you away." This is because, shooting arrows with a bow, indicates the general service of purification and clarification (*Avodat HaBirurim*). This is as explained in the appendixes to Torah Ohr,[546] that the drawing back of the bow, is for the purpose of propelling the arrow to a greater distance.[547] That is, the further back one pulls the bow, the greater distance will the arrow be propelled. It is this same way with the toil in the service of purification and clarification (*Avodat HaBirurim*), (which is the service of the rebounding light (*Ohr Chozer*)). That is, to the extent that one was involved in the lower, the higher he can reach.

This then, is the meaning of what Yehonatan said to David, "If I say to the lad, 'Behold, the arrows are on this side of you!' then you yourself may take the arrows and return, for it is well with you and as *HaShem*-יהו"ה lives there is no concern." In other words, if the process of purification and clarification has been completed, "then all is well with you-*Shalom Lecha*-שלום לך," meaning that,[548] "There is peace-*Shalom*-שלום in the [heavenly] entourage above, and there is peace-*Shalom*-שלום in the [earthly] entourage below," and thus, "there is no concern," for the process of purification and

[546] Torah Ohr, Hosafot 103a
[547] Also see Shaar HaYichud – The Gate of Unity, Ch. 36 and the notes there.
[548] Talmud Bavli, Sanhedrin 99b

clarification (*Avodat HaBirurim*) has been completed. The verse therefore continues, "As *HaShem*-יהו״ה lives," indicating that a revelation of the, "day that will be entirely Shabbat and rest for everlasting life" is already possible.[549]

"But if I say this to the boy, 'Behold, the arrows are beyond you!'" – indicating that the process of purification and clarification (*Avodat HaBirurim*) has not been completed – "then go, for *HaShem*-יהו״ה has sent you away." That is, go and be involved in the process of purification and clarification (*Avodat HaBirurim*), and do not ask yourself where you will derive the strength for this, "for *HaShem*-יהו״ה has sent you." In other words, you do not do so through your own strength, but rather, as the emissary of the Holy One, blessed is He. For, the entire matter of the service of *HaShem*-יהו״ה, blessed is He, is that one is charged as the emissary of the Holy One, blessed is He. This is as our sages, of blessed memory, stated,[550] "Honor the commandments-*Mitzvot*, for they are My emissaries."

Now, Yehonatan specifically needed to clarify this matter itself with his father, king Shaul, (as to whether or not the process of clarification and purification (*Avodat HaBirurim*) was complete). For, "upon their entrance into the land of Israel, the Jewish people were commanded three *mitzvot*; to appoint a king, to cut off the seed of Amalek and to construct the Chosen House (the Holy Temple)."[551]

---

[549] Talmud Bavli, Tamid 33b
[550] Midrash Tanchuma Vayigash 6; Likkutei Torah Vayikra 2a
[551] Talmud Bavli, Sanhedrin 20b

Now, the first commandment, of appointing a king, was fulfilled with the appointment of king Shaul, since he was the first king of the Jewish people. Had he wiped out the seed of Amalek, then, at that time, they would have also come to the matter of constructing the Chosen House (the Holy Temple). [The entire lengthiness of the exile is solely due to the fact that Shaul did not cut off the seed of Amalek and allowed Agag to live.[552]] Nevertheless, it is because of this that Yehonatan needed to clarify with his father, king Shaul, as to whether the work of purification and clarification (*Avodat HaBirurim*) was completed, since it was his responsibility to complete this matter of purification and clarification (*Avodat HaBirurim*).

Now, the sign that he gave David for this, was specifically the matter of the bow-*Keshet*-קשת. This[553] may be understood from the statement in Zohar,[554] "Do not look forward to the heels of Moshiach until you see this rainbow-*Keshet*-קשת with all of its colors illuminating in the world. Only then should you look forward to Moshiach."

Now, at first glance, this passage is not understood, since the rainbow-*Keshet*-קשת is the sign of the covenant that there will be no more worldwide floods (*Mabul*).[555] In other words, the need for this sign is to indicate that the world is in an undesirable state. This is why Rabbi Shimon bar Yochai stated that one of his sublime qualities is that no rainbow-

---

[552] Samuel I 15:9
[553] See *Hemshech* 5672 Ibid. p. 1,305-1,306
[554] Zohar I 72b
[555] Genesis 9:12 and on

Keshet-קשת appeared in all his days.[556] This being the case, what is the relationship between the rainbow-Keshet-קשת and the footsteps of Moshiach?

This matter may be understood by the fact that the rainbow-Keshet-קשת will specifically be accompanied by, "all its illuminating colors." As explained by his honorable holiness, the Rebbe, the Tzemach Tzeddek,[557] this matter refers to the revelation from the inner aspect of the Ancient One (Atik), through which the darkness itself is caused to illuminate. In other words, the clouds themselves will cause an abundance of colors, similar to the revelation of the coming future, in which, "night will illuminate as the day." Thus, "When you see this rainbow-Keshet-קשת with all its colors illuminating in the world, then you should look forward to the footsteps of Moshiach."

Now, we must point out the terms that were specifically used is that one should then, "look forward to the **heels** of Moshiach." For, the matter of Moshiach himself is that the darkness will illuminate, in and of itself, as explained above. However, such is not the case with the matter of, "the rainbow-Keshet-קשת and all its brilliant colors," in which case, the illumination of the darkness is due to the abundance and strength of the sunlight. This is why it is only referred to as the aspect of the "**heels** of Moshiach."

---

[556] Midrash Bereishit Rabba 35:2; Talmud Yerushalmi Berachot 9:2

[557] See Ohr HaTorah Noach 72a; Ohr HaTorah Bereishit 21b and on; Ohr HaTorah Noach Vol. 3, p. 651a and on.

The *Haftorah* concludes with the words,[558] "Each man kissed the other and they wept with one another, until David greatly magnified-*Higdeel*-הגדיל." Now, Yehonatan the son of Shaul, corresponds to the matter of comprehension (*Hasagah*), which is the matter of, "Shaul from *Rechovot HaNahar*-The Breadth of the River,"[559] which refers to the faculty of understanding-*Binah*. In contrast, the matter of David is that he,[560] "established the Yoke of Torah," and[561] "the Yoke of Repentance-*Teshuvah*," specifically in a way of accepting the yoke. This then, is the meaning of the words, "until David greatly magnified-*Higdeel*-הגדיל," that is, until such time that there will be a revelation of the matter of, "the magnification and wondrousness that *HaShem*-יהו״ה does in the earth,"[562] which is the revelation of His Hidden Essential Self (*He'elem HaAtzmi*), blessed is He, may it happen speedily in our days!

---

[558] Shmuel I 20:41

[559] Genesis 36:37; Etz Chaim Shaar 8 (Shaar Drushei Nekudot) Ch. 4

[560] See Midrash Bamidbar Rabba 18:21; Midrash Shmuel Ch. 29; Tanna D'Vei Eliyahu Rabba Ch. 2

[561] Talmud Bavli Mo'ed Katan 16b; Commentaries to Midrash Bamidbar Rabba Ibid.

[562] See the language of the Alter Rebbe in his Igrot Kodesh – Num. 70 p. 230 and on (and see elsewhere, Num. 59 etc.)

Discourse 9

"U'Sefartem Lachem -
You shall count for yourselves"

Delivered on Lag BaOmer, 5711
By the grace of *HaShem*, blessed is He,

1.

The verse states,[563] "You shall count for yourselves – from the morrow of the day of rest, from the day when you bring the Omer of the waving – they shall be seven complete weeks." In other words, first there is the commandment-*mitzvah* to bring, "the Omer of the wave offering", followed by the commandment-*mitzvah* to count the Omer. This is as stated,[564] "It is a commandment to count days and is also a commandment to count weeks." In other words, this *mitzvah* takes place between the bringing of the Omer offering and the holiday of *Shavuot*.

However, we must understand why the verse states, "You shall count for yourselves – from the morrow of the day of rest." For, at first glance, since what is meant is the day after the [first day of] Passover,[565] the verse should have stated, "from the morrow of the Passover." Why then does the verse

---

[563] Leviticus 23:15
[564] Talmud Bavli, Menachot 66a
[565] Talmud Bavli, Menachot 65b

state, "from the morrow of the day of rest (*HaShabbat*)," when what is meant is the holiday of Passover? This question is further strengthened by the fact that the Sadducees actually erred, stating that the verse means the day after Shabbat of [the count of] Creation. As a result, our sages, of blessed memory, had to argue with them and bring proofs demonstrating that the intended meaning of the verse is the day after the [first day of] Passover (*Pesach*).[566] This being so, why did the Torah not simply specify, "the morrow of the Passover," instead of stating, "the morrow of the day of rest (*HaShabbat*)"?

2.

This may be understood by prefacing with a general explanation of the matter of the counting the Omer. It states in Mishnah[567] that, "all other meal offerings are brought from wheat, whereas this meal offering (of the *Sotah*) and the meal offering of the Omer, are brought from barley." The reason that the meal offering of the *Sotah* is brought from barley, which is considered to be animal fodder, is explained in the Mishnah. Namely, that just as her actions were animalistic, so too, her offering is of animal fodder. Nevertheless, we still must understand why the Omer offering differs from all other meal offerings and is specifically brought from barley. The well-known explanation[568] is that the service of the Omer meal

---

[566] Ibid.

[567] Talmud Bavli, Sotah 14a

[568] See discourse entitled "*Mashcheni*" 5655 (Sefer HaMaamarim 5655 p. 172 and on); 5668 (Sefer HaMaamarim 5668 p. 272 and on); Shabbat Parshat Bamidbar

offering, relates to the matter of the purification and clarification (*Birur*) of the animalistic soul.

The explanation[569] of the matter, is that the revelation of the first day of the Passover is from the aspect of an arousal from *HaShem*-יהו"ה above, of His own accord, as the verse states,[570] "When you take the people out of Egypt, you will serve God on this mountain." This indicates that the matter of service of *HaShem*-יהו"ה, blessed is He, from below to Above, only began after the exodus from Egypt, whereas in the exodus from Egypt itself, the awakening was from *HaShem*-יהו"ה above to below.

It is about this that the verse states,[571] "Draw me; we will run after You; the King has brought me into His chambers, we will rejoice and be glad in You etc." The words, "Draw me," refer to the revelations of the exodus from Egypt, that were in a manner of an awakening from *HaShem*-יהו"ה above, in which the King, King of kings, revealed Himself to them.[572] In other words, while they were in Egypt, the Jewish people were sunken into the forty-nine gates of impurity. Nevertheless, the King, King of kings, revealed Himself to them and redeemed them from Egypt, which is this matter of, "Draw me," and is an awakening from *HaShem*-יהו"ה above to below.

5701 (Sefer HaMaamarim 5701 p. 119 and on); Discourse entitled "*Lehavin Inyan Sefirat HaOmer*" and discourse entitled "*Mashcheni*" 5718 (Sefer HaMaamarim 5718 p. 210 and on; p. 218 and on).

[569] See Likkutei Torah Vayikra 3a; Emor 35b and elsewhere.

[570] Exodus 3:12

[571] Song of Songs 1:4; See discourses entitled "*Mashcheni*" ibid.; Ohr HaTorah Shir HaShirim Vol. 1, p. 59 & p. 75.

[572] Haggadah for Pesach – "*Matzah Zu*"

It is for this reason that the word, "Draw me-*Mashcheini*-מֹשְׁכֵנִי" is written in the singular form. This is because this revelation from Above affected a movement in the Godly soul only, since only the Godly soul can sense revelations from Above. Their animalistic soul, however, remained in its original state and standing.

It is also because of this that it states about the exodus from Egypt,[573] "the people had fled." The Alter Rebbe explained this[574] as follows, "At first glance, it seems strange. Why would it have been so? Had they demanded of Pharaoh that he set them free forever, would he not have been forced to do so? Rather, the explanation of the matter is that the evil that was in the [animalistic] souls of the Jewish people was still in its full strength, in the left chamber of the heart etc." This is because the revelation from Above only affected movement within their Godly soul, whereas their animalistic soul remained in its former strength. Thus, the flight and rush to leave was necessary because of the animalistic soul. The reason is because the revelation of the exodus from Egypt was in a manner of illumination from Above to below. In other words, the Jewish people, in and of themselves, were not fitting receptacles for this, and thus, they only sensed the revelation in their Godly souls.

However, after the revelation of the exodus from Egypt there was the matter of the counting of the Omer, which is the service of *HaShem*-יהו"ה, blessed is He, from below to Above.

---

[573] Exodus 14:5
[574] Tanya Ch. 31; Likkutei Torah Vayikra 3a; Emor 35b

It is about this that the verse continues, "we will run after You." In other words, this is not in a way of, "Draw me-*Mashcheini*-משכני," from Above to below, but rather, this running is of their own accord, which is the service from below to Above. Now, since this kind of service is from below to Above, it applies to the animalistic soul as well, and thus, the term used is, "**we** will run-*Narutzah*-נרוצה," in the plural form. For, this kind of service even causes movement in the animalistic soul.

Additionally, this is also the reason for the specific use of the term, "we will **run**-*Narutzah*-נרוצה," which is specifically a term of, "alacrity-*Merutzah*-מרוצה." For, when the service of *HaShem*-יהו"ה, blessed is He, also involves the animalistic soul, it is performed in a way of "alacrity-*Merutzah*-מרוצה." This is because the nature of the animalistic soul is such, that when it is drawn to something, it is drawn to it with zeal, specifically in a way of "alacrity-*Merutzah*-מרוצה." In other words, it is not typical of the animalistic soul to do the things that it is drawn to, little by little. It rather does so in a way of zeal and "alacrity-*Merutzah*-מרוצה." That is, either it altogether is not drawn to matters of Godliness, but if it is drawn to them, it does so in a way of "alacrity-*Merutzah*-מרוצה." (That is, when he finally **is** affected to be drawn to Godliness, it happens in a way of "alacrity-*Merutzah*-מרוצה.")

Beyond this, when the animalistic soul indeed is drawn to matters of Godliness in a way of "alacrity-*Merutzah*-מרוצה," the Godly soul is also affected to develop this matter of "alacrity-*Merutzah*-מרוצה." For, in and of itself, the Godly soul does not have this quality of "alacrity-*Merutzah*-מרוצה." As a result, its gravitation toward Godliness is measured and limited. However, through the alacrity of the animalistic soul, the Godly soul too is affected with additional light and illumination, so that it too develops this matter of "alacrity-*Merutzah*-מרוצה," beyond measure and limitation. This then, is why the verse uses the term, "we will run-*Narutzah*-נרוצה," in the plural form. That is, this matter of running (should not only be a quality of the animalistic soul, but should also be) developed in the Godly soul.

However, the general principle of the words,[575] "we will run after You," refers to the toil in the service of refining and clarifying the animalistic soul, which is the service of counting the days of the Omer (*Sefirat HaOmer*) in a manner of ascension from below to Above. This service is preparatory to the giving of the Torah, as indicated by the continuation of the verse, "the King has brought me into His chambers."

3.

In even greater detail, the refining of the animalistic soul consists of two general matters, that is, the refining of the intellect and the refining of the emotions. These two aspects correspond to the two matters of offering the Omer and counting of the Omer.[576]

Now, the actual service of bringing the Omer offering, corresponds to refining the intellect of the animalistic soul. For,

---

[575] Song of Songs 1:4
[576] Discourse entitled "*Mashcheini*" 5701 (Sefer HaMaamarim 5701, p. 123).

in addition to the general matter that the Omer offering was brought from barley, which is considered to be animal fodder and indicates the refinement of the animalistic soul, beyond that, amongst the various kinds of animal fodder, it is specifically brought from grain, which indicates the intellect. This is understood from the teaching of our sages, of blessed memory,[577] "A child does not know how to call, 'father-*Abba*,' until he has tasted the taste of grain." However, in this case, it refers to the matter of the intellect of the animalistic soul, for since its primary aspect is emotional, its intellect also is tied to its emotions. It is for this reason that even the grain (the intellect) is specifically animal fodder (meaning that it is intellect as it relates to emotions).

Now, after the Omer offering has been brought, which is the matter of the refinement of the intellect of the animalistic soul, it then is followed by the service of the refinement of the emotions of the animalistic soul, through the counting of the Omer, "by the count of days and by the count of weeks."[578] In other words, the offering of the Omer, which is the matter of the refinement of intellect as it relates to emotions, was only on the first day, the 16th of Nissan. In contrast, the counting of the Omer, which is the matter of the refinement of the emotions themselves, are not sufficiently refined through the general refinement, but rather, every particular emotive quality requires its specific refinement, in and of itself. Moreover, this

---

[577] Talmud Bavli, Brachot 40a; Matnot Kehunah to Bereishit Rabba 15:7; Mevo She'arim Shaar 5, Vol. 1, Ch. 12 in the Hagahot Tzemach.
[578] Talmud Bavli, Menachot 66a

refinement requires great detail, in that each particular emotional quality must be refined as it is included in each of the other seven particular emotive qualities.

This indicates that the general refinement is only in an encompassing manner (*Makif*), and therefore does not relate to practical action. Thus, the primary service, in actuality, is in a way of advancing little by little, specifically by one's own strength, which is the particular and detailed refinement of each emotive quality as it includes all seven emotive qualities. It is specifically through this that his service of *HaShem-הוי׳ה*, blessed is He, comes to be in a way of,[579] "Know Him in all your ways." In other words, it is through this kind of refinement that all the particulars of one's thoughts, speech and action, come to be as they should be.

It is for this reason that the *mitzvah* of counting the Omer is not only, "by the count of the week," which refers only to the refinement of each emotive quality in general. Rather, the primary *mitzvah* is, "by the count of the day," which refers to the refinement of each particular emotive quality, such as kindness-*Chessed* within kindness-*Chessed*, and majesty-*Hod* within majesty-*Hod*, concluding with the emotive quality of kingship-*Malchut* within kingship-*Malchut*.

Through this we may explain the view of Rabbeinu Yerucham,[580] who states that, in our times, there is a distinction between the *mitzvah* to count the days and the *mitzvah* to count

---

[579] Proverbs 3:6
[580] See Toldot Adam V'Chavah, Toldot Adam, Netiv 5, Chelek 4 (43c in Vinezia 5713 edition).

the weeks. For, there are those[581] who state that even during the time of exile[582] the commandment to count the Omer (*Sefirat HaOmer*) is biblical. There are others,[583] on the other hand, who state that during the time of exile, the commandment of counting the Omer (*Sefirat HaOmer*) is rabbinic. However, Rabbeinu Yerucham, makes a distinction between the counting of the days and the counting of the weeks, and states that the counting of the days is a biblical requirement, even during the time of exile, whereas the count of weeks is rabbinic.

This may be understood according to the above explanation, namely, that the count of the weeks is the matter of refining each general emotive quality, whereas the count of the days is the refinement of each particular emotive quality, as it is in each general emotive attribute. Based on this, it is understood that since the count of the days, which is the refinement of each particular emotive quality, is applicable to one's actual service of *HaShem*-יהו"ה, blessed is He, that is, in one's actual thoughts, speech and actions (as mentioned above), it therefore applies and is necessary during all periods and at all times. Thus, the obligation to count the days applies even in our times, as a biblical requirement.

This is not the case, however, with the count of the weeks, which is the matter of the refinement of the general

---

[581] Rambam Hilchot Tmidin uMusafin 7:22; Chinuch Mitzvah 306 and elsewhere.

[582] In which the Holy Temple is not standing, and no Omer offering is performed.

[583] See Tosefot to Talmud Bavli, Menachot 66a; Mateh Moshe 667; Birkei Yosef, Orach Chayim 489:1; Shulchan Aruch of the Alter Rebbe, Orach Chaim 489:2 & 17 and elsewhere.

emotive qualities. In and of itself, this kind of service does not relate or directly affect one's actual thoughts, speech and action. This is so, even though there is an advantage in this, over and above the service of counting the days, since it is the refinement of the emotive quality in its general totality, which is of a loftier nature. On the other hand, since it is a loftier service, it does not directly relate to tangible action. Thus, during the time of exile we are incapable of refining the totality of the quality, in general. Rather, the power that was given to us is only in relation to tangible action.

4.

Now, the explanation[584] of the matter of the inter-inclusion of the emotive qualities with each other, is that each emotive quality includes all seven emotive qualities within it. An example is the quality of kindness-*Chessed*. In addition to the general quality of kindness-*Chessed* itself, which is the matter of love of *HaShem*-יהו"ה, blessed is He, it also includes all the other emotive qualities in it.

For example, the quality of kindness-*Chessed* within kindness-*Chessed* is that, due to his love of *HaShem*-יהו"ה, blessed is He, he also will love whoever loves *HaShem*-יהו"ה. That is, if he sees someone who is occupied in the study of Torah and the fulfillment of the *mitzvot* with fear of Heaven, he will be roused with love towards him. Similarly, because of his

---

[584] See the discourses entitled "*Mashcheini*" 5655, 5678, and 5701 ibid.

love of *HaShem*-יהו"ה, blessed is He, his own involvement in matters of Torah and the fulfillment of the *mitzvot*, will be with zeal and alacrity.

The quality of judgment-*Gevurah* that is within kindness-*Chessed* is when his love of *HaShem*-יהו"ה, blessed is He, becomes pronounced and expressed relative to the opposing line, that is, he will despise all those who oppose *HaShem*-יהו"ה, blessed is He.

The quality of beauty-*Tiferet* that is within kindness-*Chessed* is the matter of the beautification and pride that arises from the quality of kindness-*Chessed*. For example, if he sees a person who studies Torah and fulfills the *mitzvot* in a pleasant and sweet manner (with delight), he takes pride in the beauty of Torah and *mitzvot*, in the measure (and to the extent that) the study of Torah can positively effect a person.

Furthermore, in addition to the inclusion of these three primary emotive qualities (kindness-*Chessed*, judgment-*Gevurah*, and beauty-*Tiferet* – *ChaGa"T*), the general quality of kindness-*Chessed* also includes the offshoots of these primary qualities, (that is, the emotive qualities of conquest-*Netzach*, majesty-*Hod*, and foundation-*Yesod*).

For example, the attribute of conquest-*Netzach* of the attribute of kindness-*Chessed* is when, because of his love of *HaShem*-יהו"ה, blessed is He, even when he faces obstacles and impediments, he nevertheless conquers himself, to overcome all obstacles and adversity in his service of *HaShem*-יהו"ה, blessed is He. Additionally, whenever there is any external opposition and he is overpowered and does not have strength, as in the verse,[585] "The multitudes rise up against me," nevertheless, because of his love of HaShem-יהו"ה, blessed is He, he will battle with those who oppose HaShem-יהו"ה, which is the matter of majesty-*Hod* within the quality of kindness-*Chessed*.

The matter of foundation-*Yesod* of kindness-*Chessed*, is that even if, for whatever reason, he does not feel drawn to Torah and *mitzvot*, nevertheless, because of his love of HaShem-יהו"ה, blessed is He, he will bind himself to Torah and *mitzvot* with all his soul, until he rouses a yearning and desire for Torah and the fulfillment of the commandments. He does so, to the point that all his thoughts, speech and action are solely invested and preoccupied with Torah and the fulfillment of the *mitzvot*, which is the matter of kingship-*Malchut* of kindness-*Chessed*.

Now, just as the attribute of kindness-*Chessed* includes all the other emotive qualities within it, so is it with each of the other emotive qualities. They each include all the other qualities.

Now, just as each of the emotive qualities of the Godly soul include all the other seven emotive qualities, it likewise is so with the animalistic soul, in that,[586] "God created one thing opposite the other." Thus, the quality of kindness-*Chessed* of kindness-*Chessed* of the animalistic soul, is the matter of his love for physical things, which is pronounced and manifest in the revealed yearnings and desires for physicality.

---

[585] Psalms 3:2
[586] Ecclesiastes 7:14; Tanya Ch. 6 and elsewhere.

The quality of judgment-*Gevurah* of kindness-*Chessed* of the animalistic soul, is that because of his love of physical things, he despises anything that opposes his desires for these matters. For example, if someone were to tell him, "It is inappropriate for you to be absorbed in these animalistic matters that are unbecoming of a human being," he will despise that person.

The quality of beauty-*Tiferet* of kindness-*Chessed* of the animalistic soul is that, in addition to the fact that he is drawn to physical matters, beyond that, he also takes pride, is excited (brags and is enthused) by the fact that he is drawn to physical matters.

The attribute of conquest-*Netzach* of kindness-*Chessed* of the animalistic soul, is that even if, for whatever reason, he lacks the pull to physical things, he conquers himself and arouses his desire. Beyond that, when there is any kind of external adversity, such as people who embarrass and degrade him, such as saying, "Look how a Jew, a son of Avraham, Yitzchak and Yaakov, is so deeply absorbed in animalistic behavior, even in forbidden matters," he nevertheless battles with himself, so that this should not distract him from fulfilling his lusts. This is the attribute of majesty-*Hod* of kindness-*Chessed* of the animalistic soul.

His lust thus becomes so great that he becomes completely bonded to the object of his lust, which is the matter of foundation-*Yesod* of kindness-*Chessed* of the animalistic soul. This continues to the point that all his thoughts, speech and actions are invested in coarse matters and he descends from level to level, until he comes into the category of forbidden matters entirely, which is the matter of kingship-*Malchut* of the attribute of kindness-*Chessed* of the animalistic soul.

5.

Now, the primary matter of refining the particulars of the emotive qualities is completed on the 33rd day of the Omer (*Lag BaOmer*-ל"ג בעומר),[587] which is the aspect of majesty-*Hod* within majesty-*Hod*. This is because this quality concludes the primary aspect of the emotive qualities.[588] The explanation is that majesty-*Hod* within majesty-*Hod* is the lowest level of the matter of acknowledgement and submission (*Hoda'ah*) itself,[589] in that he acknowledges and submits to the truth, even without understanding it intellectually.

An example for this is two people, one of whom is extremely wise and possesses a wondrous wisdom that is entirely beyond that of the masses, and another who is significantly less wise. In other words, although the second person has some general relationship to matters of intellect, nevertheless, he too does not understand the wondrous wisdom of the great sage. Nevertheless, because he indeed has some relationship to matters of intellect, although he does not fully understand the intellectual matter he hears from the great sage, he nonetheless recognizes that it is an extremely wondrous and

---

[587] See Siddur Im Divrei Elokim Chayim, Shaar Lag BaOmer 303c and on.
[588] See Shaar HaYichud – The Gate of Unity Ch. 36, and the notes there.
[589] The term majesty-*Hod*-הוד is related to the term submission or acknowledgement-*Hoda'ah*-הודאה.

deep intellectual matter. Therefore, although it is not possible to say that he actually knows or grasps it, nonetheless, he acknowledges it to be true (even though he does not understand), and submits to the wisdom of the great sage. This is because he can sense that this is an extremely deep and wondrous matter, and since he, at least, has some relationship to matters of intellect, at the very least, he understands that he must submit to the wisdom of the great sage, whether or not he fully comprehends it.

Now, in regard to a simpler person, who is not at all intellectual, it is not applicable to say about him that he even understands why he must acknowledge and submit to the wisdom of the great sage. Just the fact that he does acknowledge and submit to him, is itself acknowledgement and submission.[590]

This aspect is the matter of majesty-*Hod*-הוד of majesty-*Hod*-הוד, meaning a submission-*Hoda'ah*-הודאה of the submission-*Hoda'ah*-הודאה. In other words, it is when the majesty-*Hod*-הוד itself (the submission and acknowledgement-*Hoda'ah*-הודאה) is not because of his intellectual faculties of wisdom-*Chochmah*, understanding-*Binah* and knowledge-*Da'at* (*ChaBa"D*), nor is it because of his emotive faculties of kindness-*Chessed*, judgment-*Gevurah* or beauty-*Tiferet* (*ChaGa"T*). Instead, it is solely the matter of submission-*Hoda'ah*-הודאה itself.

---

[590] In other words, he acknowledges and submits that he must acknowledge and submit.

229

This is similar to our recitation of, *Modim D'Rabbanan*,[591] "We submit to You... that we submit to You." In other words, it is the aspect of submission and acknowledgement-*Hoda'ah*-הודאה of submission and acknowledgement-*Hoda'ah*-הודאה. This is the lowest level of holiness and it is regarding this that our sages, of blessed memory, stated,[592] "One who does not bow during the blessing of *Modim*-מודים, will not rise upon the resurrection of the dead." For, even if a person is lacking the matter of knowledge of *HaShem*-יהו"ה, blessed is He, nevertheless, since he at least knows that he must submit to *HaShem*-יהו"ה, there still is hope for him. Moreover, even if he is lacking in this knowledge itself, he nevertheless is able to cause himself to submit, just out of submission alone, without knowledge. That is, he can, at the very least, attain the level of majesty-*Hod*-הוד of majesty-*Hod*-הוד, meaning a submission-*Hoda'ah*-הודאה of the submission-*Hoda'ah*-הודאה, and therefore there is hope for him.

However, "One who does not bow during the blessing of *Modim*-מודים," indicates that he even lacks this manner of submission-*Hoda'ah*-הודאה of the submission-*Hoda'ah*-הודאה, and, "his spine turns into a snake,"[593] indicating that he has no connection to matters of holiness.

From the above, we can now understand the connection between the 33rd day of the Omer (*Lag BaOmer*-ל"ג בעומר) and Rabbi Shimon bar Yochai. Rabbi Shimon bar Yochai affected

[591] The "Rabbinic acknowledgement" (*Modim dRabbanan*) recited during the repetition of the *Shmonah Esreh* prayer.
[592] Talmud Bavli, Bava Kamma 16a; Zohar II 100a & Zohar III 164a
[593] Talmud Bavli, Bava Kamma 16a ibid.

a bond between the Depth of the heights (*Omek Rom*) and the depths below (*Omek Tachat*) (as explained before[594]). Because of this, the revelation of the Depth of the Heights (*Omek Rom*), at its very root in the Height of all heights, was specifically on the 33rd day of the Omer (*Lag BaOmer*-ל"ג בעומר), which corresponds to the *Sefirah* of majesty-*Hod*-הוד within majesty-*Hod*-הוד, which is the lowest level of service of *HaShem*-יהו"ה. For, with this attribute there is a completion of the service of refining the primary aspects of the emotive qualities, and it then is possible for the, "pipes," to be opened, so that a drawing forth and revelation of the Root of all roots from the Height of all heights, can occur, through which every single Jew attains a revelation of the inner aspect of Torah.

The power that causes this, "opening of the pipe," is specifically through the service of *HaShem*-יהו"ה, blessed is He, in a way of majesty-*Hod*-הוד of majesty-*Hod*-הוד, which is the matter of submission to *HaShem*-יהו"ה and accepting the yoke of the kingdom of Heaven upon oneself, that is, the yoke of Torah[595] (as explained before[596]). In other words, he does not take the restrictions of time and place into consideration whatsoever, in that his whole service of *HaShem*-יהו"ה is not according to the limitations of reason and intellect. Thus, not only do time and space not conceal or hide Godliness from him,

---

[594] In the Sicha talk that preceded this discourse, printed in Torat Menachem Vol. 3, p. 75 (chapter 5).

[595] See Midrash Bamidbar Rabba 18:21; Midrash Shmuel Ch. 29; *Hemshech* 5666 p. 406-407.

[596] In the Sicha talk that preceded this discourse, printed in Torat Menachem Vol. 3, p. 72 and on (chapter 2 and on).

but on the contrary, even within the constraints of time and space he actualizes the matter of,[597] "You shall count for yourselves-*U'Sephartem Lachem*-וספרתם לכם."[598]

6.

It is for this reason that the verse specifically states,[599] "You shall count for yourselves – from the morrow of the day of rest." The explanation is that the entire chaining down of the worlds (*Hishtalshelut*) was established in a manner of front (*Kadimah*) and back (*Achor*), that is, in a way of, "reaching and not reaching"[600] (*Mati V'Lo Mati*). In general, this refers to the matter of time and the ordering of the times.[601]

Now, for there to be this matter of, "You shall count for yourselves," which refers to the refinement of the entire chaining down of the worlds (*Hishtalshelut*), up to and including the aspect of the "depth below" (*Omek Tachat*), the power and ability to actualize this is from the aspect of, "from the morrow of the day of rest," which transcends the entire matter of time.[602]

---

[597] Leviticus 23:15

[598] The term count-*Sphar*-ספר is related to the term to "shine-*Sapir*-ספיר," indicating that he even causes time and space, and all therein, to radiate and be illuminated with the Godliness that brings it into being and vitalizes it at every moment.

[599] Leviticus 23:15

[600] Zohar I 16b; Etz Chaim Shaar 7 (Shaar Mati V'Lo Mati)

[601] Sefer HaMitzvot of the Tzemach Tzeddek 57b & 59a

[602] See Likkutei Torah Emor 35d; Ohr HaTorah Vayikra Vol. 1 p. 167 & Vol. 3, p. 869 and elsewhere.

This is because the highest level within time is the matter of the day of rest – Shabbat. That is, following the six mundane days of the week, comes the day of rest – Shabbat, which is sanctified and holy relative to all the other days. This is as stated,[603] "Shabbat is established as holy and sanctified." Even so, it still is within the category of time, as the verse states,[604] "In six-days *HaShem*-יהו״ה made heavens and earth and on the seventh day He rested and was refreshed." Now, since it still is within the category of time, even though it is a time of holiness, its holiness is only sufficient to transform itself,[605] but is insufficient in transforming the folly of the opposing side of evil.

Thus, when it comes to the matter of, "You shall count for yourselves," which is the matter of refinement, even to the point of transforming the, "depths of below" (*Omek Tachat*), the power and ability to actualize this, specifically comes from the aspect of, "from **the morrow** of the day of rest – Shabbat." That is, the strength to accomplish this even transcends the matter of Shabbat, which, "is established as holy and sanctified." That is, it must be drawn from higher than the entire chaining down of the worlds (*Hishtalshelut*).

The explanation is that at the time of the exodus from Egypt, there was an awakening from *HaShem*-יהו״ה Above, as previously explained regarding the verse,[606] "the people had fled." This also was a general preparation for the giving of the

---

603 Talmud Bavli, Beitzah 17a
604 Exodus 31:17
605 A play on Talmud Bavli Bechorot 5a
606 Exodus 14:5

Torah, through the fact that the King, King of kings, the Holy One, blessed is He, revealed Himself to them and redeemed them. We recite this in the Haggadah,[607] "I and not an angel... I and not a Saraph... I and not a messenger... I and no other!" That is, the Holy One, blessed is He, in His full glory, redeemed the Jewish people from Egypt, Himself.

The reason[608] is that, since the Jewish people were sunken in the depths of the forty-nine gates of impurity, if anyone else, other than *HaShem*-יהו"ה Himself, would have come to redeem them, even if he were coming from the loftiest levels of holiness, not only would he not have been able to take the Jewish people out, but on the contrary etc.[609] It therefore was specifically necessary for the King, King of kings, the Holy One, blessed is He, Himself to come, for He utterly transcends everything and has no relation whatsoever to the chaining down of the worlds (*Hishtalshelut*). This is the meaning of the verse,[610] "And *HaShem*-יהו"י will pass over," which refers to the matter of a leap (*Dilug*) that transcends the entire chaining down of the worlds (*Hishtalshelut*).[611]

---

[607] Haggadah for Pesach - "*Vayotzi'einu*"

[608] Siddur of the Arizal, Haggadah shel Pesach; Likkutei Torah Tzav 12c and elsewhere.

[609] It is explained (in the Likkutei Torah Tzav 12c and on ibid.) that had the exodus from Egypt been by the hand of an emissary, it would have been possible for the extraneous husks of evil (*Kelipot*) to derive influence and become strengthened, God forbid.

[610] Exodus 12:23

[611] See Likkutei Torah, Shir HaShirim 15b; Discourse entitled "*Kol Dodi*" (1 & 2) and discourse entitled "*U'Sefartem*" 5636 (Sefer HaMaamarim 5636 p. 164 and on; p. 169 and on; p. 211).

It is the same when the Jewish people were given the commandment to count the Omer, which applies to all time. That is, when they were told, "You shall count-*U'Sephartem*-וספרתם for yourselves," meaning that they should illuminate and shine-*Sphurim*-ספורים for all forty-nine days, in that they are to be refined and purified,[612] they were informed that they would be given the ability to do so, "from the **morrow** of the day of rest – Shabbat." That is, they were given the ability to do this from **beyond** the order of the chaining down of the worlds (*Hishtalshelut*) entirely, even beyond all the levels of the side of holiness, and even beyond the level of "Shabbat which is established as holy and sanctified."

Thus, when this aspect of "the morrow of the day of rest" is drawn forth, and the service of "You shall illuminate-*U'Sephartem*-וספרתם yourselves" is performed, they then are capable of finally coming to the subsequent aspect of,[613] "the King has brought me into His chambers," which refers to the giving of the Torah. For, it is specifically then that the revelation of[614] "I am-*Anochi*-אנכי,"[615] which is an acronym for "I have placed My soul in My writings-*Ana Nafshi Katavit Yahavit*-אנא נפשי כתבית יהבית," took place. That is, we were given the very Essential Self of *HaShem*-יהו"ה, the Singular Intrinsic Unlimited Being Himself, blessed is He.

---

[612] Likkutei Torah, Emor ibid; Pardes Rimonim Shaar 8, Ch. 2

[613] Song of Songs 1:4

[614] Exodus 20:2; Talmud Bavli Shabbat 105a (Ein Yaakov version of the text); Likkutei Torah Shlach 48d and on; Tanya Ch. 47

[615] The first word of the Ten Commandments (Exodus 20:2) that states, "I am HaShem, your God-*Anochi HaShem Elohe"cha*-אנכי יהו"ה אלהי"ך."

7.

However, in preparation for this, there is the intermediary matter of the 33rd day of the Omer (*Lag BaOmer*), which is when a revelation of the inner aspect of the Torah takes place.[616] In other words, although according to the order of the chaining down (*Hishtalshelut*) of Torah study, one is to first study the revealed aspects of Torah and only afterward come to study the inner aspects of Torah, nonetheless, he should know that the very matter that gives him the ability to learn in this order, is the fact that it was preceded by the matter of the 33rd day of the Omer (*Lag BaOmer*-ל"ג בעומר). In other words, the revelation of the inner aspects of Torah is what empowers the study of the revealed aspects of Torah, for them to be learned properly, as they should be. This is true, even though it is through the revealed aspects of Torah, that one comes to the inner aspect of Torah.

The explanation is as follows: King David requested,[617] "Open my eyes-*Gal Einai*-ג"ל עיני, that I may behold wondrous things (*Nifla'ot*-נפלאות) from Your Torah." Although he certainly did not only study the revealed aspects of Torah, but also its inner aspects, nevertheless, he did not arrive at the level of beholding, "wondrous things-*Nifla'ot*-נפלאות from Your Torah." The reason is because these, "wonders-*Nifla'ot*-נפלאות"

---

[616] Sefer HaMaamarim 5704 p. 211; See discourse entitled "*LeHaveen Inyan Hilulah d'Rashbi*" and discourse entitled "*Gal Einei*" 5737 (Sefer HaMaamarim 5737 p. 214; p. 216; p. 230).

[617] Psalms 119:18; Also see *Hemshech* entitled "*Chayav Adam*" 5638, Ch. 23 and on (*Sefer HaMaamarim* 5638 p. 147 and on).

will only be revealed in the coming future.[618] As stated about the coming future,[619] "Like the days when you went out of Egypt, I will show you wonders-*Nifla'ot*-נפלאות." The word "wonders-*Nifla'ot*-נפלאות" divides into "*Nun*-נ-50 wonders-*Pla'ot*-פלאות,"[620] and refers to the Fiftieth Gate of Understanding (*Sha'ar HaNun*-שער הנו"ן), which will be revealed in the coming future.[621]

Nevertheless, this revelation began on the 33rd day of the Omer (*Lag BaOmer*-ל"ג בעומר), through Rabbi Shimon bar Yochai. For it was he who, "opened the pipe," thus allowing for the fulfillment of, "Open my eyes-*Gal Einai*-ג"ל עיני that I may behold wondrous things-*Nifla'ot*-נ"פלאות from Your Torah." This is specifically true of the day of his passing, on the 33rd day of the Omer – *Lag BaOmer*-ל"ג בעומר – upon which there was this matter of, "Open my eyes-*Gal Einai*-ג"ל עיני."[622] For, although it is true that throughout his life Rabbi Shimon bar Yochai taught the secrets of the Torah, nonetheless, on the day of his passing, he revealed, "hidden secrets that were never revealed before."[623] It thus is as he stated,[624] "There will not be another generation like his generation until the generation of Moshiach," for in that time, there will be the complete revelation of what Rabbi Shimon bar Yochai began to open up.

---

[618] See Rashi commentary to Song of Songs 1:2; Likkutei Torah Tzav 17a and on.

[619] Micah 7:15

[620] Zohar I 261b

[621] See Ohr HaTorah Na"Ch to Micah 7:15 (Vol. 1 p. 487).

[622] See Pri Etz Chaim, Shaar Sefirat HaOmer, Ch. 7

[623] See Idra Zuta, Zohar III 287b; 290a; 291a

[624] Zohar II 147a; Zohar III 58a & 159a

Now, it is well known that each and every year there is a reawakening of all the matters and the general state that took place in the original event.[625] Thus, as we stand here today, on the 33rd day of the Omer (*Lag BaOmer*-ל"ג בעומר) and are moved to bond ourselves to the study of the inner teachings of Torah, to follow in the way paved by Rabbi Shimon bar Yochai and to draw it forth throughout the whole year, then this is indeed a preparation and introduction to the giving of the Torah, in which,[626] "the King has brought me into His chambers."

It is also an auspicious time to request, actualize (and invite) that the request of King David be fulfilled, namely,[627] "Open my eyes that I may behold wondrous things (*Nifla'ot*-נפלאות) from **Your** Torah." That is, all of Your Torah, both the study of the revealed parts of Torah and the study of the secrets of Torah, should be with the revelation of wonders-*Nifla'ot*-נפלאות, culminating with the coming of our righteous Moshiach, speedily in our days, who will study the inner aspects of Torah with the entire Jewish people.[628]

---

[625] See RaMa"Z in the book Tikkun Shovevim, cited and explained in the book Lev David (of the ChiDa"H), Ch. 29.

[626] Song of Songs 1:4

[627] Psalms 119:18; Also see *Hemshech* entitled "*Chayav Adam*" 5638, Ch. 23 and on (*Sefer HaMaamarim* 5638 p. 147 and on).

[628] Likkutei Torah Tzav Ibid.

Discourse 10

"V'Heet'halachti BeTochechem -
I will walk within you"

Delivered on Shabbat Mevarchim Sivan,
Parshat Bechukotai, 5711
By the grace of *HaShem*, blessed is He,

1.

The verse states,[629] "I will walk within you, I will be a God for you and you will be a people for Me. I am *HaShem*-יהו״ה your God, who took you out of the land of Egypt, from being their slaves; I broke the rods of your yoke and I caused you to walk upright." Now, we must understand the greatness of the matter of, "I will walk within you," for which reason the portion begins with the words,[630] "If you will walk in the way of My decrees," only then, "I will walk within you." For, there is another verse that states,[631] "You shall walk after *HaShem*-יהו״ה your God." Similarly, the verse states,[632] "to love *HaShem*-יהו״ה your God, to walk in all His ways and cleave to Him," about which our sages, of blessed memory, stated,[633]

---

[629] Leviticus 26:12-13
[630] Leviticus 26:3
[631] Deuteronomy 13:5
[632] Deuteronomy 11:22
[633] Sifri to Deuteronomy 11:22; Rambam Hilchot De'ot 1:5; Sefer HaMitzvot of the Rambam, positive commandment 8; Shulchan Aruch of the Alter Rebbe,

"Just as He is compassionate, so too, you be compassionate; Just as He is merciful, so too, you be merciful etc." This being the case, there already is a **constant** requirement of, "walking in the ways of the Holy One, blessed is He." What exactly is newly introduced by the matter of, "I will walk within you," that specifically only happens, "If you walk in the way of My decrees?"

We also must understand the meaning of the conclusion of the verse, "and I caused you to walk upright," meaning,[634] "upright in stature." The Talmud[635] presents two views regarding the words "VaOleich Etchem Komemiyut- ואולך אתכם קוממיות," which can also be read in the future tense, "And I will cause you walk upright." One view is that in the coming future, the Jewish people will have the stature of one-hundred cubits, corresponding to the measure of the Sanctuary (Heichal) and its walls, which are one-hundred cubits. The second view is that the term "upright-Komemiyut-קוממיות," in the plural, indicates two times the "height-komot" of Adam, the first man, which is two-hundred cubits. Now, we must understand what all this means, and what its superiority is, over and above the constant requirement to walk in His ways, mentioned above.

We also must understand an additional matter of superiority that we find regarding these promises, "If you walk in the way of My decrees" then "I will walk within you... and will cause you to walk upright," in relation to all the other

Orach Chayim 156:3; Also see Mechilta Beshalach 15:2; Talmud Bavli, Shabbat 133b.
[634] Rashi to Leviticus 26:13
[635] Talmud Bavli, Bava Batra 75a; Sanhedrin 100a

promises stated in this Torah Portion. That is, all the other promises do not dependent on any specific time, such as the coming future, but can be fulfilled at any and all times. In other words, **at all times** that the Jewish people, "walk in the way of My decrees...I will provide your rains in their time and the land will give its produce and the tree of the field will give its fruit."[636] The same applies to all of *HaShem's*-יהו"ה other promises. Proof of this can be found in Tractate Ta'anit,[637] that in the times of Shimon ben Shetach the wheat grew as big as kidneys, similar to what will happen in the coming future.[638] However, regarding this matter of the wheat growing as big as kidneys, it could be said that this was just a foretaste of how it will be in the coming future.

Nevertheless, we find[639] that even regarding *HaShem's*-יהו"ה promise, "I will provide peace in the land...and no sword will pass through your land,"[640] that based on this promise, King Yoshiyahu did not allow Pharaoh to pass peacefully through the land of Israel, on his way to wage war against Nebuchadnezzar. This is because he understood the words, "**no** sword will pass through your land," to not just mean a warring sword, since the verse already promised, "I will provide peace in the land," and the intent of the additional words, "no sword will pass through your land," which at first glance seem to be

---

[636] Leviticus 26:4 and on
[637] Talmud Bavli, Taanit 23a
[638] Deuteronomy 32:14; Talmud Bavli, Ketuvot 111b
[639] Talmud Bavli, Taanit 22a
[640] Leviticus 26:6

superfluous, comes to include even a sword that wishes to peaceably pass through the land.

The reality of *HaShem*'s-יהו״ה promise was so engrained in Yoshiyahu, in a way of such simplicity, that he did not even consult with the prophet Jeremiah about his decision. And although he was punished for it, the punishment was not because he had misinterpreted the verses, but only because his generation was unworthy of this blessing.[641] However, barring this, the promise itself should have been fulfilled, even at that time.

Through these examples, it is understood that the promises in this Torah portion are not dependent upon any specific time, such that they should only occur in the coming future. In contrast, about the promise mentioned above, that "I will walk within you... and I will cause you to walk upright," the Ramban[642] and Rabbeinu Bachaya[643] both wrote, "Know, that the Jewish people never attained these blessings in their totality (neither in the time of the first Holy Temple, nor in the time of the second Holy Temple). This is true both of the Jewish people as a whole, as well as the special individuals amongst them (even including those special individuals who attained perfection). Rather, this will only happen in the coming redemption, in the times of the Third Holy Temple."

Therefore, we must further understand the superiority of this matter of, "I will walk within you," (in contrast to the

---

[641] Talmud Bavli, Taanit 23a ibid.
[642] Ramban to Leviticus 26:12
[643] Rabbeinu Bachaya to Parshat Bechukotai 26:9,13

constant presence of *HaShem*-יהו"ה, mentioned before, that is accessible at all times), and "I will cause you to walk upright," (with the upright stature and the doubled stature). We must understand why this only will be completed to perfection specifically in the coming future, when the true and complete redemption comes about, may it be speedily in our times.

The general matter[644] may be understood from the use of the term, "*VeHeet'halachti*-והתהלכתי," as opposed to the term "*VeHalachti*-והלכתי." Although both terms mean, "I will walk," nonetheless, the term "*VeHeet'halachti*-והתהלכתי" is a usage of emphasis, in a doubled manner, which indicates a constant, "walking within you." In other words, the use of the term "*VeHeet'halachti*-והתהלכתי" means, "I will walk within you continuously." Moreover, the doubled term "*VeHeet'halachti*-והתהלכתי" indicates two modes of "walking," a walking from Above to below and a walking from below to Above, and that they both happen simultaneously, just as they are included in a single term. This also explains the words, "and I will cause you to walk upright-*Komemiyut*-קוממיות," which also is in the plural form and doubled. It likewise indicates two "heights-*Komot*-קומות," in the plural, as mentioned above, and that both come as one, as they too are included in a single term.

---

[644] Imrei Beinah Shaar HaKriyat Shema, Ch. 88; Discourse entitled "*VeHeet'halachti*" of the Alter Rebbe in Hanachot HaRav Pinchas p. 157; 5569 p. 131 and on; Maamarei Admor HaEmtza'ee Vayikra Vol. 2 p. 786 and on & p. 876 and on; Ohr HaTorah Vayikra Vol. 2, p. 640, p. 654, p. 677, p. 682, and elsewhere.

2.

Now, in order to understand this superiority of the term "*VeHeet'halachti*-והתהלכתי*," which indicates the two forms of "walking" at the same time, we must first preface with the explanation of the difference between these two forms of "walking," and the advantage that each has over the other.

This may be understood through the well-known[645] analogy of two people, one standing above, on top of a high mountain and the other, standing below, in a valley. These two can meet in two ways. Either the one above descends below or the one below ascends above.

Now, the difference between these two ways is as follows: In order for the one below to ascend above, there are certain preconditions.[646] Firstly, he must know all the paths and ways by which to ascend the mountain. Secondly, he must have great strength and stamina to ascend the mountain. Thirdly, he must have the appropriate clothing to ascend the mountain. That is, not only should his garments not obstruct his ascent, but in addition, they should actually assist him in his ascent.

This may likewise be understood in man's service of *HaShem*-יהו״ה, blessed is He, as it states,[647] "Who may ascend the mountain of *HaShem*-יהו״ה etc." Thus, in man's ascension of "the mountain of *HaShem*-יהו״ה," there likewise are several prerequisites. Firstly, he must know all the paths and ways by

---

[645] See Likkutei Torah Re'eh 26a & 28b

[646] See *Hemshech* 5672 Vol. 2, p. 777 and on; Sefer HaMaamarim 5698 p. 149; Sefer HaSichot 5699 p. 316

[647] Psalms 24:3

which to ascend the mountain. In other words, he must know the path of *HaShem*-יהו״ה, blessed is He, which refers to the matter of Torah and *mitzvot* generally. In this, one must know the correct pathways. Namely, his study of Torah must be with the proper approach, and beyond that, it must be for the sake of the Name of *HaShem*-יהו״ה, blessed is He, and not for any selfish motives.[648]

It is about this that Talmud states,[649] "What is the meaning of the verse,[650] 'And the faith of your times shall be the strength of your salvations, wisdom, and knowledge; the fear of *HaShem*-יהו״ה is His treasure.' 'Faith' refers to the Mishnaic order of *Zera'im*-Seeds. 'Your times' refers to the Mishnaic order of *Mo'ed*-Festivals. 'Strength' refers to the Mishnaic order of *Nashim*-Women. 'Salvations' refers to the Mishnaic order of *Nezikin*-Damages. 'Wisdom' refers to the Mishnaic order of *Kodashim*-Consecrated Items. 'Knowledge' refers to the Mishnaic order of *Taharot*-Purity. However, even if a person studies all these, 'the fear of *HaShem*-יהו״ה is His treasure.'" In other words, the **primary** matter is the fear of *HaShem*-יהו״ה.

This is as further indicated in the continuation of the Talmudic discussion there, which states: "When a person is brought to judgment after departing from this world, they ask him: 'Did you conduct your business honestly? Did you

---

[648] See Kuntres Etz HaChayim, Ch. 12; Also see Tzavaat HaRivash translated as The Way of the Baal Shem Tov, Section 95 (also see Sections 2, 55, 65, and elsewhere).

[649] Talmud Bavli, Shabbat 31a

[650] Isaiah 33:6

245

designate times for the study of Torah? Did you bring children into the world? Did you await the salvation? Did you engage in wisdom? Did you understand one matter from another? Even if he did all these, if the fear of *HaShem*-יהו"ה is his treasure, then he is worthy, but if not, then he is not. This is analogous[651] to a man who said to his agent: 'Bring a *kor* of wheat up to the attic storeroom for me.' He went and brought it up for him. He said to the agent: 'Did you mix a *kav* of *chomton* into it for me?' He responded, 'no.' He then said to him: 'It would have been preferable if you had not brought it up at all.'" The *kav* of *chomton* is a preservative that keeps the worms away from the wheat (as Rashi explains). In other words, this agent had no reason, understanding or comprehension etc., which are the primary aspects that lead to fear of *HaShem*-יהו"ה and the acceptance of the yoke of Heaven.

How much more so is it the case, that one's learning must not be in a manner of studying the Torah of *HaShem*-יהו"ה, but not fulfilling what he studies. (This certainly applies to a person whose Torah learning is only in order to argue and vex his fellows.[652]) For, regarding such people the verse states,[653] "But to the wicked God said: 'To what purpose do you recount My decrees and bear My covenant upon your lips? For you hate discipline and have thrown My words behind you.'" In other words, if he is not meritorious, his Torah study becomes the

---

[651] Also see Likkutei Torah Vayikra 6a; Shlach 46c and on, and elsewhere.

[652] See Tosefot entitled "*HaOseh*" to Brachot 17a; Also see Likkutei Sichot Vol. 20, p. 50 and on.

[653] Psalms 50:16-17

very opposite of an elixir of life for him,[654] and in doing so, he actually increases the vitality of the external husks of evil (*Kelipah*), at least temporarily, as stated by the Alter Rebbe in the laws of Torah study.[655]

The same applies to ones fulfillment of the *mitzvot*. They must specifically be performed as properly as they should be. This is as stated in Talmud,[656] that there can be a person who fulfills the commandment of honoring his father and mother, but receives purgatory because of it, since the way he honors them is actually degrading to them. The same applies to the fulfillment of all other commandments as well. They must be fulfilled properly and only for the sake of the Name of *HaShem*-יהו"ה, absent of any selfish motives.

Now, in addition to knowing the pathways (*Drachim*-דרכים) of *HaShem*-יהו"ה, one must also know the trails (*Netivot*-נתיבות). The difference between the two,[657] is that the pathways (*Drachim*-דרכים) are like paved and well-trodden roads, upon which the masses travel. In contrast, the trails (*Netivot*-נתיבות) are very narrow and untrodden paths. In other words, the trails (*Netivot*-נתיבות) by which one ascends the mountain of *HaShem*-יהו"ה, blessed is He, is the matter of grasping actual Godliness, through which one is automatically brought to love

---

[654] Talmud Bavli, Yoma 72b

[655] Hilchot Talmud Torah 4:3

[656] Talmud Bavli, Kiddushin 31a

[657] See Ohr HaTorah Na"Ch Vol. 1 p. 554; Also see Tzava'at HaRivash translated into English as The Way of the Baal Shem Tov, Num. 140.

and fear *HaShem*-יהו"ה,[658] blessed is He, by which he ascends the mountain of *HaShem*-יהו"ה.

Now, all the above, is only in regard to ones Godly soul. However, to be able to cause his animalistic soul to also ascend with him, there is a second prerequisite, namely, that he must have great strength.[659] In other words, not only should he not allow his "materiality[660] to crouch under its burden,"[661] but on the contrary, he even must take his animalistic soul along with him.

The third requirement is that he must garb himself with the appropriate clothing. In other words, not only should his garments not be obstructive,[662] but he must don garments that will assist his ascent. The explanation is that the garments refer to the letters of thought and the letters of speech and action.[663] They have two aspects; the vitality and feeling manifest in the letters and the letters themselves. The refinement and rectification of the vitality in the letters, is accomplished through serving *HaShem*-יהו"ה, blessed is He, with love and fear. That is, through contemplation (*Hitbonenut*) in matters of

---

[658] See Rambam, Hilchot Yesodei HaTorah 2:2; Also see Kuntres HaHitpa'alut of the Mittler Rebbe, translated as Divine Inspiration for a lengthy explanation of all levels of attainment of love and fear of *HaShem*-יהו"ה, blessed is He, that result from different levels of grasp and comprehension of Godliness through *Hitbonenut* contemplation.

[659] Mishnah Avot 4:1; Rambam Hilchot Yesodei HaTorah 7:1

[660] Igrot Kodesh of the Rebbe Rayatz, Vol. 3 p. 325; HaYom Yom 28 Shvat. The word "donkey-*Chamor*-חמור" of this verse is being translated homiletically as "materiality-*Chomer*-חומר." (Also see Tzava'at HaRivash translated as The Way of The Baal Shem Tov, Section 100.)

[661] Exodus 23:5

[662] See Likkutei Torah Teitzei 37c; Sefer HaMitzvot of the Tzemach Tzeddek 107b.

[663] See Tanya, Ch. 4

the comprehension of Godliness, love and fear of *HaShem*-יהו"ה are born in him,[664] and these are the, "wings by which he flies up."[665]

However, the rectification of the letters themselves is accomplished through tears, as stated,[666] "O' wall of the daughter of Zion, shed tears like a river." The tears are brought about by his mind being crushed. This happens when he contemplates how he was separate from the Essential Being of the Unlimited One, *HaShem*-יהו"ה, blessed is He, (even if only temporarily, nevertheless, the fact that he subsequently repented, does not change the fact that, at that time, he could have been bonded with the Essential Being of the Unlimited One, *HaShem*-יהו"ה, blessed is He, but was separate from the Essential Self of *HaShem*-יהו"ה). This causes his heart to be crushed and his mind to be crushed, through which he is brought to tears. For, this is something that he is incapable of expressing in letters and his mind cannot bear it. These tears rectify the letters themselves, in that they tear down the wall of the side of evil, and rebuild the, "wall of the daughter of Zion."

---

[664] Rambam, Hilchot Yesodei HaTorah 2:1-2; Also see Kuntres HaHitpa'alut of the Mittler Rebbe, translated as Divine Inspiration for a lengthy explanation of all levels of attainment of love and fear of *HaShem*-יהו"ה, blessed is He, that result from different levels of grasp and comprehension of Godliness through *Hitbonenut* contemplation. Also see Shaar HaYichud of the Mittler Rebbe, translated as The Gate of Unity, Ch. 1-6 regarding the approach and method of *Hitbonenut* contemplation itself, and the resultant levels of love and fear of *HaShem*-יהו"ה, blessed is He, that are the automatic result of proper contemplation.

[665] Tikkunei Zohar, Tikkun 10 (25b); Tanya Ch. 40 (55b); Shaar HaYichud – The Gate of Unity, Ch. 6 ibid.; Also see at greater length in the first eleven chapters of Derech Chayim of the Mittler Rebbe, translated as The Path of Life.

[666] Lamentations 2:18; Shaarei Orah of the Mittler Rebbe, discourse entitled "*B'Chaf Hey b'Kislev*" Ch. 11-12; Sefer HaMaamarim 5665 p. 216; *Hemshech* 5666 p. 266.

Thus, it is specifically when he has attained all three abovementioned preconditions and prerequisites, that he has the appropriate garments, he has great strength, and he knows the pathways and trails, specifically then, he can ascend the mountain of *HaShem*-יהו״ה, blessed is He.

The same is true regarding the matter of ascension to the Garden of Eden (*Gan Eden*),[667] which is called,[668] "the mountain of *HaShem*-יהו״ה." For, just as a physical mountain is inanimate, but rises high above, so likewise, the matter of the Garden of Eden (*Gan Eden*) is that it is the ascension from below to Above.[669] Now, in order for a person to ascend from this world to the Garden of Eden, he must traverse the River of Fire (*Nahar Deenor*) specifically. This is because to enter the Garden of Eden one must first forget all the visions of this world.[670] In the same manner, even the ascension from the lower Garden of Eden (*Gan Eden HaTachton*) to the upper Garden of Eden (*Gan Eden HaElyon*) requires traversing the River of Fire (*Nahar Deenor*). This likewise, is in order to forget the visions of the lower Garden of Eden. For, even the visions of the lower Garden of Eden are distracting and confusing, relative to those of the upper Garden of Eden.[671]

---

[667] This refers to the Supernal levels of comprehension and grasp of Godliness. See Ginat Egoz of Rabbi Yosef Gikatilla, translated into English as HaShem is One, Vol. 1, The Gate of the Sanctuary, and Vol. 2, section entitled "The seven letters בג״ד כפר״ת correspond to the seven chambers of purgatory."

[668] Also see *Hemshech* 5672 ibid. pg. 779.

[669] See Ateret Rosh, Shaar Rosh HaShanah Ch. 24; Maamarei Admor HaEmtza'ee, Dvarim Vol. 2, p. 664; Drushei Chatunah Vol. 1 p. 210 & p. 304.

[670] See Zohar I 201a; II 211b & 247a; Torah Ohr, Yitro 69c; Maamarei Admor HaEmtza'ee Vayikra Vol. 2 p. 821 and on.

[671] See Zohar ibid.

This is similar[672] to what we find in relation to Rabbi Zeira,[673] that, "when he ascended to the Land of Israel and needed to study the Jerusalem Talmud, he fasted one-hundred fasts in order to forget the Babylonian Talmud." This is because,[674] "the way of the Babylonian Talmud is like the verse,[675] 'He has made me dwell in dark places, as those that have been long dead.'" In other words, it is confusing relative to the Jerusalem Talmud. It is the same with the Garden of Eden. That is, the ascent from the lower Garden of Eden to the upper Garden of Eden is through traversing the River of Fire (*Nehar Deenor*) in order to forget the visions of the lower Garden of Eden, which are confusing relative to the upper Garden of Eden.[676]

Now, in addition to the matter of the River of Fire (*Nehar Deenor*), there is also the matter of the pillar that stands between the lower and upper Gardens of Eden and connects them.[677] It is through this pillar that he becomes subsumed in essence to the higher level.[678] This matter likewise applies to

---

[672] See Torah Ohr, Yitro ibid.; *Hemshech* 5666 p. 13; Also see the later discourse of this year entitled "*The Torah preceded this world by two thousand years.*"

[673] Talmud Bavli, Bava Metziyah 85a

[674] Talmud Bavli, Sanhedrin 24a

[675] Lamentations 3:6

[676] That is, the comparison between the lower Garden of Eden and the upper Garden of Eden are like the comparison between the body and the soul. (See Ginat Egoz of Rabbi Yosef Gikatilla, translated as HaShem is One, Vol. 2 ibid.)

[677] See the famous letter written by the Baal Shem Tov to his brother-in-law, Rabbi Gershon Kitover (Keter Shem Tov 1) translated in the introduction to The Way of The Baal Shem Tov. Also see Rambam Hilchot Yesodei HaTorah 1:1.

[678] See Maamarei Admor HaEmtza'ee Vayikra Vol. 2, p. 822; Torah Ohr Yitro Ibid.; *Hemshech* 5666 p. 15; *Hemshech* 5672 p. 780 and on; Sefer HaMaamarim 5698 p. 212.

the myriads of different levels of the lower Garden of Eden and the upper Garden of Eden. For, as known,[679] although we generally mention only two levels of the Garden of Eden, in reality, there are myriads of levels to no end, which is the matter of the three ascensions that one is to make each day, during the three prayers of the day. Thus, since there are innumerable levels through which one ascends from one rung to the higher rung, this likewise requires that each ascent is preceded by the nullification of the previous level, through which he then is able to ascend to an even higher level, to no end. This is the meaning of the teaching,[680] "Torah scholars have no rest, even in the coming world, as stated,[681] 'They go from strength to strength, every one of them appears before God in Zion.'"

Thus, the general matter of ascensions in the Garden of Eden depends on the manner in which one serves *HaShem*-יהו״ה, blessed is He, below. In other words, according to the manner that the soul serves *HaShem*-יהו״ה, as it is in this lowly world, will be the manner of its ascent in the Garden of Eden. Thus, there are souls who only merit to ascend to the lower Garden of Eden, and there are souls who ascend to the upper Garden of Eden. Nevertheless, even the souls who merit to ascend to the upper Garden of Eden, must first pass through the lower Garden of Eden, and so on. All this is regarding the path of ascent, from below to Above, which is dependent on how the

---

[679] Torah Ohr Tetzaveh 81c
[680] Talmud Bavli, Brachot 64a; Mo'ed Katan
[681] Psalms 84:8

lower one prepares himself and the manner of his service of
HaShem-יהו"ה, blessed is He.

3.

However, the journey from Above to below does not
require the aforementioned preconditions, since, The One
Above certainly knows the pathways (*Drachim*) and trails
(*Netivot*), and He also has great strength. In other words, aside
for the fact that to descend from Above to below one does not
need great strength, and the only strength he needs, is to restrain
Himself and descend, the One Above is certainly strong.
Moreover, the requirement of garments is not relevant for the
descent below. Moreover, not only are they not necessary to
the One Above, but they likewise are not relevant from the
angle of the one below, in that the garments of the one below
are not relevant in this case.

For example, this is like the giving of the Torah, which
was in a manner of drawing down from Above to below, as it
states,[682] "And *HaShem*-יהו"ה descended upon Mount Sinai," in
which the state of the lower ones was not relevant. For, about
the exodus from Egypt it states,[683] "the people fled." This is
explained (in Tanya[684]) as follows, "At first glance, it seems
strange: Why would it have been so? Had they demanded of
Pharaoh that he set them free forever, would he not have been

---

[682] Exodus 19:20
[683] Exodus 14:5
[684] Tanya Ch. 31; Likkutei Torah Vayikra 3a; Emor 35b; Also see the prior
discourse 9 entitled "*U'Sefartem Lachem* – You shall count for yourselves."

forced to do so? Rather, the explanation of the matter is that the evil that was in the souls of the Jewish people was still strong in the left chamber of the heart etc." Thus, on account of the body and the animalistic soul, it was necessary for there to be this aspect of "fleeing." Even though this was subsequently followed by the service of *HaShem*-יהו״ה, blessed is He, through the counting of the Omer (*Sefirat HaOmer*),[685] nevertheless, the revelations of the giving of the Torah were entirely beyond comparison to their service of the counting of the Omer (*Sefirat HaOmer*).

We thus find that the general revelation of the giving of the Torah was in a manner of descent from Above to below, wherein the state of the lower was irrelevant. Moreover, this revelation from Above to below caused their impurities (*Zuhamah*) to cease,[686] and brought them to the state of purity that preceded the sin of the Tree of the knowledge of good and evil. Thus, the drawing forth to below was in such a manner that they heard,[687] "I am *HaShem*-יהו״ה your God," from all four directions.[688]

We likewise find that the resurrection of the dead (*Tchiyat HaMeitim*) will also be in such a way, in that it will be a drawing forth from Above to below. This is why our sages, of blessed memory, stated,[689] "All Israelites have a share in the

---

[685] Which is accompanied by the refinement of the emotive attributes as discussed in the prior discourse.

[686] Talmud Bavli, Shabbat 146a – This refers to the contamination (*Zuhamah*) imparted by the Snake when it seduced Chavah to eat of the Tree of Knowledge.

[687] Exodus 20:2; Deuteronomy 5:6

[688] Midrash Shmot Rabba 5:9; Zohar III 229b (Ra'aya Mehemna)

[689] Mishnah Sanhedrin 11:10

coming world (*Olam HaBa*)" (excluding those who are enumerated there). In other words, the matter of the resurrection of the dead (*Tchiyat HaMeitim*) applies to, and will occur for all the Jewish people. Moreover, it is will not be like how it is in the Garden of Eden (*Gan Eden*), in which there are many different levels, as explained before. Rather, it will be in such a way that all Jews will have a share in the coming world, because the resurrection of the dead (*Tchiyat HaMeitim*) is in a way of descent from Above to below, in which case the state and level of the lower is entirely irrelevant.[690]

This may be better understood by way of analogy to a great king sitting in his royal hall, garbed in his royal garments and wearing the crown of kingship upon his head. The commonfolk of the nation all remain standing outside and all their requests must be submitted to various ministers and clerics, who then transmit their requests to the king. This is because the commonfolk cannot simply enter into the king's royal chamber, of their own accord. Moreover, even if a person does merit entry into the hall of the king, there are limits as to how far he may enter, whether into the outer court or the inner court, or into the inner sanctum of the king himself. At times, however, the king desires to present himself to the people, in which case, he exits his royal hall and stands at the entrance, presenting himself in full revelation to the nation. That is, the king reveals himself to everyone, as he is, in his elevated purity

---

[690] See Imrei Binah Ibid.; Torah Ohr Yitro 73b; *Hemshech* 5672 Ibid. p. 779 and on; Sefer HaMaamarim 5698 p. 212 and on; Discourse entitled "*Lehavin Inyan Techiyat HaMeitim*" and "*Ata Hareita*" of the year 5746 (Torat Menachem, Sefer HaMaamarim Iyar p. 221 and on; Sivan p. 345) and elsewhere.

and refinement, garbed in his royal garments and insignia and wearing the crown of kingship, in his full glory and majesty. However, when he reveals himself in this manner, the people are gripped with awe and fear and are utterly nullified before him, to the point that it is not applicable to speak to him about their affairs or to submit supplications and petitions to him.

Now, there is yet another way the king reveals himself. This is when the king dons common clothing and even speaks with the commonfolk of the nation about simple matters. In such a case, he descends to their level and they can to speak to him about matters that relate to them. In addition, they can submit their requests directly to him. In other words, even though the people know that this is the very same king who previously was garbed in royal, stately garments, including the crown of kingship, nevertheless, since he currently is in simple garments and speaks to them of simple matters, the effect in them is that they can discuss their affairs with him in detail and submit their requests directly to him.

We thus find that it is specifically when the king reveals himself in simple garments, that there is an even greater revelation of his essential being, even more than when he is garbed in his royal garments and wearing the crown of kingship. On the contrary, the whole reason that he wears simple garments is specifically because he wants the people to speak directly to him about their concerns, according to their own level. He desires this to such an extent, that he entirely forgoes his royal garments and crown of kingship, indicating that it is specifically this, that is his very essence. It is because of this that the union between the nation and the king, is with the very essence and being of the king himself.[691]

From this analogy, we may understand the comparison Above, in Godliness. Namely, that the revelation of the giving of the Torah is like the revelation of the King, blessed is He, in His full glory and majesty. It is for this reason that this revelation caused a complete nullification in them, as it states,[692] "With each and every utterance of the Holy One, blessed is He, the souls of the Jewish people left their bodies... and He needed to revive them with the dew-*Tal*-טל that will revive the dead in the coming future," specifically.[693]

In contrast, following the giving of the Torah, the fulfillment of the *mitzvot* is with physical objects and is comparable to the revelation of the King when he garbs Himself in common clothes. In other words, this is the meaning of the fact that the *mitzvot* are garbed in physical matters. Nevertheless, it is specifically in this that His Essential Being,

---

[691] In other words, it transcends all the formalities that would accompany meeting with the king in his royal hall, as discussed above.

[692] Talmud Bavli, Shabbat 88b

[693] This refers to the true knowledge of the absolute Oneness of *HaShem-HaShem Echad*-יהו"ה אחד-39 which shares the same numerical value as the Dew-*Tal*-טל-39. The Talmud (Bavli Taanit 4a) relates that the Jewish people entreated *HaShem* to be a blessing as the rain, as in the verse (Hosea 6:3) "And let us know, eagerly strive to know *HaShem*. His going forth is sure as the morning, and He will come to us as the rain." To this *HaShem* responded, "My daughter, you request [my manifestation by comparing me to] the matter [of rain] which sometimes is desirable and sometimes not desirable. However, I will be for you, like that which is always desirable, as stated (Hosea 14:6) 'I will be as the dew-*Tal*-ל"ט' to Israel.'" In other words, dew is constant and unchanging, just as "HaShem is One" is constant and unchanging. We thus understand the relationship between the ל"ט-dew-39 and יהו"ה אח"ד-*HaShem Echad-HaShem* is One-39. (See Ginat Egoz of Rabbi Yosef Gikatilla, translated into English under the title HaShem is One, Volume 1, The Gate of Intrinsic Being.)

blessed is He, is found. This is as we are taught,[694] "There is utterly no thought that can grasp Him whatsoever, except for when He is grasped through Torah and its commandments." In other words, through the fulfillment of Torah and *mitzvot*, one grasps the very Essential Being of *HaShem*-יהו"ה Himself, blessed is He, in the most literal sense, something that cannot be grasped even by the primordial thought (*Machshavah HaKedooma*) of primordial man (*Adam Kadmon*).[695] Thus, it is specifically the physical fulfillment of Torah and *mitzvot*, that is the receptacle for the resurrection of the dead (*Techiyat HaMeitim*), which will specifically be brought about by the Essential Being of *HaShem*-יהו"ה Himself, blessed is He.

4.

Now, each of these two kinds of traveling, mentioned above, from below to Above and from Above to below, has an advantage that the other does not have. For, in the travel from below to Above, it is quite possible that his travel is only according to his strength, and only according to the measure of his service of *HaShem*-יהו"ה, blessed is He. Moreover, this kind of "travel" is generally only to the root of how *HaShem*-יהו"ה, blessed is He, fills all worlds (*Memale Kol Almin*). Thus, relative to this type of "travel," there is an advantage to the travel from Above to below, since in that case, the One Above is drawn down **as He is**, which is a revelation of how *HaShem*-

694 Introduction to Tikkunei Zohar 17a; See Tanya Ch. 4
695 See Shaar HaYichud translated as The Gate of Unity, Ch. 17-19.

יהו"ה, blessed is He, utterly transcends all worlds (*Sovev Kol Almin*).

On the other hand, there is a disadvantage to the descent from Above to below, in that He does not become entirely one with the one below, since this union is not due to the efforts and service of *HaShem*-יהו"ה, of the one below. Thus, in comparison, there is an advantage to the "travel" from below to Above, in that in this case, the lower one fully absorbs the illumination of the Upper One, blessed is He, in an inner way.

However, based on all the above, we may now understand the great exaltedness of the matter conveyed by the doubled language, "*VeHeet'halachti*-והתהלכתי" as opposed to the term "*VeHalachti*-והלכתי." That is, it includes both kinds of "travel," both from Above to below, as well as from below to Above, as they are both included in a single word and a single matter. This is brought about through a revelation of an aspect of *HaShem*-יהו"ה that transcends both.

The explanation of the matter is as follows: In both the aforementioned modes of, "travel," the existence of the lower being is distinct, as a separate being. This is true not only in regard to the ascent of the lower being from below to Above, which refers to the ascent of the how *HaShem*-יהו"ה, blessed is He fills all worlds (*Memale*) to the aspect of how *HaShem*-יהו"ה, blessed is He utterly transcends all worlds (*Sovev*). Generally, this is referred to as the matter of the ascension of the feminine waters (*Ha'ala'at Mayim Nukvin*), in which case, the subsequent beneficence that is drawn forth, is commensurate to the measure of the ascent, to the extent that the lower being has become a receptacle for the drawing forth of influence.

However, this is likewise so, even in the "traveling," from Above to below, which refers to the drawing forth of how HaShem-יהו״ה, blessed is He, utterly transcends the worlds (*Sovev*) into how He fills the worlds (*Memale*). That is, although in this drawing forth, there is no need for the ascension of the feminine waters (*Mayim Nukvin*), nevertheless, there still must be a refinement of the recipient.

In other words, since the root of this drawing forth is from the illumination and revelation of His light, as it is to Himself, blessed is He,[696] therefore, even though it is an illumination of His light to Himself, which entirely transcends any relation to worlds, nevertheless, from the very fact that we must negate any relation to worlds (in the fact that we say that the matter of this revelation is an illumination of His light to Himself), it is understood that this revelation still has some relation to worlds, in the sense that there are worlds that He transcends and to whom this revelation is negated.

It is thus applicable to state that the lower being is a receptacle for this light of HaShem-יהו״ה, at least in a way of negation, and because of this, for this illumination from Above to below to be, at the very least, there still must be some kind of refinement in the recipient. (This is so, even though this revelation does not require an ascension of the feminine waters (*Mayim Nukvin*), as mentioned above.)

---

[696] See *Hemshech* 5666 p. 515 and on; Also see the prior discourse 1 entitled "*Bati LeGani*" 5711, Ch. 1.

Because of this we find that even in regard to the coming future, in which there will be a revelation from Above to below, there nevertheless will still be different levels, as stated,[697] "They will all know Me, from their smallest to their greatest." That is, even though the revelation will be in a way of,[698] "the earth will be filled with the knowledge of *HaShem*-יהו״ה as the waters cover the ocean floor," there will nonetheless be different levels, "from their smallest to their greatest." This is because even in the "travel" from Above to below, the refinement of the lower being is necessary.

Moreover, the very description of, "travel from Above to below" entails the two distinct categories of "Above" and "below" and that the One Above becomes revealed in the one below. This is because the root of this drawing forth is from the aspect of the light, as it is to Himself, blessed is He, and although it entirely is a revelation to Himself alone, nonetheless, because it already is in the category of light and illumination, there already is some relation to worlds,[699] and it already possesses the parameters of Above and below.

In contrast, the matter conveyed by the doubled language, "*VeHeet'halachti*-והתהלכתי," is that it includes both aspects in a single word, and is thus in a manner in which there is no division between Above and below at all, but both are equal. This is because this drawing forth is from the very Essential Being of *HaShem*-יהו״ה Himself, blessed is He, who

---

698 Isaiah 11:9
699 Even if only in negation (*Shlilah*), as mentioned above.

is the root of all light and illumination. Moreover, in reality, it is inappropriate to even describe Him as the source of illumination, given that to *HaShem*-יהו״ה, blessed is He, it is all entirely equal. It thus is understood, that this level of revelation does not require the refinement of the recipient at all, but rather, it is entirely within His capacity to reveal Himself to everyone, blessed is He, on whatever level they may be.

Such revelation will specifically happen in the coming future, with the resurrection of the dead, at which time the revelation will be to everyone equally, to the point that it even will be revealed to the created being (*Yesh HaNivra*), that his very existence is the True Being (*Yesh HaAmeetee*) of *HaShem*-יהו״ה, blessed is He. In other words, even with a created being (*Yesh HaNivra*) who senses himself as existing intrinsically, this sense of being itself, is due to the fact that his very existence is from the Singular Preexistent Being whose existence is Intrinsic and Essential to Him, blessed is He.[700] Thus, in the coming future, it will be revealed in the created being (*Yesh HaNivra*) that he is entirely one with the True Being (*Yesh HaAmeetee*) of *HaShem*-יהו״ה, blessed is He.[701]

This also explains our recitation of the four praises,[702] "There is none comparable to You, and none aside for You; There is nothing without You, and who is like You?" We continue, "There is none comparable to You, *HaShem*-יהו״ה our

---

See Biurei HaZohar of the Mittler Rebbe, *Beshalach* 43c; Sefer HaMaamarim 5677 p. 151; Also see the prior discourse 1 entitled "*Bati LeGani*" 5711, Ch. 4.

[701] Also see Sefer HaSichot 5752 Vol. 2, p. 349 and the notes there.

[702] In the *Yotzer* blessings of the Shabbat morning prayers.

God – in this world; and nothing aside for You, our King – in the life of the coming world; There is nothing without you, our Redeemer – in the days of Moshiach; and there is none who can be likened to You, our Deliverer – in the era of the resurrection of the dead."

Now,[703] the explanation of the words, "there is nothing aside for You," (in the life of the coming world) and "there is nothing without you" (in the days of Moshiach), is that there is utterly no existence aside for the existence of the True Being, *HaShem*-יהו״ה, blessed is He. In other words, even though there is some novel existence, nevertheless, it is utterly nullified to *HaShem*-יהו״ה, whether it is the nullification that it is, "nothing-*Ein*-אין," (as in, "there is nothing aside for You") or whether it is a nullification in a way of being, "nothing without You-*Efes*-אפס" (as in "there is nothing without You").

This is not the case with the other two forms of praise that, "there is none comparable to You, *HaShem*-יהו״ה our God" (in this world) and "there is none who can be likened to You, our Deliverer" (in the era of the resurrection of the dead). In other words, the explanation of these two latter praises is that there is indeed the existence of an "other," only that it is in such a way that, "there is none comparable to You" and "there is none who can be likened to You." In other words, this is due to the fact that the created being (*Yesh HaNivra*) is himself entirely one with the True Being (*Yesh HaAmeetee*). However, in this itself, there are two possible extremes, that are two

---

[703] See *Hemshech* 5672 ibid. p. 781; Discourse entitled "*Ein Aroch*" 5652 (Sefer HaMaamarim 5652, p. 6 and on).

diametric opposites of each other. That is, when we say "there is none comparable to You, *HaShem*-יהו״ה our God – in this world," even though, it is true, that in reality the created being (*Yesh HaNivra*) is himself entirely one with the True Being (*Yesh HaAmeetee*), nonetheless, in this world this is concealed and hidden. However, through our service of *HaShem*-יהו״ה in this world, in toiling to remove all concealments and coverings, we then will arrive at the revelation of, "there is none who can be likened to You, our Deliverer – in the era of the resurrection of the dead." There will then indeed be a revelation of the reality that the created being (*Yesh HaNivra*) is himself entirely one with the True Being (*Yesh HaAmeetee*), blessed is He.

5.

This then, is the meaning of the words, "I will cause you to walk upright-*VaOleich Etchem Komemiyut*- ואולך אתכם קוממיות," in which the term "upright-*Komemiyut*-קוממיות" is in the plural, indicating two times the "height-*komot*" of Adam, the first man. That is, it refers to the stature-*Komah*-קומה of the direct light (*Ohr Yashar*), as well as the stature-*Komah*-קומה of the rebounding light (*Ohr Chozer*). That is, it refers to the service of *HaShem*-יהו״ה by the Godly soul together with the animalistic soul, as well as the animalistic soul's service of *HaShem*-יהו״ה, blessed is He, in and of itself.

In the coming future, both these aspects will be entirely unified in one word, which refers to the matter of the inclusion and unification of Above and below, as one! This will be due to the revelation of the Singular Preexistent Intrinsic and Essential Being of *HaShem*-יהו״ה Himself, blessed is He. As previously explained, even special individuals who attained perfection did not attain this level, for as we see, even the stature-*Komah*-קומה of the first man, *Adam* himself, was only one-hundred cubits. Thus, this will specifically happen in the coming future, that the stature of the Jewish people will be twice that of Adam, the first man. This refers to the inclusion and unification of both aspects of Above and below, so that they are entirely one, due to the revelation of the Singular Preexistent Intrinsic and Essential Being of *HaShem*-יהו״ה Himself, blessed is He.

Discourse 11

"Alpayim Shanah Kadmah Torah L'Briyato Shel Olam -
The Torah preceded the creation of the world by two-
thousand years"

Delivered on the second day of *Shavuot*, 5711
By the grace of *HaShem*, blessed is He,

1.

It says in Midrash,[704] "The Torah preceded the creation
of the world by two-thousand years, as it states,[705] 'I was with
Him as His nursling, I was delights day by day,' and a day of
the Holy One, blessed is He, is one thousand years." His
honorable holiness, my father-in-law, the Rebbe, said that we
must understand this matter of the Torah preceding the world
by two-thousand years and analyzed this teaching to
precision.[706] Is it not so, that time itself is a novel creation[707]
that was brought into being out of nothing by the Holy One,
blessed is He, together with the rest of the novel creation of the

---

[704] Midrash Tehillim 90:7; Also see Bereishit Rabba 8:2; Tanchuma Vayeshev 4; Zohar II 49a; Discourse entitled *"Ita b'Medrash Tehillim"* (Sefer HaMaamarim 5708 p. 272 and on).

[705] Proverbs 8:30

[706] In the discourse entitled *"Amar Rav Huna b'Shem Resh Lakish Alpayim Shanah"* of the year 5704, printed in Kuntres Chag HaShavuot 5711 (and subsequently printed in Sefer HaMaamarim 5711 p. 262 and on; Sefer HaMaamarim 5704 p. 198 and on).

[707] See Ginat Egoz of Rabbi Yosef Gikatilla, translated as HaShem is One, Volume 3, at length.

world out of nothing?[708] This being the case, what is the meaning of the statement that Torah preceded the creation of the world by two-thousand years?

We should preface that this teaching of our sages, of blessed memory, was also questioned in many earlier works.[709] They question this based on the fact that time is measured according to the celestial luminaries and the stars and constellations. This is as stated,[710] "And they shall serve as signs, and for appointed times, and for days and years." This being the case, how is it applicable for there to be a matter of two thousand years before the creation of the celestial luminaries?

The general answer given to this, is that what is meant in stating "two-thousand years," is that it is according to how we measure time today, after creation. In other words, had the luminaries, which are the instruments by which time is measured, been formed then, the measurement of the amount of time would have been like two-thousand years, by our measurement of time.

However, on a deeper level, the question relates to the very essence of time itself, which is the change of past, present and future. That is, with the passage of a small amount of time, a small amount of change takes place, and with a greater

---

[708] See Siddur Im Divrei Elokim Chayim, Shaar HaKriyat Shema 75d and on; Likkutei Sichot Vol. 17, p. 59 note 52; Igrot Kodesh Vol. 1 p. 293 and on; Vol. 2 p. 224.

[709] See the various citations in Sefer HaChakirah of the Tzemach Tzeddek 111b and on, and elsewhere.

[710] Genesis 1:14

passage of time, greater change take place. However, this matter is only applicable within the novelty of the existence of created beings, who undergo change in their existence. However, it is self-understood, that before the creation of the world, when novel created beings did not yet exist, there was no matter of time and change. This being the case, what is the meaning of this matter of time in relation to Torah, that, "Torah preceded the creation of the world by two thousand years"?

In other words, the absence of change, which is the matter of the eternality of Torah, is in such a way that even though it may exist within the parameters of time, nevertheless, time does not cause any weakening in it, whatsoever. It therefore is understood that just as time does not affect Torah negatively in any way, so also, it does not affect it positively. This being the case, what difference does it make whether the measure of time was two-thousand years, or more or less than that?

The answer is that even though Torah is eternal and remains unchanged by time, nonetheless, since it is indeed found within time, and relates to all other matters that are within time, therefore, relative to those matters, a relationship to time is ascribed to it.[711]

However, in truth, the question is even deeper. For, time itself is a novel creation that is newly brought into being out of nothing. That is, just as the existence of space is novel, in that it is not preexistent or intrinsic, the same is true of time.

---

[711] See Likkutei Torah, Drushim L'Shabbat Shuvah 67c; Sefer HaMaamarim

Its existence is novel, meaning that it did not exist before creation. Moreover, as known, time and space are intertwined.[712] This being the case, the question is strengthened. What is meant by this teaching that, "The Torah preceded the creation of the world by two-thousand years?"

Now, his honorable holiness, my father-in-law, the Rebbe, explains that what is meant, is not that Torah preceded the world in time, but that it preceded the world in **level**. He further explains that this precedence of the Torah by, "two-thousand years-*Alpayim Shanah*-אלפיים שנה," refers to the two aspects of "learning-*Aleph*-אלף" which are,[713] "I will teach you wisdom-*A'Alephcha Chochmah*-חכמה אאלפך," and,[714] "I will teach you understanding-*A'Alephcha Binah*-אאלפך בינה." That is, it refers to the aspects of intellect (*Mochin*) that transcend the worlds.[715] For, as stated,[716] "In six days *HaShem*-יהו״ה made the heavens and the earth," indicating that the creation of the heavens and the earth was preceded by the creation of the six days, these being the six emotive qualities[717] through which *HaShem*-יהו״ה made the heavens and the earth. The "heavens"

---

[712] See Ginat Egoz by Rabbi Yosef Gikatilla, translated as HaShem is One, Vol. 3 (and at greater length in the Gate entitled "The Gate explaining that *HaShem*, blessed Is He, is the place-*Makom*-מקום of all beings.") Also see Tanya, Shaar HaYichud VeHaEmunah Ch. 7; Likkutei Torah Brachah 98a and elsewhere.

[713] Job 33:33

[714] Talmud Bavli Shabbat 104a

[715] See Likkutei Torah Shir HaShirim 1d and on; *Hemshech* entitled "*VeHechereem*" 5631 (Sefer HaMaamarim 5631 p. 289). Also see the Petach HaShaar to Imrei Binah of the Mittler Rebbe, translated as The Gateway to Understanding.

[716] Exodus 20:11; 31:17

[717] Zohar I 247a; Zohar III 298b; and elsewhere.

refer to the upper worlds, whereas "the earth" refers to the lower world.

However, the intellect transcends the worlds, and is for Himself, blessed is He. This is similar to how it is in man below. His emotive qualities specifically relate to his fellow. That is, the general matter of emotions is that they are specifically applicable when there is an "other." If this is so regarding the arousal of the emotions themselves, then it certainly is so regarding the effects of the emotions as they manifest into action, in which case, there certainly must specifically be the existence of an "other." However, this is not so regarding intellect. For, aside for the fact that there does not need to be an "other" for the arousal of the intellectual faculties, even the effects of the intellect do not require an "other." Moreover, in actually, the presence of an "other" is a distraction to the intellect, since the intellect is entirely internal, unto oneself.

It thus is understood how it is Above in Godliness. The matter of the emotive qualities is in relation to the worlds, whereas the intellect is in relation to Himself, blessed is He. Moreover, although in His Essential Being, *HaShem*-יהו"ה, blessed is He, does not require the matter of light or illumination altogether, in that He transcends the world of Emanation-*Atzilut*, and He certainly does not require the intellectual faculties of wisdom-*Chochmah* and understanding-*Binah* (the "two-thousand years"), nonetheless, they are drawn forth in this order. That is, there first must be the drawing forth of the light and illumination, as it is to Himself (which is the matter of the intellect) and only afterwards can there be an illumination of light that relates to an "other" (which is the matter of the emotions). This then, is the meaning of the teaching,[718] "The Torah preceded the creation of the world by two-thousand years (*Alpayim Shanah*-שנה אלפיים), as it states,[719] 'I was with Him as His nursling, I was delights day by day.'" That is, the Torah is rooted in the aspect of the Upper intellect of *HaShem*-יהו"ה, that transcends the worlds.

2.

Now, we still must further understand this teaching of our sages that, "The Torah preceded the creation of the world by two-thousand years." Why is the level of the Torah, as it is in the state of, "delights day by day," important, (which is the part of the verse from which they derived the two-thousand years, as they stated, "a day of the Holy One, blessed is He, is one thousand years")? Is it not more relevant how the Torah was in an even loftier state, indicated by the first half of the verse,[720] "I was with Him as His nursling"? For, the order of this verse is from Above to below, and the first half of the verse states, "I was with Him as His nursling,"[721] referring to how the

---

[718] Midrash Tehillim 90:7; Also see Bereishit Rabba 8:2; Tanchuma Vayeshev 4; Zohar II 49a; Discourse entitled "*Ita b'Medrash Tehillim*" (Sefer HaMaamarim 5708 p. 272 and on).

[719] Proverbs 8:30

[720] Proverbs 8:30

[721] The words "I was with Him as His nursling-*VaEheyeh Etzlo Amon*- ואהיה אצלו אמון" indicates the initial revelation of the light of the Oneness of *HaShem*-יהו"ה, blessed is He, with the name *Eheye"h*-אהי"ה which corresponds to the attribute of the Crown-*Keter*, and thus transcends the faculties of wisdom-*Chochmah* and

Torah was in the Essential Being of *HaShem*-יהו"ה Himself, blessed is He. Only afterwards does it continue and state, "I was delights day by day," which refers to how the Torah was drawn forth into the aspect of intellect, which are the faculties of wisdom-*Chochmah* and understanding-*Binah*.

It then lists various other levels of descent, until it finally states,[722] "My delights are with the sons of man," which refers to the Torah, as it descended down below. We thus find that the most elevated and superior level of Torah is at the beginning of the verse, which states, "I was with Him as His nursling." We must therefore understand why, in this teaching of our sages, they expounded about the level of Torah, as it is in the aspect of, "delights day by day," but did not expound about the higher, superior level of, "I was with Him as His nursling."

Now, at first glance, we might say that the order indicated by the verse is actually from below to Above. For, in explanation of the words, "I was with Him as His nursling-*VaEheyeh Etzlo Amon*-ואהיה אצלו אמון," the Midrash states

---

understanding-*Binah*. This is indicated by the fact that the name *Eheye"h*-אהי"ה-21 is the first of *HaShem's*-יהו"ה names of Being-*Havayah*-הוי"ה in that it is the very first derivative of the Preexistent Intrinsic Essential Name of *HaShem*-יהו"ה Himself, blessed is He, and is the same as the truncated name *Yeh"o*-יה"ו-21. This name *Yeh"o*-יה"ו indicates the absolute Oneness of *HaShem*-יהו"ה אח"ד-39 in that the letters יהו"ה א"א ה"א-39 are equal to *HaShem* is One-יהו"ה אח"ד-39. Additionally, the usage in this verse with the prefix *Vav*-ו-6, as in *VaEheye"h*-ואהי"ה-27 is inclusive of all ז"ך-27 letters of the *Aleph-Beit*, which are the letters through which the Torah, and all of creation, were subsequently brought forth. Thus, the former half of the verse, "I was with Him as His nursling-*VaEheyeh Etzlo Amon*-ואהיה אצלו אמון," indicates the most elevated and superior level of the Essential Torah of *HaShem*-יהו"ה. (See Ginat Egoz of Rabbi Yosef Gikatilla, translated as HaShem is One, Volume 1, The Gate of Intrinsic Being.)

[722] Proverbs 8:31

273

that,[723] "The Torah is saying, 'I was the craftsman's tool-*Kli Umanuto*-כלי אומנתו of the Holy One, blessed is He... He gazed into the Torah and created the world.'" Based on this, we find that the beginning of the verse, "I was with Him as His nursling-*VaEheyeh Etzlo Amon*-ואהיה אצלו אמון," is the level of Torah that relates to how *HaShem*-יהו״ה, blessed is He, brings the world into existence out of nothing.

The verse then lists the level of, "delights day by day," which refers to the Torah as it comes into the aspects of intellect, wisdom-*Chochmah* and understanding-*Binah*, that transcend the world. (It concludes with the words, "My delights are with the sons of man," which refers to the Torah that was given below, and actually is the highest level, since it is specifically through man's service of *HaShem*-יהו״ה below, that one is elevated to the highest level, as explained before.)

However, in reality, the first part of the verse, "I was with Him as His nursling-*VaEheyeh Etzlo Amon*- ואהיה אצלו אמון," is actually the highest and most superior level of Torah. This is understood from the explanation of Rashi,[724] that the word, "*Amon*-אמון," shares the same root as the word,[725] "brought up-*HaEmunim*-האמנים," and thus means, "brought up with Him." We therefore must say that even in the aspect of how the Torah is the craftsman's tool-*Kli Umnuto*-כלי אומנתו of the Holy One, blessed is He, it also is a much higher and superior level.

---

[723] Midrash Bereishit Rabba 1:1
[724] Rashi to Provers 8:30
[725] Meaning to be raised and brought up, like a child. Lamentations 4:5

The explanation is as follows:[726]   At times Torah states,[727] "By the word of *HaShem*-יהו"ה the heavens were made," indicating that the existence of the worlds is from the aspect of the speech of *HaShem*-יהו"ה, blessed is He.   At other times, Torah states,[728] "Whatever *HaShem*-יהו"ה desired, He did," indicating that the existence of the worlds is from the aspect of the will and desire of *HaShem*-יהו"ה, blessed is He.

Now, it is explained[729] that every created being consists of both substance (*Chomer*) and form (*Tzurah*). The substance (*Chomer*) is the tangible body of the created being, and is made, "by the word of *HaShem*-יהו"ה," meaning, the attribute of speech-*Dibur*. In contrast, the form (*Tzurah*) of the created being is made by the will and desire of *HaShem*-יהו"ה, blessed is He, and it is this level that is drawn forth and causes the nullification of the created being to *HaShem*-יהו"ה, blessed is He. Thus, when it states that, "the Torah is the craftsman's tool-*Kli Umanuto*-כלי אומנתו of the Holy One, blessed is He," it is in regard to the fact that through it, the form (*Tzurah*) of the created beings is brought into existence, which relates to the nullification and sublimation of the creatures to their Creator, *HaShem*-יהו"ה, blessed is He.

We may additionally say that the existence of the created beings that is drawn forth through Torah (which is the craftsman's tool of the Holy One, blessed is He), also relates to

---

[726] See Sefer HaMaamarim 5665, p. 73 and on.

[727] Psalms 33:6

[728] Psalms 135:6

[729] See Ginat Egoz of Rabbi Yosef Gikatilla, translated as HaShem is One; Also see Torah Ohr Miketz 41d

the existence of their substance (*Chomer*). This is as explained in Iggeret HaKodesh,[730] that the existence of tangible created beings (*Yesh*) is solely and specifically dependent on the power of the Singular Intrinsic Essential Being of *HaShem*-יהו"ה Himself, blessed is He, who Himself is not preceded by any cause, God forbid. Thus, it is within His ability alone to create something out of absolute nothingness. This then, is what is meant by the fact that the world is brought into existence through Torah, since Torah is rooted in the Singular Intrinsic Essential Being of *HaShem*-יהו"ה, Himself, blessed is He.[731]

It thus is understood that, in fact, the order of the verse is, from Above to below, meaning that the highest and most superior level of Torah is the aspect of, "I was with Him as His nursling-*VaEheyeh Etzlo Amon*-ואהיה אצלו אמון." This being so, we still do not understand why our sages, of blessed memory, selected the superiority of the Torah, in that, "it preceded the creation of the world by two-thousand years," which only relates to the lower level, expressed as, "I was delights day by day." Why did they not discuss the first and higher level of, "I was with Him as His nursling-*VaEheyeh Etzlo Amon*- ואהיה אצלו אמון"?

Now, there is yet another matter that we must understand regarding the words, "*VaEheyeh Etzlo Amon*- ואהיה אצלו אמון," in that the term "*Eheyeh*-אהיה" is generally used in the future tense and therefore reads, "I **will be** with Him as His nursling." Now, the explanation of this verse (in other words,

---

[730] Tanya, Iggeret HaKodesh, Epistle 20 (p. 130b)
[731] Also see *Hemshech* 5672, Vol. 1, p. 356.

the abovementioned teaching of our sages, of blessed memory, that is under discussion, in which this verse is mentioned) was taught in the times of the Amora'im, if not earlier, at the time of the giving of the Torah. For, as known, all insights that a seasoned Torah scholar is destined to derive from Torah, were given to Moshe at Sinai.[732] This being the case, the verse should have been stated in the past tense ("I was-*Hayeetee*-הייתי"), and we must therefore understand why it was specifically stated in the future tense ("I will be-*Eheyeh*-אהיה").

Now, it is true that according to the rules of grammar, the explanation is that the prefix letter *Vav*-ו ("*VaEheyeh*-וָאהיה") modifies the word from future tense to past tense[733] (as well as to present tense). Nevertheless, the Zohar states[734] that this verse, "*VaEheyeh Etzlo Amon*-ואהיה אצלו אמון" is similar to the verse,[735] "I will be that I will be-*Eheyeh Asher Eheyeh*- אהיה אשר אהיה," which the Zohar explained to mean, "I am destined to be revealed," in the coming future. According to this, it is understood that the verse specifically uses the word, "*VaEheyeh*-ואהיה" in the future tense. We therefore must understand why this matter was stated in the future tense.

---

[732] Talmud Bavli, Megillah 19b; Midrash Shmot Rabba 47; See notes to Likkutei Sichot Vol. 19, p. 252.

[733] See Gur Aryeh Al HaTorah, Shmot 1:17; Also See Ginat Egoz of Rabbi Yosef Gikatilla translated as HaShem Is One, Vol. 1, section on the name *Eheye"h*-אהי"ה.

[734] Zohar III 65b

[735] Exodus 3:14

3.

Now, to understand this, we must first explain the five matters enumerated in these verses. Namely, (1) "I was with Him as His nursling," (2) "I was delights day by day," (3) "I played before Him at all times," (4) "playing in the inhabited areas of His earth," and (5) "My delights are with the children of man." About this, it is explained that the first part of the verse, which states, "I was with Him as His nursling-*VaEheyeh Etzlo Amon*-ואהיה אצלו אמון," refers to the Torah, as it is in the Essential Being of *HaShem*-יהו"ה, blessed is He, as indicated by the word, "**with** Him-*Etzlo*-אצלו."

The continuation, that states, "I was delights day by day-*VaEheyeh Sha'ashu'im Yom Yom*-ואהיה שעשועים יום יום," refers to the Torah, as it is drawn into the aspect of the intellect, that is, wisdom-*Chochmah* and understanding-*Binah*, which include all intellect in general. It is about this level that the term, "delights-*Sha'ashu'im*-שעשועים" is used. (It nonetheless does not use the term "**My** delight-*Sha'ashu'ay*-שעשועי," which refers to the **Essential** Delights (*Sha'ashu'im HaAtzmiyim*), but instead uses the lesser, general term, "delights-*Sha'ashu'im*-שעשועים.") For, even as the Torah descends to the aspect of the intellect, there still is an aspect of pleasure in it.

As known, our sages, of blessed memory, were very precise[736] when they said,[737] "The Torah came out from the upper wisdom." That is, it "**came out**" from the upper wisdom, meaning that it was **revealed** through the quality of wisdom-*Chochmah*. However, it is rooted much higher than wisdom-*Chochmah*, in the aspect of the Upper Pleasure (*Ta'anug*). Therefore, even as it comes to be revealed in the intellectual faculties of wisdom-*Chochmah* and understanding-*Binah*, there is an aspect of, "delights-*Sha'ashu'im*-שעשועים."

Additionally, as we are taught,[738] "The revelation of the pleasure of the Ancient One-*Atik* is in understanding-*Binah*." This also is the inner meaning of the verse,[739] "The Levite shall serve Him-*Hoo*-הוא." Since the word, "Him-*Hoo*-הוא" is in the third person it refers to the Ancient One-*Atik*,[740] and indicates

---

[736] Likkutei Torah Bamidbar 7c; Ohr HaTorah Bereishit Vol. 6 1,023b; Sefer HaMaamarim 5696 p. 8 and various other places.

[737] Zohar II 62a, 85a, 121a and elsewhere.

[738] Zohar III 178b; Torah Ohr Lech Lecha 11b and on, and elsewhere.

[739] Numbers 18:23

[740] Zohar III 178b ibid. and Torah Ohr Lech Lecha ibid. Also see Ginat Egoz of Rabbi Yosef Gikatilla, translated in English as HaShem is One, Vol. 2. It is explained there, that the word "Him-*Hoo*-הוא," which has a numerical value of "In Me-*Bi*-ב"י-12" (Gen. 22:16) is inclusive of all the numerals up until and including ב"י-12 (which is known as *Cheshbon Kidmi*). Thus, א"ב ג"ד ה"ו ז"ח ט"י י"א י"ב is equal to 78, which is the numerical value of, "He is and He was and He will Be-*Hoveh V'Hayah V'Yihiyeh*-הוה והיה ויהיה-78" that shares the same letters as, three times the Name *HaShem*-יהו"ה. יהו"ה-יהו"ה-יהו"ה in all three tenses. That is, *HaShem*-יהו"ה is, *HaShem*-יהו"ה was, *HaShem*-יהו"ה will be. Thus, the verse may be read, "And the Levite shall serve He Who Is and Was and Will be," which is the aspect of the eternality of the Singular Intrinsic Essential Being, *HaShem*-יהו"ה Himself, blessed is He, the Eternal One, blessed is He.

that the revelation of the Ancient One-*Atik* is specifically in understanding-*Binah*.[741]

Beyond this, the beginning of the revelation of the pleasure and the essence of the pleasure, is in the aspect of wisdom-*Chochmah*. This is the meaning of the statement,[742] "The face of Rabbi Avahu would light up when he would find an additional-*Tosefta* teaching." The term, "additional-Tosefta teaching," indicates the novelty of the discovery, which is the aspect of the insight of the faculty of wisdom-*Chochmah*.[743] The effect of the insight of wisdom-*Chochmah* is that it draws forth pleasure (*Ta'anug*), and is the reason his face would light up.

As also known, this matter is referred to as the Garden of Eden (*Gan Eden*). For, as known,[744] the insight of wisdom-*Chochmah* is called by the term Eden-עדן, whereas the comprehension of understanding-*Binah*, is called by the term the Garden of Eden-*Gan Eden*-גן עדן. In other words, although understanding-*Binah* is the aspect of the river-*Nahar*,[745] about which it states,[746] "A river issued from Eden to water the

---

[741] For a lengthier explanation of this matter and this verse, see Shaar HaYichud of the Mittler, translated into English as The Gate of Unity, Ch. 40 (Vol. 2).

[742] Talmud Yerushalmi Shabbat 8:1 and elsewhere.

[743] See Likkutei Torah, Masei 93b; Sefer HaMaamarim 5657 p. 266 and elsewhere.

[744] See Sefer HaMaamarim 5665 ibid. and Maamarei Admor HaZaken and Ohr HaTorah Shir HaShirim ibid. Also see Ginat Egoz of Rabbi Yosef Gikatilla, translated as HaShem is One, Vol. 1, The Gate of The Sanctuary, and Vol. 2, section entitled "The seven letters בג״ד כפר״ת correspond to the seven chambers of purgatory."

[745] See Likkutei Torah, Shir HaShirim 39b and elsewhere.

[746] Genesis 2:10

garden" (and is actually higher than the aspect of the Garden), nevertheless, this itself demonstrates that understanding-*Binah* is not the aspect of Eden itself, but is only the aspect of the "river" that issues from Eden. In contrast, wisdom-*Chochmah* is Eden itself. This is because the **root** of Torah is even more elevated than the wisdom-*Chochmah*, and thus, even as it is manifest within the aspect of wisdom-*Chochmah*, and even as it "comes forth from wisdom-*Chochmah*," it still possesses this aspect of "delights-*Sha'ashu'im*-שעשועים."

The verse then continues, "I played-*Mesacheket*-משחקת before Him at all times." The root of the word "*Mesacheket*-משחקת" is "laughter-*Schok*-שחק," and refers to the actual **revelation** of the pleasure. (It is about this[747] that our sages, of blessed memory, stated,[748] "It is forbidden for a person to fill his mouth with laughter-*Schok*-שחק in this world." They specifically used the term "laughter-*Schok*-שחק." In other words, even though the service of *HaShem*-יהו"ה, blessed is He, must be with joy, as it states,[749] "because you did not serve *HaShem*-יהו"ה your God with joy," and even beyond that, as the verse continues, "and with goodness of heart," it nevertheless is, "forbidden for one to fill his mouth with laughter-*Schok*-שחק." This is because it indicates that he feels the joy in a sensory manner to a very great extent.) Thus, this matter specifically relates to the emotions. For, the drawing forth of pleasure in the intellect is not as revealed, and is primarily

---

[747] See the notes of the Tzemach Tzeddek to Maamarei Admor HaZaken ibid. (p. 178), and Ohr HaTorah Shir HaShirim ibid. (p. 179).
[748] Talmud Bavli, Brachot 31a
[749] Deuteronomy 28:47

experienced in the illumination of the face alone. In contrast, it is specifically in the emotions that the pleasure comes to be felt and revealed to a much greater extent.

The verse then continues, "playing in the inhabited areas of His earth-*Artzo*-ארצו." This refers to the manifestation of the Torah within the *Sefirah* of kingship-*Malchut*, which is the aspect of the "earth-*Aretz*-ארץ." For, the attribute of kingship-*Malchut* is the root of the creatures of the worlds of Creation-*Briyah*, Formation-*Yetzirah*, and Action-*Asiyah*.

The verse then concludes, "My delights are with the children of man." This refers to the Torah as it is drawn down, specifically here below. It is specifically in **this** aspect of Torah that it says, "**My** delights-*Sha'ashu'ay*-שעשועי," which refers to the Essential Delights of *HaShem*-יהו״ה **Himself**, blessed is He. For, it is specifically through our study of Torah here below, that we can reach the aspect of, "The delights of The King in His Essential Self" (*Sha'ashu'ey HaMelech B'Atzmuto*).[750]

4.

The explanation of the matter is as follows:[751] As known, there generally are two ways by which Godliness is drawn forth, the way of direct light (*Ohr Yashar*) and the way of rebounding light (*Ohr Chozer*). The same applies in the study of Torah.[752] That is, one may study Torah in a way of

---

[750] Emek HaMelech Shaar 1; Likkutei Torah, Shir HaShirim 27a
[751] See *Hemshech* 5666 p. 91 and on, and p. 94 and on.
[752] See *Hemshech* 5666 ibid. p. 80 and on.

direct light (*Ohr Yashar*), meaning that he studies and understands what he studies, or one may study Torah in a way of rebounding light (*Ohr Chozer*), meaning that he studies and does not understand what he studies, or that questions arise for him, because of what he has learned somewhere else in Torah. He then must toil to overcome the questions and concealments.

This is the general difference between the Jerusalem Talmud and the Babylonian Talmud.[753] That is, in the Jerusalem Talmud there are not so many questions, nor are there an abundance of lengthy dissections and back and forth debates. Rather, the manner of study is in a way of direct light (*Ohr Yashar*). In contrast, the Babylonian Talmud is full of many questions. As our sages, of blessed memory, stated,[754] "The verse,[755] 'He has made me dwell in darkness' refers to the Babylonian Talmud." This is because the manner of study in the Babylonian Talmud is that of rebounding light (*Ohr Chozer*).

Now, as known, the manner of study in a way of rebounding light (*Ohr Chozer*) actually reaches much higher, beyond comparison to study in a manner of direct light (*Ohr Yashar*). This may be understood by what we find regarding the advantage of the Jerusalem Talmud over the Babylonian Talmud. It is to such an extent that Rabbi Zeira,[756] "fasted one-hundred fasts in order to forget the Babylonian Talmud." It is

---

[753] See *Hemshech* 5666 ibid. p. 90 and on; Also see Shaarei Orah of the Mittler Rebbe, discourse entitled "On the twenty-fifth of Kislev," Ch. 54 and on.

[754] Talmud Bavli, Sanhedrin 24a

[755] Lamentations 3:6

[756] Talmud Bavli, Bava Metziyah 85a

understood from this that the Babylonian Talmud cannot at all be compared to the Jerusalem Talmud. For, if the ascension from the Babylonian Talmud to the Jerusalem Talmud was merely a matter of gradation and ascension from one level to the next level, he would not have had to forget the Babylonian Talmud in order to study the Jerusalem Talmud. Thus, from the fact that to study the Jerusalem Talmud it was necessary for him to forget the perspective of the Babylonian Talmud, it is understood that this is not just a matter of gradual ascent, but is an ascent that is entirely beyond comparison. However, through this, we also can understand the advantage of the Babylonian Talmud over the Jerusalem Talmud, that is, that the superiority of the rebounding light (*Ohr Chozer*), also is an advantage that is entirely beyond comparison.

Now, Torah study in the manner of rebounding light (*Ohr Chozer*) is actually comprised of two approaches.[757] The first, is that one toils in his Torah study, in order to understand what he studies. Now, although there is very great toil in this, the toil itself is not a matter of intellectual understanding at all. For, the matter of intellect is that it descends from above to below, rather than from below to above. Additionally, the essential toil itself is not at all a matter of intellect, but actually transcends intellect. Nonetheless, his toil is specifically in matters of intellect.

The second approach is that he studies in order to know the, "deeds that he should do."[758] In other words, his desire is

[757] See *Hemshech* 5666 p. 390 and on, p. 410 and on, p. 421.
[758] Exodus 18:20

to grasp the Supernal Intention of the Singular Intrinsic Essential Being of *HaShem*-יהו"ה Himself, blessed is He. He therefore is fearful that perhaps his intention is not properly aligned with the Supernal Desire of *HaShem*-יהו"ה, blessed is He, and he therefore is gripped with fear and dread that he may come to err. This moves him to be completely focused and to toil to an even greater extent. This kind of toil is altogether not a matter of intellect.

Now, at first glance, it may appear that in this second approach to Torah study, it is not applicable for it to be pleasurable. For, regarding the first approach, it makes sense that even though he greatly toils, investing his whole being into his study of Torah (with complete devotion) to the point that he feels that his life is worthless without grasping it, nevertheless, because he toils to grasp its intellect, the matter of delight and pleasure is applicable in it. However, such is not the case with the second approach, in which he is not actually moved by the intellect of it at all. Rather, his entire being is that of total constriction. It therefore does not seem applicable that there would be any pleasure in it at all. However, in truth, there is indeed a matter of pleasure, even in this approach to Torah study.

By way of analogy, this may be understood by the difference between a minister and a servant, both of whom fulfill the will of the king. The minister knows that the king conducts the kingdom with goodness. Therefore, out of love of country, he fulfills the directives and responsibilities set upon him by the king. In other words, because the minister knows that by fulfilling the directives of the king, he will benefit the country, he fulfills his orders with vitality and pleasure in carrying them out. However, such is not the case, with the servant who fulfills the directives of the king. The servant is not at all an entity unto himself. Rather, his entire reason for being is solely to fulfill the will of his master. In this, he has neither intellectual understanding, nor emotional feelings, and seemingly, he should not have any pleasure from it at all.

However, in truth, it must be said that the servant indeed has (concealed) pleasure in fulfilling the directives of the king. We observe this by the fact that he wants to fulfill the king's directives in the most optimal manner, in a way of beauty and perfection, and with added splendor. This demonstrates that he actually does have pleasure in it. For, regarding his essential acceptance of the yoke of the king upon himself (and his servitude to him), it would have been sufficient for him to merely fulfill the king's directives, as they are, without the added aspect of beautification and splendor at all. However, from the fact that he strives to beautify his fulfillment of the king's directives, with additional splendor, it must be said that he has pleasure in it (albeit in concealed way).

Moreover, it could be said that the pleasure of the servant is the pleasure of the king himself. In other words, since the servant has no independence as an entity unto himself at all, and on the contrary, is nothing of his own, therefore, his entire reason for being is only to fulfill the will of his master. This being so, his pleasure is the pleasure of his master himself, meaning that what moves him is his master's pleasure. Thus, his master's pleasure is found in him.

Thus, in the analogue, it is understood that when a person learns Torah specifically to fulfill it in actuality, even though his toil is in a way of the constriction of the soul, nevertheless, in truth, he has (concealed) pleasure in it. On the contrary, since he has no ulterior motives in this study, being that it is only for the purpose of properly actualizing the will of *HaShem*-יהו״ה, blessed is He, therefore, his pleasure in it is the Upper Supernal Pleasure of *HaShem*-יהו״ה Himself, blessed is He. That is, it is the Upper Pleasure of *HaShem*-יהו״ה Himself that is felt within him and moves him.

The explanation is that through the second approach to Torah study, that of the rebounding light (*Ohr Chozer*), we reach the very Essential Pleasure of the One Above, blessed is He, which is the inner aspect of the pleasure of the Ancient One-*Atik Yomin* Himself, literally.[759] Such is not the case with the first approach, through which we only reach the inner aspect of "wisdom-*Abba*, within which the inner aspect of the Ancient One-*Atik Yomin* is manifest."[760] Although what is meant here, is not that the inner aspect of wisdom-*Abba* garbs or conceals the inner aspect of the pleasure-*Atik*, nonetheless, it only is how the inner aspect of the pleasure-*Atik* is drawn into the inner aspect of wisdom-*Abba*. In other words, it is not the inner aspect of the pleasure of the Ancient One-*Atik Yomin* Himself.

---

[759] See *Hemshech* 5666 ibid. p. 97; Sefer HaMaamarim 5696 p. 8 and on.

[760] Pri Etz Chaim, Shaar HaKriyat Shma, Ch. 15; Likkutei Torah Netzavim 49d; *Hemshech* 5666 p. 95 and on.

The difference between the two may be compared to the difference between a sensory, composite pleasure[761] (*Ta'anug Murkav*) and a simple, essential pleasure (*Ta'anug Pashut*).[762] This is similar to what is explained[763] about the coming future. That is, it sometimes states,[764] "In the coming future, the Holy One, blessed is He, will make a feast-*Ariston* (which, as explained, is the "morning meal"[765]) for His servants, the righteous *Tzaddikim*." At other times, it states,[766] "The coming world is not like this world. In the coming world there is no eating or drinking etc." Now, it is explained that these represent two levels in the revelation of the coming future. That is, at first there will be a revelation of composite and tangible pleasure, which is the matter of the "feast-*Ariston*." Afterwards there will be the revelation of the simple and essential pleasure of *HaShem*-יהו״ה Himself, which is not felt whatsoever. This is the matter of the coming world, in which, "there will be no eating or drinking etc."

5.

This then, is the meaning of the conclusion of the verse, "My delights are with the children of man." That is, it is specifically through the study of Torah here below ("with the

---

[761] Like the pleasure in fulfilling one's needs and desires.
[762] Like the pleasure in life itself.
[763] *Hemshech* 5666 ibid.
[764] Midrash Vayikra Rabba 13:3
[765] Matnat Kehunah commentary to Vayikra Rabbi 13:3
[766] Talmud Bavli, Brachot 17a

children of man") whereby the study is in a manner of rebounding light (*Ohr Chozer*), primarily in the second approach to study, mentioned above, that one reaches the aspect of, "**My** delights-*Sha'ashu'ay*-שעשועי," referring to the Essential Delights (*Sha'ashu'im HaAtzmiyim*), and "The delights of the King in His Essence" (*Sha'ashu'ey HaMelech B'Atzmuto*). This refers to the matter of Torah, as it is in the Singular Preexistent Intrinsic Essential Being of *HaShem*-יהו"ה Himself, blessed is He, referred to in the first part of the verse, "I was with Him as His nursling-*VaEheyeh Etzlo Amon*- ואהיה אצלו אמון."[767]

With this in mind, we may now understand why the verse states, "**I will be** with Him as His nursling-*VaEheyeh Etzlo Amon*-ואהיה אצלו אמון," specifically using the term "*Eheyeh*-אהיה," in the future tense, as explained above, for this matter will specifically be revealed in the coming future. In other words, although even now, the Torah is drawn forth as it is in the Essential Being of *HaShem*-יהו"ה, blessed is He, through which additional illuminations are added to the world of Emanation-*Atzilut*, nonetheless, this will specifically be revealed in the coming future.

This is why our sages, of blessed memory, expounded on the level of Torah that preceded the world by two thousand years, which is only the aspect of, "I was delights day by day-*VaEheyeh Sha'ashu'im Yom Yom*-ואהיה שעשועים יום יום," and did not expound on the level of, "I was with Him as His nursling-

---

[767] See Sefer HaMaamarim 5696 ibid.

*VaEheyeh Etzlo Amon-*ואהיה אצלו אמון." This is because the level of Torah reflected in the words, "I was with Him as His nursling-*VaEheyeh Etzlo Amon-*ואהיה אצלו אמון," is Torah as it is in the Essential Being of *HaShem-*יהו"ה Himself, blessed is He. In other words, this aspect of Torah is not something separate unto itself, but is rather the very essence of Torah, as it is entirely one with the Essential Self of *HaShem-*יהו"ה Himself, because of His Essential Being, and not because of the Torah.

This is also the meaning of what his honorable holiness, my father-in-law, the Rebbe, said in the name of the Alter Rebbe,[768] that at the giving of the Torah, three things were given. The first is the revealed aspects of the Torah, the second is the secrets of the Torah, and the third is the ability to serve *HaShem-*יהו"ה, blessed is He.

The explanation is that the revealed aspects of Torah, refer to what is currently revealed. The secrets of the Torah refer to the hidden reasons (*Ta'amim-*טעמים) of Torah, that will be revealed in the coming future, and is the aspect of the tangibly felt pleasure, mentioned above.[769] The ability to serve *HaShem-*יהו"ה, blessed is He, which is in the manner of reflective light (*Ohr Chozer*), entirely transcends intellect, including even the hidden reasons (*Ta'amim-*טעמים) of Torah that will be revealed in the coming future, since it reaches all the way to the Singular Intrinsic Essential Being of *HaShem-*

---

[768] Sefer HaSichot 5705 p. 102
[769] It is explained that the word for reason-*Ta'am-*טעם also means flavor-*Ta'am-*טעם, which is the aspect of the tangibly felt pleasure.

יהו״ה Himself, blessed is He. As explained above, this will only become fully revealed in the coming future.

Nevertheless, this matter was also present at the giving of the Torah. For, since there will not be another giving of the Torah,[770] it is understood that all these matters were already given at the giving of the Torah, only that they will become revealed in the coming future.

---

[770] See Sefer HaMaamarim 5647 p. 87; 5656 p. 356; *Hemshech* 5666 p. 23, p. 546; *Hemshech* 5672 Vol. 1, p. 366; Sefer HaMaamarim 5679 p. 291; 5685 p. 199; 5709 p. 51.

Discourse 12

"*Shlach Lecha Anashim -*
Send forth men, for yourself"

Delivered on Shabbat Parshat Shlach,
Shabbat Mevarchim Tammuz, 5711
By the grace of *HaShem*, blessed is He,

1.

The verse states,[771] "Send forth men for yourself, and let them spy out the Land of Canaan that I give to the Children of Israel." Rashi comments[772] on the words, "Send forth men for yourself," stating, "According to your own understanding. I am not commanding you, but if you wish, you may send." Now, from the fact that Moshe did indeed send the spies (as it subsequently states,[773] "Moshe sent them forth… to spy out the land,") we must say that according to his understanding, it was necessary to send the spies. Now, it is true, that the Torah states later,[774] "All of you approached me and said, 'Let us send men ahead of us and let them spy out the Land for us…' and the idea was good in my eyes." Nevertheless, our sages, of blessed memory, stated,[775] "This is comparable to a person who says to

---

[771] Numbers 13:2
[772] Rashi to Numbers 13:2
[773] Ibid. 13:3-16
[774] Deuteronomy 1:22-23
[775] Sifri and Rashi commentary to Deuteronomy 1:22-23

his fellow, 'Sell me your donkey.' He replies, 'Yes.' He then says, 'At least, will you give it to me to test it?' He replies, 'Yes.' 'May I test it on mountains and hills?' Again, he replies, 'Yes.' When he sees that the fellow withholds nothing from him, the purchaser thinks to himself, 'He is confident that I will not find any defect in his donkey,' and he immediately says to him, 'Take the money, I have no need to test it now.' Similarly, Moshe told the Jewish people, "I too consented to your words, thinking that perhaps you would reconsider when you saw that I did not withhold it from you, but you did not reconsider." Now, this seems to indicate that Moshe only agreed to send the spies so that the people would see that he is not withholding them from inspecting the Land, and so that they would reconsider (Since they did not reconsider, he had no choice but to send them).

Nevertheless, from the fact that the Holy One, blessed is He, hinged the decision to send the spies on Moshe's understanding, in stating, "Send forth men for yourself," it is understood that if Moshe's understanding was that it was not necessary to send spies, he would not have sent them. Since he did indeed send them, we must say, that according to his understanding, it indeed was necessary to send spies.

Now, this is a very astonishing matter and we must understand why Moshe felt it was necessary to send spies. For, the Talmud, in Tractate Brachot, states,[776] "It was taught regarding the verse,[777] 'Until Your nation passes through,

[776] Talmud Bavli, Brachot 4a
[777] Exodus 15:16-17

HaShem-יהו"ה, until this nation whom You have acquired passes through.' The words, 'Until Your nation passes through,' refers to the first entry into the Land (in the days of Yehoshua), whereas the words, 'until this nation You have acquired passes through,' refers to the second entry (in the days of Ezra, following the Babylonian exile).

Based on this juxtaposition, our sages, of blessed memory, stated: Israel was worthy of having a miracle performed on their behalf in the days of Ezra, just as a miracle was performed on their behalf in days of Yehoshua Bin Nun." Rashi explains that[778] the miracle that should have occurred for them, was that they should have entered the Land with, "an outstretch arm." In other words, just as they entered the Land in the times of Yehoshua, with great miracles and an outstretch arm, so likewise, this should have happened in the days of Ezra.

From this it is understood, that had they entered the Land in the days of Moshe, it would certainly have been with great miracles and with an outstretched arm! (The incident of the spies occurred in the second year after the exodus from Egypt and preceded the sin of the waters of strife (*Mei Merivah*).[779] Thus, they should have entered the Land at that time, through the leadership of Moshe.) For, when they entered the Land with Yehoshua, it was by the accompaniment of an angel. This is as our sages, of blessed memory, explained[780] about the verse,[781] "I am the commander of *HaShem*'s-יהו"ה

---

[778] Rashi to Talmud Bavli, Brachot 4a ibid.
[779] Numbers 20:12-13
[780] Midrash Tanchumah 18; Midrash Shemot Rabba 32:3; Rashi to Joshua 5:14
[781] Joshua 5:14

legion; now I have come." They stated, "I did not come in the days of your Master, Moshe, since Moshe did not agree to be accompanied by an angel, and instead told *HaShem*-יהו"ה,[782] 'If Your Presence does not come along, do not bring us up from here.'" This being the case, if Yehoshua's entry into the Land was miraculous and was with an outstretched arm, though it was only accompanied by an angel, how much more would it have been so, had the entry been with Moshe (without an angel, but rather, with *HaShem*-יהו"ה Himself, blessed is He). This certainly would have been accompanied by wondrous miracles and an outstretched arm.

Based on the above, it is not understood why Moshe thought he needed to send spies. For, if the entrance into the Land would be through wondrous miracles, what difference would it make, "if the people that dwell in it are strong or weak... or whether they live in open cities or fortified cities..." or the like?

2.

This may be understood by first explaining the general matter of entering the Land of Israel. Through this, we will be able to understand the necessity of sending spies.

Now, the general novelty that was introduced upon entering the Land, is that it was primarily then that they began to specifically fulfill the *mitzvot* in action.[783] Although, in the

---

[782] Exodus 33:15
[783] See Likkutei Torah, Shlach 36c, 47a, 41b and elsewhere.

desert, their conduct certainly was according to Torah, nonetheless, they fulfilled the commandments in a temporary manner and only a small portion of the *mitzvot* were applicable at that time. Rather, the primary matter of fulfilling the *mitzvot* in action, began upon their entrance to the Land. An example of this is the thirty-nine forms of labor that are prohibited on the day of Shabbat, "the order of which is derived according to the sequence of preparing bread,"[784] such as plowing, sowing, harvesting, winnowing etc., all of which were not applicable, since in the desert they ate, "bread that rained down from heaven."[785] Thus, the actualization of this matter was specifically introduced upon their entrance into the Land, at which point, the matter of fulfilling the *mitzvot* in action, was introduced.

Now, to understand the superiority of fulfilling the *mitzvot* in action, which began upon their entrance into the Land, we must preface with the explanation in Likkutei Torah,[786] that the service of *HaShem*-יהו״ה, blessed is He, by the righteous *Tzaddikim*, is divided into two general categories; that of the Leviathan (*Livyatan*) and that of the Behemoth (*Shor HaBar*).

About the *Tzaddikim* who are in the category of the Leviathan (*Livyatan*-לויתן), it is explained that the word, "*Livyatan*-לִוְיָתָן" is a term of bonding, as in the verse,[787] "This

---

784 Talmud Bavli, Shabbat 74b
785 Exodus 16:4
786 See Likkutei Torah, Shmini 18a and on; Maamarei Admor HaZaken Al Maamarei Razal, p. 144 and on.
787 Genesis 29:34

time my husband will accompany-*Yilveh*-ילוה me." The primary service of *HaShem*-יהו"ה, blessed is He, by this kind of *Tzaddik* (in their fulfillment of *mitzvot*) is to effect Supernal unifications with *HaShem*-יהו"ה, which is a spiritual form of service. This is also why the actual Leviathan is a fish and is "of the fish of the sea," referring to the matter of souls who are of the concealed world (*Alma D'Itkasiya*).[788] Such souls are compared to sea creatures, who are not at all separate from their root and source. Thus, even as they are below, in this world, their service of *HaShem*-יהו"ה, blessed is He, is by affecting spiritual and Supernal unifications.

The above cited Likkutei Torah gives an example of this from the service of Rabbi Shimon Bar Yochai, while he was in the cave for thirteen years.[789] While there, he certainly was incapable of fulfilling a number of the *mitzvot* in action. Now, according to Torah law, he was exempt from fulfilling those commandments, since he was a victim of circumstances that were beyond his control and his life was in jeopardy. Accordingly, "The Merciful One exempts a victim of circumstances that are beyond his control."[790] However, we cannot say that he lacked those matters that are affected through the performance of the commandments. We therefore must say that he drew these matters forth through his spiritual service of *HaShem*-יהו"ה, and through Supernal unifications to Him etc.

---

[788] Zohar III 187b

[789] Talmud Bavli, Shabbat 33b

[790] Talmud Bavli, Bava Kamma 28b; Also see the discourse entitled "*Venikdashti*," Shabbat Parshat Emor 5747 (*Hitva'aduyot* 5747 Vol. 3, p. 264).

Likkutei Torah continues and states that the Holy Ari"zal[791] was also of this category of souls, and in his notes, the Tzemach Tzeddek adds, that the Baal Shem Tov, of righteous memory, was also of this category.[792]

The matter of the Behemoth (*Shor HaBar*), on the other hand, refers to *Tzaddikim* whose service of *HaShem*-יהו"ה, blessed is He, is through the fulfillment of the commandments in action. Likkutei Torah goes on to explain,[793] that although the *Tzaddikim* who are of the aspect of the Behemoth (*Shor HaBar*) require the ascensions and elevations that are affected by the *Tzaddikim* who are of the aspect of the Leviathan (*Livyatan*), nevertheless, there is an advantage to the performance of the physical commandments specifically in action, which is the aspect of the Behemoth (*Shor HaBar*), over and above the *Tzaddikim* who serve in the manner of the Leviathan.

This accords to the verse,[794] "Many crops come through the power of the Ox." In other words, there is an advantage to the souls that are called "The Beasts of the Earth," in that they have much greater strength and abundant power. This likewise is stated about the angels called the, "Animals-*Chayot* of the Chariot-*Merkavah*," as it states,[795] "And the animals-*Chayot*

---

[791] Rabbi Yitzchak Luria, the famed master Kabbalist.

[792] See the notes of the Rebbe Rashab to the additions to the Likkutei Torah there 18b; Also see Maamarei Admor HaZaken al Maamarei Razal ibid.

[793] Likkutei Torah Shimini 18c and on.

[794] Proverbs 14:4

[795] See Musaf of Rosh HaShanah after the Kedusha of "*Keter*" beginning with the words, "And the *Chayot* etc." Also see Midrash Shemot Rabba 23:15; Bachaye Terumah 25:10 in the name of Pirke d'Rabbi Eliezer; Torah Ohr Yitro 71a and on; 72d and on.

lifted the throne," indicating that they have great strength to be capable of lifting the throne, and through this, they themselves are uplifted.[796]

This is similar to the explanation[797] of the verse,[798] "Not by bread alone does man live, but rather by everything that emanates from the mouth of *HaShem-*יהו״ה does man live." In other words, it is through the emanation of the mouth of *HaShem-*יהו״ה that is **in** the bread,[799] meaning, the Godly vitality in it, through which man lives. However, at first glance, this is not understood. Why is it that man requires that which emanates from the mouth of *HaShem-*יהו״ה, that is in the bread, when man himself also possesses the emanation of the mouth of *HaShem-*יהו״ה in himself?

It therefore is explained that the emanation of the mouth of *HaShem-*יהו״ה, blessed is He (meaning the Godly vitality) that is in the bread, is rooted in a loftier source than the Godly vitality that is in man. For, since it descended to a lower station, it is understood that its root is a more elevated source, in that the general principle is; that which is higher descends to a greater extent below.[800] Thus, it specifically is the emanation of the mouth of *HaShem-*יהו״ה within the bread, that affects a strengthening of the bond between the soul and the body.

From the above, we may understand the advantage of performing the commandments in action, specifically with

---

[796] See Torah Ohr Ibid.
[797] Likkutei Torah, Shlach 36c
[798] Deuteronomy 8:3
[799] Likkutei Torah of the Arizal to Deuteronomy 8:3 (*Eikev*).
[800] See Likkutei Torah Re'eh 19c.

physical things. Moreover, this is why even those *Tzaddikim* whose souls are in the category of the Leviathan, are also required to fulfill the commandments specifically with physical things. (It was only during certain times, when there was a specific Supernal indication from above, that they were exempt. For example, Rabbi Shimon Bar Yochai was a victim of circumstances beyond his control and was therefore incapable of fulfilling the commandments physically, which was an indication from Above that his service should be performed spiritually, through Supernal unifications to *HaShem*-יהו״ה.) This then, is the special advantage in serving *HaShem*-יהו״ה, blessed is He, from the angle of souls that are in the category of the Behemoth (*Shor HaBar*).

With all the above in mind, we may now understand the advantage of the mode of service of *HaShem*-יהו״ה, that was introduced upon the entrance of the Jewish people into the Land of Israel, in comparison to their service of *HaShem*-יהו״ה in the desert. For, when they were in the desert, they ate, "bread that rained down from heaven,"[801] and they drank water from the well of Miriam (which rolled and accompanied them in their journeys).[802] Even their garments, which were separate from their bodies, were laundered and ironed by the Clouds of Glory. Moreover, their garments actually grew together with the growth of their bodies,[803] meaning that the growth of the soul, which normally causes the growth of the body, also caused the

---

[801] Exodus 16:4
[802] Midrash Bamidbar Rabba 1:2
[803] Rashi to Deuteronomy 8:4; Pesikta d'Rav Kahana 92a

automatic growth of their garments. That is, even though a garment is something separate from the body, nevertheless, it grew together with the growth of the body.

Thus, while they were in the desert, they had no need to be involved in physical matters, and their service of *HaShem*-יהו״ה, blessed is He, was primarily in the aspects of thought (*Machshavah*)[804] and speech (*Dibur*).[805] This is as hinted at in the word for "desert-*Midbar*-מדבר" which is related to the word for "speech-*Dibur*-דבור," as indicated by the verse,[806] "And your mouth-*Midbarech*-מדברך is coveted," referring to the commandment to study Torah, which is primarily done with the speech of the mouth. This accords to the teaching of our sages, of blessed memory,[807] about the verse,[808] "For they are life to those who find them-*L'Motzeihem*-למוצאיהם," meaning, "to those who express them-*L'Motzi'eihem*-למוציאהם with their mouths." In contrast, specifically upon their entrance into the Land, the matter of fulfilling the commandments, specifically with physical action, was introduced, which is an even loftier matter.

---

[804] Likkutei Torah, Shlach 38b; See Likkutei Sichot Vol. 4, p. 1,047; Reshimot Vol. 7 p. 40, and Vol. 10, p. 24.

[805] Likkutei Torah, Shlach 38c; 37a-b; Likkutei Sichot and Reshimot ibid.

[806] Song of Songs 4:3

[807] Talmud Bavli, Eruvin 54a; Hilchot Talmud Torah of the Alter Rebbe 2:12

[808] Proverbs 4:22

3.

Now, for the service of *HaShem*-יהו״ה, blessed is He, to be specifically in a manner of fulfilling physical commandments, through which we attain the higher level, as mentioned above, for this to be, strength must specifically be given from Above. This is besides the strength given from Above, about which our sages, of blessed memory, stated,[809] "Were it not for the assistance of the Holy One, blessed is He, a person would be incapable of overcoming his evil inclination," in that this strength is given once the matter of service of *HaShem*-יהו״ה, blessed is He, has already come about, at which point, we need Divine assistance to overcome the hiddenness and concealments etc. However, even before the service of *HaShem*-יהו״ה begins, strength from Above must be given for the general matter of serving *HaShem*-יהו״ה physically, to even be. However, after this, our awakening from below affects an awakening Above. Through this, we arrive at an even loftier level of service of *HaShem*-יהו״ה, blessed is He.

To preface, these three matters in the general service of *HaShem*-יהו״ה, blessed is He, which are (1) The strength given from Above to fulfill the commandments physically, (2) the service of *HaShem*-יהו״ה itself, and (3) the awakening Above through the awakening from below, are likewise found in Torah. For, since,[810] "the Holy One, blessed is He, gazed into

---

[809] Talmud Bavli, Sukkah 52b
[810] Zohar II 161b; Zohar I 134a; Zohar III 178a

the Torah and created the world," it is understood that all these matters are rooted in Torah first.

The explanation is that, as known, there are three levels in Torah; "Inheritance-*Yerushah*," "Toil-*Yegiyah*," and "Gift-*Matanah*." Regarding "Inheritance-*Yerushah*-ירושה," it is written,[811] "The Torah that Moshe commanded us is the inheritance-*Morashah*-מורשה of the Congregation of Yaakov." In other words, Torah is the aspect of an inheritance-*Yerushah*-ירושה.

Now, we also find that Torah study specifically requires toil, as our sages, of blessed memory, taught,[812] "Prepare yourself for the study of Torah, for it is not yours by inheritance," that is, it specifically requires toil-*Yegiyah*-יגיעה.

Additionally, we find that Torah is an aspect of a gift-*Matanah*-מתנה, as in the common expression, "the giving of the Torah-*Matan Torah*-מתן תורה," which also means, "the gift of the Torah." This is like what our sages, of blessed memory, stated,[813] "At first, Moshe would study Torah and forget it, until it was gifted to him."

The explanation is that there is an aspect of Torah that is the inheritance (*Yerushah*) of every Jew, in that he is the descendent (and inheritor) of Avraham, Yitzchak and Yaakov. This is also indicated in the name of the Jewish people, Israel-ישראל, which forms the acronym, "There are six-hundred thousand letters to the Torah-*Yesh Shishim Ribo Otiyot*

---

[811] Deuteronomy 33:4
[812] Mishnah Avot 2:12 and Rashi and Midrash Shmuel commentaries there.
[813] Talmud Bavli, Nedarim 38a; Midrash Shemot Rabba 41:6

LaTorah-לתורה אותיות רבוא ששים יש."[814] That is, every single Jew has a letter in Torah, through which he receives his vitality.[815]

In addition to this, the approach to Torah study must specifically be in a way of toil (*Yegiyah*). In other words, those matters in Torah that one is capable of attaining through toil, can **only** be attained specifically through toil (*Yegiyah*). However, higher than this is the matter of the gift (*Matanah*) of Torah, which is specifically given from Above, in that it refers to the matters that one is incapable of attaining through his own effort and toil in the service of *HaShem*-יהו"ה, blessed is He.

This is similar to what we previously explained[816] about the verse,[817] "I was with Him as His nursling... My delights are with the children of man." That is, it is specifically through Torah as it is here below, that the Essential Delights (*Sha'ashu'im HaAtzmiyim*), which are the aspect of, "The delights of The King in His Essence" (*Sha'ashu'ey HaMelech B'Atzmuto*) is drawn forth.[818] As we explained, this is the meaning of the word, "**My** delights-*Sha'ashu'ay*-שעשועי," which refers back to the beginning of the verse, "I was with Him as His nursling-*Va'Eheyeh Etzlo Amon*-ואהיה אצלו אמון," and refers to the Torah as it is in the Singular Intrinsic Being of

---

[814] Megale Amukot, Ophan 186.

[815] Likkutei Torah, Bamidbar 16b; Sefer HaMaamarim 5689 p. 104

[816] In the previous discourse, entitled "The Torah preceded the creation of the world by two-thousand years," Ch. 3.

[817] Proverbs 8:30

[818] Emek HaMelech Shaar 1; Likkutei Torah, Shir HaShirim 27a

HaShem-יהו"ה Himself, blessed is He. This matter is only attainable specifically as a gift (*Matanah*).

However, in order to come to the aspect of the gift (*Matanah*) of Torah, it must first be preceded by the matter of the toil (*Yegiyah*) in Torah. This is like the saying of our sages, of blessed memory,[819] "Were it not for the fact that he caused delight in his soul, he would not have given him the gift." In other words, by first toiling in those levels that can be attained through toil, he is then given the aspect of the gift of Torah.

With this, we can also understand the statement of our sages, of blessed memory,[820] "Whosoever sits and studies Torah, the Holy One, blessed is He, sits opposite him and studies with him." They likewise stated,[821] "There are twelve hours in the day. The first three, the Holy One, blessed is He, sits and engages in the study of Torah."

Now, at first glance, this matter, that the Holy One, blessed is He, engages in Torah study specifically in the first three hours of the day, needs to be understood. Is it not so, that the Holy One, blessed is He, sits opposite whoever studies Torah, at any time? However, the explanation is that this matter of the Holy One, blessed is He, sitting opposite the person who engages in Torah study, is referring to the levels of Torah that are attainable through toil (*Yegiyah*). In contrast, the matter of the Holy One, blessed is He, studying Torah in the first three

---

[819] See Talmud Bavli, Gittin 50b; Bava Metziya 16a; See Sefer HaMaamarim 5630 p. 87 and on; *Hemshech V'Kachah* 5637 Ch. 66; Sefer HaMaamarim 5684 p. 210 and on; p. 222 and on; Likkutei Sichot Vol. 13, p. 115 and on.

[820] Tanna D'Bei Eliyahu Rabba Ch. 18; Yalkut Shimoni Eichah Remez 1,034.

[821] Talmud Bavli, Avoda Zarah 3b

hours of the day, refers to Torah in the aspect of a gift (*Matanah*). This is the matter of "the first three hours," which refers to the "three heads of the Ancient One-*Atik*,"[822] that are only drawn forth in an aspect of a gift (*Matanah*) from Above, specifically.

Now, just as these three aspects are found within Torah, they also are automatically drawn forth in the fulfillment of the commandments-*mitzvot*. The form of blessings that we recite over the fulfillment of *mitzvot* is, "Blessed are You, *HaShem*-יהו"ה our God-*Elohei"nu*-ו-אלהינ, King of the world..." His honorable holiness, my father-in-law, the Rebbe, explained this, in the name of the Alter Rebbe, that the title, "God-*Elohi"m*-אלהי"ם" is a term of strength.[823] Therefore, the meaning of the words "*HaShem*-יהו"ה our God-*Elohei"nu*-ו-אלהינ," is that *HaShem*-יהו"ה, blessed is He, is our strength and vitality.[824] This matter itself, empowers us with the ability to fulfill the *mitzvot*,[825] since the substance of the commandments themselves, is as the blessing continues, "Who has sanctified us[826] with His commandments." In other words, we take a physical object and transform it into something that is holy and sanctified unto *HaShem*-יהו"ה, blessed is He. This then, is the

---

[822] That is, the three upper Sefirot of Atik Yomin. See Shaar HaYichud – The Gate of Unity, Ch. 23-24.

[823] See Tur, Shulchan Aruch and the words of the Alter Rebbe in Orach Chaim Siman 5; Also see Ginat Egoz of Rabbi Yosef Gikatilla, Vol. 1, The Gate of The Title.

[824] See Likkutei Torah Shlach 40c; Balak 73c, and the beginning of Parshat Re'eh.

[825] See Likkutei Torah, Ve'Etchanan 2b

[826] It is further explained that the term "sanctified us-*Keedeshanu*-קדשנו" also means "betrothed us."

form of the blessing over the fulfillment of the commandments-*Mitzvot*, and must be recited, "immediately before their performance."[827]

This is then followed by the actual performance of the commandment-*Mitzvah* itself, through which there is an awakening from below that affects an awakening from Above, to the extent that an even loftier level may be reached. It is about this loftier level that our sages, of blessed memory, stated,[828] "The reward of the *mitzvah* is the *mitzvah*." That is, the highest and most superior aspect of the *mitzvah*-מצוה is the *mitzvah*-מצוה itself, in that it affects a bond and a union (*Tzavta v'Chibur*-צוותא וחבור)[829] with the commander-*Metzaveh*-מצוה of the *mitzvot*-מצוות, that is, He who wills and desires them, *HaShem*-יהו"ה Himself, blessed is He.

With all the above in mind, we may likewise understand the matter of the entrance of the Jewish people into the Land of Israel, so that they could then attain the spiritual elevation brought about specifically through the actual physical fulfillment of the commandments. To do so, one who serves *HaShem*-יהו"ה, blessed is He, must descend from his level and invest himself in physical matters, which requires that assistance be granted from Above. This then, is the matter of sending the spies, which is the granting of strength from Above to be able to perform the physical service of *HaShem*-יהו"ה upon

---

[827] Talmud Bavli, Pesachim 7b

[828] Mishnah Avot 4:2; Igrot Kodesh of the Rebbe Rayatz Vol. 10, p. 369 and on; HaYom Yom 8 Cheshvan, and elsewhere.

[829] See Likkutei Torah Bechukotai 45c; Igrot Kodesh and HaYom Yom ibid. and elsewhere.

entering the Land. About this it states,[830] "Send forth men for yourself, and let them spy out (*VeYatooroo*-ויתורו) the Land of Canaan." The term "spy out-*Yatooroo*-יתורו" is of the same root as the word, "advantage-*Yitron*-יתרון," as in the verse,[831] "The advantage-*Yitron*-יתרון of land is supreme." It thus refers to the empowerment from Above that enables the attainment of the advantage-*Yitron*-יתרון that is brought about specifically through the actual physical service of *HaShem*-יהו"ה, blessed is He.

4.

Based on the above, we may understand Moshe's supplication to *HaShem*-יהו"ה,[832] "Let me now cross over and let me see the good Land," in which he specifies, "let me see." For, at first glance, the primary aspect of his supplication was "Let me cross over," meaning that he wanted to cross over the Jordan river and actually come into the land. Why then does he continue, "and let me see"?

The question is strengthened by the words of our sages, of blessed memory, who stated,[833] "Why did our teacher Moshe greatly desire to enter into the Land of Israel? Did he need to eat of its produce or did he need to satisfy himself from its goodness? Rather, he desired to enter the land so that all of the

---

[830] Numbers 13:2
[831] Ecclesiastes 5:8
[832] Deuteronomy 3:25
[833] Talmud Bavli, Sota 14a

commandments-*mitzvot* (including those that can only be fulfilled in the Land of Israel) could be fulfilled by his hand."

This being the case, his request should only have been to enter the land to fulfill the commandments therein. Why then does he specify, "and let me see"? What exactly is this matter of sight that he desired it so greatly, and "prayed five-hundred and fifteen prayers of supplication, like the numerical value of the word, 'I implored-*VaEtchanan*-ואתחנן-515'"?[834]

The explanation[835] is that Moshe desired to affect the empowerment from Above, so that the service of *HaShem*-יהו״ה, blessed is He, could be fulfilled physically, in actuality. That is, through seeing the land, he desired to draw down the aspect of sight (*Re'iyah*), which is the aspect and level of Moshe. This is as stated,[836] "He saw the first portion-*Reishit*-ראשית for himself," through which there is an attainment of the sublimation that is caused through the sight of wisdom-*Chochmah*-חכמ״ה. This is as stated regarding Moshe,[837] "For what-*Ma"h*-מ״ה are we?"

Thus, when he saw that he could not draw forth this aspect of sight (*Re'iyah*) through seeing the Land, he said,[838] "Now, O' Israel, listen-*Shma* etc." In other words, he was only able to affect them in a manner of hearing (*Shmiyah*) alone. It is about this distinction that our sages, of blessed memory,

---

[834] Midrash Dvarim Rabba 11:10

[835] See Likkutei Torah VaEtchanan 2d and on; 3d; Ohr HaTorah VaEtchanan p. 65 and on; p. 93 and on, and elsewhere.

[836] Deuteronomy 33:21

[837] Exodus 16:7-8

[838] Deuteronomy 4:1

stated,[839] "Seeing and hearing cannot be compared to each other." For, although a person may hear about something with all its details, it is specifically when he sees it, that he takes great delight in it. This is because there is a much greater drawing forth of the inner aspect of the soul in the faculty of sight, than in the faculty of hearing. In the same manner, sight effects a much greater inner nullification of one's sense of self, than hearing does. For although, when one hears that, in the capital far away, there is a great king, with many great and glorious ministers who all are sublimated to him, this will cause him to be sublimated to the king and to fulfill his decrees, nonetheless, his reaction cannot at all compare to a person who enters the court of the king and sees all the great and glorious ministers and their sublimation to the king, with his own eyes.[840] Thus, seeing causes a much greater nullification of his sense of self. This, then, is what Moshe desired to affect in the Jewish people, that they should attain the aspect of sight (*Re'iyah*).

5.

Based on this, we may also understand the explanation in Likkutei Torah[841] about the difference between the spies that Moshe sent and the spies that Yehoshua sent. Moshe sent the spies to spy out the whole Land of Canaan, whereas Yehoshua

---

[839] Mechilta Yitro 19:19; Midrash Lekach Tov, Shlach 13:18

[840] See Tanya Ch. 42 in the note (61a).

[841] Likkutei Torah, Shlach 51c and on; Ohr HaTorah ibid. p. 439 and on; Also see the discourse entitled, "*VaYishlach Yehoshua*" 5736 (Torat Menachem, Sefer HaMaamarim, Sivan p. 380 and on; Sefer HaMaamarim 5736 p. 243 and on).

sent the spies to spy out the city of Jericho only. The name Jericho-*Yericho*-יריחו is from the root, "scent-*Rei'ach*-ריח," and refers to the garments of the soul; thought, speech and action, that are only in the category of scent-*Rei'ach*-ריח. That is, Yehoshua's purpose in sending the spies was only to empower the Jewish people with the ability to refine the garments of the soul.

In contrast, Moshe sent the spies to spy out the whole of the Land of Canaan, the land of the seven nations. His purpose was to empower the Jewish people with the ability to refine the seven emotive attributes themselves, which primarily are the aspects of love (*Ahavah*) and fear (*Yirah*). This is as mentioned in the note in the Likkutei Torah there ("see Tanya, Chapter Fourteen").

It is explained there that the "quality of the *Beinoni*-the Intermediate, is attainable to everyone and every person should strive after it." For, the service of *HaShem*-יהו"ה performed by the Intermediate-*Beinoni* is specifically in his thought, speech, and action. In other words, it goes without saying that he guards all his speech and actions, but beyond that, he even guards his thoughts, since he knows that, "thoughts of transgression are worse than transgression."[842] Thus, the quality of the Intermediate-*Beinoni* is that, "He has never committed a transgression, nor will he ever transgress."[843] This quality is applicable and attainable by every person, and everyone should strive after it. In other words, this is what is demanded of each

---

[842] Talmud Bavli, Yoma 29a; Tanya ibid. 17b.
[843] Tanya ibid. 16b.

and every Jew, and this is the empowerment that was affected by Yehoshua sending the spies.

In contrast, the service of *HaShem*-יהו״ה by the righteous-*Tzaddikim* is in the aspect of the emotive attributes of love (*Ahavah*) and fear (*Yirah*) themselves. That is, the *Tzaddik* has tremendous love for all matters of holiness (*Kedushah*), and utterly despises and is repulsed by all matters of the external husks of evil (*Kelipah*). This kind of Divine service is not applicable to everyone, but is something that comes from Above, like the teaching,[844] "You created righteous people-*Tzaddikim*," which is a matter of a gift (*Matanah*). This is as stated,[845] "I shall grant your priestly service as a gift." This empowerment was affected through the spies that were sent by Moshe.

The explanation is that since Moshe was of the aspect of sight (*Re'iyah*) and was in the (aforementioned) state of essential nullification of sense of self, he therefore had the power to send spies to the whole of the Land of Canaan. In other words, he had the capacity to refine the emotive attributes themselves. This is because, from the perspective of the sight of the true reality of *HaShem*-יהו״ה, blessed is He, there is no room for the existence of anything that opposes holiness. This is similar to how it will be in the coming future, when there will be a sight of Godliness, at which point, it no longer will be possible for anything that opposes Godliness to exist. (It is only

---

[844] Talmud Bavli, Bava Batra 16a; Tanya Ch. 14 ibid. 20a.
[845] Numbers 18:7; Tanya ibid.

313

regarding the current state of the world that the verse states,[846] "I have placed before you today the life and the good, and the death and the evil... choose life." In other words, currently, it is possible to choose the opposite of goodness and life, God forbid. Even so, one chooses life.)

Now, a similarity to this may be found in man's service of *HaShem*-יהו״ה, blessed is He, even now. This was stated by his honorable holiness, my father-in-law, the Rebbe, in the name of the teachings of ethics (*Musar*),[847] regarding the teaching,[848] "Who is wise? One who sees the consequences." That is, the advice given to a person who has difficulty overcoming his lusts, is to picture to himself (that is, he should **see** in his mind's eye) what will happen once he fulfills his lusts (that is, the consequences). He will see that nothing at all will remain of it. For, since it is physical, it inevitably decays and decomposes, until nothing is left of it at all. At that point, he will be full of regret and anguish over this deed. When he pictures this to himself, he will then be able to overcome his lust.

This is similar to what we explained before about Moshe's request,[849] "Let me cross over and let me see the good Land," in which he specifies, "let me see." That is, he wanted to affect this aspect of sight (*Re'iyah*), through which there could then be the physical service of *HaShem*-יהו״ה, blessed is He, upon the Jewish people entering the Land.

---

[846] Deuteronomy 30:15-19
[847] See Torat Menachem, Vol. 10, p. 166 note 48.
[848] Talmud Bavli, Tamid 32a
[849] Deuteronomy 3:25

6.

This then, is the meaning of the verse,[850] "Send forth men for yourself, and let them spy out the Land of Canaan that I give to the Children of Israel." That is, the sending of the spies is the matter of empowerment, to be able to serve *HaShem-*יהו״ה, blessed is He, even with physical things. The bestowal of this empowerment is through Moshe, and this is why it states, "Send forth men for yourself," meaning,[851] "According to your own understanding." For, although, "the spies themselves were all virtuous,"[852] thus far, their service of *HaShem-*יהו״ה, blessed is He, was only in spiritual form. The empowerment to serve *HaShem-*יהו״ה, blessed is He, physically, was drawn forth specifically through Moshe, since it was Moshe who had the aforementioned aspect of sight (*Re'iyah*) and the essential nullification of sense of self.

This is similar to what is explained[853] regarding the verse,[854] "And Moshe said: 'Six-hundred-thousand foot-soldiers of the people-*Ragli HaAm*-רגלי העם in whose midst I am-*Anochi b'Keerbo*-אנכי בקרבו.'" That is, even though they only are the aspect of the "feet-*Ragli*-רגלי," it is specifically through them that there is a drawing forth of the aspect of, "I

---

[850] Numbers 13:2

[851] Rashi to Numbers 13:2

[852] Rashi to Numbers 13:3

[853] See *Hemshech* 5666 p. 87; Sefer HaMaamarim 5687 p. 115; 5689 p. 69; Torah Ohr Bereishit 1b.

[854] Numbers 11:21

am-*Anochi*-אנכי" in their midst.   This shows the utter nullification of the sense of self that Moshe had, through which he sensed (and was deeply aware of) the advantage of physical service of *HaShem*-יהו"ה, blessed is He, that would come about upon entering the Land, thus actualizing this empowerment.

In contrast, the spies did not have the same degree of nullification of sense of self (*Bittul*). Therefore, they did not sense or feel the advantage of physical service of *HaShem*-יהו"ה, blessed is He. They therefore said,[855] "It is a land that devours its inhabitants." In other words, they felt that through physical service of *HaShem*-יהו"ה, blessed is He, not only would the physical not become elevated, but the opposite might occur. This is why they said,[856] "They are stronger than us-*Mimenu*-ממנו*," about which, our sages, of blessed memory, stated,[857] "Do not read, 'They are stronger than **us**-*Mimenu*-ממנו' but rather read, 'They are stronger than **Him**-*Mimeno*-ממנו,' meaning that even the "Landlord" is incapable of removing His belongings from there." While it is true that physical things possess extremely lofty sparks of Godliness in them, that fell with the shattering of the vessels (*Shevirat HaKeilim*), they argued that, nevertheless, because of the great descent, "even the "Landlord" is incapable of removing His belongings from there." In other words, even though He is the Landlord, they argued that, "He cannot remove His belongings (that is, the sparks of holiness) from there."

---

[855] Numbers 13:32
[856] Numbers 13:31
[857] Talmud Bavli, Sotah 35a; Ohr HaTorah Shlach p. 451

Such was not the case with the two spies, Yehoshua and Calev, who were sublimated and nullified to Moshe. Thus, they instead argued,[858] "But do not rebel against HaShem-יהו"ה! You should not fear the people of the Land, for they are our bread. Their protection has departed from them, and HaShem-יהו"ה is with us! Do not fear them!" In other words, they argued that, "The Landlord can certainly remove His belongings from there," meaning that He certainly can uplift even the physical. They thus argued,[859] "The Land is very, very good-Tovah HaAretz Me'od Me'od-טובה הארץ מאד מאד!" The term "very-Me'od-מאד" is repeated twice here, meaning that the first, "very-Me'od-מאד," is the aspect of serving HaShem-יהו"ה, blessed is He, "with all your being-Bechol Me'odecha- בכל מאדך,"[860] from below. The second "very-Me'od-מאד," on the other hand, is with "all Your Being-Me'od-מאד," from Above.

Yehoshua and Calev had this perspective because they were entirely sublimated and completely nullified their sense of self (Bittul) to Moshe. This is also the meaning of the verse,[861] "Calev silenced-VaYaHas-ויהס the people toward Moshe," wherein the term, "silenced-VaYaHas-ויהס" indicates the matter of sublimation and nullification (Bittul), since it is specifically through this aspect of sublimation and nullification of sense of self (Bittul) that the power to enter the Land comes about.

---

[858] Numbers 14:9
[859] Numbers 14:7; See Likkutei Torah Shlach 37a; 38c
[860] Deuteronomy 6:5
[861] Numbers 13:30

This also is the meaning of what it states about the spies that Yehoshua sent,[862] "Yehoshua bin Nun dispatched two men – spies – from Shittim, secretly-*Cheresh*-חרש, saying etc." The word, "secretly-*Cheresh*-חרש" is also a term of silence,[863] and is related to a "deaf mute-*Cheeresh*-חרש," who neither hears nor speaks. In other words, it indicates utter and total sublimation and nullification of sense of self (*Bittul B'Tachlit*). This is to say that Yehoshua too had this aspect of the inner nullification of sense of self, at the very least in the matters of thought, speech, and action. This is because the power to enter the Land depends entirely on the inner essential nullification of sense of self (*Bittul Atzmi*) that Moshe possessed, which is why he was told, "Send forth men for yourself" – "according to your own understanding."

The same principle applies to the coming redemption, which will occur through the sublimation and nullification of the sense of self to Moshe. For,[864] "there is an offshoot of Moshe in every generation." In our generation, this refers to his honorable holiness, my father-in-law, the Rebbe, the shepherd of our generation. We will enter the Land, in the most literal sense, and will become aware that, "the Land is very, very good!"

---

[862] Joshua 2:1
[863] See Likkutei Torah Shlach 52b
[864] Tikkunei Zohar, Tikkun 69, 112a

Discourse 13

"Natata L'Yerei'echa Neis LeHitnoseis -
You have given those who fear You a banner to be raised"

Delivered on the 12th of Tammuz, 5711
By the grace of *HaShem*, blessed is He,

1.

The verse states,[865] "You have given those who fear You a banner to be raised (*Neis LeHitnoseis*-נס להתנוסס) for the sake of truth, always!" In his discourse (that he sent to Russia, and has recently been printed),[866] His honorable holiness, my father-in-law, the Rebbe, cites the Targum translation,[867] "You have given those who fear You a test by which to be uplifted (*Nisa L'It'nasa'ah Beih*-נסא לאתנסאה ביה), because of the eternal truth of Avraham." He explains that this refers to serving *HaShem*-יהו"ה, blessed is He, with self-sacrifice (*Mesirat*

---

[865] Psalms 60:6
[866] The discourse entitled "*Natata L'Yerei'echa*" 12 Tammuz 5693 (that was printed with additional citations and notes by the Rebbe) in the pamphlet that was given out for 12-13 Tammuz 5711 (Kuntres 93). It was subsequently printed in Sefer HaMaamarim 5711, p. 289 and on; Sefer HaMaamarim 5693, p. 532 and on. (It was sent to Russia to be studied during the days of 12-13 Tammuz. Due to the fact that the substance of this discourse discusses the matter of self-sacrifice (*Mesirat Nefesh*) in the face of tests-*Nisyonot*, and the manner of their refinement etc., this fact was thus mentioned in the beginning of this discourse. (See the notes of the Rebbe in the aforementioned pamphlet.)
[867] Targum to Psalms 60:6

Nefesh), specifically in matters that one is challenged and tested by (*Nisyonot*-נסיונות). (These tests and challenges were given to the Jewish people specifically to uplift them-*Hitnoses-*התנוסס)[868] and it is specifically in this, that there is a distinction between this final exile and the exiles that preceded it. Namely, now, there are many more concealments, challenges and tests. However, in truth, this itself indicates the additional strength and might given to each and every Jew from Above, to be able to withstand the test and overcome it.

Moreover, this is the advantage of the strength and might given to the Jewish people in this final exile, over and above the other exiles, including the exile of Egypt (which was the root of all exiles).[869] For, regarding the exile of Egypt, it states,[870] "They did not listen to Moshe, because of distraction and hard work." (In other words, the challenges and tests of their hard labor distracted and confused them.) In contrast, in the current exile, we have been granted the strength and might to recognize the reality that these are merely tests and challenges (*Nisyonot*).

He continues and further explains[871] that the test (*Nisayon*) is that the spark of Godliness is very hidden and concealed.[872] For, the matter of a test or challenge (*Nisayon*) is

---

[868] See discourse entitled "*Natata L'Yerei'echa*" 5680 (Sefer HaMaamarim 5680, p. 105, p. 113); Sefer HaMaamarim 5689 p. 285.

[869] Midrash Bereishit Rabba 16:4; Likkutei Torah of the Arizal, VaYetzei; Sefer HaMaamarim 5684, p. 279; 5709 p. 107, and elsewhere.

[870] Exodus 6:9

[871] Sefer HaMaamarim 5680 ibid. p. 107, 5689 p. 288 and on; 5700 p. 22 and on; 5708 p. 94 and on; Discourse entitled "*Natata L'Yerei'echa*" 5736 Ch. 4.

[872] See Likkutei Torah, Re'eh, discourse entitled "*Acharei*" and its explanation 19b and on; Sefer HaMitzvot of the Tzemach Tzeddek 185b and on.

unlike all other physical matters that become refined. That is, in regard to other physical matters, the refinement is through working with them, through which the Godly element in them becomes refined and included in Godliness. However, such is not the case with challenges and tests (*Nisayon*), wherein the manner of refinement is not through working with the thing, but rather, is through working on oneself.

In other words, the test (*Nisayon*) has no independent existence of its own. Rather, it is just that something has been placed in his way, to conceal and obstruct. Thus, one's entire engagement when dealing with such tests and challenges (*Nisyonot*) is to work on himself, to awaken the essential strength he has within himself. This must be done until he utterly nullifies all obstructions and obstacles. (The above are the words of his honorable holiness, my father-in-law, the Rebbe, at the beginning of his discourse, albeit in a very short summary.)

The essential point is that it is specifically in this final exile, in the doubled and quadrupled darkness of the "heels of Moshiach," at the very end of the hiddenness and concealment, that the Jewish people have been bestowed with even greater strength not to become confounded by the tests and challenges. In other words, through awakening the essential strength that we have within ourselves, which is an essential strength, and more so, is an essential nullification of awareness of self,[873] the obstacle and challenge automatically becomes nullified of itself

---

[873] Sefer HaMaamarim 5680 p. 108

(and it can be said that this is why specifically tests and challenges (*Nisyonot*), cause much greater ascension).

2.

The explanation of the matter is as follows: In every type of service of *HaShem*-יהו״ה, blessed is He, be it the service of refinement (*Birurim*) or the service of overcoming tests (*Nisyonot*), there are three matters. The first is the thing with which the service must be performed. The second is the Jew himself, whose responsibility is to perform the service. The third, is the manner in which the service should be performed, whether it is with the thing that requires refinement (*Birur*), or whether it is the thing within which the test (*Nisayon*) is garbed. However, in each of these matters, there is a difference between service that is called, "the service of refinement" (*Avodat HaBirurim*) and service that is called, "the service of tests" (*Avodat HaNisyonot*).

Now, the explanation is that, "the service of refinement" (*Avodat HaBirurim*) is such, that there is a refinement of the spark of Godliness that exists in the thing being refined itself, which is not the case with "the service of tests," (*Avodat HaNisyonot*), in which, that through which the test (*Nisayon*) is made, has no actual existence.[874] (As mentioned above, the test (*Nisayon*) itself, has no independent existence, in and of itself, but is only there to conceal and obstruct.) Nevertheless, since

---

[874] See *Hemshech* 5672 Vol. 2, p. 681; Sefer HaMaamarim 5689, 5700, 5708 ibid.; Discourse entitled "*Natata L'Yerei'echa*" 5736, Ch. 4.

there indeed is a matter of a test (*Nisayon*), it must be said that there is a spark of holiness there. For, without the spark of holiness, there could not even be an imaginary existence that conceals and obstructs.

This is further understood from the abovementioned discourse regarding the matter of tests (*Nisyonot*), in that it states about the Egyptian exile,[875] "They did not listen to Moshe, because of distraction and hard work." For, in the hard labor of the Jewish people in Egypt, there certainly were many sparks of holiness, that were refined and subsequently elevated when they left Egypt.[876] As known[877] about of the teaching of our sages, regarding the verse,[878] "And they emptied Egypt," that,[879] "They made Egypt like a trap with no bait and like a deep sea with no fish." In other words, they utterly emptied it of all sparks of holiness.

However, the spark of holiness that exists in a test (*Nisayon*) is in a much greater state of concealment and hiddenness. This is why the primary matter of tests and challenges (*Nisyonot*) is mainly during the time of the, "heels of Moshiach," of this final exile. That is, toward the very end of this exile. For, it is at this time that refinement of even the minutest and final sparks of holiness is necessary, as the concealment and hiddenness in them is to a much greater

---

[875] Exodus 6:9

[876] See Kanfei Yonah Vol. 3, Siman 58; Megaleh Amukot, Ophan 58, and elsewhere. Also see Sefer HaMaamarim 5689 p. 287.

[877] Torah Ohr, Bo 60c and elsewhere.

[878] Exodus 12:36

[879] Talmud Bavli, Brachot 9b

extent.[880] In other words, the sparks of holiness found in the challenges and tests (*Nisyonot*) are garbed and consumed in concealment and hiddenness, to such an extent that they do not illuminate at all. Because of this, they cannot even be called "light-*Ohr*-אור." Thus, at times, we find that it states[881] that the spark of holiness can itself become "darkness-*Choshech*-חושך," similar to the Halachic principle that,[882] "once milk imparts flavor to a piece of meat, the meat becomes non-kosher, in and of itself."[883]

Thus, the difference between something that needs refinement (*Birur*) and something that is a test (*Nisayon*), is that the spark of holiness in the thing being refined, can be called a spark of "light-*Ohr*-אור," since it possesses an element of illumination and light. In contrast, in a test (*Nisayon*), nothing remains of the spark of holiness except that it exists, being that all its other aspects (other than its essential existence) have become "non-kosher, in and of themselves."

Now, based on the above distinction between something that is being refined (*Birur*) and something that is a test (*Nisayon*), there likewise is a difference in the person performing the service and in the manner of his service. For, in regard to the matter of tests (*Nisyonot*), a person must grapple with himself, meaning with his own essential being, and not

---

880 See Sefer HaMaamarim 5680, p. 107

881 Sefer HaMaamarim 5665 p. 104; Sefer HaMaamarim 5670 p. 104; *Hemshech* 5672 Vol. 2, p. 477; Sefer HaMaamarim 5680 p. 108.

882 Talmud Bavli 108a

883 And can then render other meat that it is mixed with it, as non-kosher. This is known as "*Chatichah Atzmah Na'aseit Neveilah*-חתיכה עצמה נעשית נבילה."

324

with other matters that are only external expressions of himself. (This is similar to the spark of holiness in the thing that is a test (*Nisayon*), in which only its essential being remains intact.) Moreover, the way of this service is not one of battle, nor is it the give and take of question and answer, through which refinement and ascension are affected. Rather, the approach is specifically an awakening of one's inner essential strength and inner essential sublimation to *HaShem-יהו״ה*, blessed is He.

3.

Now, in greater detail, the beginning of the service of *HaShem-יהו״ה*, blessed is He, in a way of refinement (*Birurim*), is during prayer. This is as stated,[884] "The time of prayer is a time of battle." In other words, although, generally speaking, the service of refinement (*Avodat HaBirurim*) is while eating, drinking and involvement with all other physical aspects of one's being, nevertheless, for a person not to be pulled down by these involvements, but on the contrary, to cause an ascent of the physical things, to refine and elevate the sparks of Godliness manifest within them, he must first cause a general weakening, both in himself, meaning in his body and animalistic soul, as well as in the physicality and materiality of the world.

This is accomplished through the service of *HaShem-יהו״ה*, blessed is He, during prayer, which is, "a time of battle," by which he causes a general weakening of his body and

---

[884] Zohar as cited in Likkutei Torah Teitzei 34c, 35c

animalistic soul. This is accomplished through contemplation (*Hitbonenut*) that precedes prayer and the subsequent contemplation (*Hitbonenut*) during prayer itself. For example, when he contemplates the manner in which the *Ophanim* and *Chayot* angels are utterly nullified to *HaShem-יהו״ה*, blessed is He, and are entirely in His service and that they are the root of the animalistic soul, this causes a general weakening of his body and animalistic soul, and thus automatically also affects his portion of the world at large.

This is the reason[885] why it is forbidden to eat and tend to one's own affairs before praying.[886] For, before he has caused this general weakening in himself and in his portion in the world, there is room for concern that not only will he not be able to elevate the physical matters he engages in, but more so, the physical matters will lower him and pull him down. Thus, only after one has served *HaShem-יהו״ה*, blessed is He, in prayer, is it followed by serving *HaShem-יהו״ה* through the morning meal of bread[887] and all other matters that pertain to the service of refinement (*Avodat HaBirurim*). For, after he has caused the general weakening of the body and animalistic soul, which is the beginning of the battle, he then is able to continue to the second stage of the battle, this being,[888] "one who wishes to eat bread must do so by the blade of the sword." This refers

---

[885] See Likkutei Torah, Pinchas 79d and on; Maamarei Admor HaZaken al Parshiot HaTorah Vol. 2, p. 747; Ohr HaTorah Bereishit Vol. 6, p. 1,020a and on; Sefer HaMaamarim 5689 p. 126 and on, and elsewhere.

[886] Talmud Bavli, Brachot 10b; 14a

[887] See Talmud Bavli, Bava Metzia 107b

[888] Zohar III 188b (Parshat Balak, Yenuka)

to the involvement and refinement of physical matters (*Birurim*).

Now, the beginning of the service of refinement (*Avodat HaBirurim*), which is the (aforementioned) service of prayer, is by way of contemplation (*Hitbonenut*).[889] The reason is that since the sparks of holiness in the things being refined are such, that besides their essential state of existence, all their other aspects also have an element of light and holiness, it therefore is possible to wage battle with them, through the give and take of questions and answers, until they are refined and elevated.

This is not the case, however, with the service of tests (*Avodat HaNisyonot*), since in this case, the spark of holiness in the test (*Nisayon*) is in such a way that it has "become non-kosher, in and of itself." That is, the spark itself has become dark, like the darkness of the three completely impure husks of evil (*Shalosh Kelipot HaTmei'ot*), God forbid. In this case, it is impossible to approach the test in a manner of the battle of give and take, since there is no element in it by which to take hold, to even begin waging battle. Rather, this way of service requires that one awaken his innermost essential strength and sublimation to *HaShem*-יהו"ה, blessed is He, with the realization that there is no other way at all but to stand up to the test, since no path is open before him, except to overcome it.

However, because his service in this is from his innermost essential strength and sublimation to *HaShem*-יהו"ה,

---

blessed is He, and not because of other, more limited expressions of the soul, such as illuminations and revelations, or even service that accords to reason and intellect, but instead, is only because of his essential self, it therefore is within the power and ability of the essence to extract the spark of holiness in the thing that he is tested with. This is because essentially, the spark that is within it is indeed whole, as explained above.

4.

Now, it is for these reasons that the service of tests (*Avodat HaNisyonot*) is tied to the aspect of the singular *Yechidah*-essence of the soul.[890] That is, it is within the power of the singular *Yechidah*-essence of the soul to even transform the singular *Yechidah*-essence of the opposing side, that is, the singular *Yechidah*-essence of the animalistic soul. It is sometimes explained[891] that with the illumination of the singular *Yechidah*-essence of the soul, there no longer is an aspect of a test (*Nisayon*) whatsoever. Thus, the only element of a test (*Nisayon*) that remains, is to awaken and come to serve *HaShem*-יהו"ה, blessed is He, with the singular *Yechidah*-essence of his soul. However, once he, in fact, reveals the singular *Yechidah*-essence of his soul, his service of *HaShem*-יהו"ה, blessed is He, no longer is in the way of a test whatsoever.

---

[890] Sefer HaMaamarim 5680 p. 109 and on; Also see the discourse entitled "*Natata L'Yerei'echa*" 5736, Ch. 2.

[891] See discourse entitled "*Padah BeShalom*" of the Mittler Rebbe, Ch. 9 (Shaarei Teshuvah 54c and on), cited in Sefer HaMaamarim 5680 p. 110; Sefer HaMaamarim 5700, p. 41.

The explanation is that the *Nefesh, Ru'ach* and *Neshamah* levels of the soul, are the inner powers of the soul and are the aspects of the intellect and below.[892] Above them, however, are the aspects of the encompassing light of the *Chayah* level of the soul and the encompassing light of the singular *Yechidah*-essence of the soul. The encompassing light of the *Chayah* of the soul, is the aspect of desire (*Ratzon*), whereas the encompassing light of the singular *Yechidah* of the soul, is the aspect of pleasure (*Ta'anug*).

Now, the way of service in a manner of the give and take of battle, is only applicable in service of *HaShem*-יהו״ה, blessed is He, in the aspects of the intellect and below. However, this is not so with service of *HaShem*-יהו״ה from the aspects of desire (*Ratzon*) and pleasure (*Ta'anug*), in which case, the give and take of the intellect is altogether not applicable. For, this is a matter of either-or, that is, either he takes pleasure in it or not. In other words, if one's service of *HaShem*-יהו״ה, blessed is He, is from the *Yechidah*-essence of his soul, which is the power of pleasure, because he has great delight in this, there is no room for the give and take of questions and answers, which is the matter of battle.

Thus, when one's service of *HaShem*-יהו״ה is from the aspect of the *Yechidah*-essence of his soul, it even transforms the *Yechidah*-essence of the animalistic soul into holiness. In other words, it pulls the pleasure of the animalistic soul out of physical matters, and it goes without saying, that it pulls it away

---

[892] See Sefer HaMaamarim 5680 p. 279 and on; Discourse entitled "*Ka'asher Yarim Moshe*" 5730, and elsewhere.

from coarse materiality. He then has total equanimity (*Hishtavut*) towards all physical and material matters, and thus all matters that he is tested by, become entirely nullified. This is explained by the Alter Rebbe in Iggeret HaKodesh of Tanya,[893] that "the truly faithful is not perturbed by any sufferings in the world, and regarding all matters of the world, 'yes' and 'no' are equal to him, with true equanimity."

In other words, the reason that a person is pained and worried over any lacking in matters relating to his children, health and livelihood, is only because these matters are not in a state of equanimity for him. However, if he has attained a state of total equanimity towards these matters this is not the case. For, he is concerned only with matters that relate to Torah and *mitzvot*, and from the perspective of Torah,[894] "Whatever the Merciful One does, He does for the best!" Therefore, he has total equanimity towards everything that he might be tested with, and thus, the test (*Nisayon*) is automatically nullified completely.

This then, clarifies and explains the above statement, that if the service of *HaShem*-יהו"ה, blessed is He, is from the aspect of the *Yechidah*-essence of the soul, it is not in a way of a test at all. This is because he has brought himself to total and complete equanimity toward everything that happens to him.

---

893 Tanya, Iggeret HaKodesh, Epistle 11
894 Talmud Bavli, Brachot 60b

5.

Now, although we explained before that the spark of holiness that exists within the test (*Nisayon*) is in a state of utter concealment, to the point that all that remains of the spark is its essential existence alone (and as mentioned, this is the general distinction between tests (*Nisyonot*) and refinements (*Birurim*), from which all the other differences between them stem), on the other hand, it is known[895] that the loftier something is, the greater its descent below. Thus, because this spark descended below to such a degree that nothing remains of it except for its existence, it is therefore understood that in this itself, the Highest of the high can be found.

By way of example, this may be compared to the explanation given regarding to the matter of self-sacrifice (*Mesirat Nefesh*) in these latter generations. In earlier generations, matters of intellect were openly revealed, and the effect of intellect is that it conceals the matter of self-sacrifice (*Mesirat Nefesh*). The latter generations, however, do not fall into this category. Thus, just as it is much easier to have self-sacrifice (*Mesirat Nefesh*) in one's heels, than to have self-sacrifice in one's head, so likewise, it is easier to affect self-sacrifice (*Mesirat Nefesh*) in the generation of the, "heels of Moshiach," than it was in earlier generations, who were on a much loftier level.

---

[895] See Likkutei Torah, Re'eh, discourse entitled "*Acharei*" and its explanation 19b and on; Sefer HaMitzvot of the Tzemach Tzeddek 185b and on.

The same can be said of the spark of holiness in the test (*Nisayon*). That is, because nothing remains of it, but its existence alone, therefore, the Highest of the high can be found in it to an even greater extent.

6.

With all the above, we may now understand the verse,[896] "for *HaShem*-יהו"ה your God, is testing you, to know whether you love *HaShem*-יהו"ה your God with all your heart and with all your soul." In other words, in order for a person to attain knowledge-*Da'at* and perception-*Re'iyah* of Godliness ("to know-*LaDa'at*-לדעת"), which is the ultimate intention in the coming of Moshiach, this is attained specifically through the matter of tests ("*HaShem*-יהו"ה your God is testing-*MeNaseh*-מנסה you").

The reason is because, in the matter of tests (*Nisyonot*), the spark of Godliness is concealed and hidden to a much greater extent, and it thus is impossible to refine it by way of the give and take of battle. Rather, one's service of *HaShem*-יהו"ה must be with the full strength of his essential self and with the sublimation of his essential self to *HaShem*-יהו"ה, blessed is He, through which he comes to reveal the singular *Yechidah*-essence of his soul.

When there then is a revelation of the *Yechidah*-essence of his Godly soul, this likewise transforms the *Yechidah*-

---

[896] Deuteronomy 13:4

essence of his animalistic soul. The automatic effect is that he will have absolute equanimity towards all matters that pertain to his children, his health, and his livelihood, through which the test is utterly nullified (as explained above). It is at this point that the Godly spark within the test becomes revealed and returns to holiness. Moreover, it actually is elevated to a much loftier level, in that whatever descended lower is, in fact, much loftier.

7.

Now, this is also the reason that specifically following the tests of the doubled and quadrupled darkness of this final exile (after which, the prophecy,[897] "I will remove the spirit of impurity from the land" will be fulfilled), during which time we refine the most final sparks that are in the greatest state of concealment and hiddenness, we will subsequently arrive at the fulfillment of the prophecy that,[898] "the earth will be filled with the knowledge of *HaShem*-יהו״ה as the water covers the ocean floor." That is, the promise of Torah will be revealed, namely, that, "*HaShem*-יהו״ה your God is testing you, **to know**." In other words, the ultimate purpose of the tests (*Nisayon*) is to reveal the knowledge of *HaShem's*-יהו״ה Godliness, as in the verse,[899] "**know** the God of your father."

---

[897] Zachariah 13:2
[898] Isaiah 11:9
[899] Chronicles I 28:9

We therefore were given this service of tests (*Avodat HaNisyonot*) – not as it was in the time of the Egyptian exile, which was only a manner of confusion. Rather, it will be as explained by his honorable holiness, my father-in-law, the Rebbe, in his discourse, that in this exile we have been given the strength to recognize the reality that they are nothing but tests (*Nisyonot*)." In other words, we have the ability to stand up to the test (*Nisayon*) through an essential awakening and the arousal of our essential strength and sublimation to *HaShem*-יהו״ה, blessed is He. We therefore can stand up to the test (*Nisayon*) in such a way that we actually can extract the sparks of holiness in them, through which we merit to come to, "know *HaShem*-יהו״ה your God!"

In other words, the test (*Nisayon*) has no independent existence in and of itself. Rather, the whole reason that "*HaShem*-יהו״ה your God, is testing you" is specifically so that you should come "to know-*LaDa'at*," and to come to the state and standing of, "the earth will be filled with the knowledge of *HaShem*-יהו״ה!"

Therefore, if we stand up against all concealment and hiddenness, and if our service of *HaShem*-יהו״ה, blessed is He, is not in the way of the give and take of battle, but we instead approach every matter with our essential strength and our essential sublimation to *HaShem*-יהו״ה, blessed is He, that is, that we recognize the reality that, "In and of myself I have no existence whatsoever (I truly am nothing), nonetheless, since I am engaged in the service of *HaShem*-יהו״ה, blessed is He, I will not be shaken or moved by anything. I know that it is impossible to do otherwise and that this matter must be carried out!" If this is the approach, then the test (*Nisayon*) becomes nullified and the spark of holiness that was concealed in it, becomes refined and elevated.

Through this, we bring about revelation of Godliness in the world at large, so that speedily in our days, this revelation will come about in the most literal sense, through the coming of our righteous Moshiach. The preparation for this must be carried out by every single one of us during the time of exile, particularly during this final exile, and more particularly, during the "heels of Moshiach," which is the very end of the exile. In other words, when each and every one will carry out his service of *HaShem-*יהו״ה, blessed is He, with essential strength, and with essential sublimation to *HaShem-*יהו״ה, blessed is He, then we all will speedily merit, that in our times, all the revelations and illuminations of the Singular Essential Being of *HaShem-*יהו״ה, the Unlimited One Himself, blessed is He, will be revealed, through our righteous Moshiach! May this be speedily in our days, Amen!

Discourse 14

"*Tzav Et B'nei Yisroel* -
Command the children of Israel"

Delivered on Shabbat Parashat Pinchas,
Shabbat Mevarchim Menachem-Av, 5711
By the grace of *HaShem*, blessed is He,

1.

The verse states,[900] "Command the children of Israel and say to them: Take care to offer Me My offering of My food for My fire offerings, My pleasing aroma in its appointed time." Sifri comments on this,[901] "What is stated above this verse?[902] Our teacher Moshe said, 'Let *HaShem*-יהו״ה, the God of the spirits of all flesh, appoint a man over the congregation, who will go forth before them and come before them, who will lead them out and bring them in, so that the congregation of *HaShem*-יהו״ה will not be like a flock without a shepherd.' The Holy One, blessed is He, said to him, 'Before you command Me regarding My children (which is unnecessary), command My children regarding Me.'"

Now, from the fact that before Moshe's passing, the Holy One, blessed is He, told him to, "Command My children

---

[900] Numbers 28:2
[901] Sifri Pinchas 24 in Rashi ibid.; Also see Midrash Shir HaShirim Rabba 1:3
[902] Numbers 27:16-17

regarding Me," specifically about the matter of sacrificial offerings (*Korbanot*), it is understood that the sacrificial offerings (*Korbanot*) are primary to the service of *HaShem-יהו״ה*, blessed is He.

However, this needs to be understood. For we find that the Prophets admonished the Jewish people,[903] "Does *HaShem-יהו״ה* delight in burnt-offerings and feast-offerings as (He does) in obedience to the voice of *HaShem-יהו״ה*? Surely, to obey is better than a choice offering, to be attentive is better than the fat of rams." It likewise states,[904] "For I desire kindness, not sacrifice; and knowledge of God, rather than burnt-offerings." This seems to indicate that the primary matter is obedience (*Shmo'a-שמוע*) and kindness (*Chessed-חסד*), rather than sacrificial offerings.

In addition, we must understand the matter of sacrificial offerings, in and of themselves. The very first sacrificial offering that the Jewish people were commanded through Moshe, was the daily *Tamid*-offering. About the daily-*Tamid* offerings, our sages, of blessed memory stated,[905] "The daily *Tamid*-offering of the morning atones for the sins of the previous night and the daily *Tamid*-offering of dusk atones for the sins of that day." The well-known question is,[906] how can the sacrificial offering of an animal atone for the sins of man?

---

[903] Samuel I 15:22

[904] Hosea 6:6

[905] Midrash Tanchuma Pinchas 13, Bamidbar Rabba 21:21; Tanya Iggeret HaTeshuvah Ch. 11 (100b).

[906] See Maamarei Admor HaZaken 5567 p. 289 and notes there; Ohr HaTorah Matot p. 1,255 and elsewhere.

In the words of our sages, of blessed memory,[907] "If the man sinned, in what way did the animal sin?" However, the explanation[908] is that atonement comes about when the man contemplates that whatever is done to the animal should have fittingly been done to him.[909]

This also applies to the matter of prayer (*Tefillah*[910]), which was established in place of the sacrificial offerings, as our sages, of blessed memory, stated,[911] "The *Tefillah*-prayer was instituted corresponding to the daily *Tamid* offerings." It is similarly explained in Likkutei Torah,[912] that in the burnt offerings (*Korban Olah*), they would offer the flesh (*Basar*), the veins (*Gidin*), and the bones (*Atzamot*). It explains there that the bones are drawn from the brain, the flesh is drawn from the blood, which mainly resides in the heart, and the flesh is drawn from the blood. It explains these matters there in relation to prayer (*Tefillah*), which corresponds to the sacrificial offerings.

That is, the contemplation (*Hitbonenut*) into the matter that relative to the Unlimited Light of *HaShem*-יהו"ה Himself, blessed is He, the worlds (and their entire chaining down – *Seder Hishtalshelut*) take up no space and their entire existence is nullified and sublimated to Him, in that before Him they literally are nothing, corresponds to the aspect of the bones,

---

[907] Talmud Bavli, Yoma 22b

[908] Ohr HaTorah, Matot ibid. Sefer HaMaamarim 5698 p. 227 and elsewhere.

[909] See Ramban to Leviticus 1:9; Rekanti to the beginning of Vayikra, cited in the Shnei Luchot HaBrit in his Mesechet Taanit 211b; Also see Rashi to Genesis 22:13.

[910] Referring to the silent Amidah prayer.

[911] Talmud Bavli, Brachot 26b

[912] Likkutei Torah Pinchas 77d and on

which are drawn from the brain. In contrast, the awakening of the emotions of love (*Ahavah*) and fear (*Yirah*) of *HaShem*-יהו"ה, blessed is He, that is brought about through contemplation (*Hitbonenut*),[913] is the aspect of the flesh that is drawn from the blood of the heart. For, the emotions are a mere glimmer of the grasp of the intellect of the brain, as it is drawn to be manifest in the heart by way of the veins and arteries, through which the bones and flesh are bonded.

Now, based on the above, we find that there is an advantage to prayer, over and above the sacrificial offerings. For, the matter of the offerings is that it is only **as if** everything being done to the animal is being done to the man. In contrast, in prayer, the actual service of the sacrificial offerings is being done within the soul of man himself, in the most literal sense. For, the contemplation (*Hitbonenut*) and awakening (*Hit'orerut*) of love and fear, are themselves the matters of offering the bones, veins and flesh, literally, as stated above. This being the case, we would think that prayer is a loftier level than the sacrificial offerings.[914] However, we nevertheless find that the sacrificial offerings are loftier than prayer. We recite

---

[913] See Rambam Hilchot Yesodei HaTorah (Laws of the Foundations of the Torah) 2:2; For an explanation of all of the states of love and fear of *HaShem*, blessed is He, which are awakened through the above *Hitbonenut*-contemplation, see Kuntres HaHitpaalut of the Mittler Rebbe, translated as Divine Inspiration. For an elucidation of the methodology and approach to *Hitbonenut*-contemplation, as well as the entire subject matter that one is to contemplate, see Shaar HaYichud of the Mittler Rebbe, translated as The Gate of Unity.

[914] See Torah Ohr, Vayechi 46b; Torat Chaim 95a and on; Ohr HaTorah ibid. Vol. 6, p. 1,129a and on; p. 1,137a and on; Vol. 7 p. 1,269a and on; *Hemshech* entitled "*VeKachah*" 5637 Ch. 19; Derech Chaim, Shaar HaTefilah Ch. 92.

this in our prayers,[915] "May it be desirable before You, *HaShem*-יהו"ה our God and the God of our fathers, that the Holy Temple will be built speedily, in our days," where we will then be able to bring the sacrificial offerings (*Korbanot*).

Additionally, according to the explanation given for the advantage of the sacrificial offerings (*Korbanot*), namely, that the spark of Godliness in the animal is rooted in a loftier source,[916] since whatever is higher descends lower,[917] it makes sense that the primary advantage of the sacrificial offerings was specifically in the first and second Holy Temples, at which time the Godly spark in the physical animal had descended very low, but not in the sacrificial offerings of the coming future, about which the verse states[918] "I will remove the spirit of impurity from the land."

Nevertheless, we find that the primary advantage of sacrificial offerings will specifically be in the coming future. This is as we recite in our prayer Liturgy,[919] "There we will offer our obligatory sacrifices to You, the daily burnt-offerings according to their order and the additional-*Musaf* offerings according to their rule... we will prepare and offer them to You with love and in accordance with the commandments that You desire..." This seems to indicate that specifically in the coming

---

[915] At the conclusion of the *Shemoneh Esreh* prayer.

[916] See Maamarei Admor HaZaken 5567 p. 289 and notes there; Ohr HaTorah Matot p. 1,255 and elsewhere.

[917] See Likkutei Torah Re'eh 19c

[918] Zachariah 13:2

[919] In the *Musaf* liturgy

future the service of the sacrificial offerings will be completed to perfection.

Now, this needs to be understood, because from either angle, this matter requires clarification. If we examine it from the spiritual perspective, it would seem that the primary advantage should be in the matter of prayer. However, if we examine it from the physical angle, it would seem that the primary advantage should be in the sacrificial offerings of the first and second Holy Temples. Why then do we say that, specifically the sacrificial offerings of the coming future will be completed to perfection, "in accordance with the commandments that You desire"?

2.

To understand this, we must preface with the following. As known,[920] the ultimate purpose in creating the worlds is that,[921] "The Holy One, blessed is He, desired to have a dwelling place for Himself in the lower worlds." The explanation of a, "dwelling place," is that, just as the totality of one's essential self and being dwells in his home,[922] so likewise, "The Holy One, blessed is He" – meaning, the Essential Self of the Unlimited One, HaShem-יהו"ה Himself, blessed is He –

See Sefer HaMaamarim 5670, p. 214 and on;

[921] Midrash Tanchumah Naso 16; Bechukotai 3; Bereishit Rabba Ch. 3; Bamidbar Rabba Ch. 13; Tanya, Ch. 36

[922] See Maamarei Admor HaZaken 5565 Vol. 1, p. 489 (and with the notes in Ohr HaTorah Shir HaShirim Vol. 2, p. 680); Ohr HaTorah Balak p. 997; Sefer HaMaamarim 5635 Vol. 2, p. 353; *Hemshech* 5666 p. 3.

"desires to have a dwelling place for Himself in the lower worlds," specifically.

This is also the meaning of the teaching of our sages, of blessed memory, about the verse,[923] "I have come to My garden-*Gani*-גני," meaning,[924] "'to My wedding canopy-*Genuni*-גנוני,' that the **essential root** of the Indwelling Presence of *HaShem*-יהו"ה, the *Shechinah*, was in the lowest world." They specifically used the term, "The **essential root** of the Indwelling Presence of *HaShem*-יהו"ה," as opposed to the general term "the Indwelling Presence of *HaShem*-יהו"ה-*Shechinah*," which only refers only to revelations of Godliness. Rather, the "**essential root** of the Indwelling Presence of *HaShem*-יהו"ה-*Shechinah*," refers to the Essential Self of the Unlimited One, *HaShem*-יהו"ה Himself, blessed is He. It is specifically about this that it states, "The Holy One, blessed is He, desired to have a dwelling place **for Himself** in the lower worlds."

This matter is accomplished through man's service of *HaShem*-יהו"ה, blessed is He, here below. This is similar to how it was originally, when the, "the essential root of the *Shechinah*-The Indwelling Presence of *HaShem*-יהו"ה was in the lowest world." For, even then, there was a matter of service of *HaShem*-יהו"ה, blessed is He, as it states,[925] "And *HaShem*-יהו"ה

---

923 Song of Songs 5:1

924 Midrash Rabba, Shir HaShirim 5:1; See the discourse entitled "I have come to My garden-*Bati LeGani*" 5710 (Sefer HaMaamarim 5710 p. 111 and on) and the first discourse by the same title from this year.

God, took the man (*Adam*) and placed him in the Garden of Eden, to work it and to guard it."

The explanation is that the verse states,[926] "God ceased from all the work that God created to be done-*La'asot*-לעשות." Our sages, of blessed memory, commented on the word, "to be done-*La'asot*-לעשות," and said that this means,[927] "To be done-*La'asot*-לעשות and to be repaired-*LeTakken*-לתקן." In other words, there are two aspects to everything. The first aspect is what it is, in and of itself. The second aspect is added to it through man's work in the service of *HaShem*-יהו״ה, blessed is He. This even applies to the Garden of Eden, which transcends the world. For, as known, the floor of the Garden of Eden is the spirituality of the physicality of the world.[928] That is, there is the aspect of the Garden of Eden as it is, in and of itself, and there is what is added to it through man's service of *HaShem*-יהו״ה, blessed is He, here below.

The explanation is that the Garden of Eden is loftier than this world.[929] This is because the world is connected to the aspect of the emotive attributes, as it states,[930] "For I said, the world is built of kindness-*Chessed*." In contrast, generally speaking, the Garden of Eden is the world of Creation-*Briyah*, wherein there is an illumination of the wisdom-*Chochmah*,

---

[926] Genesis 2:3

[927] Bereishit Rabba 11:6 and the commentaries there; Rashi to Genesis 2:3

[928] See Maamarei Admor HaEmtza'ee, Vayikra Vol. 2, p. 703; Sefer HaMaamarim 5662 p. 299; Discourse entitled "*Vayikach HaShem Elokim*" 5712; Ohr HaTorah Bereishit Vol. 7, p. 1,163a and on, and elsewhere.

[929] See Biurei HaZohar of the Mittler Rebbe, Acharei 75a; Sefer HaMaamarim 5698 p. 222.

[930] Psalms 89:3; Ohr HaTorah (*Yahal Ohr*) to Psalms 89:3; Sefer HaMaamarim 5698 p. 220 and on;

understanding-*Binah*, and knowledge-*Da'at* of the Unlimited One, blessed is He. (That is, it is **His** wisdom-*Chochmah*, **His** understanding-*Binah*, and **His** knowledge-*Da'at.*) In other words, it is the aspect of the intellect (*Mochin*), and as known, intellect transcends emotions. This is why the drawing forth of intellect to the emotions is specifically through the narrowing of the neck (*Meitzar HaGaron*). In other words, in order for the emotions to come into existence from the intellect, there must first be the concealment of the intellect. Only then is it possible for the emotions to come forth into existence. It is therefore understood that there is a vast difference between the emotions and the intellect, when compared to each other. Because of this, there must first be a concealment of the intellect, until a state of neither intellect nor emotions, and only afterwards can there be the existence of emotions.

In the same way, we may understand the vast distance in comparison between this world, the existence of which is from the emotive attributes, in comparison to the Garden of Eden, in which there is an illumination of the aspect of the intellect. Moreover, in this world there only is the knowledge of *HaShem's*-יהו"ה existence (*Yediyat HaMetziyut*), but not any grasp of His Essential Being itself (*Hasagat HaMahut*).[931] This applies to both the spiritual, as well as the material matters of this world. There is no grasp of His Essential Being in their existence, neither physically nor spiritually.

---

[931] See Likkutei Torah Ve'Etchanan 6a and on; Also see the introduction and opening gateway – *Petach HaSha'ar* – to Imrei Binah of the Mittler Rebbe, translated and adapted into English under the title, The Gateway to Understanding, Chapter 22 and on.

This is because the essential being of every novel creature is the Godly power manifest within it. For, if the power of the Actor would be withdrawn from the acted upon, the acted upon would revert to utter nothingness.[932] Thus, because the very existence of the novel creature is the Godly power manifest within it, and there is no grasp of the Godly power itself, we therefore find that amongst the physical, there is no grasp of HaShem's-יהו"ה Essential Being (*Hasagat HaMahut*) whatsoever, but only the knowledge of His existence (*Yediyat HaMetziyut*).

However, such is not the case in the Garden of Eden, in which there is actual grasp of the Essential Being of HaShem's-יהו"ה Godliness.[933] This is similar to the teaching that in the Garden of Eden,[934] "The righteous delight in the ray of the *Shechinah*-The Indwelling Presence of HaShem-יהו"ה. That is, their delight is specifically in the grasp of His Essential Being (*Hasagat HaMahut*).[935]

Now, although this world cannot in any way be compared to the Garden of Eden, nevertheless, it is specifically through the service of HaShem-יהו"ה, blessed is He, in this world, that we bring about additional illumination of Godly light in the Garden of Eden. For, the revelations in the Garden of Eden (that is, "their delight in the ray of the *Shechinah*-The

---

[932] See Tanya, Shaar HaYichud V'HaEmunah, Ch. 1, and elsewhere; Also see Ginat Egoz of Rabbi Yosef Gikatilla, translated as HaShem is One, Volume 1.

[933] See Torah Ohr, Chaye Sarah 16a; Sefer HaMaamarim 5698 p. 224 and on.

[934] Talmud Bavli, Brachot 17a

[935] See Ginat Egoz of Rabbi Yosef Gikatilla, translated as HaShem is One, Vol. 1, The Gate of The Sanctuary

Indwelling Presence of *HaShem*-יהו״ה), is from the ray of the Torah learning and service of *HaShem*-יהו״ה that they accomplished in this world.[936]   Moreover, it is just an illumination of a light and ray (*Ohr V'Ziv*),[937] affected through their service of *HaShem*-יהו״ה, blessed is He, here below.

This is similar to what we explained before, in the discourse entitled, "I have come to My garden – *Bati LeGani*,"[938] regarding the matter of the additional illumination in the world of Emanation-*Atzilut*, caused through man's service of *HaShem*-יהו״ה, blessed is He, here below. That is, the illuminations of light in the world of Emanation-*Atzilut* are comparable to something that is placed in storage. That is, their purpose is not for the world of Emanation-*Atzilut*, but rather, for the needs of this lower world. Thus, they are not actually revealed in the world of Emanation-*Atzilut*.

The same is true of the revelation in the Garden of Eden. It is only the aspect of a ray (*Ziv*) of the Torah and *mitzvot* that the righteous fulfilled in this world.   Nonetheless, it is specifically this that adds additional light and illumination in the Garden of Eden.

To further explain, the novel introduction of illumination in the Garden of Eden through man's service of *HaShem*-יהו״ה, blessed is He, in this world, is an illumination that is drawn forth from the aspect of how *HaShem*-יהו״ה, blessed is He, transcends all worlds (*Sovev Kol Almin*). That is,

---

[936] Tanya, Ch. 39 (52b)
[937] See Ohr HaTorah Bamidbar p. 9.
[938] See the prior discourse, Ch. 5.

in the Garden of Eden itself, there only is an illumination of how *HaShem*-יהו"ה, blessed is He, fills all worlds (*Memale Kol Almin*).[939] This is why the Garden of Eden is called,[940] "The clear world – *Olam Barur*." This is because, in the Garden of Eden, all matters are in their proper place and order and everything is according to its proper state and station. This is also why in the Garden of Eden repentance (*Teshuvah*) is no longer effective. This is because repentance (*Teshuvah*) is the transformation of one's self from one state of being to another state of being, which is entirely inapplicable to the Garden of Eden, since it is, "a clear world," within which there is an illumination of how *HaShem*-יהו"ה, blessed is He, fills all worlds (*Memale Kol Almin*).

That is, the aspect of how *HaShem*-יהו"ה, blessed is He, fills all worlds (*Memale Kol Almin*) is the aspect of lights (*Orot*) and vessels (*Keilim*), wherein the lights (*Orot*) are commensurate to the capacity of the vessels (*Keilim*) to receive them, and the vessels can only contain the illumination of light appropriate to them, and no more. Thus, the novel introduction of illumination in the Garden of Eden, caused specifically by man's service of *HaShem*-יהו"ה, blessed is He, in this world, is that an illumination from the aspect of how *HaShem*-יהו"ה, blessed is He, transcends all worlds (*Sovev Kol Almin*) is drawn forth.

---

[939] Likkutei Torah, Pinchas 75c
[940] Talmud Bavli, Pesachim 50a

3.

Now, the primary service of *HaShem*-יהו״ה, blessed is He, by which this lower world becomes a dwelling place for His Presence, is specifically the service of the sacrificial offerings (*Korbanot*).[941] The same is true of the service of *HaShem*-יהו״ה, blessed is He, at the very beginning of creation, about which it states,[942] "And *HaShem*-יהו״ה God, took the man (*Adam*) and placed him in the Garden of Eden, to work it and guard it." Our sages, of blessed memory, explained[943] that the term, "to guard it-*Leshamrah*-לְשָׁמְרָהּ," refers to the sacrificial offerings, about which its states,[944] "You shall take care-*Tishmeru*-תִּשְׁמְרוּ to offer it to Me at its appointed time."

This may be understood as follows: We explained before that the "dwelling place" means that the Intrinsic Essential Being of the Unlimited One, *HaShem*-יהו״ה Himself, blessed is He, will be here below. Moreover, the matter of a "dwelling place" is that the drawing down of His Presence will not just be in a transcendent manner (*Makif*), but rather, that it will be drawn into the creatures in an inner manner (*Pnimi*) that is openly revealed. In order to bring this about it is necessary to remove the hiddenness and concealments, because as long as there is hiddenness and concealment, the drawing down is only

---

[941] See discourse entitled "I have come to My garden – *Bati Legani*" 5732, Ch. 4, and note 22 there.

[942] Genesis 2:15

[943] Midrash Bereishit Rabba 16:5; Also see Likkutei Torah Shir HaShirim 48d and on.

[944] Numbers 28:2

in a transcendent manner (*Makif*), or the drawing down is in an inner manner (*Pnimi*), but remains concealed and is not openly revealed. It therefore is necessary to remove the hiddenness and concealment, at which point the drawing down will be both in an inner manner (*Pnimi*) and will be openly revealed, since there will be nothing to obstruct it from being openly revealed.

Now, this is specifically accomplished through the service of sacrificial offerings (*Korbanot*) to *HaShem-יהו"ה*, blessed is He. For, when they were offered, it was openly revealed that the physical animal was subsumed and consumed by a fire from above, which is the aspect of the, "Fiery Lion that consumed the sacrifices."[945] Additionally, the term, "sacrifice-*Korban-קרבן*" is of the same root as, "bringing close-*Kiruv-קירוב*,"[946] and refers to bringing the faculties and senses of man close to Godliness, that is, that Godliness is drawn into the creatures in an inner way.

Moreover, the drawing forth that comes about from the sacrifices (*Korbanot*) is the drawing down of the Essential Intrinsic Being of *HaShem-יהו"ה*, the Unlimited One Himself, blessed is He. This is as stated,[947] "The mystery of sacrifice ascends to the mystery of the Unlimited One (*Ein Sof*)," that is, to the mystery of the Singular Intrinsic Essential Being of *HaShem-יהו"ה*, the Unlimited One Himself, blessed is He! This is evident from the precise usage of the term, "the mystery of

---

[945] Zohar III 32b; Talmud Bavli Yoma 21b; Likkutei Torah Bamidbar 11a

[946] See Sefer HaBahir, Section 46 (p. 109); Zohar III 5a; Shnei Luchot HaBrit note 10; Pri Etz Chaim, Shaar HaTefilah Ch. 5

[947] Zohar II 239a; Zohar III 26b

the Unlimited One-*Ein Sof*-אין סוף," as opposed to, "the mystery
of the Light of the Unlimited One – *Ohr Ein Sof*-אור אין סוף."

Thus, the primary service of *HaShem*-יהו"ה, blessed is
He, that actualizes His dwelling in the lower worlds, is the
service of the sacrificial offerings (*Korbanot*). For, it is through
this service that we reach the aspect of the very Essence of His
Being, blessed is He, and moreover, we draw Him forth in an
inner manner within creation, in a way of open revelation!

Because of this, the superiority of the sacrificial
offerings (*Korbanot*) is primarily when they are performed in
actuality, that is, specifically with a physical animal, and not
only through prayer. This is because it is specifically through
the offering of a physical animal, that it becomes openly
revealed that the animal is consumed in the Upper Fire, as
mentioned above. Similarly, it is for this reason that the initial
service of *HaShem*-יהו"ה, blessed is He, at the beginning of
creation, was with the matter of sacrificial offerings
(*Korbanot*). For, it is specifically through this that the intent in
creation is fulfilled, namely, that "The Holy One, blessed is He,
desired to have a dwelling place for Himself in the lower
worlds."

This is also the reason for the specific usage of the term
"and He placed him-*VaYanicheihu*-ויניחהו" in the verse,[948] "And
HaShem-יהו"ה God, took the man (*Adam*) and placed him in the
Garden of Eden, to work it and to guard it." For, it is through

---

[948] Genesis 2:15

351

the sacrificial offerings that the matter of "satisfaction-*Naycha*-ניי חא" comes about.[949]

4.

Now, in the service of the sacrificial offerings itself, there is a superiority to how it was at the beginning of creation, in the Garden of Eden. For, as explained before, the Garden of Eden is the spiritual aspect within the physical world. In other words, although it is part of the physicality of the world, it is the spiritual of the physical, within which there was no existence of evil at all (in that evil was external to the Garden of Eden). It is thus understood that the service of the sacrificial offerings in the Garden of Eden was not a matter of refinement (*Birurim*), but was rather the matter of drawing forth Godliness.

(This is similar to how it was in the times of Shlomo (Solomon), about whom it states,[950] "Behold, a son will be born to you, he will be a man of calm, and I shall calm him of all his surrounding enemies. For his name will be Shlomo-His Peace." That is, for him, the matter of refinement (*Birurim*) was automatic.)[951]

However, after the sin of the Tree of the knowledge of good and evil (*Eitz HaDa'at*), it states,[952] "And He banished man," meaning that,[953] "He was judged to be punished by

---

[949] See Likkutei Torah, Shir HaShirim 49a

[950] Chronicles I 22:9

[951] See Torah Ohr, Bereishit 6a; Likkutei Torah Bamidbar 4a, and elsewhere.

[952] Genesis 3:24

[953] Midrash Bereishit Rabba 19:9; Petichta to Eicha Rabbati 4

banishment." The is because in the Garden of Eden, the existence of evil is not applicable.[954] Although the simple reason the Torah gives for his banishment is,[955] "Lest he put forth his hand and take also of the Tree of Life, and eat and live forever," nevertheless, this reason, in and of itself, does not necessitate that the punishment should specifically be through banishment, and *HaShem*-יהו"ה, the All-Present One, blessed is He, has many methods available at His disposal, besides banishment. Rather, the inner reason that he was specifically banished, is because in the Garden of Eden the existence of evil is not applicable.

Because of this, it states,[956] "So *HaShem*-יהו"ה God banished him from the Garden of Eden to work the earth from which he was taken." That is, since it was the earth from which he was taken that caused him to come to sin, therefore, instead of his service of *HaShem*-יהו"ה in the Garden of Eden, in which his toil was to draw forth Godliness, he was instead given to toil in the earth, which is the matter of the service of refinement (*Avodat HaBirurim*).

This then, is the advantage of the service of the sacrificial offerings (*Korbanot*) as they were in the Garden of Eden. Namely, the primary matter of the service of *HaShem*-יהו"ה, blessed is He, as it was in the Garden of Eden, was to draw forth Godliness, without any involvement or relationship to evil altogether. This likewise will be the service of the

[954] Maamarei Admor HaEmtza'ee, Vayikra Vol. 2, p. 703; Sefer HaMaamarim 5662 p. 299; Discourse entitled "*Vayikach HaShem Elokim*" 5712 and elsewhere.
[955] Genesis 3:22
[956] Genesis 3:23

sacrificial offerings (*Korbanot*) of the coming future. For, since,[957] "I will remove the spirit of impurity from the land," the sacrificial offerings will no longer be for the service of refinement (*Avodat HaBirurim*), for that will have been completed. Rather, as it was in the Garden of Eden at the beginning of creation, they will be to draw forth Godliness.

5.

However, the **essential completion** of the service of *HaShem*-יהו"ה, blessed is He, through sacrificial offerings, will specifically be attained to perfection in the coming future. For, then, the sacrificial offerings (*Korbanot*) will be on an even loftier level than the sacrificial offerings of the Garden of Eden.

More particularly, it states about the sacrificial offerings, "My bread, for My fire... you shall take care to offer to Me." Three matters are enumerated here: The word "My bread-*Lachmi*-לחמי" refers to that which is presented in offering. "You shall take care-*Tishmeru*-תשמרו," refers to the one who brings the offering and, "for My fire-*L'Ishay*-לאשי" refers to the Upper Fire. In other words, according to that which is brought in the offering and the one who brings the offering, so likewise will be the manner of drawing forth of the Upper Fire from Above. In the coming future, all three matters will be completed to perfection, and thus, at that time, the matter of

---

[957] Zachariah 13:2

sacrificial offerings (*Korbanot*) will reach the ultimate level of perfection.

The explanation is that the sacrificial offerings of the Garden of Eden preceded the giving of the Torah. Thus, at that time the edict that,[958] "The Romans shall not descend to Syria and the Syrians shall not ascend to Rome," was still in effect, meaning that, "The upper did not descend to the lower and the lower did not ascend to the upper." This is why it states that,[959] "all of the *mitzvot* performed by our forefathers were only in the aspect of a scent." In other words, the drawing forth of the Essence, that occurred at the giving of the Torah, had not yet happened. As explained by the Rebbe Rashab,[960] whose soul is in Eden, the matter of scent also applied to Adam, even though, actually, his service was loftier than that of the forefathers, being that he was,[961] "formed by the hand of the Holy One, blessed is He," and that he was in the Garden of Eden itself.

Now, it can be said that the novelty of this is that even though he was, "formed by the hand of the Holy One, blessed is He," nevertheless, his service of *HaShem*-יהו"ה, was only in this manner of a scent. For, in regard to the soul, every Jew is equal. As the Alter Rebbe explained in Tanya,[962] the Godly soul, "is, literally, a portion of Godliness from Above,[963] as written,[964] 'And He blew into his nostrils a soul of life,' and we

---

[958] Midrash Tanchuma Va'era 15; Shmot Rabba 12:3
[959] Midrash Shir HaShirim Rabba 1:3
[960] Sefer HaMaamarim 5670, p. 217
[961] See Midrash Bereishit Rabba 24:5 and elsewhere.
[962] Tanya, Ch. 2
[963] Job 31:2
[964] Genesis 2:7

recite,[965] 'You blew into me,' and as it states in the Zohar,[966] 'He who blows, blows from within himself,' meaning from his inwardness and innermost being."

The superiority of Adam, however, was that even in regard to his body, he was, "formed by the hand of the Holy One, blessed is He." In other words, even as his body was down here in this world, below ten handbreadths, nevertheless, he was, "formed by the hand of the Holy One, blessed is He," who "is above ten handbreadths."[967] In other words, we find that, in Adam, there was a bond between the Upper and the lower.

The novelty is that, even so, his service of *HaShem*-יהו"ה, blessed is He, was only the aspect of scent. This is because the aforementioned edict that, "the Upper shall not descend to the lower and the lower shall not ascend to the Upper," had not yet been nullified. Rather, the nullification of this edict only happened through the giving of the Torah, which was a drawing forth of the Essential Being of *HaShem*-יהו"ה, blessed is He, in the most literal sense. For, this is the meaning of,[968] "I am *HaShem-Anochi HaShem*-יהו"ה אנכ"י," which is an acronym for,[969] "I have placed My soul in My writings-*Ana Nafshi Katavit Yahavit*-אֲנָא נַפְשִׁי כַּתְבִית יָהַבִית."

It is for this reason that the general matter of the giving of the Torah was actually much loftier than the state and

---

Morning blessings Liturgy

[966] Cited in Tanya ibid. in the name of the Zohar; See Igrot Kodesh, Vol. 20, p. 131.

[967] Talmud Bavli, Sukkah 5a

[968] Exodus 20:2; Deuteronomy 5:6; The first word of the Ten Commandments that states, "I am *HaShem*, your God-*Anochi HaShem Elohe"cha*-אנכי יהו"ה אלהי"ך."

[969] Talmud Bavli, Shabbat 105a (Ein Yaakov)

standing of the Garden of Eden at the beginning of creation. This is as understood from the teaching of our sages,[970] of blessed memory, regarding the verse,[971] "And there was morning and there was evening, the sixth day-*HaShishi*-הַשִּׁשִׁי." They asked, "Why do I require the superfluous letter *Hey*-ה? It teaches that the Holy One, blessed is He, established a condition with the act of creation, and said, 'If Israel accepts the Torah, you will exist; and if not, then I will return the world to chaos and disorder.'" This is because it was specifically at the giving of the Torah that there was a drawing forth of the Essential Being of *HaShem*-יהו"ה Himself, blessed is He.

Thus, although there was great superiority to the service of *HaShem*-יהו"ה through the sacrificial offerings (*Korbanot*) of the Garden of Eden, and it was not a matter of refinement (since in the Garden of Eden there is no existence of evil to refine) but was rather a matter of drawing forth Godliness, nevertheless, it did not yet affect a drawing forth of the true Essential Being of *HaShem*-יהו"ה Himself, blessed is He.

On the other hand, although the service of *HaShem*-יהו"ה with sacrificial offerings of the first and second Holy Temples occurred after the giving of the Torah, at which point there was a drawing forth of the Essential Being of *HaShem*-יהו"ה Himself, blessed is He, nevertheless, because after the sin of the Tree of the knowledge of good and evil there came to be an admixture of good and evil, the primary aspect of the sacrificial service at that time was the matter of refinement (*Birurim*).

---

[970] Talmud Bavli, Shabbat 88a; Rashi to Genesis 1:31
[971] Genesis 1:31

In contrast, with the coming of Moshiach both superior elements will be present.[972] For, it states regarding the coming future,[973] "I will remove the spirit of impurity from the land," and in that time the three completely impure husks of evil (*Shalosh Kelipot HaTmei'ot*) will be nullified. This is the meaning of the verse,[974] "And the wolf shall dwell with the lamb." That is, there will be a matter of refinement even of the wolf (an impure animal), which is of the three completely impure husks of evil. It thus is understood that the shining husk (*Kelipat Nogah*), which is the intermediary between holiness and the three completely impure husks, will certainly be elevated to a much higher level.

This being the case, we thus find that in the coming future, both the animal that is being brought in sacrifice, as well as the man bringing the sacrifice, will be on a much loftier level. This automatically necessitates that the purpose of the sacrificial offerings of that time will not be for the service of refinement (*Avodat HaBirurim*), but rather, in order to draw forth Godliness, like in the Garden of Eden. Moreover, they also will possess the superiority that followed the giving of the Torah, namely, that they will bring about a drawing forth of the Singular Intrinsic Essential Being of *HaShem*-יהו"ה Himself, blessed is He! They will therefore be even loftier than the sacrificial offerings (*Korbanot*) of the Garden of Eden! Thus, it is specifically in regard to the sacrificial offerings of the

---

[972] Also see discourse entitled "*Tzav et b'nei Yisroel*" 5615; Sefer HaMaamarim 5635, Vol. 2, p. 386 and note 205.
[973] Zachariah 13:2
[974] Isaiah 11:6

coming future that it states,[975] "There we will offer to You... in accordance with the commandments that You desire." For, then there will be the fulfillment of the primary desire and primary matter of, "a dwelling place for Himself, blessed is He, in the lower worlds."

6.

Now, the complete perfection of the service of *HaShem*-יהו"ה, blessed is He, with the sacrificial offerings of the coming future, is accomplished specifically through the toil in service of *HaShem*-יהו"ה in exile.[976] This is in accordance with the known principle[977] that the cause is loftier than that which is caused by it, since it is specifically in its power to cause that which is effected. We may thus understand the great superiority of our service of *HaShem*-יהו"ה, blessed is He, during exile, since it is specifically through such service that we come to the complete perfection in the service of the sacrificial offerings, "in accordance with the commandments that You desire."

It can be said that this is the meaning of the verse,[978] "All of her pursuers overtook her in dire straits-*Heeseegoohah Bein HaMitzarim*-המצרים בין השיגוה." This is to say that it is specifically when we are, "in dire straits-*Bein HaMitzarim*- בין המצרים," that we are given the ability to attain the level of

---

[975] In the *Musaf* liturgy
[976] Tanya Ch. 37
[977] See *Hemshech* entitled "*VeKachah*" 5637 Ch. 15
[978] Lamentations 1:3; Also see Ohr HaTorah, Na"Ch Vol. 2 to Lamentations 1:3 (p. 1,035 and on).

"*Heeseegoohah*-השׂיגוה," which refers to the attainment of the loftiest levels of "grasp-*Hasagah*-השׂגה," until we finally attain the time in which we will serve *HaShem*-יהו״ה, blessed is He, with the sacrificial offerings (*Korbanot*) of the coming future, which are the culmination and perfect completion of the "dwelling place in the lower worlds," with the coming of our righteous Moshiach, may it be speedily in our days!

Discourse 15

"VeHayah Eikev Tishme'un -
And it shall come to pass, that because you listen"

Delivered on Shabbat Parshat Eikev,
Shabbat Mevarchim Elul, 5711
By the grace of *HaShem*, blessed is He,

1.

The verse states,[979] "And it shall be, that because you listen to these ordinances, to keep and do them; that *HaShem*-יהו"ה your God, will safeguard for you, the covenant and the kindness that He swore unto your forefathers. He will love you, bless you and increase you. He will bless the fruit of your womb and the fruit of your Land..."

Now, we must understand[980] the inner theme of these three matters, the covenant (*Brit*-ברית), the kindness (*Chessed*-חסד), and the oath (*Shvu'ah*-שבועה). According to the simple understanding of the verse, this matter seems to be conditional. That is, "**Because** you listen to these ordinances etc., then He will safeguard for you, the covenant and the kindness that He swore etc. Now, we must understand this, for these matters are not at all dependent on conditions, but rather are unconditional.

---

[979] Deuteronomy 7:12-13
[980] See the discourse by the same title 5673 (*Hemshech* 5672 Vol. 1, p. 355).

This is because the matter of a covenant (*Brit*-ברית)[981] is like two friends who make a covenant between each other, that in the event that something comes between them, to stop their love (for example, if one of them acts improperly towards the other), it nevertheless, will not diminish their love for each other at all. We thus find that the matter of a covenant (*Brit*-ברית) is unconditional.

The same is true of the oath (*Shvu'ah*-שבועה). It too is unconditional. For example, this is similar to the oath that the Jewish people took to fulfill the commandments of *HaShem*-יהו"ה.[982] That is, even if there are obstacles and hindrances to the fulfillment of the commandments, the purpose of the oath (*Shvu'ah*-שבועה) is that, because of it, one remains entirely unmoved by any hindrances and fulfills the commandments nonetheless.[983] This likewise is true of the oath (*Shvu'ah*-שבועה) of *HaShem*-יהו"ה, blessed is He,[984] as it states,[985] "'In Myself I have sworn,' said *HaShem*-יהו"ה etc.," and it similarly states,[986] "As You swore to our forefathers from the days of old." The intention of this oath, is that regardless of the state

---

[981] See Likkutei Torah, Netzavim 44b and elsewhere.

[982] Talmud Bavli, Nedarim 8a; Kuntres U'Maayan, Maamar 14, Ch. 1

[983] See Kli Yakar to Deuteronomy 7:12; Discourse by the same title 5634 (Sefer HaMaamarim 5634, p. 290).

[984] See Likkutei Torah, Shmini Atzeret 83b and on; Maamarei Admor HaZaken, Ethalech Liozhna p. 205; Sefer HaMaamarim 5635 p. 434; Kitzurim V'Ha'arot L'Tanya p. 52 and on; Sefer HaMaamarim 5698 p. 239 and on.

[985] Genesis 22:16

[986] Micah 7:20

and standing of the Jewish people, the Holy One, blessed is He, has bound Himself to fulfilling His oath.[987]

The same is so regarding the matter of kindness (*Chessed*-חסד), which also is unconditional. Kindness (*Chessed*) is the indiscriminate bestowal of influence to all, not only to the worthy, but even to the unworthy.[988] To further explain, the difference between the qualities of kindness-*Chessed*, judgment-*Gevurah*, and mercy-*Rachamim* is well known. Namely, that the attribute of judgment-*Gevurah* means that *HaShem*-יהו״ה, blessed is He, is exacting, even with those who are worthy. The attribute of mercy-*Rachamim* means that even if someone is unworthy, nevertheless, *HaShem*-יהו״ה, blessed is He, bestows His influence upon him. However, in the case of mercy-*Rachamim*, the distinction between one who is worthy and one who is unworthy is apparent and taken into consideration. In contrast, the attribute of kindness-*Chessed* means that *HaShem*-יהו״ה, blessed is He, bestows his influence to all without any consideration as to whether the beneficiaries of the kindness are worthy or not.

This being the case, that these matters are unconditional, why then does the verse state, "And it shall come to pass, that **because** you listen to these ordinances, to keep and do them, that "*HaShem*-יהו״ה your God, will safeguard for you, the **covenant** and the **kindness** that He **swore** unto your forefathers"?

---

[987] See the lengthy explanation of this in Ginat Egoz of Rabbi Yosef Gikatilla, translated as HaShem is One, Volume 2.

[988] Likkutei Torah, Dvarim 1d; Igrot Kodesh of the Rebbe Rashab Vol. 1, p. 74 and on; Sefer HaMaamarim 5709 p. 8 and on.

Additionally, we must understand why the Torah specifically uses the word, "And it shall come to pass, that **because**-*Eikev*-עקב you listen." That is, if it is indeed conditional, then the word, "**if**-*Im*-אם" would have been more appropriate. That is, it could have said, "And it shall come to pass, that **if**-*Im*-אם you listen." This would be similar to the verse,[989] "And it shall come to pass, that if-*Im*-אם you listen diligently to My commandments etc." Why then does this verse specifically use the word, "because-*Eikev*-עקב," stating, "And it shall come to pass, that because-*Eikev*-עקב you listen"?

Now, (based on the words of Midrash Tanchuma that the word *Eikev*-עקב means "heel") Rashi comments that,[990] "If you will heed the minor commandments that one tramples with his heels [and considers to be of minor importance]." However, this too must be understood, since according to this explanation, the continuation of the verse is not understood. Namely, the verse continues, "because you listen to these ordinances," specifying the commandments that are known as "ordinances-*Mishpatim*-משפטים."

As known, there are three categories of commandments-*mitzvot*: Testimonies-*Eidot*-עדות, Decrees-*Chukim*-חוקים, and Ordinances-*Mishpatim*-משפטים. The laws known as Ordinances-*Mishpatim*-משפטים are those laws that are imperative by reason and intellect, even without having been commanded. Testimonies-*Eidot*-עדות are laws that, once they are commanded, make intellectual sense, even though we

---

989 Deuteronomy 11:13
990 Rashi to

would never have come to do them of our own volition, had they not been commanded. Nevertheless, once they are commanded, it makes intellectual sense to fulfill them, because of what they commemorate and attest to, such as the commandments that recall and attest to the exodus from Egypt.

Decrees-*Chukim*-חוקים, on the other hand, are those commandments about which, "the nations of the world taunt Israel, saying, 'What is this commandment and what purpose does it serve?'"[991] In other words, these are commandments that make no sense to human intellect whatsoever, but are done solely because they are the decrees of *HaShem*-יהו״ה, blessed is He, as it states,[992] "They are statutes that I have engraved and the decrees that I have decreed etc." This being the case, when the Torah mentions the commandments that, "one tramples with his heels," and considers to be of minor importance, it should have instead mentioned "Decrees-*Chukim*-חוקים" or "Testimonies-*Eidot*-עדות." Why then did it specifically mention "Ordinances-*Mishpatim*-משפטים?"

2.

To understand this, we must preface[993] with the teaching in Zohar that,[994] "There are three levels that are bound one to the other; the Jewish people are bound to the Torah and the

---

[991] Rashi to Numbers 19:2; Midrash Bamidbar Rabba 19:8
[992] Midrash Bamidbar Rabba, beginning of Parshat Chukat.
[993] See *Hemshech* 5672 Ibid. p. 356 and on; Torat Menachem, Sefer HaMaamarim Iyar, p. 284 and on and the citations there.
[994] Zohar III 73a

Torah is bound to the Holy One, blessed is He. Each is a level upon a level, with a concealed aspect and a revealed aspect." In other words, this bond is not only in the concealed aspect of the Jewish people, which are the elevated powers of the soul itself, but even in the revealed aspect of the Jewish people, meaning in the revealed powers of the soul. In other words, this teaching does not only relate to the Godly soul of the Jew, but rather, through it, even the revealed powers of the animalistic soul of the Jew become bonded to Torah and to the Holy One, blessed is He.

To further explain,[995] the term, "binding-*Hitkashrut*-התקשרות" (or in the language of the Zohar, "*Mitkashran*-מתקשראן") is only applicable in regard to two things that are separate from each other. In contrast, in regard to something that is one, the term "binding-*Hitkashrut*-התקשרות" is not an appropriate term. Instead, the term "adhesion-*Dveikut*-דביקות" should be used. An example of this is the bond that exists between light-*Ohr*-אור and its luminary-*Ma'or*-מאור, in which the light is not a separate entity from the luminary at all, but is merely the revelation of the luminary itself. It therefore would be inappropriate to use the word, "binding-*Hitkashrut*-התקשרות" in regard to their bond, but rather, the term "adhesion-*Dveikut*-דביקות," which indicates that they are essentially bound and unified as one.

In the same manner, the soul as it is above, is in a state of adhesion-*Dveikut*-דביקות to Godliness. As Tanya specifies,[996]

---

[995] See Likkutei Sichot Vol. 9, p. 73 and note 15 there.
[996] Tanya, Ch. 37 (48a)

"Even if the soul becomes perfectly righteous in this world, serving *HaShem*-יהו"ה with fear and love and delighting in the abundant love of Him, it will not attain the level of **its adhesion-*Dveikut*-דביקות** to *HaShem*-יהו"ה, with the same fear and love that the soul experienced before it descended into the physical world, not even a fraction of it."

It is only when the soul descends and comes to a state of seeming independence of existence, that it becomes applicable to use the term "binding-*Hitkashrut*-התקשרות." In other words, as long as the soul is in a state of, "she is pure-*Tehorah Hee*-טהורה היא,"[997] it is in a state of adhesion-*Dveikut*-דביקות to Godliness. However, when it comes to a state of, "You created it, You formed it, You blew it into me and You preserve it within me,"[998] it then is in a state of "somethingness" and has a sense of independent existence, in which case, its bond to Godliness is in a state of being "bound-*Hitkashrut*-התקשרות" to Godliness. It is about these aspects of the soul that Zohar states, "There are three levels that are bound to each other, the Jewish people are bound to the Torah and the Torah is bound to the Holy One, blessed is He."

Albeit, there is an advantage to the matter of, "binding-*Hitkashrut*-התקשרות" below, over and above the matter of "adhesion-*Dveikut*-דביקות" Above. That is, it is specifically through the matter of "binding-*Hitkashrut*-התקשרות" below, that we come to attain an even loftier level.

---

[997] Elokai Neshamah blessing in the morning prayers (Talmud Brachot 60b); See Likkutei Torah Re'eh 27a.

[998] Continuation of the Elokai Neshamah blessing.

This matter may be understood by the explanation of the verse that states,[999] "I am black, but beautiful, O' daughters of Jerusalem." "Daughters of Jerusalem" refers to the soul as it is Above.[1000] That is, as the soul is Above, it is called, "The daughters of Jerusalem-*Bnot Yerushalyim*-בנות ירושלים," since it is in a state of, "complete and perfect fear-*Yirah Shelimah*-יראה שלימה" of *HaShem*-יהו"ה, blessed is He (The name "*Yerushalayim*-ירושלים" means, "perfect fear-*Yirah Shalem*-יראה שלם.")[1001] This refers to what we previously cited from Tanya, that,[1002] "Even if the soul becomes perfectly righteous (*Tzaddik*) in this world, serving *HaShem*-יהו"ה with fear and love of Him, and delighting in the abundant love of Him, it will not attain the level of its adhesion-*Dveikut*-דביקות to *HaShem*-יהו"ה, with the fear and love that it experienced before descending into the physical world, not even a fraction of it." In other words, it is only as the soul is Above that it is in a state of "perfect fear-*Yirah Shelimah*-יראה שלימה," and it is about this that the souls of the Jewish people are called, "the daughters of Jerusalem-*Bnot Yerushalyim*-בנות ירושלים."

More specifically, the term, "daughters of Jerusalem-*Bnot Yerushalyim*-בנות ירושלים," refers to the souls as they are in the aspect of kingship-*Malchut* of the world of Emanation-*Atzilut*.[1003] This is because matters of love and fear of *HaShem*-יהו"ה, blessed is He, are not applicable in levels that are higher

---

[999] Song of Songs 1:5
[1000] Likkutei Torah, Shir HaShirim 6c.
[1001] Midrash Bereishit Rabba 56:10
[1002] Tanya, Ch. 37 (48a)
[1003] Likkutei Torah, Shir HaShirim Ibid. 7b.

than the *Sefirah* of kingship-*Malchut*. This is because, higher than the *Sefirah* of kingship-*Malchut* there is no existence of a separate being for there to be "one who loves" or "one who fears." Rather, it is only in kingship-*Malchut* of Emanation-*Atzilut*, which is the aspect of the revelation of the world of Emanation-*Atzilut*, that is, the aspect that there is something-*Yesh* that is emanated, that the matter of fear is applicable.

It is because of this that the verse states, "I am black, but beautiful." In other words, this statement is said by the soul, as it is below, to the souls, as they are Above (wherein they are called "the daughters of Jerusalem-*Bnot Yerushalayim*- בנות ירושלים.") The words, "I am black" refer to the darkening and concealment of light and illumination, in that the soul is in a state of separateness from the Essential Being of *HaShem*-יהו"ה, the Unlimited One, Himself, blessed is He.

Moreover, she even is separate from the aspect of "the daughters of Jerusalem-*Bnot Yerushalayim*-בנות ירושלים," mentioned above, in that she is not in a state of "perfect fear-*Yirah Shalem*-יראה שלם" of *HaShem*-יהו"ה, blessed is He. For, "even if the soul becomes perfectly righteous in this world... it will not attain the level of its adhesion-*Dveikut*-דביקות to *HaShem*-יהו"ה, with the fear and love, that the soul experienced before it descended into the physical world, not even to a fraction of it."

The reason is because the body is incapable of withstanding this. Thus, as the soul exists and resides in the body, it is self-understood that it is very distant from perfect fear (*Yirah Shalem*-יראה שלם) of *HaShem*-יהו"ה. Moreover, it resides and exists in,[1004] "a parched and thirsty land with no water." In other words, in this physical world, the possibility exists for the soul to come to transgress positive commandments and even to transgress matters that the advice is to sit idly, rather than to transgress.[1005]

Even so, (though I am black) "I am beautiful." In other words, it is specifically when the soul is here below that it is in the ultimate state of attractiveness and beauty. That is, it is specifically because of the concealment and hiddenness of Godliness, as the soul exists below, that it is roused with great thirst for Godliness, with passionate love of *HaShem*-יהו״ה, blessed is He, like "flames of fire,"[1006] referring to the level of ultimate beauty of the love. (This is in contrast to the soul, as it is Above, where there are no concealments and hiddenness, and it is not in a state of thirst for Godliness.) Thus, as the soul exists below, it is in the ultimate state of beauty (and "attractiveness").

3.

However, this needs to be understood, because at first glance, the advantage that the soul has as a result of its descent below, that due to the concealment and hiddenness it becomes roused with thirst and love, "like flames of fire," is only applicable to the matter of **love** of *HaShem*-יהו״ה, blessed is He.

[1004] Psalms 63:2
[1005] In other words, prohibitive commandments.

However, the matter of fear of *HaShem*-יהו"ה, blessed is He, applies to how the soul is Above, and is a much loftier matter. This is because the matter of fear of *HaShem*-יהו"ה comes about through the recognition and awareness of *HaShem's*-יהו"ה exaltedness, blessed is He, and it is specifically through this, that fear of *HaShem*-יהו"ה is aroused. This is experienced by the soul specifically as it is Above. Since the matter of Godliness is revealed there, the exaltedness of *HaShem's*-יהו"ה, blessed is He, is felt there, thus causing an arousal of fear in the soul. Such is not the case if the soul is below, where there are no revelations etc.

Additionally, for the arousal of love, comprehension and understanding are adequate, in and of themselves, to awaken the love. For, when a person understands and comprehends that something is good for him, he will be awakened to love and pursue it. This is because it is natural to be drawn after all things that benefit him. Thus, when he grasps that Godliness is good for him, he is roused with love of *HaShem*-יהו"ה, blessed is He.

In contrast, in regard fear of *HaShem*-יהו"ה, comprehension alone is inadequate to arouse it. Rather, there must be a recognition and bond with the One he fears. This is because the matter of fear (*Yirah*-יראה) is one of self-nullification (*Bittul*), which is the opposite of one's sense of independent existence. Therefore, understanding and comprehension alone are inadequate, but rather, there must specifically be a recognition and bond (*Hitkashrut*-התקשרות) with *HaShem*-יהו"ה for it to be aroused. This requires great toil, as in the teaching of our sages, of blessed memory,[1007] "Woe to mortal flesh who did not toil with fear." (Which is not the case regarding love of HaShem-יהו״ה, blessed is He, which is awakened through understanding and comprehension and does not require the same degree of great toil-Yegiyah-יגיעה).

From this it is understood that the essential matter of fear of HaShem-יהו״ה, blessed is He, specifically applies to the soul as it is Above. For since above there are revelations of Godliness, the soul as it is above, possesses the aspects of recognition and bonding to Godliness, through which the fear-Yirah-יראה of HaShem-יהו״ה is brought about. Such is not the case as the soul is below, where there are no revelations of Godliness through which it can come to the recognition and bonding. This being the case, as the soul is below, how can it come to the matter of fear-Yirah-יראה?

We must therefore understand the matter of, "I am black, but beautiful," as it applies to fear of HaShem-יהו״ה, blessed is He. For, as stated above, the **ultimate** beauty of fear of HaShem-יהו״ה, is specifically as the soul is below. This being the case, we must say that this matter of beauty not only applies to the love of HaShem-יהו״ה, but also to the fear of HaShem-יהו״ה. For, as we explained before, the unity of the souls of the Jewish people with HaShem-יהו״ה, blessed is He, as they are below, is called "binding-Hitkashrut-התקשרות," and as known, a "permanent knot" is a doubled knot. That is, it has two knots,

---

Reishit Chochmah, Shaar HaYirah, Ch. 12, cited in Tanya Iggeret HaKodesh, Epistle 18 (p. 126b).

one over the other.[1008] These refer to the two matters of love (*Ahavah*) and fear (*Yirah*) of *HaShem*-יהו״ה, blessed is He. As explained in Tanya,[1009] just as a bird cannot fly with a single wing, but requires two wings, so likewise the matter of ascension is not possible except through the medium of both fear and love of *HaShem*-יהו״ה, blessed is He. We therefore must understand what it is that is beautiful ("attractive") in the fear-*Yirah* of *HaShem*-יהו״ה as it is specifically here below.

However, the explanation is that, even though the essential nullification of fear of *HaShem*-יהו״ה is much stronger as the soul is Above, nevertheless, **what** the fear is, is loftier as it is below, since below, the nullification (*Bitul*) is through setting aside one's sense of self, which is more applicable to the soul as it is below, where it has a sense of separate existence.

This is explained elsewhere[1010] regarding the distinction between the nullification of self in the aspect of, "there is nothing but Him alone,"[1011] and the nullification of self in the aspect of, "In His Presence everything is regarded as nothing."[1012] That is, the nullification of the light (*Ohr*) to the Luminary is in an aspect that it is, "regarded as nothing." In contrast, the nullification of, "there is nothing but Him alone –

[1008] See Ginat Egoz of Rabbi Yosef Gikatilla, translated as HaShem is One, Volume 1, section entitled "The Name *Eheye"h*-אהי״ה which is drawn from the reality of the Name of *HaShem*-יהו״ה." Also see Shaltei Giborim Shabbat Ch. 15; Rama to Orach Chayim 317:1; Shulchan Aruch of the Alter Rebbe ibid 2-3, and elsewhere.

[1009] Tanya, Ch. 41 (p. 57b)

[1010] See Sefer HaMaamarim 5661 p. 197 and on; 5692 p. 110 and on.

[1011] Deuteronomy 4:39

[1012] Zohar I 11b; Tanya Ch. 20 and elsewhere.

Ein Od Milvado" (the loftier level) is specifically in the aspect of a tangible something-*Yesh*.

In other words, as the soul is Above, it's nullification of sense of self is in an aspect of, "In His Presence everything is regarded as nothing." That is, through contemplation that the Source is continuously enlivening him and that he cannot compare to Him, his sense of self becomes nullified, **as if** he does not exist. However, since he too is Godliness, he is not utterly nullified of his existence in a way of, "there is nothing but Him alone – *Ein Od Milvado*."

In contrast, when one's soul is below, in a world of concealments and hiddenness, when he comes to the recognition (and realization) that this is not true reality, he then becomes completely nullified in the knowledge that only the Singular Intrinsic and Essential Being of *HaShem*-יהו"ה, the Unlimited One, exists and, "there is nothing but Him alone – *Ein Od Milvado*."[1013]

This is the advantage of fear of *HaShem*-יהו"ה as the soul is specifically below. That is, even though the essential fear of *HaShem*-יהו"ה is greater as the soul is Above, nevertheless, **wha**t the fear is, is much loftier, specifically when the soul is below. We therefore say that the matter of, "I am black, but beautiful" also applies to the matter of fear of *HaShem*-יהו"ה (*Yirah*).

[1013] Deuteronomy 4:35

374

4.

Now, just as in the first "knot," of the Jewish people with the Holy One, blessed is He, there is an advantage in the connection of the soul, specifically as it is below, so also, in the second "knot" of the Torah with the Holy One, blessed is He, there is an advantage in the connection of the Torah, specifically as it is below.

This[1014] is so, even though the Torah is the Supernal will and wisdom of the Holy One, blessed is He. Nonetheless, in its descent below it only is in the aspect of the excess of the Upper Wisdom of *HaShem*-יהו״ה, blessed is He, as in the teaching,[1015] "The excess of the Upper Wisdom-*Chochmah*, is Torah." This is because the Torah descended to become manifest within human intellect and matters of this world,[1016] including even false arguments, to the point that a person can study Torah and completely forget about the **Giver** of the Torah, blessed is He.[1017] More so, one's approach to Torah study could be in such a way that he is undeserving, in which case, it becomes the opposite of an elixir of life for him.[1018] All this is because, as the Torah is below, it is in a state of seemingly separate existence.

[1014] See *Hemshech* 5672 ibid. p. 364 and on.

[1015] Midrash Bereishit Rabba 17:5; *Hemshech* 5672 ibid. p. 350 and on.

[1016] See Tanya Ch. 5

[1017] See Ra"N to Talmud Bavli, Nedarim 81a and Ba"Ch to Orach Chayim, Siman 47.

[1018] Talmud Bavli, Yoma 72b

Now, this matter does not only apply to the revealed aspect of Torah, but also to the concealed aspect of Torah, meaning the concealed of the revealed. This refers to Torah as it is studied by the souls in the Garden of Eden, such as the laws pertaining to plagues, impurities, sacrificial offerings and, "one who exchanges a cow for a donkey,"[1019] and the like. In all of them the Torah is explaining matters that relate to the chaining down of the worlds, meaning that they are in a state of tangible existence.

In other words, what is meant by descent in relation to Torah, not only applies to its descent to this world, but also applies to all the worlds that follow the restraint-*Tzimtzum* of the Unlimited light of *HaShem*-יהו"ה, in general. Before the restraint-*Tzimtzum*, there altogether was no "room" for the existence of worlds,[1020] and it is only with the restraint-*Tzimtzum* that "room" was created for their existence. Thus, even in the Garden of Eden, the Torah discusses and explains the particular matters as they relate to the order of the chaining down of the worlds (*Hishtalshelut*).

Now, since the restraint-*Tzimtzum* of the Unlimited light of *HaShem*-יהו"ה was in a manner of the complete withdrawal (*Siluk*) of illumination, it is understood that the Torah that follows the restraint-*Tzimtzum*, does not fall into the category of "adhesion-*Dveikut*-דביקות," but rather falls into the category of "binding-*Hitkashrut*-התקשרות." This is certainly the case regarding Torah as it is below, in this world, wherein it certainly

---

[1019] Talmud Bavli, Bava Metzia 100a
[1020] See Etz Chaim, Shaar 1 (Drush Igullim V'Yosher) Anaf 1.

is inapplicable to consider it to be in the category of "adhesion-*Dveikut*-דביקות."

Now, although the words of Torah do not contract spiritual impurity,[1021] this is because Torah does not actually become manifest within the physical (*Hitlabshut*). This accords with the well-known difference between Torah and prayer-*Tefillah*. That is, prayer is in a way of manifestation (*Hitlabshut*), being that the contemplations of prayer are in the aspect of Godliness as it relates to worlds, and the contemplations of prayer are in such a way that he truly grasps these matters in his mind very well. In contrast, Torah does not actually come forth in a way of manifestation (*Hitlabshut*).

The same is true of the difference between Torah and *mitzvot*. That is, the *mitzvot* become manifest in actual physical things. Torah, on the other hand, does not manifest in actual physical things at all, but only **discusses** them. Thus, it does not truly manifest in them in a way of actual manifestation (*Hitlabshut*), but only in a transcendent, encompassing manner (*Makif*). This is why words of Torah do not contract spiritual impurity.

Nevertheless, because the Torah is indeed drawn forth into matters of the world, even if only in a transcendent, encompassing manner (*Makif*), it is therefore inapplicable to use the term "adhesion-*Dveikut*-דביקות" in relation to it. Rather, only the term "binding-*Hitkashrut*-התקשרות" applies to it. Nonetheless, it is specifically in the descent of Torah below,

---

[1021] Talmud Bavli, Brachot 22a

when it is in the category of "binding-*Hitkashrut*-התקשרות," that the aspect of the Singular Intrinsic and Essential Being of *HaShem*-יהו״ה Himself, the Unlimited One, blessed is He, is drawn within it (in the same manner that we explained regarding the Jewish people).

Now, this is specifically drawn forth to the Torah by the Jewish people. In other words, there first is a bond (*Hitkashrut*-התקשרות) of the Jewish people to the Holy One, blessed is He, through Torah. However, through this bond, an additional illumination of light is caused within Torah itself. For,[1022] "At the outset, when a person does it, he does it for his own soul." This refers to the study of Torah before prayer, which is the matter of Godly contemplation-*Hitbonenut*. This affects that his prayers cause actual refinement in his soul, through which he binds himself to the Singular Intrinsic and Essential Being of *HaShem*-יהו״ה, the Unlimited One Himself, blessed is He.

This is then followed by Torah study after the prayers, which is the study of Torah for the sake of the Name of *HaShem*-יהו״ה, blessed is He, that is within Torah itself, meaning that he binds the Torah itself to the Singular Intrinsic and Essential Being of *HaShem*-יהו״ה, blessed is He. In other words, by virtue of the fact that the Torah caused him to be bonded to *HaShem*-יהו״ה Himself, blessed is He, he likewise affects a bond of the Torah to *HaShem*-יהו״ה Himself, blessed is He.

[1022] Talmud Bavli, Pesachim 68b

This then, is the meaning of the teaching in Zohar that,[1023] "There are three levels that are bound one to the other, the Jewish people are bound to the Torah and the Torah is bound to the Holy One, blessed is He." In other words, this refers to the bond of the Torah and the Jewish people to *HaShem*-יהו"ה, blessed is He, even as they are in a state of separate existence, so that even then, they are bound to the Holy One, blessed is He.

Moreover, this is true in both, "the concealed aspect and the revealed aspect." In other words, this bond is not only in the revealed aspect of the Jewish people, the revealed aspect of Torah and the revealed aspect of the Holy One, blessed is He. Rather, this bond is affected even in the concealed and inner aspect, that is, the inner aspect of the souls of the Jewish people, the inner aspect of Torah and the inner aspect of Godliness. That is, the advantage of this bond is caused specifically through the aspect of "binding-*Hitkashrut*-התקשרות," that is specifically brought about through the descent below.

5.

This, then, is the meaning of the verse,[1024] "And it shall come to pass, that because you listen to these ordinances, and you observe and perform them; *HaShem*-יהו"ה your God, will safeguard for you the covenant and the kindness that He swore to your forefathers." For, the matter of the covenant (*Brit*-ברית)

[1023] Zohar III 73a
[1024] Deuteronomy 7:12-13

applies even if one of the two friends is not conducting himself as he should. The love nevertheless remains in place, as it was initially. The same is true of the kindness (Chessed-חסד), which, as explained above, is the indiscriminate bestowal of goodness, even to the unworthy. This refers to the, "True kindness," which is the aspect of kindness-Chessed of the Ancient One-Atik, blessed is He, about which it states, "There is no left side in this Holy Ancient One."[1025] This likewise is the matter of the oath (Shvu'ah-שבועה), in which HaShem-יהו"ה obligates Himself, as if He has no choice, so to speak (as mentioned above).

All these matters are entirely beyond reason and intellect, meaning that they completely transcend the chaining down of the worlds (Hishtalshelut). This level is specifically attained through our service of HaShem-יהו"ה, blessed is He, in a manner of, "And it shall come to pass, that because-Eikev-עקב you listen," which, as explained above, also means "heel-Eikev-עקב." In other words, this verse is not making a conditional statement at all, but only comes to inform us of the order and manner of serving HaShem-יהו"ה, blessed is He. Namely, that the aspect that transcends the chaining down of the worlds (Histhalshelut), is specifically in the, "hcel-Eikev-עקב."

To further explain, there are two aspects in the soul, Yisroel-ישראל and Yaakov-יעקב.[1026] The name Yisroel-ישראל spells the words, "My head-Li Rosh-לי ראש,"[1027] and refers to

---

Zohar III 129a; 289a
See Likkutei Torah Balak 70c and on, and elsewhere.
Shaar HaPesukim of the Arizal, Vayishlach 32:29; Likkutei Torah Shlach 48b and on; Sefer HaMitzvot of the Tzemach Tzedek 15b, citing the Zohar.

the aspect of the head of the soul. In contrast, the name *Yaakov*-יעקב divides into "*Yud Eikev*-יו"ד עקב,"[1028] and refers to the heel-*Eikev*-עקב of the soul.[1029]

The same matter applies to time and space. The heel-*Eikev*-עקב refers to the time and space of the, "heels of Moshiach-*Ikveta D'Meshicha*-עקבתא דמשיחא,"[1030] about which it states,[1031] "We have not seen our signs; there is no longer a prophet, and there is none among us who knows for how long," and,[1032] "I clothe the heavens in darkness and make sackcloth their garment."

However, there nonetheless is the aspect of "you listen-*Tishme'un*-תשמעון to these ordinances," wherein "listening-*Tishme'un*-תשמעון" refers to the matter of understanding and comprehension.[1033] More particularly, the verse specifies that this listening is specifically, "to these ordinances-*Mishpatim*-משפטים." This refers to the "judgement-*Mishpat*-משפט, by which a person judges himself,"[1034] meaning that he reflects and contemplates the ultimate purpose of his own existence and the manner of how he came to be in the state that he is in. In other words, he contemplates the fact that, at its root, his soul is hewn

---

[1028] Etz Chaim, Shaar 3, Ch. 2; Torah Ohr VaYeitze 21a.

[1029] See Ohr HaTorah, Eikev, p. 490; p. 502; p. 505.

[1030] See Ohr HaTorah ibid. p. 479; 491; 504 (citing Ohr HaMe'ir Eikev).

[1031] Psalms 74:9

[1032] Isaiah 50:3; Torah Ohr, Veyeishev 28d

[1033] Hearing-*Shmiyah*-שמיעה refers to the faculty of understanding-*Binah*, whereas Seeing-*Re'iyah*-ראיה refers to the faculty of insight and wisdom-*Chochmah*. (See Shaar HaYichud, translated as The Gate of Unity, Ch. 5 and elsewhere.)

[1034] See discourse by the same title 5674 (*Hemshech* 5672 Vol. 1 p. 589); Torah Ohr Beshalach 63b; Sefer HaMaamarim 5689 p. 133.

from beneath the Throne of Glory,[1035] and even beyond that, from the state of, "the soul that You have placed within me is pure."[1036] He thus contemplates,[1037] "From where did you come?" From this he subsequently comes to contemplate his current situation, and that he is in a state about which Torah states,[1038] "[He] dwells within them even in their impurities," and,[1039] "They were exiled to Edom and the Indwelling Presence (*Shechinah*) accompanies them." In other words, no matter where a Jew goes and wherever he may find himself, he is accompanied by his spark of Godliness (and pulls it along with him). Through contemplating all this, at some point or another, he will become aroused to complete repentance, especially since strength for this is given to him from Above, through the Supernal heralds who cry out,[1040] "Return, O' wayward children."

It is through contemplating all this, which is the aforementioned matter of, "judgments-*Mishpatim*-משפטים," that even though he is in the aspect of the, "heel-*Eikev*-עקב," meaning the heel of the soul and the heel of the time and space of the, "heels of Moshiach-*Ikveta D'Meshicha*-עקבתא דמשיחא," he will come to a state of listening-*Tishme'un*-תשמעון, keeping-*U'Shmartem*-ושמרתם and "doing-*Ve'Asitem*-ועשיתם." These three aspects, mentioned in the verse, refer to the three garments

---

[1035] Zohar III 29b; 123b and elsewhere.
[1036] Elokai Neshama blessing in the morning prayer liturgy.
[1037] Mishnah Avot 3:1
[1038] Leviticus 16:16
[1039] Sifri to Masei 35:34
[1040] Jeremiah 3:14, 3:22; Zohar III 126a; Maamarei Admor HaEmtza'ee Vayikra Vol. 1, p. 9

of the soul; thought (*Machshavah*), speech (*Dibur*), and action (*Ma'aseh*).[1041]   As mentioned above, "Listening-*Tishme'un*-תשמעון," refers to the matter of understanding and comprehension and is thus the garment of thought. The term "Keeping-*U'Shmartem*-ושמרתם" refers to speech, as indicated by our sages, of blessed memory, that the words,[1042] "'Keep them-*Shamor*-שמור' refers to the Mishnah," and thus refers to,[1043] "the study of Torah, which is equal to all the commandments" and is done specifically through speech. The term "doing-*Ve'Asitem*-ועשיתם," clearly refers to action-*Ma'aseh*-מעשה.

Thus, it is through the above that, "*HaShem*-יהו"ה your God, will safeguard for you the covenant (*Brit*-ברית) and the kindness (*Chessed*-חסד) that He swore (*Shvu'ah*-שבועה) to your forefathers," all of which are matters that transcend the chaining down of the worlds (*Hishtalshelut*).

This also explains the connection between this Torah portion to the seven weeks of consolation.[1044]   Namely, this is hinted at in the specific use of the term, "And it shall come to pass-*VeHayah*-והיה," about which it states,[1045] "The term 'And it shall come to pass-*VeHayah*-והיה' is always a term of joy."[1046]

[1041] See Ohr HaTorah Eikev p. 479 and p. 491 and on.

[1042] Sifri to Re'eh 11:32; 11:1; Rashi there 12:28 and elsewhere.

[1043] Mishnah Pe'ah 1:1

[1044] The seven weeks of consolation refers to the seven weeks between the 9th of Av and Rosh HaShanah.

[1045] Midrash Bereishit Rabba 42:3 (Likkutei Torah Re'eh 30d) and elsewhere. Ohr HaMe'ir, Eikev.

[1046] The term "And it shall come to pass-*VeHayah*-והיה" is one of the permutations of the Singular Name of *HaShem*-יהו"ה, blessed is He, except that the letters *Vav-Hey*-ו"ה precede the letters *Yud-Hey*-י"ה. While the letters *Yud-Hey*-י"ה

For then, both the, "heel-*Eikev*-עקב," of the soul and the time and space of the, "heels of Moshiach-*Ikveta D'Meshicha*- עקבתא דמשיחא," will be in a state of "listening-*Tishme'un*-תשמעון." This will affect a drawing forth from Above, as the verse continues, "*HaShem*-יהו״ה your God, will safeguard for you, the covenant and the kindness that He swore to your forefathers," which is a drawing forth that entirely transcends the chaining down of the worlds (*Hishtalshelut*).

Moreover, all this will be drawn forth below, physically, in accordance with the continuation of the verse, "He will love you, bless you, and multiply you, and He will bless the fruit of your womb and the fruit of your Land; your grain, your wine, and your oil; the offspring of your cattle and the flocks of your sheep and goats; on the Land that He swore to your forefathers, to give you."

---

correspond and refer to the judgments of the intellect, the letters *Vav-Hey*-ה״ו-11 correspond and refer to a revelation of the kindness and mercy of *HaShem*-יהו״ה blessed is He, Himself, Who utterly transcends the chaining down of the Ten Sefirot. (See at length in Ginat Egoz of Rabbi Yosef Gikatilla, translated as HaShem is One, Volumes 2 & 3, as well as Likkutei Torah Re'eh 30d ibid.)

Discourse 16

"Atem Nitzavim Hayom Kulchem, Lifnei HaShem -
You are standing this day, all of you, before *HaShem-*יהו״ה"

Delivered on Shabbat Parashat Nitzavim, 28 Elul, 5711
By the grace of *HaShem*, blessed is He,

1.

The verse states,[1047] "You are standing this day, all of
you, before *HaShem-*יהו״ה your God; your leaders, your tribes,
your elders, your officers – all the men of Israel. Your young
children, your wives and your proselyte who is in your camp,
from your wood-cutter to your water-drawer." Now, this Torah
portion is always read on the Shabbat preceding Rosh
HaShanah (biblical New Year).[1048] This is the meaning of the
words, "You are standing **this** day-*Hayom-*היום," referring to
the Day of Judgment, which is Rosh HaShanah.[1049] This is as
we recite on Rosh HaShanah,[1050] "**This** day-*HaYom-*היום is the
beginning of Your works." This is similar to the teaching of
our sages, of blessed memory, about the verse,[1051] "you are all

---

[1047] Deuteronomy 29:9-10
[1048] See Tosefot to Tractate Megillah 31b; Rambam Hilchot Tefilah 13:2; Tur
and Shulchan Aruch, Orach Chayim 428:4; Likkutei Torah, Nitzavim 44a.
[1049] Pa'aneach Raza Nitzavim; Megale Amukot Nitzavim 60d (entitled
"*Asiri*"); Also see Zohar II 32b and RaMaZ commentary there; Zohar III 231b.
[1050] Musaf prayer of Rosh HaShanah
[1051] Deuteronomy 4:4

alive this day-*HaYom*-היום," that,[1052] "Even on the day that the whole rest of the world is dead, you (the Jewish People) will live."

Now, for this matter of, "you are standing this day" to come about, (as it states in the continuation of the verse) there must be the matter of, "all of you-*Kulchem*-כולכם." In other words, all the Jewish people must be in a state of inclusion and oneness,[1053] in which no difference between individuals is recognized, but instead, they are one complete stature.[1054] It is specifically through this that we come to the aspect of, "You are standing this day-*HaYom*-היום," meaning that, "Even on the day when everyone in the whole world is dead, you will live."

However,[1055] we must understand the continuation of the verse, that specifies, "your leaders, your tribes, your elders, your officers – all of the men of Israel; your young children, your wives, and your proselyte who is in your camp, from your wood-cutter to your water-drawer." At first glance, this seems to be superfluous, since the verse already stated, "all of you-*Kulchem*-כולכם," which already includes all the particulars of the Jewish people. Why then does the verse continue by specifying ten categories of the Jewish people?

This question is further compounded by the fact that, as we just explained, the primary meaning of the word, "all of you-*Kulchem*-כולכם," is that the Jewish people should be as one

---

[1052] Talmud Bavli, Sanhedrin 90b
[1053] Midrash Tanchuma, Nitzavim 1
[1054] See Likkutei Torah, Nitzavim ibid.
[1055] Also see the discourse entitled "*Atem Nitzavim*" 5675 (*Hemshech* 5672 Vol. 2, p. 1,131).

complete stature, without focusing on the particular differences between them. Based on this, the continuation of the verse, that specifies distinct levels within the Jewish people, seems to contradict the first part of the verse that indicates the matter of "all of you-*Kulchem*-כולכם."

Now, we cannot say that the continuation of the verse; "your leaders, your tribes, your elders etc.," is not coming to segregate each of these categories unto itself, but rather, only comes to explain the meaning of the word "all of you-*Kulchem*-כולכם," in order to indicate to us that "all of you" means, "your leaders, your tribes, your elders etc." For, if that was the case, the verse could have simply stated, "From your leaders to your water-drawers." However, since the verse indeed specifies all ten categories, it is understood that it is not merely to clarify the meaning of the word, "all of you-*Kulchem*-כולכם." Rather, it comes to specify particular levels, each category unto itself.

From this it is understood that the service of *HaShem*-יהו"ה, blessed is He, on Rosh HaShanah, has two aspects. The first aspect is the oneness of the whole (*Klal*) of Israel, in that they are one complete stature. The second aspect is the division of the particulars, that is, each and every individual, in and of himself.[1056]

[1056] Also see Likkutei Sichot Vol. 4, p. 1,141; Vol. 23, p. 57.

2.

To better understand this, we must preface with the well-known principle that the primary aspect of man's service of *HaShem*-יהו"ה, blessed is He, is to draw down the illuminations of light (*Orot*) into vessels (*Keilim*). For, the ultimate intention of *HaShem*-יהו"ה, blessed is He, in creation, is, "to have a dwelling place for Himself in the lowest world."[1057] The preparation for this is through the manifestation of lights (*Orot*) within vessels (*Keilim*).

The explanation[1058] is that lights (*Orot*), which are an aspect of illumination and revelation, are in a state of ascension to their Source, and therefore, their adhesion (*Dveikut*) to their Source is recognizable.[1059] In contrast, vessels (*Keilim*) come through the restraint and cessation of the light etc. and are in an aspect of concealment. Therefore, their adhesion (*Dveikut*) to their Source is not recognizable.[1060] This being so, lights (*Orot*) and vessels (*Keilim*) seem to be two diametric opposites. If so, how can they possibly bond together? The answer[1061] is that

---

[1057] Midrash Tanchuma Naso 16; Bechukotai 3; Bereishit Rabba end of Ch. 3; Bamidbar Rabba 13:6; Tanya Ch. 36, and elsewhere.

[1058] See the discourse entitled "*Atem Nitzavim*" 5675 (*Hemshech* 5672 Vol. 2, p. 1,133 and on). Also ibid. Vol. 1, p. 483; Also see the discourse entitled "*Ani LeDodi*" 5679 (p. 652); 5693 (Sefer HaMaamarim Kuntreisim Vol. 3, p. 104; Sefer HaMaamarim 5693 p. 542); Sefer HaErechim Chabad, Vol. 4, p. 395-396 and the additional citations there.

[1059] The very existence of light testifies to the existence of the luminary, for example, if you look out the window and see daylight, you know that the sun is out, because light cannot exist without a luminary.

[1060] Also see Sefer HaMaamarim 5662, p. 229 and on.

[1061] See *Hemshech* 5672 Vol. 1, p. 178 and on; Sefer HaMaamarim 5649 p. 243 and on; and elsewhere.

since the light feels the advantage of the vessel over the light, through this, the effect of the light is that this advantage is also felt in the vessel.

In other words, light is the matter of revelation. Therefore, to whatever matter light is drawn, it feels (and reveals within it) its advantage over the light. This is the meaning of the above statement that the light feels the advantage of the vessel, which is the matter of concealment.

The advantage of the vessels over the lights, is that they are rooted in the aspect of the ability of HaShem-יהו"ה, the Unlimited One, blessed is He, **not** to illuminate, which is an even greater display of His might than the aspect of His ability to illuminate.[1062] However, because, in and of itself, the vessel is an aspect of concealment, the adhesion (Dveikut) of the vessels to their source is not recognizable and the superior advantage of the vessel is not felt.

Thus, it is specifically and only through the illumination of light, which is the matter of revelation, and which feels the superiority of the vessel,[1063] that it also reveals the superiority of the vessel, within the vessel itself. Through this, it then is possible for there to be a bond between the lights (Orot) and the vessels (Keilim), due to the illumination of light.

This is likewise the case from the angle of the vessel itself. For, since the matter of the vessel (Kli) is that it is nullified and sublimated to everything that is not a vessel,[1064]

[1062] See Sefer HaMaamarim 5670 p. 33; Hemshech 5672 Vol. 2, p. 1,000; Also see Hemshech 5666 p. 188; Sefer HaSichot Torat Shalom p. 148 & 152;

[1063] See Sefer HaMaamarim 5670 p. 39; Sefer HaMaamarim 5689 p. 348;

[1064] See Hemshech 5672 Vol. 2, p. 1,013; Vol. 1, p. 177.

and is particularly nullified and sublimated to the illumination of light that reveals its own superiority within it (since on its own, it is the aspect of concealment, and it is specifically the light that reveals its superiority, it thus is sublimated and nullified to a much greater extent to the light and illumination) and thus there can be a bond between the lights (*Orot*) and the vessels (*Keilim*), even from the angle of the vessel.

3.

Now, the root of the matter of this bond between the lights (*Orot*) and vessels (*Keilim*) is due to their root in the name *HaShem*-יהו״ה, blessed is He, and His title God-*Elohi"m*-אלהי״ם. The Name *HaShem*-יהו״ה, blessed is He, is the root of the lights (*Orot*), whereas His title God-*Elohi"m*-אלהי״ם, is the root of the vessels (*Keilim*).[1065] Thus, it is due to the unity of *HaShem*-יהו״ה, blessed is He, with His title God-*Elohi"m*-אלהי״ם, that there is a drawing forth of this matter of a bond between the lights (*Orot*) and vessels (*Keilim*).

The explanation[1066] of this may be understood by the verse,[1067] "For a sun and a shield is *HaShem*-יהו״ה God-*Elohi"m*-אלהי״ם." Now, a shield has two effects. The first is the concealment of the sunlight and the second is that through

---

[1065] See Torah Ohr, Yitro 69d; Also see discourse entitled "*Atem Nitzavim*" 5721 (Sefer HaMaamarim 5721 p. 240 and on).

[1066] See the discourse entitled "*Atem Nitzavim*" 5675 (*Hemshech* 5672 Vol. 2, p. 1,132 and on).

[1067] Psalms 84:12; Also see Tanya Shaar HaYichud VeHaEmunah Ch. 4 and on; Ohr HaTorah (*Yahal Ohr*) Tehillim to Psalms 84:12.

the concealment of the essential light, light can be revealed below. It is the same way with His Essential Intrinsic Name *HaShem*-יהו״ה, blessed is He, and His title God-*Elohi"m*-אלהי״ם. That is, the title God-*Elohi"m*-אלהי״ם conceals the light of the Essential Name *HaShem*-יהו״ה, blessed is He, the effect of which, is that a revelation of the light of *HaShem*-יהו״ה, blessed is He, becomes possible within vessels (*Keilim*).

However, this is not in a way that one overpowers the other. For, if that were the case, then at times there would be an overpowering of the Essential Name *HaShem*-יהו״ה, blessed is He, in which case there would be the absolute and total revelation of *HaShem*-יהו״ה, blessed is He and blessed is His name, without limit. Or alternatively, if at times there would be an overpowering of His title God-*Elohi"m*-אלהי״ם, there would be an aspect of complete concealment.

However, since in reality, although the title God-*Elohi"m*-אלהי״ם conceals the Essential Name *HaShem*-יהו״ה, blessed is He, nevertheless, it is specifically through it, that there is an illumination and revelation of the Essential Name *HaShem*-יהו״ה, blessed is He. We therefore must say that it is not in a manner of one overpowering the other. Rather, it is in a way that they are appropriate and fitting to each other and therefore fully operate as One. Thus, it is it possible for the lights (*Orot*) and vessels (*Keilim*) to bond.

The explanation is that the Essential Name *HaShem*-יהו״ה, blessed is He, is the matter of revelation, and that ultimately there should be a revelation of the Light of the Singular Intrinsic Being, *HaShem*-יהו״ה, the Unlimited One

Himself, blessed is He, everywhere, even in the lowest of the lowest place. This revelation is only possible through the manifestation of *HaShem's*-יהו"ה title God-*Elohi"m*-אלהי"ם, which is specifically the aspect of the vessels (*Keilim*).

We thus find that the matter of revelation is accomplished specifically through an initial concealment. In the same manner, the purpose of His title God-*Elohi"m*-אלהי"ם is not to conceal the revelation of His Essential Name *HaShem*-יהו"ה, blessed is He, but on the contrary, it is specifically through the initial concealment that a revelation of the Name *HaShem*-יהו"ה, blessed is He, all the way down, is possible.

We therefore find that the matter of concealment is for the purpose of bringing about revelation in a complete and perfect manner.[1068]   Thus, in truth, His Essential Name *HaShem*-יהו"ה and His title God-*Elohi"m*-אלהי"ם, are utterly

---

[1068] See Shaar HaYichud of the Mittler Rebbe, translated as The Gate of Unity, Ch. 12-13 where it is explained that the purpose of the restraint (*Tzimtzum*) is actually for the purpose of the ultimate revelation. This is compared to a teacher who restrains and constricts his own understanding of the subject, and draws forth a limited line of explanation according to the capacity of the student. Ultimately, his intention in teaching the student the diminished illumination of his intellect is so that the student should come to understand the subject in the same manner and to the same extent as the teacher, and not solely a diminished understanding. However, were he to reveal the entirety of the subject according to his own understanding, rather than a restrained and diminished illumination according to the capacity of the student, then the student would not understand anything at all. In the same manner, the intent of the restraint (*Tzimtzum*) of the illumination of the Singular Preexistent Intrinsic Name of *HaShem*-יהו"ה, blessed is He, is ultimately for the purpose of the revelation of the true reality of *HaShem*-יהו"ה, and not concealment.

included with one another,[1069] to the point that HaShem-יהו"ה and God-Elohi"m-אלהי"ם are entirely One."[1070]

The same principle applies in regard to the root of the matter of the restraint-Tzimtzum and the revelation of the line-Kav that followed the restraint-Tzimtzum. For, the actual intention in the restraint-Tzimtzum is to reveal. In other words, even the very first restraint-Tzimtzum, which differs from all subsequent restraints, since they are only a diminishment of illumination, whereas the first restraint-Tzimtzum is in a way of complete withdrawal (Siluk) of illumination,[1071] nevertheless, the intent, even in the very first restraint-Tzimtzum is actually for the purpose of revelation.

The same is true of the aspect of the light of the line-Kav, within which the matter of restraint-Tzimtzum is felt. For, before the restraint-Tzimtzum, the light of HaShem-יהו"ה, blessed is He, illuminated limitlessly, whereas after the restraint-Tzimtzum, the revelation of His light is by way of a

---

[1069] The inclusion of the title God-Elohi"m-אלהי"ם-86 in the Singular Essential Name of HaShem-יהו"ה-26 Himself, blessed is He, is hinted at in the Name of HaShem-יהו"ה-26 which has a numerical value of כ"ו-26. This numeral כ"ו-26 possesses, in a concealed manner, the numeral פ"ו-86 which is the numerical value of God-Elohi"m-אלהי"ם-86. For, when the letters כ"ו-26 are spelled out, כ"ף ו"ו, we see the כ"ו-26 contains פ"ו-86. This is similarly the case with the expanded name of HaShem-יהו"ה which is called the name of Ma"H-מ"ה-45 and is spelled as follows: יו"ד ה"א וא"ו ה"א. We see that this name of Ma"H-מ"ה likewise includes the title God-Elohi"m-אלהי"ם-86 in it, for when ה"מ-45 is spelled out Mem-Hey-מ"ם ה"א-86 it equals פ"ו-86, which is the same as the title God-Elohi"m-אלהי"ם-86. We thus see that the title God-Elohi"m-אלהי"ם-86 is utterly bound to and dependent upon the Singular Preexistent Intrinsic Name of HaShem-יהו"ה Himself, blessed is He. (See Ginat Egoz of Rabbi Yosef Gikatilla, translated as HaShem is One, Volume 1.)

[1070] Zohar II 26b; Also see Sefer HaMaamarim 5657, p. 45 and on; 5698 p. 271 and on. Also see Shaar HaYichud, translated as The Gate of Unity, Ch. 12-13 ibid.

[1071] Likkutei Torah, Hosafot to Vayikra 51c, 53d, and elsewhere.

thin line (*Kav Dak*) of revelation,[1072] which is caused by the restraint-*Tzimtzum*. Nevertheless, its purpose is to reveal, since the actual illumination of the line-*Kav* is not drawn from the restraint-*Tzimtzum* itself, but is rather from the aspect of the vastness of the encompassing circle (*Igul HaGadol*) that precedes the restraint-*Tzimtzum*.[1073]

We thus find that, in the restraint-*Tzimtzum* itself, the intention is specifically to reveal, and that in the thin band of revelation of the line-*Kav*, the aspect of the restraint-*Tzimtzum* is felt.[1074] This is likewise drawn forth in the Name *HaShem*-יהו״ה, blessed is He, and His title God-*Elohi"m*-אלהי״ם, in that they are not two separate things in a way that the one overpowers the other, or that they are in conflict with each other, God forbid, but rather, they are completely bonded as one. This is likewise drawn forth in the lights (*Orot*) and vessels (*Keilim*), so that there is a bond between them.

Now, this matter is likewise drawn forth in man's service of *HaShem*-יהו״ה, blessed is He, in order to bring about a bond between the Godly soul and the animalistic soul.[1075] For, the Godly soul and the animalic soul are actually diametric opposites of each other. On the one hand, the Godly soul is in a state of ascension and is compared to fire which ascends

---

[1072] Etz Chaim, Shaar 1 (Drush Iggulim V'Yosher) Anaf 2; Mevo She'arim Shaar 1, Vol. 1, Ch. 2, and elsewhere.

[1073] See the citations in the prior note, as well as Sefer HaMaamarim 5661, p. 161 and p. 177. Also see Shaar HaYichud translated as The Gate of Unity, Ch. 14-15 at length.

[1074] In that though it is revelation, it is only a thin band of revelation.

[1075] Zohar II 26b; Also see the discourse entitled "*Atem Nitzavim*" 5675 (*Hemshech* 5672 Vol. 2, p. 1,134 and on).

above to cleave to its Source.[1076] This is as stated,[1077] "For, *HaShem*-יהו״ה your God is a consuming fire." In contrast, the animalistic soul is of,[1078] "the spirit of the beast that descends down." Nevertheless, the ultimate intent and purpose is to transform the animalistic soul itself into Godliness, so that the Godly soul will be able to function in its service of *HaShem*-יהו״ה through the animalistic soul itself.[1079] This matter is accomplished through the Godly soul causing the animalistic soul to realize it's advantage over the Godly soul, in that it possesses an even loftier spark of Godliness, only that it fell further down.[1080] Moreover, the animalistic soul itself possesses nullification and sublimation that is similar to that of an animal, in that it is nullified and sublimated to the Godly soul. It thus is possible for there to be a bond between the Godly soul and the animalistic soul.

4.

Now, the abovementioned matter, that the Godly soul transforms the animalistic soul into holiness, is the same matter as the manifestation of lights (*Orot*) within vessels (*Keilim*). In other words, the ten powers of the Godly soul manifest within

---

[1076] See at great length in Ginat Egoz of Rabbi Yosef Gikatilla, translated as HaShem is One, Volume 2.

[1077] Deuteronomy 4:24

[1078] Ecclesiastes 3:21

[1079] See Torah Ohr, Mikeitz 39d

[1080] See the citations in Sefer HaMafteichot of the works of the Alter Rebbe (printed by Kehot 5741), the section entitled, "*Kol HaGavo'ah*-כל הגבוה" etc.; Also see Siddur Im Divrei Elokim Chayim, 71d, 303c; Shaarei Orah, 58a and on; 65a and on; and elsewhere.

and fill the powers of the animalistic soul, so that they become filled with the powers of the Godly soul.[1081] However, as known, the ultimate intention is to come to the aspect of simple desire (*Ratzon Pashut*) that transcends intellect and reason, meaning that it transcends the manifestation of lights (*Orot*) within vessels (*Keilim*).

(To clarify, what is meant by this is not that the simple desire (*Ratzon Pashut*) should not be expressed in vessels, but rather, that even the simple desire (*Ratzon Pashut*), which utterly transcends the aspect of vessels, should be drawn into the vessels in a way of illumination of lights (*Orot*) within vessels (*Keilim*). In other words, what is meant, is that even the illumination of lights (*Orot*) within vessels (*Keilim*) should be according to the simple desire (*Ratzon Pashut*) which transcends reason and understanding, and is higher than the manifestation of lights within vessels.)

Now, the revelation of this aspect comes from Above. For, it is not something that is within man's power to accomplish on his own, but is solely something that is granted as a gift from Above. In other words, after a person has toiled in his service of *HaShem*-יהו״ה, blessed is He, to transform his animalistic soul into holiness, so that the powers of his animalistic soul become filled by the powers of the Godly soul, which indeed is a service that everyone is capable of attaining by their own efforts, then subsequently, the aforementioned aspect of the simple desire (*Ratzon Pashut*) from Above, is

---

[1081] See Tanya Ch. 9

drawn to him. It is about this that the verse states,[1082] "I shall grant your priestly service as a gift."

5.

In explanation, our sages, of blessed memory, stated,[1083] "The attribute of flesh and blood is unlike the attribute of the Holy One, blessed is He. The attribute of flesh and blood is that an empty vessel holds what is put into it, whereas a full vessel does not. The attribute of the Holy One, blessed is He, is that a full vessel holds, whereas an empty vessel does not." Now, in various places[1084] it is explained that these two attributes exist in man's service of *HaShem*-יהו״ה, blessed is He, except that, "the attribute of flesh and blood" refers to the service of *HaShem*-יהו״ה in a manner that one is capable of attaining through his own efforts, whereas, "the attribute of the Holy One, blessed is He," refers to the service of *HaShem*-יהו״ה, that is drawn from Above. It is about this that our sages, of blessed memory, stated that the attribute of flesh and blood is that an empty vessel holds, but a full vessel does not hold.

To further clarify, it states that, "the arguments of the animalistic soul precede"[1085] the arguments of the Godly soul. In other words, the animalistic soul manifests in man first and

---

[1082] Numbers 18:7; Tanya, Iggeret HaKodesh, Epistle 18 (p. 126b); Also see *Hemshech* 5672 ibid, p. 1,130.

[1083] Talmud Bavli, Brachot 40a

[1084] Sefer HaMaamarim 5634 p. 302 and on; Discourse entitled "*Ani LeDodi*" ibid. (Sefer HaMaamarim 5679, p. 651 and on; Sefer HaMaamarim Kuntreisim Vol. 3, p. 101 and on; Sefer HaMaamarim 56932 p. 537 and on) and elsewhere.

[1085] See Zohar I 189a; Midrash Kohelet Rabba 4:13

thus becomes entrenched in him.[1086] Additionally, over time, it becomes strengthened within him, since he uses it regularly, in eating, drinking and other worldly matters.[1087] As a result, man is a "full vessel," meaning that he is full of all kinds of desires. He rationalizes to himself, "I want this thing and I need that thing and I cannot exist without this other thing etc." It is about this that our sages, of blessed memory, stated, "A full vessel does not hold." In other words, when he is a, "full vessel" – and it goes without saying that this is so if he is full of forbidden matters that cloud his mind and confuse him – but even if he is full of permissible matters, only that they are not for the sake of the Name of *HaShem*-יהו"ה, blessed is He – then, as a result of the fact that he is a, "full vessel," he will not hold.

It therefore is necessary to be an empty vessel, meaning that he must empty himself of all his physical matters, and should not even desire permissible matters, not even things that are necessary to him. (This applies not only to things that he imagines are necessary, but even things that he actually needs.) Even in things that he needs according to Torah, his desire should only be for the spirituality in them.

This then, is the meaning of, "an empty vessel." That is, it is not that he is entirely empty of all physicality, meaning that he does not eat and drink and the like, but rather, that he has utterly no desire whatsoever for the physicality of these things at all, but only for their spirituality. He then is called an

---

[1086] That is, the animalistic soul is actively revealed within a person at birth. On the other hand, one's Godly soul only begins to be actively revealed upon reaching adolescence.

[1087] See Tanya, Ch. 13 (18b).

"empty vessel," since he empties himself of the physicality of these things.

This may be further understood by explaining the teaching of our sages that, "the attribute of flesh and blood is that an empty vessel holds, whereas a full vessel does not hold," as it relates to physical influence, since this is the attribute of man of flesh and blood, in the most literal sense. We observe that when person is a, "full vessel," meaning that he is full of lusts and desires etc., he then is incapable of even holding blessings of physical beneficence. For, since the ultimate intent in the creation of man is for his spiritual service of *HaShem*-יהו״ה, blessed is He, which he is not involved in, he therefore cannot hold physical blessings either, since physicality is not his true reason for being.

However, if he is an "empty vessel," meaning that he has emptied himself of all interest in physicality, then he is even capable of holding physical beneficence. For, even though the purpose of his creation is for his spiritual service of *HaShem*-יהו״ה, blessed is He, and physicality is not his purpose for being, nevertheless, since he is an "empty vessel" and has no desire in physical things, but only for the spirituality within them, and this is his only motivation in involving himself with physical matters altogether, then even his physicality becomes spiritual (and spirituality is his only motivation, for which he was created). He therefore is capable of holding the bestowal of physical beneficence too.

Moreover, he can actually hold limitless bestowal of physical beneficence. For, although he is limited in space, he nevertheless can contain abundant influence, since his physicality has become spiritual, and spirituality does not take up space. (This is as is explained in the Chassidic teaching on the Torah portion of *Nitzavim*,[1088] with the analogy that several powers of the soul, such as desire, intellect and thought, can all be contained in a single brain.) As a result of this, he is capable of holding unlimited bestowal of physical beneficence.

From this we may also understand the matter of, "an empty vessel holds," as it applies to the attribute of flesh and blood in man's service of *HaShem*-יהו״ה, blessed is He. (That is, man's service of *HaShem*-יהו״ה, blessed is He, by his own strength.) What is meant by an, "empty vessel," is not that he does not eat or drink and the like, but rather, that even when he engages in eating and drinking and attending to all his physical needs, he has utterly no desire for the physicality of these things. That is, not only does he have no desire for permissible things, but even the things that he must necessarily do, he does only for their spiritual benefits.

He is therefore called an "empty vessel," because since his physicality is not physicality, he is entirely empty of physical things. Then, when he is an "empty vessel," as we have learned, an "empty vessel can hold." In other words, he contains the spiritual influence that is bestowed upon him, meaning, that he now is capable of toiling in the service of *HaShem*-יהו״ה, blessed is He, and transforming his animalistic soul to holiness, to the point that all the powers of his

---

[1088] Likkutei Torah, Nitzvaim 49a

animalistic soul become entirely filled by the powers of his Godly soul.

Only afterwards, does he come to the service of HaShem-יהו״ה, blessed is He, according to, "the attribute of the Holy One, blessed is He, is that a full vessel will hold." In other words, after he has attained the furthest extent of what he is capable of, on his own, in his service of HaShem-יהו״ה, blessed is He, meaning, that he has become, "a full vessel," and all the powers of his animalistic soul have become entirely filled with the powers of the Godly soul, only then is he capable of containing even that which man cannot contain on his own, but is given to him as a gift from Above. This refers to the aspect of the simple desire (*Ratzon Pashut*) that entirely transcends intellect and reason, and transcends the manifestation of lights (*Orot*) within vessels (*Keilim*). That is to say, this is when the light of HaShem-יהו״ה, blessed is He, which entirely transcends manifestation within vessels, is also drawn within vessels. Beyond this, it is even drawn into the physical, in which case the physicality itself is in an entirely different manner, in a state of limitlessness.

This is similar to what we find in regard to the Manna, the bread that descended from Heaven.[1089] That is, although the portion of Manna was the measure of an Omer,[1090] it nevertheless was in a way of limitlessness, in that,[1091] "one gathered more and one gathered less, but when they came home

---

[1089] Exodus 16:4; See *Hemshech* 5672 ibid.
[1090] Exodus 16:16
[1091] Rashi to Exodus 16:17

and measured, it was exactly equal to an Omer, which was a great miracle that occurred with the Manna." The same is true in regard to the influence from *HaShem*-יהו"ה, blessed is He, that transcends the manifestation of lights (*Orot*) within vessels (*Keilim*). That is, even as it comes to be drawn within vessels (*Keilim*) and physicality, it nevertheless remains in a state of limitlessness (*Bli Gvul*)!

6.

Now, just as in the individual service of *HaShem*-יהו"ה of every person, there is an aspect of service of *HaShem*-יהו"ה in a way of bonding the lights (*Orot*) and vessels (*Keilim*) and there also is an aspect of service of *HaShem*-יהו"ה that utterly transcends reason and intellect, so likewise, it is the same way with the complete stature of the Jewish people as a whole. In this too, there are two aspects of service of *HaShem*-יהו"ה, blessed is He. That is, there is the service of *HaShem*-יהו"ה in a way of manifestation of lights (*Orot*) within vessels (*Keilim*), which is in a limited manner. Because of this there are many different levels and aspects, as reflected in the ten general categories of the Jewish people, "your leaders, your tribes, your elders, and your officers – all of the men of Israel; your small children, your wives, and your proselyte who is in your camp, from your wood-cutter to your water-drawer."

However, there also is the aspect of service of *HaShem*-יהו"ה, that entirely transcends reason and intellect and is entirely limitless (*Bli Gvul*). In this aspect, division of particular levels is inapplicable, but rather, it is the aspect of the inclusiveness and oneness of the whole (*Klal*).

This,[1092] then, is the meaning of the verse,[1093] "You are standing this day, all of you, before *HaShem*-יהו"ה your God etc." As mentioned, this Torah portion is always read before Rosh HaShanah, at which time it is necessary for there to be a general drawing forth of influence from the First and Primary Cause, *HaShem*-יהו"ה, blessed is He.[1094] There thus must be the aspect of the service of *HaShem*-יהו"ה, blessed is He, in the way of inclusiveness and oneness of the whole (*Klal*). This is as we recite,[1095] "Bless us, our Father, all of us are as one." In other words, the blessing is drawn forth specifically when we are all as one, which is the aspect of the inclusive whole (*Klal*). Therefore, it is specifically on Rosh HaShanah that there must be this aspect of, "You are standing this day, all of you- *Kulchem*-כולכם," without any division into different levels.

However, since *HaShem's*-יהו"ה Supernal intention is specifically that there should be a drawing forth of lights (*Orot*) within vessels (*Keilim*), the verse continues, "your leaders, your tribes, your elders, and your officers – all of the men of Israel; your young children, your wives, and your proselyte who is in your camp, from your wood-cutter to the your water-drawer." This refers to the service of *HaShem*-יהו"ה, blessed is He, throughout the rest of the year (after the general service of the whole (*Klal*) that takes place on Rosh HaShanah). In other

---

[1092] See *Hemshech* 5672 ibid. p. 1,139 and on.

[1093] Deuteronomy 29:9-10

[1094] See Siddur Im Divrei Elokim Chaim, p. 246a and on; and elsewhere.

[1095] In the "*Seem Shalom*" blessing at the end of the Shmonah Esreh.

words, this specifically refers to the manifestation within vessels (*Keilim*).

Moreover, since His Supernal intention is that the aspect of the light of *HaShem*-יהו״ה, blessed is He, which entirely transcends manifestation in vessels (*Keilim*), should also be drawn forth within the aspect of vessels (*Keilim*) – meaning that the aspect of the general whole (*Klal*) that transcends particular divisions should be drawn into the particulars (*Prat*) – the verse therefore states both, "all of you-*Kulchem*-כולכם," and then continues, "your leaders, your tribes, your elders and your officers – all of the men of Israel; your young children, your wives, and your proselyte who is in your camp, from your wood-cutter, to your water-drawer." In other words, the general whole (*Klal*) should be drawn into all of the particulars (*Prat*).

Now, the explanation of this in regard to our service of *HaShem*-יהו״ה, blessed is He, is as known,[1096] that the acceptance of the yoke of Heaven on Rosh HaShanah is not the same as the acceptance of the yoke of Heaven throughout the rest of the year. For, on Rosh HaShanah, the *mitzvah* of the day is itself the acceptance of the yoke of Heaven, and is the general acceptance of the yoke of Heaven that entirely transcends reason and intellect, which is the aforementioned service of *HaShem*-יהו״ה, blessed is He, in the way of the general inclusive whole (*Klal*). It is for this reason that in his discourses,[1097] his

---

[1096] See *Hemshech* 5672 Vol. 1, p. 144 and on; Sefer HaMaamarim 5656 p. 264 and on; and elsewhere.

[1097] See Sefer HaMaamarim 5688 p. 6; 5697 p. 310; Sefer HaSichot 5696 p. 144; Igrot Kodesh of the Previous Rebbe, Vol. 4, p. 132 & p. 416; Also see the discourse entitled "*Atem Nitzavim*" 5712; Igrot Kodesh, Vol. 3, p. 468.

honorable holiness, the Rebbe Rashab, repeatedly mentions the preciousness and importance of every moment of Rosh HaShanah, and that not even a single moment should be wasted. Rather, it is imperative that we fill the time with the letters of Torah, prayer, and the recitation of Psalms. The reason is because, when serving *HaShem*-יהו״ה with the recitation of the letters themselves, everyone is equal.[1098] (In other words, this is unlike matters of comprehension, in which there are many different levels.) Thus, this is the service of *HaShem*-יהו״ה, blessed is He, in the way of the inclusive whole (*Klal*) that transcends the division of particulars (*Prat*). Through this we will merit to be inscribed and sealed for a good and sweet year, with openly apparent and revealed goodness!

[1098] This itself sheds light on the advantage and superiority of the vessels (*Keilim*) mentioned before, in that they are the first of *HaShem*'s-יהו״ה creations. For, the vessels (*Keilim*) refer to the 27-ך״ז letters of the *Aleph-Beit* themselves, which are the containers through which the entirety of creation was brought forth into existence an all levels equally. As mentioned before, this superiority is hinted at in the highest level of Torah indicated by the verse, "And I was with Him as His nursling-*VaEheyeh Etzlo Amon*-ואהי״ה אצלו אמון," wherein the word "*VaEheyeh*-ואהיה-27" refers to the 27-ך״ז letters of the *Aleph-Beit*. (See Ginat Egoz of Rabbi Yosef Gikatilla, translated as HaShem is One Vol. 1, section entitled "The Name *Eheye"h*-אהי״ה which is drawn from the reality of the name of *HaShem*-יהו״ה," and Volumes 2 & 3 at length. Also see Tanya, Shaar HaYichud VeHaEmunah, Ch. 1, Ch. 5, and elsewhere. Shaar HaYichud of the Mittler Rebbe, translated as The Gate of Unity, Ch. 43-44.)

Made in the USA
Middletown, DE
14 October 2023

40769880R00225